THE ROUTLEDGE COMPANION
TO ENGLISH LANGUAGE STUDIES

D0494339

'An indispensible resource for students and scholars. It offers both a systematic overview of approaches to the analysis of language and its use in specific social contexts and an in-depth exploration of the key debates currently dominating English language studies'

Rodney Jones, City University of Hong Kong

'This volume is extremely valuable for all those who are interested in what the editors call the changing global role of English. The range and mix of themes is most impressive'

Alan Scott Partington, Università di Bologna, Italy

The Routledge Companion to English Language Studies is an accessible guide to the major topics, debates and issues in this rapidly expanding field. The first part provides a comprehensive overview of the study of the English language and the second part includes chapters on a wide range of topics, from globalisation to sexuality to food packaging, contributed by well-known language specialists from a wide range of backgrounds.

This volume provides critical overviews of:

- approaches to researching, describing and analysing English
- the position of English as a global language
- the use of English in texts, practices and discourses
- variation and diversity throughout the English-speaking world.

The Routledge Companion to English Language Studies is fully cross-referenced throughout with useful definitions of key terms and concepts, and also includes helpful suggestions for further reading.

The volume will be of interest to those teaching English or wishing to check, consolidate or update their knowledge, and is essential reading for all students of English Language Studies.

Janet Maybin is a senior lecturer in Language and Communication at the Open University. She is co-editor of *Using English*, also published by Routledge, and *The Art of English: Everyday Creativity* with Joan Swann.

Joan Swann is a senior lecturer and director of the Centre for Language and Communication at the Open University. She is co-author of *A Dictionary of Sociolinguistics* and *Introducing Sociolinguistics*.

THE ROUTLEDGE COMPANION TO ENGLISH LANGUAGE STUDIES

Edited by
Janet Maybin and Joan Swann

Routledge
Taylor & Francis Group

LONDON AND NEW YORK

First published 2010
by Routledge
2 Park Square, Milton Park, Abingdon, Oxon OX14 4RN

Simultaneously published in the USA and Canada
by Routledge
270 Madison Ave, New York 10016

Routledge is an imprint of the Taylor & Francis Group, an informa business

Typeset in Times New Roman by
Book Now Ltd, London
Printed and bound in Great Britain by
TJ International Ltd, Padstow, Cornwall

British Library Cataloguing in Publication Data
A catalogue record for this book is available from the British Library

Library of Congress Cataloging in Publication Data
The routledge companion to English language
studies/edited by Janet Maybin and Joan Swann.
p. cm.— (Routledge companions)
1. English language—History. 2. English language—Study
and teaching. I. Maybin, Janet, 1950– II. Swann, Joan.

PE1075.R67 2009
420′.9—dc22   2008044854

ISBN10: 0–415–40173–9 (hbk)
ISBN10: 0–415–40338–3 (pbk)
ISBN10: 0–203–87895–7 (ebk)

ISBN13: 978–0–415–40173–9 (hbk)
ISBN13: 978–0–415–40338–2 (pbk)
ISBN13: 978–0–203–87895–8 (ebk)

CONTENTS

CONTENTS

ILLUSTRATIONS

FIGURES

TABLES

CONTRIBUTORS

Richard Andrews is Professor of English at the Institute of Education, London. He is the author of *The Problem with Poetry* (1991) and *Teaching and Learning Argument* (1995) as well as a number of edited collections, the most recent of which is the Sage *Handbook of E-learning Research*, with Caroline Haythornthwaite (2007).

Susan Bassnett (FRSL) is Professor in the Centre for Translation and Comparative Cultural Studies, which she founded in the 1980s at Warwick University. Author of over 20 books, including *Translation Studies* (third edition, 2002), recent publications are *The Translator as Writer* (2006, ed. with Bush), and *Translation in Global News* (2008, with Bielsa).

Selim Ben Said is a doctoral candidate in Applied Linguistics at the Pennsylvania State University. He has been teaching courses in Arabic, French and English as a Second Language. He is currently working on his dissertation, which examines multilingualism on street signs in the post-colonial north-African context of Tunisia.

Deborah Cameron is Rupert Murdoch Professor of Language and Communication at Oxford University. A sociolinguist with a particular interest in language, gender and sexuality, her publications include *Language and Sexuality* (2003, with Kulick), *The Language and Sexuality Reader* (2006, ed. with Kulik), *On Language and Sexual Politics* (2006) and *The Myth of Mars and Venus* (2007).

Suresh Canagarajah is the Kirby Professor in Language Learning and Director of the Migration Studies Project at Pennsylvania State University. Publications include *Resisting Linguistic Imperialism in English Teaching* (1999) *Geopolitics of Academic Writing* (2002) and *Reclaiming the Local in Language Policy and Practice* (ed., 2005).

Caroline Coffin is a Reader in the Centre for Language and Communication at the Open University, UK. Working primarily within Systemic Functional Linguistics, her research covers educational and other contexts. Recent books include *Analysing English in a global context* (2001, ed. with Burns) and *Historical Discourse: The Language of Time, Cause and Evaluation* (2006).

Guy Cook is Professor of Language and Education at the Open University. He has published extensively on applied linguistics, discourse analysis, English-language teaching, literary stylistics, and the language of public debate and persuasion. Recent books are: *Genetically Modified Language* (2004); *The Discourse of Advertising* (second edition, 2001); *Language Play, Language Learning* (2000).

Brenda Danet is Professor Emerita of Sociology and Communication, Hebrew University of Jerusalem, and a Research Affiliate in Anthropology, Yale University. Her book *Cyberpl@y: Communicating Online* (2001) was short-listed for the Katherine Briggs folklore prize in 2002. With Susan C. Herring she co-edited *The Multilingual Internet: Language, Culture, and Communication Online* (2007).

Diana Eades is a Research Fellow at the University of New England, Australia and works on language in the legal system, particularly the use of English by, to and about Australian Aboriginal people. Her latest book, which takes a critical sociolinguistic perspective, is *Courtroom Talk and Neocolonial Control* (2008).

Ann Hewings is a Senior Lecturer in the Open University Centre for Language and Communication. She has worked in English language teaching and materials production in the UK and internationally. Her research interests include academic literacy in higher education, especially disciplinarity. She is co-author (with Martin Hewings) of *Grammar and Context* (2005).

Busi Makoni holds a PhD in Applied Linguistics from Edinburgh University. Her interests are in second language acquisition, sociolinguistics, language planning and language rights. She has published in the *Journal of Second Language Research, Southern African Journal of African Languages, Per Linguam, Current Issues in Language Planning* and the *International Multilingual Research Journal*.

Sinfree Makoni is an Associate Professor of Applied Linguistics at Penn State University. He is co-editor of *Disinventing and Reconstituting Languages* (2006, with Pennycook). Recent research has been published in the *International Multilingual Research Journal, Language in Society, Current Issues in Language Planning* and the *Journal of Language, Identity, and Education*.

Janet Maybin is a Senior Lecturer in Language and Communication at the Open University. Publications include *Children's Voices* (Palgrave 2006), *The Art of English: everyday texts and practices* (co-edited with Swann, Palgrave, 2006) and *Using English* (co-edited with Mercer and Hewings, Routledge 2007).

Barbara Mayor is a Lecturer in the Centre for Language and Communication at the Open University. Her research interests include the pragmatics of bilingual interaction and cross-cultural differences in the use of English as a global language of education. Recent publications include *Learning English* (2007, ed. with Mercer and Swann).

Rajend Mesthrie is Professor of Linguistics at the University of Cape Town. Publications include the *Concise Encyclopedia of Sociolinguistics* (2001), *Language in South Africa* (2002), *A Dictionary of Sociolinguistics* (2004, with Swann, Deumert and Lillis) and *World Englishes* (2008, with Bhatt).

Sarah North is a Senior Lecturer in the Centre for Language and Communication at the Open University. With interests in computer-mediated communication and English for academic purposes, she has published in several journals and in *IELTS Collected Papers: Research in Speaking and Writing Assessment* (2007, Taylor and Falvey eds) and *Language and Literacy: Functional Approaches* (Whittaker, O'Donnell and McCabe eds, 2006).

Kieran O'Halloran is a Senior Lecturer in Linguistics in the Centre for Language and Communication at the Open University, UK. Publications include: *Critical Discourse Analysis and Language Cognition* (2003), *Applying English Grammar: Functional and Corpus Approaches* (2004, ed. with Coffin and Hewings) and *The Art of English: Literary Creativity* (2006, ed. with Goodman).

Alastair Pennycook is Professor of Language Studies at the University of Technology Sydney. Publications include *The Cultural Politics of English as an International Language* (1994), *English and the Discourses of Colonialism* (1998), *Critical Applied Linguistics: A Critical Introduction* (2001) and *Global Englishes and Transcultural Flows* (2007).

Rob Pope is Professor of English at Oxford Brookes University and a UK National Teaching Fellow. His work seeks to bridge – or jump – the gaps between the critical and the creative, and his publications include *Textual Intervention: Critical and Creative Strategies for Literary Studies* (1995) and *Creativity: Theory, History, Practice* (2005).

Celia Roberts is Professor of Applied Linguistics at King's College, University of London. Her interests are in language and cultural processes in institutional contexts and their practical relevance to real world situations of disadvantage. Publications include *Language and Discrimination* (1992, with Jupp and Davies), *Achieving Understanding* (1996, with Bremer *et al.*) and *Talk, Work and Institutional Order* (1999, with Sarangi).

Mark Sebba is Reader in Sociolinguistics and Language Contact in the Department of Linguistics and English Language at Lancaster University. His interests are in bilingualism, pidgin and creole studies, written bilingual and multilingual texts and the Sociolinguistics of Orthography. He has recently published *Spelling and Society: The Culture and Politics of Orthography Around the World* (2007).

Brian Street is Professor of Language in Education at King's College, University of London and Visiting Professor of Education in the Graduate School of Education, University of Pennsylvania. Recent publications include: *Literacy: An Advanced Resource Book* (2007, with Lefstein) and *On Ethnography: Approaches to Language and Literacy Research* (2008, with Heath).

Joan Swann is a Senior Lecturer and Director of the Centre for Language and Communication at the Open University. Publications include *A Dictionary of Sociolinguistics* (with Deumert, Lillis and Mesthrie, Edinburgh University Press 2004), *The Art of English: everyday texts and practices* (co-edited with Maybin, Palgrave 2006) and *Introducing Sociolinguistics* (with Mesthrie, Deumert and Leap, 2nd edn in press 2008).

ACKNOWLEDGEMENTS

We would like to thank Carol Johns-MacKenzie for her expert help with formatting the manuscript.

We are indebted to the people and archives listed below for permission to reproduce original material. Every effort has been made to trace copyright-holders. Any omissions brought to our attention will be remedied in future editions.

Figure 2.1 Reproduced with the kind permission of HarperCollins Publishers.

Figure 2.3 Reproduced with the kind permission of Equinox Publishing Limited.

Figure 2.6 Reproduced with the kind permission of News Group Newspapers Ltd.

Figure 2.7 Reproduced with the kind permission of News Group Newspapers Ltd.

Figure 4.1 Reproduced with the kind permission of J.D.A. Widdowson and Clive Upton.

Figure 4.2 Reproduced with permission from the publisher of Dictionary of Regional English Vol. 1 – A–C, edited by Frederick G. Cassidy, p. 11, Cambridge, Mass.: The Belnap press of Harvard University Press. Copyright © 1985 by President and Fellows of Harvard College.

Figure 4.3 Reproduced with the kind permission of Mouton de Gruyter.

Figure 4.4 Reproduced with the kind permission of University of Pennsylvania Press.

Pg 128. 'The Actual Dialogue' by Mongane Wally Serote. Reprinted with permission from DALRO (South Africa) © 2009 on behalf of the author.

Pg 131. 'A Hard Rain's A-Gonna Fall' by Bob Dylan. Copyright 1963; renewed 1991 Special Rider Music. All rights reserved. International copyright secured. Reprinted by permission.

Figure 8.1 Brenda Danet (2001) *Cyberpl@y: Communicating Online*, Oxford: Berg. Reproduced with kind permission.

Figure 8.2 Reproduced with the kind permission of Guava (www.guava.com).

Figure 8.3 Brenda Danet (2001) *Cyberpl@y: Communicating Online*, Oxford: Berg. Reproduced with kind permission.

Figure 8.4 Reproduced with the kind permission of Jukka K. Korpela.

1

INTRODUCTION

JANET MAYBIN AND JOAN SWANN

The Companion to English Language Studies is designed as a resource for those studying English language at undergraduate or postgraduate level. It will also be of interest to those teaching English, and others who wish to check, consolidate or update their knowledge of an area of English Language Studies. The book focuses mainly on contemporary English Language Studies (for more detailed accounts of the history of English, see the suggestions in Further Reading at the end of Part I) and draws on work by language specialists from a range of backgrounds. It takes into account the contemporary position of English in the world and recent developments in the study of the English language and its use, as we explain below.

First, English is affected by its position as a global language, at a point in history when we are witnessing accelerating globalisation, mass movements of peoples and increasing intercultural communication on an unprecedented scale. On the one hand, the number of speakers of English is increasing: it has been estimated that one in four people in the world currently speaks English (Graddol 2006) and that English will be spoken by three billion people, or 40 per cent of the global population, in 2040 (Crystal 2004). On the other hand, it is also the case that the global dominance of English has been challenged by other languages, for instance Mandarin. Furthermore, the dramatic increase in the number of speakers of English predicted by Crystal relates mainly to those who speak English as an additional language rather than to native speakers. English is spoken within multilingual contexts across the globe, and the study of English in such contexts is raising new questions about scholarly concepts and explanations which have been previously accepted within the field.

In addition to addressing the dynamic global role of English, the contents of this volume reflect an important two-way conceptual shift that occurred towards the end of the twentieth century, i.e. the 'social turn' in language studies and a parallel 'turn to discourse' in the social sciences more generally. These two 'turns' both involved an increasing interest among researchers and theorists in the 'processual', 'constitutive' and 'ideological' dimensions of language. Increasingly, language use is seen not simply as reflecting the identities of its speakers, and the cultural contexts in which it is spoken, but as reproducing institutions, identities and cultures. The discursive turn within the social sciences has involved recognition of the significance of discourse, or particular ways of speaking and writing, for the articulation and local management of a range of social processes. References to a 'postmodern turn' are also found among researchers who emphasise the fluid and dynamic nature of language, and the highly contextualised nature of language meaning.

Within language studies, a social approach has been evident in the academic area of sociolinguistics from its inception in the 1960s, and in linguistic anthropology for rather longer. But social concerns are now much more salient, even in fields such as grammar. There is increasing interest in English as a means of communication, with all the contingent social and cultural factors which this entails, and an increasing tendency to conceptualise language and literacy as ideological social practice. English language specialists now share with psychologists, sociologists, anthropologists and historians areas of interest such as language and identity, power and ideology, and the politics of representation, and they also draw on a shared body of critical theory. The social turn in language studies is evident in the more socially-orientated and contextualised studies discussed in the chapters within Part I of the book, and in social, contextual and critical approaches presented in the chapters within Part II.

The changing global role of English, processes of globalisation and intellectual trends in the academy are all reshaping the nature of English Language Studies, and reinvigorating the ways in which English is conceptualised, described and analysed.

CONTENT AND STRUCTURE

This section sets out the content of the book and explains features designed to help readers find their way around the material.

This volume is divided into two parts: Part I on *The fabric of English* outlines major approaches to the description and analysis of language, with a particular focus on English. Part II, brings together contributions from a variety of scholars, each addressing contemporary issues or debates within an area of English Language Studies. Across the book as a whole, our aim is to introduce a range of ways in which English may be researched and understood, and to show how different research traditions construct 'English language' as an academic subject and an object of enquiry.

PART I THE FABRIC OF ENGLISH

In this first part of the book, authors seek to locate and critically account for different research traditions, different languages of description and analysis, and different linguistic processes that have been the object of description and analysis. The aim is to provide an understanding of a variety of approaches to the study of English/language, and also an awareness of their affordances – what they can offer to the study of English – and their limitations.

Part I begins with a chapter by Caroline Coffin and Kieran O'Halloran on *Describing English*. The chapter introduces different descriptive levels: the sounds of language, the writing system, word structure and sentence structure, linguistic and pragmatic meaning, that have been drawn on in the analysis of English. Later sections provide a historical account of traditional grammatical descriptions of English, as well as discussing newer approaches – corpus linguistics and systemic functional linguistics (SFL) – that have challenged some traditional descriptive categories. SFL in particular, in its integration of aspects of social context with linguistic analysis, also provides a grammatical example of the social turn in language studies referred to above. Coffin and O'Halloran explore the motivations for different approaches and also address their strengths and limitations.

Traditional grammar has tended to look at linguistic structures at clause level or below, but both corpus linguistics and systemic functional linguistics have also been drawn on to analyse the structure of longer sequences of language. In Chapter 3, on *Texts and practices*, Ann Hewings and Sarah North continue and develop this focus. The chapter examines a range of approaches to analysing spoken, written and 'multimodal' communication, including relatively 'textual' approaches that study the formal properties of texts; more 'contextualised' approaches that take greater account of the socio-historical contexts in which texts are produced and understood; and 'critical' approaches that highlight power as a significant dimension in language use.

Like other languages, English is highly dynamic, changing through time and varying geographically and socially. Variation and change in English have been studied systematically within sociolinguistics, and this is the subject of Chapter 4, *From variation to hybridity*. In this chapter Rajend Mesthrie and Joan Swann distinguish regional variation, social variation and stylistic variation, in which speakers vary their speaking style in different contexts. The chapter also examines the status and use of English in bi- and multilingual contexts, the development of 'New Englishes' in different parts of the world, and the relationship between English and globalisation. It looks at different approaches to the study of variation and change, for instance quantitative approaches that seek to establish general patterns of use and qualitative (and also more contextualised) approaches that pay greater attention to how speakers manage linguistic resources within specific interactions.

While these chapters examine different aspects of the fabric of English, there are also continuities between them. For instance, in describing variation and change in English, Chapter 4 works within the principle of linguistic levels of description discussed in Chapter 2 (in this case the focus is mainly on sound). In exploring how, in interacting with others, speakers draw on the variability of language as a communicative resource, Chapter 4 also comes close to some of the concerns evident in Chapter 3. We deal with 'interactional sociolinguistics' and 'ethnographic approaches' to the analysis of spoken interaction in both chapters, preferring a small amount of repetition to the unhelpful relegation of these approaches to one chapter or the other.

PART II ISSUES AND DEBATES

Whereas Part I provides a systematic overview of three broad areas in the study and analysis of language, in Part II the authors had a relatively free rein to explore topics that exemplify current issues and debates in English Language Studies. In many cases, these chapters extend ideas about language, or draw on analytical traditions that were introduced in Part I.

The chapters highlight a number of recurring themes in contemporary English Language Studies. First, as we suggested above, English can no longer be treated either as part of a monolingual world, or as an uncontested dominant world language. In a postcolonial global context, English is often studied alongside and in connection with other languages, and its diverse and hybrid forms provide a focus for research in contexts where multilingualism is the norm. Second, there is a particular interest in the ideological dimension of English, for instance in the context of its relationship with other languages, its embedding in social practices and its role in the constitution of individual identities. Third, there is a significant focus on institutional dimensions of English: for instance how English is implicated within sites of struggle and exclusion in habitual institutional practice in courts, workplaces, schools and universities. A fourth theme relates to the creativity inherent in a great deal of language use, as well as the capacity for language play, evident in both 'serious' and more 'frivolous' contexts (from literary texts to food packaging to online code-switching). In combination, these themes challenge any conception of language that would see this as simply (or even mainly) transactional (i.e. having to do with the communication of ideas). They also confront the unsettled relationship between the social and the individual, or between structure and agency, which continues to preoccupy language researchers as well as those working in other disciplines. A final theme has as its focus the material properties of language, or more accurately English texts, and in particular the way verbal language interacts with other communicative modes. As mentioned in Chapter 3, while studies of English still focus mainly on the verbal, in practice English is encountered in 'multimodal' contexts where verbal language works alongside a range of other elements in the creation of meaning (e.g. spoken language alongside posture, gesture and facial expression, voice quality; written language alongside graphic conventions, layout, visual imagery).

The specific coverage of each chapter is outlined briefly below.

In Chapter 5, Alastair Pennycook provides a critical perspective on English and globalisation, extending discussion in Chapter 4. Pennycook argues that contemporary processes of globalisation 'demand that we rethink what we mean by language, language spread, native speakers or multilingualism'. Pointing to ways in which English is linked to inequitable global relations at the same time as it is being appropriated for local uses, he discusses the contrasting ways in which English has been conceptualised as a global language: as a threat to other languages, a lingua franca and a collection of world Englishes.

The focus of Chapter 6, by Rob Pope, is creativity in language. Contemporary research has identified 'literary-like' creativity as a pervasive feature of everyday language – a finding that problematises the distinctiveness of literary language. Pope seeks to develop a working model of creativity which is dynamic and dialogic, involving transformations rather than 'creation from nothing', and which can incorporate a dialogue between linguistic creativity and literary creation. He applies these ideas to a reading of examples from poetry and song.

Chapter 7 looks at the use of persuasive language, evident in various contemporary genres from adverts to political discourse. Applying Aristotle's tripartite division of persuasive rhetoric to the speeches of Brutus and Anthony in Shakespeare's *Julius Caesar*, Guy Cook then examines the contemporary persuasive genre of food marketing, and its use of 'the most contemporary media and the most ancient of techniques'. Considering examples of packaging and promotion from both mass-produced and organic products, he analyses their artful mixture of stories, poetry and images (pathos), appeals to scientific evidence (logos) and use of celebrity personalities (ethos).

English is currently used by around a third of world internet-users, within different forms of synchronous and asynchronous computer-mediated communication. In Chapter 8, Brenda Danet reviews the distinctive features of 'computer-mediated English', stressing its tendency to be informal and playful. While early internet technology favoured the use of English, and it is still the default language in many internet contexts, she points out that code-switching and mixing are common in multilingual contexts, and that linguistic diversity is an increasingly prominent feature of online discourse.

In Chapter 9 Suresh Canagarajah and Selim Ben Said focus on English as a language of education in multilingual contexts. Canagarajah and Ben Said discuss how recent forms of globalisation have challenged Kachru's (1986) conceptualisation of inner, outer and expanding circles of English speakers, complicating the distinctions between speakers of English as a second or foreign language. They argue that social and technological changes have produced new pedagogical imperatives for teachers, new challenges for educational language policies and the need to redefine the scholarly constructs that explain English language learning.

Continuing the focus on education, in Chapter 10 Richard Andrews looks at English as an academic subject in school, taking developments in England as a case study. Andrews reviews the changing position of 'English' as a subject over the past 50 or so years, from the emphasis on expressiveness and personal voice in the 1960s to the early 1980s, through a greater understanding of the processes of written English and of the importance of spoken English in the later part of the twentieth century, to current tensions between curricular and assessment demands on the one hand, and the interest in rhetoric, multimodality and new technologies in the wider society on the other.

In Chapter 11, Celia Roberts discusses institutional discourse, taking a broadly critical discursive approach that examines the ways in which institutions are created and maintained through talk and texts, and their uses within shared habitual practices which are also sites of struggle and exclusion. Drawing on research from a range of disciplinary perspectives (ethnographic approaches, sociolinguistics, conversation analysis and critical discourse analysis) Roberts provides illustrations from diverse institutional contexts, including courtroom testimony, a gate-keeping interview between a counsellor and student, consultations between patients and health care professionals and a job interview.

In Chapter 12 Diana Eades examines one institutional context, the legal system, drawing on sociolinguistic research which examines how language use can affect the delivery of justice. Focusing particularly on the use of English in the courtroom, Eades provides illustrations from her own work on legal cases involving Australian Aboriginal defendants and witnesses. She argues that subtle differences between Aboriginal and standard English, and different communicative practices such as the use of silence, can lead to significant miscarriages of justice. She also discusses the use of sociolinguistic expertise in the legal system, suggesting that this may sometimes be misappropriated by legal professionals.

The focus of Chapter 13 is on language, gender and sexuality. This area has provided some of the most exciting recent research on the complex relationship between language and identity. Deborah Cameron addresses certain 'myths' about women's and men's language, arguing that the relationship between language and gender/sexuality is mediated by social networks, habitual activities, identity and social status. It is distinctions between different kinds of femininity or masculinity, and between specific rather than generic sexual identities, which are most likely to affect stylistic choices. Cameron argues that speakers choose from an array of linguistic options which have symbolic value in relation to widely accepted notions of feminine and masculine speech, in the context of the mutual constitution of gender and heterosexuality.

In Chapter 14, Barbara Mayor discusses children's learning of English, comparing and contrasting insights from 'nativist', 'empiricist' and 'social' perspectives on language acquisition. Mayor points out that most English speakers today acquire 'bilingualism as a first language' (Swain 1972) and stresses the challenges that observations of bilingual acquisition pose to conventional assumptions about the neurological organisation of languages, and about the links between languages and cultures.

Chapter 15 discusses contemporary approaches to the study of literacy. Brian Street reviews the shift from a cognitivist view of literacy in terms of individual skills and competencies, to a social practices or ideological approach, which places more emphasis on the nature and significance of literacy in specific contexts. Using examples from Grahamstown, South Africa and London, England, he discusses research which applies a social practices approach to the study of academic literacies, in combination with insights from research on teaching English as an additional language (EAL) and work on multimodality.

In Chapter 16 Mark Sebba discusses English orthography, particularly spelling. Departing from its usual treatment by linguists or educationalists, Sebba draws on Street's work (see Chapter 15 above), to treat spelling in English as a social practice which is associated with particular beliefs and values. He examines the twentieth century preoccupation with correctness, and the social meanings attributed to deviations from standard spelling conventions. He shows how such deviations are used to create identities, and discusses the currently expanding range of genres where variant spellings are tolerated or valued.

Taking as a context the position of English as a global language (see also Chapter 5 above), in Chapter 17 Busi Makoni and Sinfree Makoni critically review dominant research traditions into the use of English in Africa. Makoni and Makoni discuss a recent approach, 'vague linguistique', whose goal is to capture dynamic and evolving relationships between English, African languages and other semiotic systems. They apply this approach in an analysis of multi-modal data from taxi culture in Accra and Johannesburg.

Chapter 18 focuses on translation between English and other languages. Susan Bassnett traces the roots of the reluctance of native English speakers to embrace other languages, contrasting this with the central, though often overlooked, role of translation in the English Literature canon. She discusses how translation studies, emerging in the late 1970s alongside other radical approaches to English literary and language studies, has highlighted the creative nature of translation and its central importance as a shaping force in English literary history.

SOME STYLISTIC FEATURES IN PART I THE FABRIC OF ENGLISH

While *The Companion to English Language Studies* deals with a range of challenging ideas, we have tried to keep the structure simple and user-friendly (decidedly unpostmodern, in fact). In Part I, which provides some essential groundwork in English Language Studies, chapters include the following features, designed to help readers track significant concepts and issues.

KEY CONCEPTS

First, within each chapter, important concepts are set in **bold** where they are introduced and defined. These are also represented as bold terms in the index, so that readers can easily find the location of explanations/definitions.

BOXES

For those terms that need a fuller definition, or where we want to group related terms, we use separate boxed text to avoid interrupting the flow of discussion in the chapters.

CROSS-REFERENCING

Within each chapter, we include cross-referencing to allow readers to track ideas across chapters.

FURTHER READING

Chapter authors have also included suggestions for further reading. For ease of reference, these are included in a combined list at the end of Part I.

Part I
THE FABRIC OF ENGLISH

2

DESCRIBING ENGLISH

CAROLINE COFFIN AND KIERAN O'HALLORAN

2.1 INTRODUCTION

There are many ways of carving up and describing English. In this chapter, both authors start by providing a brief overview of the different linguistic levels that typify the way many linguists have traditionally approached English structure. Then Caroline Coffin takes a historical perspective and, focusing on grammar in particular, reflects on why particular views on language structure came to dominate at different historical points. The chapter then goes on to discuss some exciting contemporary perspectives and methods of examination. Kieran O'Halloran looks at **corpus linguistics**. A corpus is a large electronic database of texts, e.g. The Bank of English is a corpus of 450 million words; The British National Corpus consists of 100 million words. In the past 10 to 20 years, technology has developed to allow quick searches of corpora. Instead of relying on their intuitions of how language is used, or on small amounts of data, linguists can now make empirically robust statements about widespread language use. Indeed, corpus-based linguistics is challenging traditional ways of describing and classifying language structure. Coffin also considers the impact of **systemic functional linguistics**, a theory which puts in central position the relationship between grammatical structure and the texts and social contexts in which language is used. She indicates how such an orientation departs from traditional ways of describing English. Finally, O'Halloran takes stock and considers some of the strengths and weaknesses of these approaches to describing English.

GRAMMAR AND GRAMMARS

Grammar is used in two broad senses in linguistics: first, it refers to aspects of the structure of language (either language as a faculty or the structure of a particular language – e.g. the grammar of English). Second, it refers to a particular approach to the study of linguistic structure. We look at grammar in both senses in this chapter.

Grammar usually refers to two levels of linguistic structure: sentence structure (syntax) and word structure (morphology), although sometimes it is used more broadly to include other linguistic levels.

Whereas traditionally grammar has been distinguished from **lexis** (adjective **lexical**), referring to the vocabulary system of a language, some recent grammatical descriptions seek to combine these levels of analysis:

---

the term **lexicogrammar** may be found in such cases. More recent grammatical descriptions may also be applied above the level of the sentence, to incorporate the structure of longer sequences of text.

2.2 LINGUISTIC STRUCTURES: A TRADITIONAL VIEW

GRAMMAR: MORPHOLOGY AND SYNTAX

In this section we provide a brief introduction to how linguistic structures have traditionally been identified according to different levels of analysis and discuss, in turn, grammar, semantics and pragmatics, the sounds of language and the writing system.

Consider the following from a satire on radio disc jockeys (DJs). Smashie (Mike Smash) and Nicey (Dave Nice) are both DJs at the fictitious British radio station, Radio Fab FM:

SMASHIE: At Radio Fab in the late 60s, the powers that be . . . or be-ed at the time . . . or is it 'were'? . . . er . . . anyway . . . they was . . . er . . . and these powers moved my show to a slot that abutted Nicey's.

> (From *Smashie and Nicey: End of an Era* BBC by Harry Enfield and Paul Whitehouse)

Smashie is clearly confused about the past of *powers that be*? But what exactly is it? It is difficult to decide because *powers that be* is a **formulaic sequence**, a fixed expression in other words. It signals the present tense ('be' is present subjunctive), but trying to convert it to the past tense disrupts the fixedness of the expression. Once this has happened, it is hard to know how to proceed because we usually only deal with *powers that be*. Smashie attempts to find the past tense. The Radio Fab DJ knows that *be* is a verb and needs to be changed in some way to indicate past meaning. He thus knows that *be* needs to have its **morphology** changed but is not sure which verb form to use.

Morphology is the study of word structure which includes the way in which words are related to other words and the way in which many words can be subdivided into smaller meaningful units called **morphemes**. *Cooked*, for example, has two morphemes, *cook* providing the core meaning and *-ed* signalling past tense or past participle. Similarly, *book* in *books* signals the core meaning and *s* signals the plural form. A morpheme is a unit of grammar and is not the same as a syllable. That is, a word may have several syllables but be a single morpheme (e.g. *catastrophe*), or be a single syllable and contain two morphemes (e.g. *cook-ed* or *work-ed*).

There are a number of aspects of word structure to consider including **inflection** and **derivation**. Inflection deals with word structure that is determined by the role of words in sentences. For example, the present tense of the verb 'work' uses the form *works* for third person singular (she works, he works, it works) and the form *work* in all other cases (I, you and they work). Derivation is concerned with the creation of new words with different meanings, e.g. *mistreat* from *treat*.

Linguistic forms are combined into utterances via grammatical rules, or **syntax**, to produce well-formed sentences. In standard English, the combination of third person plural subject pronoun with past tense of the verb *to be* is realised as *they were*. Thus Smashie utters non-standard syntax in the extract above when he says 'they was'.

The syntax of 'they was', or 'they were', involves the **grammatical** word – *they*. Pronouns such as *they* along with other grammatical words such as prepositions (e.g. *on, in, at*), conjunctions (e.g. *if, because, since*), determiners (e.g. *a, the*) are a relatively small finite set. Grammatical words provide the structure or glue for texts while **lexical words** such as *cat, language, power* provide the building blocks of text. Lexical words are the main carriers of meaning in a text, and are from a very large set: the vocabulary we use (also referred to as **lexis**).

Lexical and grammatical words can be combined into **phrases**: units of meaning which consist of a **head** (i.e. the core element) plus **modifiers** which go round the head. Phrases in the example above include (heads underlined): *at Radio Fab, in the late 60s, the powers that be, at the time*. Lexical and grammatical words can be combined into longer units of meaning which normally consist of a verb plus other elements: e.g. subject, object. These units of meaning are known as **clauses**; e.g. *these powers moved my show* (verb underlined).

To sum up, syntax is concerned with the way words work together to constitute phrases or clauses. Key aspects of syntax include negation, the formation of questions, the coordination and subordination of clauses and passivisation.

MEANING: SEMANTICS AND PRAGMATICS

Consider another extract from *Smashie and Nicey: End of an Era*. This time the DJs are addressing a TV audience on the topic of punk rock:

NICEY: The early 70s were halcyon days but then in 1976 a cancer appeared, Smashie.
SMASHIE: No, I'm sorry mate I object to that description.
NICEY: Oh, er, a cancer appeared – Smashie, tell them about the cancer.
[laughter]

This short dialogue shows the distinction between **semantic** meaning and **pragmatic** meaning.

Semantic meanings are encoded in the lexis and grammar of a language. These are the meanings that are found in dictionaries and grammar books, and to know a language is to know what these are. As an example, take 'The green van has arrived'. If we didn't know what *van* denotes, we could find out by going to a dictionary and read that it is a 'covered motor vehicle for transporting goods by road'. But what a word denotes is not the same as knowing what it means in particular utterances. To establish this we need to know the situation in which the utterance occurs. One possible situation is as follows: it's near Christmas and a husband is at the window of their front room, while his wife and children are watching television. He has just spotted the arrival of a green van outside their house, which he and his wife are expecting: it is a delivery van from a toy shop. The husband relays semantic meaning when he utters 'The green van has arrived'. But what is the significance of this information in this situation? In other words, what pragmatic meanings need to be generated? The husband prefers to use 'the green van' to communicate the arrival of the toys to his wife so as not to spoil the surprise for the children. His wife, with knowledge of the semantic meanings of English, and knowledge of this situation, is able to generate relevant pragmatic meaning. Another way of looking at this is to say that she generates a relevant context in order to process this information (for the pragmatics scholars, Dan Sperber and Deidre Wilson (e.g. Sperber and Wilson 1995) context is defined as aspects of a situation which are relevant to communication). In a different time and place and with different participants, 'the green van has arrived' may have a very different pragmatic meaning but its semantic meaning would remain more or less the same.

In the extract above, Smashie and Nicey play on the distinction between semantic and pragmatic meaning. *Cancer* has two potential semantic meanings: 'malignant growth caused by abnormal and uncontrolled cell division' and, metaphorically, 'an evil influence that spreads dangerously'. *Cancer* has the latter semantic meaning here. However, when Nicey uses the term (to refer to the rise of punk rock in the mid-1970s) there is a pragmatic misunderstanding. From the proximity of *cancer* to *Smashie* at the end of Nicey's utterance, Smashie makes a false inference in thinking that Nicey is referring to him as a cancer. The inferences we make from the situation we are in, taking our bearings from semantic meaning, are known as pragmatic meanings. Clearly, Smashie should have made the inference that *Smashie* at the end of the utterance was only a cue for him to take his turn.

THE SOUNDS OF LANGUAGE: PHONETICS AND PHONOLOGY

The dialogue between Smashie and Nicey, presented here as a written transcript, was, of course, originally spoken. Clearly, absent in any transcript are meanings which are communicated through sound. A speaker's accent, for example, provides useful sociolinguistic information regarding their social class and geographical origin whilst intonation can convey attitude (such as surprise or irony) as well as making clear whether a clause is a statement or a question. Accents may also have characteristic intonation patterns. A feature known as 'high rising tone' (where statements end with rising intonation) occurs in many varieties of English, particularly amongst younger speakers.

Phonetics and phonology are ways of describing and analysing the sounds of language. Whereas **phonetics** is about the physical production and perception of speech sounds, **phonology** is concerned with the sound *system* of a language: individual speech sounds that are recognised as distinctive within a language, referred to as **phonemes**, as well as phenomena such as intonation, stress and syllable structure. In English, for example, /p/ and /b/ are distinctive phonemes. Using one rather than the other in a word produces a change of meaning, as in *pack* versus *back*, *rip* versus *rib*. But languages make different phonemic distinctions. This may be illustrated with respect to aspiration. 'Aspiration' refers to a puff of air accompanying the articulation of certain sounds. In English /k/ (the initial sound in *cat*) may be pronounced with a greater or lesser degree of aspiration, but this makes no difference to its phonemic status – it is still regarded as the same phoneme; in Hindi, by contrast, aspiration does make a difference – it produces a different phoneme. So *kana* and *khana* are two different words in Hindi (respectively 'one-eyed' and 'to eat').

In English the sounds [kʰ] and [k] (pronounced with or without aspiration) would be regarded as different **allophones** or realisations of the same phoneme.

Whilst the phoneme can be seen as part of an abstract sound system, phonetics is concerned with the actual articulation of sound. Phonetic symbols within the International Phonetic Alphabet are a universal (i.e. not language specific) system of symbols. They enable linguists to transcribe actual sounds both within and across languages and language varieties. A symbol such as [t] for instance, will represent a voiceless stop consonant made between the tongue and the alveolar ridge as in English *tea* or Arabic *kitab* or Chinese *tan*. The sounds are not identical, but diacritics can be added to indicate more precisely how they are produced.

Conventionally, square brackets are used to transcribe phonetic symbols – [p], [kʰ], [t]; and slashes to transcribe phonemic symbols – /p/, /k/, /t/.

THE WRITING SYSTEM OR ORTHOGRAPHY

Smashie and Nicey had a 'catchphrase' they would use to describe one another: 'Smashie/Nicey, what a guy, does a lot of work for charity, but doesn't like to talk about it'. The satire on celebrity disc jockeys here was that actually both of them wanted their listeners to know that they did a lot of work for charity, and would inconspicuously prompt whichever of the two was presenting on air to say so. Both characters pronounced the /t/ in *charity* so that it sounded more like a diminished [d], and Smashie especially made its pronunciation sound quite nauseating, something like ChARIdee. The word developed a life of its own in the 1990s as people in the UK started to use it to indicate a cynical and/or playful take on how celebrities raised money for charity, i.e. it is as good for them as it is for the cause. This form of *charity* thus carries evaluative meaning, and continues to be used:

I HOPE all the 'alternative' (i.e. not funny) comedians who slagged off Jeremy Beadle over the past two decades are feeling suitably sheepish.
It's only since he died this week that we truly discovered what a remarkable man Jeremy was . . . [Alternative comedians] scoffed at his work for **char-i-dee**, but Jeremy raised £100 million for good causes.

(Lorraine Kelly, The Sun, 2 February 2008: 21)

References to such celebrity charity activity often use nonstandard spellings, as in Lorraine Kelly's *char-i-dee*. Figure 2.1 shows 'concordance lines' from the 450-million-word Bank of English corpus (collected over the period 1999–2003) which reveal several different spellings in magazines and newspapers. Concordance lines provide the co-texts for a particular word (i.e. the immediate textual environment). There are 37 instances of *char-i-dee* or similar spellings.

The concordance lines in Figure 2.1 seem to show that the spelling has yet to standardise since the following are variants of this relatively new expression: <charidddeee>, <chariddy>, <charidee>, <charidy> (researchers often use the < > convention to represent spelling). Nevertheless, the corpus information is useful here since it provides an indication that <charidee>, as the most common spelling, may well emerge as the standard one should British English lexicographers choose to 'officialise' it. Spelling in English, both standard and nonstandard, may be studied as an aspect of **orthography**.

Orthography describes or defines the set of symbols used in any particular writing system, for example, alphabetic letters, characters, numerals and punctuation marks. Orthography is also concerned with the rules for writing the symbols. Depending on the nature of the writing system, these may include punctuation, spelling and capitalisation. Thus, while 'orthography' in colloquial terms is often used synonymously with spelling, spelling is only part of orthography.

It is useful to compare phonology and orthography. Whereas a phoneme (phonological symbol) such as /s/ will always stand for the same sound (as in the initial sound in *sun*), the letter (orthographic symbol) <s> can represent different sounds (*cats*, *dogs*). It may also combine with other letters to represent further sounds (as in *wash*). In English, the relationship between letters (orthography) and phonemes (phonology) is far from simple since English has (approximately, depending on the variety) a set of 44 phonemes, which have to be orthographically represented by the 26 letters of the English alphabet. Mark Sebba discusses how the relationship between 'sound' and 'spelling' may be manipulated to a range of effects (see Chapter 16).

In this section, we have used an extended example from Smashie and Nicey to show how linguists have described the structure of English (and other languages) according to different linguistic levels. In the next section, Coffin provides a historical perspective on grammar, contrasting traditional and more recent approaches to the description and analysis of English structure.

Mike Smash hosted a fantabulous 'charidddeee special' on Radio Fab FM or
unconsciousness by Punk. A rush of 'Chariddy' to the head knocked together a
a good £2 in change for various 'chariddy' collectors outside the ground-and
won't be on hand to sell kisses for 'chariddy'. <p> However, Wavey Davy Cottrell
of the popular quiz and all for "charidee", of course. <p> The BBC
next month raising money for charidee. Their parents are people like
goody two-shoes. Yet far from their charidee work elevating them, their Smashy
true - why, he even did it all for charidee, the National Autistic Society.
we give millions of tins of them to charidee? <p> <!--email--> <hl> I'll be
Frame it? Wear it? Auction it for charidee? <p> "And now we come to Lot No23,
out. <p> It might be great for charidee, but it didn't half make the sin
is, all this endless work for "charidee" gets on my nerves. <p> Macca and
their royalties to Comic Relief. O Charidee, what comic crimes have been
research. Of course any list of 'charidee' activities would be incomplete
website, with the proceeds going to charidee (Dean Kamen's own, in fact).
lot of driving ... and all for charidee. * Mr Tony's foreword to his
the 25p a call costs, 15p goes to charidee, which will bring back much needed
It. Worth mentioning here (it's for charidee) is Five Go Mad in the Kitchen,
want to degrade themselves for 'charidee' then good luck to them. But what
of ours did a lot of work for charidee ... <p> NEW MODEL ARMY <p>
THE BANDS are pulling together for charidee, from clueless rockers to reggae
friends are doing a lot of work for charidee and they do like to talk about it!
<p> They do a lot of duff work for charidee. (Craig mclean) <p> Goodbye Mr
reasons why I must be kind to this 'charidee' record, even though it has some
Blackburn and glam be-decked Jimmy 'Charidee' Saville and features the likes of
<p> (Island/All formats) <p> CHARIDEE RECORDS have been a bit of a joke
<h> They can't do a lot for charidee ... </h> <p> Back to the Planet
WITH CAPTIONS </c> <h> George's charidee 45 </h> <p> GEORGE MICHAEL is
TEENAGE FANCLUB for an exclusive 'charidee' single-and they do want to talk
together and dash off a couple of charidee tracks. The Fannies are currently
season and do some decent work for charidee. Last year Glasters, NME and
which includes a pop star-studded charidee mission organised by our wry host.
INN at <zz1> address <zz0> host a charidee extravaganza this Thursday 23 June
with at the end of the day. <h> CHARIDEE PETS </h> <zz1> photo <zz0> <p>
Duets and help raise money for AIDS charidees. Me? I'd pay them not to release
BY LINDSEY TANNER Last October, Charidy Crabtree's doctor had her swallow
</c> <h> THEY DO AN AWFUL LOT FOR CHARIDY ... </h> <p> Famiglia Christiana,

Figure 2.1 Concordance lines for 'charidee' and variants from The Bank of English®.

2.3 DESCRIBING ENGLISH STRUCTURE: A HISTORICAL VIEW

FROM THE TRADITIONAL TO THE CONTEMPORARY

It is important to recognise that the descriptions of levels identified by linguists
are not 'theory free'. First, the divisions themselves can be challenged. Second,
different linguists have different ideas about, for example, syntax or semantics.
In Section 2.2 we outlined the kinds of issues and areas that are generally tackled
in relation to each of the levels. It is important to acknowledge, however, that
(for example) morphology as an aspect of linguistic structure should always
be distinguished from *the study of* morphology. Michael Halliday, the chief

architect of systemic functional linguistics (see Section 2.5), makes the following point in relation to grammar:

> English ... tends to confuse the study of a phenomenon with the phenomenon itself. So while the term 'grammar' is commonly used ... to mean the wording system, the central processing unit of a natural language, it is also used indiscriminately to mean the study of that system ... I have been calling the study of grammar 'grammatics' in order to make the distinction clearer. A grammatics is thus a theory for explaining grammar.
>
> (Halliday 2002: 369)

In this section I would like to step back and reflect on why language and grammar can be, and have been, examined and described in a multiplicity of ways. Taking a historical approach, I will look at some of the most persistent and influential approaches or 'grammatics' that have shaped the way the English language is described and therefore 'seen'. I will consider how these approaches have developed partly as a consequence of historical context (including the different means for collecting and analysing language data) and partly as a result of the changing purposes of the linguists and grammarians who stand behind the theories.

TRADITIONAL GRAMMAR

Traditional grammar is a somewhat loose 'umbrella term' covering a range of approaches to the study of language. Historically, traditional approaches have focused more on single sentences than on sentences combined together to form texts and more on form than on meaning. The labelling used is often based on **word classes** – for example, *noun, verb, adjective, adverb, noun phrase, preposition phrase*, etc. – and as such tells us what kind of thing the item of language is and something about its potential to appear in different kinds of clause structure. Some labelling is more functionally oriented, for example, *subject, complement, adjunct*. This type of labelling shows what something is doing in a particular structure and makes it possible to discern grammatical relations between parts of a structure (see Martin 2004 for a full discussion of 'function' versus 'structure' labelling). In traditional grammar, the evidence for such categories has tended to come from introspection and precedent.

Traditional approaches to English grammar have a long history, with the basic terminology and system of classification being based on the work of early Greek and Roman philosophers. The Greeks had a dual purpose in developing grammars. First, they saw grammar as an important tool which could be used for studying Greek Literature and, second, they were driven by intellectual curiosity – they wanted to understand the structure of their language. The grammatical system developed by the Greeks was applied to Latin by the Romans – largely unmodified. Latin grammars were influential across Europe throughout the

Middle Ages, as during this period Latin was the medium for all education. However, it was also in this period that vernacular languages began to be used for writing and learning and thus there was an interest in developing grammars for describing particular European languages. As a consequence, Latin grammar was adopted and (to some extent) adapted in order to describe English.

Grammars of English using terminology and concepts derived from Latin and Greek grammar persisted throughout the eighteenth and nineteenth centuries. This was despite the fact that in many respects English has a different structure to that of Latin and Greek. Furthermore, these grammars were restricted to accounts of formal, written, literary language rather than taking into consideration the different varieties of spoken language. At this historical point, the main motivation for developing such grammars was to reform and standardise language. Through the process of standardisation, English could then be codified, i.e. official rules for grammar, orthography, pronunciation and vocabulary could be set up. Where variants for a certain aspect of the language existed, e.g. different ways of spelling a word, decisions on which variant to promote would be made. A secondary aim was to simplify and rework the grammars for pedagogical purposes. In the nineteenth and early twentieth century, school students were taught traditional grammar in order to 'parse' sentences (i.e. label the parts of speech in a sentence such as noun, verb, adjective, etc.) and to identify 'correct' from 'incorrect' English.

In the latter part of the twentieth century, the study of traditional grammar as part of the school curriculum fell from favour in countries such as the UK and Australia, but in recent years it has been making a come back, albeit in a less prescriptive form and with a greater emphasis on communicative effect. In the UK for example, aspects of traditional grammar feature in school English curriculum documents and in the National Literacy Strategy. More broadly, traditional grammar provides a conceptual base and terminology for the development (and understanding) of other grammars such as systemic functional grammar, to be discussed further below.

STRUCTURAL LINGUISTICS

Structural approaches to the description of language developed in the 1930s (following somewhat different directions in North America and Europe) within the relatively new discipline of **linguistics** and within a context where empirical, scientific, objective methods were particularly prized. The aims of structural linguists were quite different to those of traditional grammarians. They wished to develop descriptions of different languages that were free of preconceived notions of what a language should contain and how it should operate. In their view language constituted a set of behaviour patterns common to the members of a particular community. In particular (in contrast to traditional grammarians), their goal was to categorise the different structural patterns which occur in everyday language use. By the 1930s, technology was available for recording authentic speech. Structural linguists were particularly interested in the sound system as evidenced in the precise description of phonemes in Leonard Bloomfield's seminal work, *Language* (1933).

Structural linguists provided alternative ways of describing language. First, compared to traditional grammar, a greater emphasis was given to the structural characteristics of a linguistic element (e.g. *walked* is a verb because it contains the suffix *ed*; *boy* is a noun because the inflection *s* indicates plural form) and where it is located in the structure of a sentence (e.g. *the* is a word which comes before a noun). In order to capture this different way of classifying language, new terminology was developed. Within the American tradition of structuralism, Charles Fries distinguished **form words** and **function words** (corresponding to the distinction between lexical and grammatical words referred to in Section 2.2). Whilst form words include classes such as:

Class 1 – words that pattern like 'girl', 'musical', 'shop', etc.;
Class 2 – words that pattern like 'walk', 'sing', 'appear', etc.;

function words comprise groups such as:

Group A – words that pattern like 'a' and 'the' in English sentences;
Group B – words that pattern like 'is' (auxiliary) . . . and so on.

A second significant difference in the structuralist approach is a focus on sentence patterns or syntax – the way in which native speakers of the language arrange words in a particular order. In analysing the sentence, a process called **immediate constituent** (IC) analysis is used. The sentence is divided into successive layers, or constituents, until, in the final layer, each constituent consists of only a word or meaningful part of a word (i.e. a morpheme):

Villager | s | search | ed | the | country | side | for | many | day | s

At this level, the unit of analysis is the 'tagmeme' – a unit of grammatical arrangement that can be described in terms of slots (grammatical positions within a sentence such as subject or object) and fillers (the class of items grammatically acceptable in each slot, e.g. nouns and pronouns would be possible fillers of the subject position). In the example above, *Villagers* is a subject slot and the filler is a noun.

The structuralist approach stimulated some strong critical reaction. This is perhaps not surprising, given that it was the first major challenge to traditional grammatical descriptions. It is curious to note, however, that for some critics not only was the approach a challenge to existing theory but a challenge to language use itself. For example, Sherwood, a Professor of Composition at Oregon University at the time, argued:

the old grammar is seen to stand for values that are often a good deal more defensible than their opposites. It stands for order, logic, and consistency; for the supremacy of the written language and of the literate classes in setting linguistic standards; for continuity, tradition, and universality . . . It is not resigned to the chaos of experience but wishes to impose its own order upon it; it believes, with Orwell, in man's power to master his linguistic environment . . . it attempts to raise the illiterate to the level of the literate, not to average everyone out to a common level.

(Sherwood 1960: 276)

The pre-eminence of structuralism decreased in the late 1950s and 1960s, after the emergence of transformational generative grammar.

TRANSFORMATIONAL GENERATIVE GRAMMAR

Transformational generative grammar (TGG) emerged in the second half of the twentieth century, partly as a result of Noam Chomsky's (the main proponent) dissatisfaction with the structuralists' focus on surface features. Chomsky was particularly interested in finding a means of explaining relations between phrases with the same **surface structure** such as:

1 The barking of dogs.
2 The raising of children.

Using the notion of **deep structure**, he argued that whilst in phrases such as 1 above, *dogs bark* is the underlying deep structure, in phrases such as 2 above, *children raise* is clearly not. Rather its derivation is *they raise children*. The distinction between 'surface' and 'deep' structure is a key one in appreciating Chomsky's notion of **universal grammar**, a theory which proposes that the same deep structures underlie all human languages and are genetically programmed in the human brain. In this theory, grammar is an abstract notion, a device for producing and understanding sentences in any and all languages.

In the framework of transformational-generative grammar (of which 'Government and Binding Theory' and 'The Minimalist Program' are more recent re-workings), the structure of a sentence is represented by phrase structure 'trees' (illustrated in Figure 2.2). Such trees provide information about the sentences they represent by showing the hierarchical relations between their component parts. As Figure 2.2 demonstrates, it is possible, in such a model, to generate sentences that are syntactically but not semantically well-formed.

The type of diagramming and labelling inspired by Chomsky's work, and which is still conducted in more formal linguistic schools, provides an overview of the structure of sentences as a whole but does not show how a constituent is functioning in a particular utterance.

It is important to recognise that TGG does not set out to provide a detailed

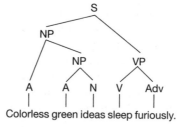

Colorless green ideas sleep furiously.

(S = sentence, NP = noun phrase, VP = verb phrase, A = adjective, N = noun, Adv = adverb)

Figure 2.2 Phrase structure tree.

description of grammatical features in a specific language such as English. Indeed Chomsky argues that there is no place for the notion of language outside the mind/brain. Rather he is interested in developing an understanding of the human 'language faculty' – the principles and parameters which can account for the way in which people acquire linguistic knowledge and produce and understand utterances, that is, develop *person-specific, internal or 'I-languages'* (Chomsky 1986).

So far, this section has shown how the different strategies of grammatical description which linguists adopt are in part dependent on what they want their grammars to do. Whereas traditional grammars often serve as **pedagogic grammars** and **reference grammars**, the work of generative linguists is more theoretically oriented. Another useful criterion in distinguishing different grammars (or more accurately 'grammatics') is whether they set out to describe or prescribe. Traditional grammar, for example, has frequently been drawn on to set out prescriptive rules for writing or speaking correct English. However, not all traditional grammars are used in this way. Those which push towards the functional, such as the 'communicative grammars' of linguists such as Quirk *et al.* (1985) are more interested in setting out common patterns of usage. Such grammars may be more accurately described as **descriptive grammars**.

Over the past 50 years, some exciting new perspectives on grammar and lexis have emerged, which will be the focus of Sections 2.4–2.6. These new approaches to theorising and describing language have been motivated partly by a growing interest in how people actually use language and partly by a recognition that traditional, more formal descriptions (often based on idealised language data) may fall short of capturing the full richness of language as a system for meaning making. Another important influence on rethinking descriptions of languages such as English has been rapid technological development. New technologies make it increasingly easy to collect, store and search vast amounts of language (i.e. a corpus) produced in a wide range of cultural and social situations. Linguists are beginning to find that existing terms, classifications and conceptualisations do not adequately capture how language 'on the ground' works, particularly spoken grammar. How, for example, would traditional descriptions classify structures illustrated in the following (naturally occurring) spoken data?

i The white house on the corner, is that where she lives?
(In this example, rather than say 'is it the white house on the corner where she lives?' or 'does she live in the white house on the corner', the speaker brings to the front of the clause *the white house on the corner* which is then picked up in the demonstrative *that.*)

ii I'm going to have steak and fries, I am.
(In this example, the speaker repeats at the end of the clause the beginning part of his utterance *I am.*)

(Examples cited Carter 2004b: 30)

Searching through large amounts of empirical spoken data has helped linguists to recognise that usage which may previously have been regarded as marginal, such as the examples above, is actually more common than previously supposed. Since traditional grammatical terms would not adequately describe the phenomena above, one solution to the problem is to develop new classifications and new terms. Ronald Carter, for example, coined the terms 'heads' to describe elements such as *The white house on the corner* in example i which are fronted in an utterance and 'tails' to describe elements such as *I am* in example ii which come at the end of an utterance. Investigation of large corpora in this way provides a basis for identifying and responding to any significant gaps or inadequacies in existing grammars and theories of language.

Sections 2.4–2.6 will consider two relatively recent 'uprisings' (if not complete 'revolutions') in relation to describing the English language. They will show how both 'movements' – corpus linguistics and systemic functional linguistics – have approached, broken up and described English in quite new ways compared to those set out above and, in so doing, have made major contributions to understanding how language is organised and structured.

2.4 Corpus Linguistics

Collocation, Phraseology, Semantic Prosody

While a speaker will have rich knowledge of how English is used in particular situations, it is, inevitably, partial knowledge since it is usually based *only* on the conversations the speaker has had, the novels they have read, the academic texts they have absorbed, etc. Rich knowledge of English allows speakers to make robust predictions about how it is generally used. And often these are fairly accurate. But, as **corpus linguistics** – the study of large bodies of language data with electronic search software – has shown, native speaker intuitions about general usage, because they are ultimately partial ones, are not always so reliable. It is often hard to know when they can be trusted and when they cannot. Large electronic corpora provide evidence of how language is actually used. The larger the corpus, and the more varied and more specific the situational uses selected for it, the better since this will provide a good sense of how a language is being used and the extent of different types of usage. Grammars based on the analysis of substantial corpora – **corpus-based grammars** – have great advantages then in providing information on the **frequency** of different types of language use. Let us look at some examples of where a corpus-based grammar can shed light on language use.

While one may be able to intuit that among the most frequently used words in English are *the* and *to*, it is much harder to intuit the most frequent patterns of lexis and grammar. This is where a large corpus is valuable. In fact, from large corpus examination, an interesting insight has flowed: languages are much more patterned than was previously recognised. One kind of pattern is **collocation** – words which commonly accompany other words. So *family* is a common collocate of *argument* as in *family argument*. In this collocation, the head noun is *argument*, which is modified by another noun, *family*. Large corpora can provide data on the most frequent and most **productive** collocates of a word. Productivity here is a different notion to frequency. It refers to the number of collocations in which a particular word is found. Biber *et al.* (1999: 592), a corpus-based grammar, indicates that *family* is one of the most productive collocate nouns in English because it combines with more than a 100 different nouns (e.g. *affair, background, barbecue, car, company, doctor, friend*). It is also relatively frequent because it occurs in noun–noun collocation over 50 times per million words.

With large corpora, one can go beyond collocation and observe longer patterns of English which are typically used. In other words, one can see more readily what the frequent **phraseologies** are in English – strings of lexis and grammar. Stubbs (2007) discovered that *world* is one of the top ten nouns in the British National Corpus (BNC), a corpus of 100 million words. He found that the reason it is so common is because it occurs in frequent phraseologies such as *the most natural thing in the world, one of the world's most gifted scientists.* Phraseologies such as these where superlatives are used, or rankings are employed, are very frequent in English but it would be difficult to see this so clearly without large corpora. The capacity to make palpable the regularity of phraseology in English has led to other exciting insights. John Sinclair (2004: 30–35) found an interesting phraseological pattern around the seemingly neutral collocation *naked eye*. His corpus investigation reveals a common phraseology, *negativity + visibility + preposition + the + naked + eye* such as in *too faint to be seen with the naked eye* or *it is not really visible to the naked eye* (ironically a phraseological regularity which is not so visible without corpus investigation!). What is very interesting here is that, while the collocation *naked eye* would seem to be neutral, in the sense of being devoid of connotational meaning, the regular phraseology in which it appears is not neutral. It carries the evaluative meanings of constraint/limitation. This type of evaluative meaning is spread over the phraseology and thus absorbs seemingly neutral meanings like *naked eye*. This corpus-illuminated type of evaluative meaning is referred to as **semantic prosody**. It is different to connotational meaning since the latter is regarded as conventionally associated with a word (e.g. *devil* has a conventionally associated negative meaning). The concept of semantic prosody has enjoyed wide currency in corpus-based linguistics (e.g. Sinclair 1991; Louw 1993; Hunston 1995; Stubbs 1996; Channell 2000; Sinclair 2004; Bednarek 2008).

There are difficulties with the concept, however. One problem is that prosodies do not necessarily carry into every situational use, or **register**. Consider *erupted* in the past tense. In the Bank of English, around 75 per cent of the instances are from the hard news register, i.e. newspaper reports of political/economic events, conflicts, disasters, wars and overwhelmingly show a preference for collocating with negative human phenomena (e.g. 'fighting erupted'; 'row erupted'). There is, in hard news, repeated evidence for a phraseology of 'abstract noun for human phenomenon + erupted (past tense)' (O'Halloran 2007). Since these meanings are overwhemingly negative, one might say there is a negative semantic prosody for 'erupted' in the past tense. However, some examples of 'erupted' in the past tense have positive associations. Consider the following extract from a sports report:

> Just as another undeserved German victory loomed, up popped Robbie Keane to score a dramatic last-minute equaliser. The pub *erupted*. Another heroic draw for the Irish to celebrate. I suspect Roy Keane would have been furious that they had failed to win.

Indeed, *erupted* in the past tense has largely positive associations in the sports report register. This, along with its largely negative associations in the hard news register, provides evidence for seeing *erupted* in **register prosody** terms rather than semantic prosody terms (see O'Halloran 2007). It should be stressed that the concept of register prosody is a probabilistic one. While the meanings around *erupted* in the past tense in hard news are overwhelmingly negative, there are a small number of instances which carry positive meanings (e.g. *fireworks erupted and champagne corks were popping* in a story about the first day of the new millennium). It may well be the case that some expressions carry a semantic prosody regardless of register (e.g. *United States of Europe*; see O'Halloran and Coffin 2004). Alternatively, other prosodies are more likely to be register-dependent.

Note that the term 'register', which we have introduced briefly here is used with slightly different meanings in different linguistic descriptions. The term is defined more fully in relation to systemic functional linguistics in Section 2.5 and we refer to it in Chapter 3.

This section has indicated how corpora provide insight into collocation and phraseology. Indeed, for Sinclair (1991), much if not most language use is collocative and phraseological, being in line with his **idiom principle**: the hearer or reader understands language in chunks, rather than as individual words in a grammatical sequence. Such chunks are difficult to define because they range from the long ('You can lead a horse to water; but you can't make him drink') to the short ('Oh no!') (Schmitt and Carter 2004: 3). To capture this variability,

Wray (2002) refers to such chunks as **formulaic sequences**: '*formulaic* carries with it some associations of "unity" and of "custom" and "habit", while *sequence* indicates that there is more than one discernible unit, of whatever kind' (Wray 2002: 9). On this broad definition, formulaic sequences can include both collocation and phraseology. To assess the speed at which formulaic sequences are read, Underwood *et al.* (2004) use measurements of eye movements. They find that the last words of formulaic sequences (e.g. *no* in *oh no*) are read more quickly than the same words when used on their own (e.g. 'No', said Jemima). This is taken to indicate that formulaic sequences are processed in reading as a whole rather than in a 'summing of parts' manner. Moreover, Wray (2002) finds both pausing and errors to be much less frequent inside formulaic sequences than outside them. Whether or not formulaic sequences are actually stored in the brain in a holistic way is a contentious issue (see Schmitt *et al.* 2004). Nevertheless, the evidence points to the fact that our language processing takes place holistically. In other words, formulaic sequence meaning would seem to have cognitive reality, and thus the idiom principle is more than mere hypothesis.

TRADITIONAL GRAMMATICAL CATEGORIES: DO THEY EXIST?

Corpus investigation has raised important questions about traditional ways of chunking, categorising and distinguishing grammar and lexis. Corpus linguists have argued that existing approaches may disguise or distort the way people produce or process linguistic information. For instance, on the basis of corpus evidence, Sinclair (1991: 82–83) queries the status of 'of' as a preposition. Typical instances of prepositional usage are *in Ipswich*, *at the same place*, *behind the masks* where the prepositions *(in, at, behind)* join noun phrases to produce adjuncts in clauses, that is, grammatical units which provide extra information, usually about time, place and manner, e.g. 'I am working *in Ipswich*'. However, Sinclair argues that large corpus investigation shows that *of* typically functions to provide 'elaboration' of the noun phrase rather than to provide extra information in a clause, e.g. ' . . . the back of the van', ' . . . a small bottle of brandy.' As Sinclair says:

> The value of frequency information shows itself here because without it a grammar could conveniently introduce *of* as a plausible, ordinary preposition, and then add what in fact is its characteristic use as an extra. But with the overwhelming pattern of usage being in nominal groups [noun phrases], this fact must dominate any good description. It may ultimately be considered distracting to regard *of* as a preposition at all.
>
> (1991: 83)

This is an important insight and shows the value of corpus investigation in allowing grammarians to reconceptualise grammatical categories. It suggests that (some) descriptive analysis that divides language into individual categories, as is the case in traditional grammars, may be misguided.

Where the basis of corpus examination is used to make arguments which attempt to overturn traditional carvings of language, this is referred to as a **corpus-driven** approach (Tognini-Bonelli 2001). In contrast, a **corpus-based** approach values the use of a large amount of empirical data in understanding how language is used but does not use this information to overhaul traditional grammatical terms. Some corpus-driven linguists go further than Sinclair and deny the possibility of grammatical categories all together. Hunston and Francis (2000: 197) and Hoey (2005: 154) argue that grammatical categories such as noun, verb, etc. are merely 'convenient short-hand' since a word's grammatical class is actually determined by the prototypical collocations and phraseologies in which it is found. In Hoey's important work, he explains this idea through comparison of the collocations of *consequence* with those of *taught* and *if*. On the basis of corpus evidence, he notes that *consequence* is usually preceded by *a*, *one*, *the* and *another* and followed by *of*, and when it is preceded by *the* it is followed by a verb such as in *The doleful consequence is that modern British society has been intensely politicised*. This is not the case for *taught* and *if*. In other words, for Hoey, the statement that '*consequence* is a noun' is shorthand for saying that it is prototypically found in collocations and phraseologies which are similar to those for *architect, table, experience, matter, book*, etc. (nouns), but not those for *taught, experienced, booked, tabled*, etc. (verbs) or *if, and, but, though*, etc. (conjunctions).

CORPUS-BASED GRAMMARS AND QUANTITATIVE AUTHORITY

Biber *et al.*'s (1999) *Longman Grammar of Spoken and Written English* is a corpus-based grammar, incorporating four broad registers: academic prose, fiction, conversation and news (this last Longman register comprising every-thing to be found in a newspaper). It represents a major advance in English grammatics since it is able to illuminate with quantitative authority how grammar varies across different situational uses (broadly defined) as will be seen below. It is thus very useful as a reference source for determining whether individual texts are typical or not with respect to an aspect of grammar in one of the 'Longman registers' covered. Figures 2.3, 2.4 and 2.5 highlight the extent to which the grammatical behaviour of the word *and* in two texts (one an academic text, the other a conversation) is typical with regard to Biber *et al.*'s (1999) findings.

And is one of the most common words in most texts of reasonable length. Its purpose is coordination: linking phrases, e.g. 'two apples and a glass of orange juice', or clauses, e.g. 'he ate two apples and drank a glass of orange juice'. In Figures 2.3 and 2.4 are reproduced two texts on the topic of cockroaches – one is from an academic source and one is a transcript of an informal conversation. In bold are all the instances of *and*.

The cockroach is probably the most obnoxious insect known to man. About half a dozen species of cockroaches have managed to acquire a relationship with man, rivalled perhaps only by lice **and** fleas. The latter are known vectors of certain rickettsial organisms (typhus) **and** rodent diseases (plague **and** murine typhus) but like the bed bug cockroaches may only be accidental carriers of pathogens. Nevertheless, there is a considerable body of evidence to incriminate a number of cockroaches as potential carriers of disease whose importance in this regard is becoming more fully recognised.

The pest status of the cockroach derives mainly from an aesthetic abhorrence of what is regarded as a loathsome intruder: its speed **and** unpredictable direction of movement, the enormous numbers to which population can increase if left undisturbed, **and** the habit of cockroaches of tainting with a characteristic odour, **and** fouling with excrement, all food **and** surfaces with which they come into contact.

Their status as pests is increased by the fact that cockroaches are usually associated with poor standards of hygiene. Thus to the vast majority of people, cockroaches in the home **and** place of work are psychologically disturbing **and** to some can cause considerable mental distress.

Cockroaches are an ancient group of insects which have existed on earth about 100 times longer than man. The status of a few pests is therefore very recent. At the present time, there are about 3,500 known species, mostly of tropical origin. As a group, they show considerable diversity of size, colouration **and** habit. Rehn rightly says that 'because cockroaches are normally seen as house-haunting pests **and** in the majority of people cause strong feeling of aversion, it is often difficult to convince the "doubting Thomas" that the number of species of cockroach which are domiciliary pests is greatly limited – in fact, less than one per cent of all known forms. Also many kinds are diurnal, with hundreds of species inhabiting tropical forests, others semi-aquatic, some living in the ground, a few wood-boring, while a dozen or so generally are found in a state of either known or suspected commensalism, in the nests of ants, wasps **and** termites. To this should be added those which inhabit caves in association with bats **and** others of the desert, some of which inhabit the burrows of rodents.'

(Source: Cornwell, P.B. (1968) *The Cockroach: A Laboratory Insect and Industrial Pest*, Vol. 1, London: Hutchinson)

Figure 2.3 Academic cockroach text.

It might initially be difficult to see how *and* is being used grammatically in the two texts as a coordinator. Using a concordancer, where all the instances of *and* can be stacked on top of one another, the difference is easier to see (Figure 2.5).

Viewing the concordance lines, one can see more readily that *and* is used mainly to link phrases in the academic text and mainly to link clauses in the conversation.

Are these typical texts with regard to *and*? Biber *et al.* (1999: section 2.4.7.3) tell us that the different uses of *and* in the cockroach texts are indeed typical in academic English and conversation. The Longman corpus-based grammar usefully identifies many other language features that distinguish conversation and academic prose (as well as the other registers of newspapers and fiction that they focus on).

But why does this pattern with *and* occur? In other words, why does *and* function differently in the two texts? One reason is that there is often a need for precision and compression in academic English, hence phrases are longer. In speech it is difficult to plan for this level of compression and precision. Hence phrases are shorter, and thus *and* doesn't function as frequently as a phrasal coordinator. Furthermore, complex subordination is often harder to manage on

S1: I hate cockroaches more than rats.

S2: I don't like cockroaches either.

S3: But cockroaches are just the thing – you just get them anywhere.

S1: Yeah but when you tread on them, they crunch. A rat just squelches.

S3: Actually, over at Manly along the promenade, if you walk along there at night, they're that big – they're huge **and** they're a different . . . brand.

S2: Big roaches are they?

S3: Yeah, they're big ones, real big ones.

S1: I remember we were sitting for our analytical chemistry exam **and** it was the final exams **and** they have sort of like bench desks where there's three to a bench normally **and** they had the middle seat empty **and** two sat either side **and** I was sitting there **and** I thought, 'Geez I can feel something on my foot.'

   And I thought, 'No, no, don't worry about it.' you know 'what on earth is this chemical equation?' **and** I am trying to think 'but there's something on my foot.' **and** I looked down **and** there was this cockroach like this – **and** I just screamed **and** jumped on the chair **and** as I did that, I knocked the bench **and** it went up **and** all Geoff's exam stuff went into the bin next to him **and** I was standing on this chair screaming **and** the exam supervisor came running over, 'what's going on there?'. **And** I said, 'there's a cockroach down there', cause you're not allowed to speak, sneeze, cough or anything in those final exams, **and** um, there's me screaming on the chair.

S3: Ran into Anna this morning, boy she gets around.

S1: Yeah, did you find out what she does?

S3: Yeah, she's part of a team.

(Source: Eggins and Slade 1997: 228)

Figure 2.4 Conversation cockroach.

the hoof in speech than it is in writing, which would also lead to more clausal coordination with *and* in speech.

While the work of Biber *et al.* (1999) represents a significant advance on traditional grammars, nevertheless its quantitative authority is less applicable if the text one is interested in is not prototypical of a Longman register. If one really wants to understand a specific use of language, a large corpus of that specific register is ultimately what is required. Furthermore, one would need to understand how that register is drawn on in a specific situation. The functional explanation of *and* given above in relation to academic writing and conversation is at something of a 'bird's-eye' level. While it is basically sound, it relates to prototypical academic writing (e.g. essays and academic journal articles) and prototypical conversation (e.g. amongst friends and thus informal). Such a functional explanation may not apply so readily if one considers more 'accessible' types of academic text (e.g. academic conference PowerPoint presentations) and takes into account disciplinary differences (e.g. humanities as opposed to science subjects) or more formal conversations (e.g. job interviews).

In Section 2.5, Coffin considers the impact of systemic functional linguistics (SFL), a theory which proposes that how grammar and lexis function is systematically linked to the specific situation in which a particular kind of text is produced as well as people's communicative purposes in relation to that text. In SFL, whilst language form is by no means disregarded, it is language function

Cockroach academic

1...   with man, rivalled perhaps only by lice [and] fleas. The latter are known vectors of
2...   certain rickettsial organisms (typhus) [and] rodent diseases (plague and murine typh
3... ms (typhus) and rodent diseases (plague [and] murine typhus) but like the bed bug coc
4...   rded as a loathsome intruder: its speed [and] unpredictable direction of movement, th
5...   ation can increase if left undisturbed, [and] the habit of cockroaches of tainting wi
6...   f tainting with a characteristic odour, [and] fouling with excrement, all food and su
7...   r, and fouling with excrement, all food [and] surfaces with which they come into cont
8...   rity of people, cockroaches in the home [and] place of work are psychologically distu
9...   of work are psychologically disturbing [and] to some can cause considerable mental d
10...   iderable diversity of size, colouration [and] habit. Rehn rightly says that 'because
11... e normally seen as house-haunting pests [and] in the majority of people cause strong
12...   mmensalism, in the nests of ants, wasps [and] termites. To this should be added thos
13...   inhabit caves in association with bats [and] others of the desert, some of which inh

Cockroach conversation

1...   night, they're that big – they're huge [and] they're a different . . . brand. Big roa
2...   tting for our analytical chemistry exam [and] it was the final exams and they have so
3...   emistry exam and it was the final exams [and] they have sort of like bench desks wher
4...   where there's three to a bench normally [and] they had the middle seat empty and two
5...   ally and they had the middle seat empty [and] two sat either side and I was sitting
6...   ddle seat empty and two sat either side [and] I was sitting there and I thought, Gee
7...   at either side and I was sitting there [and] I thought, Geez I can feel something on
8...   Geez I can feel something on my foot. [And] I thought, 'No, no, don't worry about i
9...   at on earth is this chemical equation?' [and] I am trying to think 'but there's somet
10... ink 'but there's something on my foot.' [and] I looked down and there was this cockro
11... omething on my foot.' and I looked down [and] there was this cockroach like this – an
12...   nd there was this cockroach like this – [and] I just screamed and jumped on the chair
13...   ckroach like this – and I just screamed [and] jumped on the chair and as I did that,
14... I just screamed and jumped on the chair [and] as I did that, I knocked the bench and
15...   and as I did that, I knocked the bench [and] it went up and all Geoff's exam stuff w
16... hat, I knocked the bench and it went up [and] all Geoff's exam stuff went into the bi
17...   xam stuff went into the bin next to him [and] I was standing on this chair screaming
18...   I was standing on this chair screaming [and] the exam supervisor came running over,
19...   running over, 'what's going on there?'. [And] I said, 'there's a cockroach down there
20...   cough or anything in those final exams, [and] um, there's me screaming on the chair.

Figure 2.5 Concordance lines for *and* in the two cockroach texts.

which is given central significance. Accordingly, a set of functional labels have been devised as a means of enriching structural descriptions and focusing on the meaning-making dimension of language.

2.5 THE FUNCTIONAL 'TURN': LANGUAGE, TEXT AND CONTEXT

Section 2.4 has shown how corpus-based approaches are a useful means of identifying lexical and grammatical patterns and variation within these. In this section, I will show that not all texts belonging to a broad-brush register (such as a Longman register) will necessarily display similar patterns. I will then demonstrate how an SFL approach, in which language, text and context are systematically brought together via the SFL concept of **register**, complements corpus-based and other types of grammars. I will consider how, within the SFL tradition, register has quite a specific definition and is distinct from the notion of register as used by Biber *et al.* (1999). Equally, I will show how context, or more technically **Context of Situation**, is defined in linguistic terms (rather than being used to refer more broadly to the physical and sociohistorical environment in which language is used). I will also point out some of the benefits of SFL's innovation of using grammatical labels which are functionally oriented. Aspects of this functional turn in the study of grammar, in particular the integration of social context with linguistic analysis within SFL, provide a grammatical illustration of the more general 'social turn' in language studies referred to in Chapter 1.

LINKING TEXT AND CONTEXT VIA REGISTER: AN SFL PERSPECTIVE

Figures 2.6 and 2.7 reproduce two texts which would fall within Biber *et al.*'s (1999) newspaper register and which, according to this corpus-based grammar, would be characterised by some or all of the following features:

high frequency of reporting clauses
low frequency of the personal pronoun *we*
use of slightly more present than past tense
low frequency of interrogatives.

Both texts are concerned with reductions in the number of UK prison places and both appeared in the British tabloid newspaper, *The Sun*.

Given that the texts in both Figures 2.6 and 2.7 would fall into the same newspaper register (as defined by Biber *et al.* 1999) and are concerned with the same news topic, one might predict that they would share the grammatical and lexical features outlined earlier. In fact, there are a number of differences. First, whereas in line with corpus-based predictions, the text in Figure 2.6 has several examples of reporting clauses (*He admitted, Brian Caton warned, He said*) the text in Figure 2.7 does not. Second, although Biber *et al.*'s corpus findings indicate that the most frequent tense used in the newspaper register is the present, Figure 2.6 has a greater frequency of past tense (13 instances) compared to present tense (5 instances). Figure 2.7, on the other hand, displays a higher frequency of present tense (12 instances) than past tense (4 instances). Finally, although Biber *et al.* report low frequencies of the personal pronoun *we*, it is used twice in Figure 2.6 and three times in Figure 2.7 and both are reasonably short texts. How can one account for these differences? One way is to bring to bear a theory of language use and description in which the relationship between context of situation and language use is finely tuned. Whereas registers within large-scale electronic corpora have the advantage of size, and thus, as discussed earlier, some kind of claim for representativeness can be made, the compilation may often be broad-brush (i.e. it would very time consuming to compile a huge corpus of a specific register with tightly defined variables). Since the Longman newspaper register contains everything in a newspaper, it follows that the

Promised new jail places cut

By DAVID WOODING
Whitehall Editor
Published: 28 November 2007

PRISONS face a new overcrowding crisis after the number of extra cells due this year was slashed by nearly half.

Just 1,400 more places will be finished – instead of the 2,500 promised.

Details were slipped out by Prisons Minister David Hanson while MPs were distracted over Labour's dodgy donations row.

He admitted this year's new places would have been as few as 700 – but that number was doubled when work started on a new building programme due for completion next year.

In January the Government pledged 2,500 new permanent places by the end of this year.

That target was cut to 2,200 in August.

Last night Prison Officers Association boss Brian Caton warned public safety was now under threat.

He said: *"The prison service is already in meltdown and will not be able to cope much longer. We also need more resources to rehabilitate people if we are to avoid letting them out to rape and murder.*

"Unless the Government can find some way of providing not only the spaces but the resources and staff to deal with them then the streets will no longer be safe." Ten thousand lags have already been freed early because of overcrowding, figures on Friday are expected to reveal.

At least 300 were locked up again after being caught reoffending or breaking their licence terms.

(*The Sun* online 28 November 2007: http://www.thesun.co.uk/ accessed 8 January 2008).

Figure 2.6 Newspaper report from *The Sun*.

descriptions of language variation using such a method are also often broad-brush (hence the variation in Figures 2.6 and 2.7 above). The more tightly defined notion of register within SFL facilitates more fine-grained descriptions and more systematic explanations of the relationship between aspects of the context and language use. Descriptions can also provide a much stronger focus on how language is functioning, what semantic meanings it is making and the overall communicative effect of individual texts belonging to a register. They are able to account for the language patterns in specific texts.

Within SFL, the notion of register serves to highlight three key aspects of the social context – three situational 'variables' – that relate to three general language functions which in turn relate to particular language systems. These variables turn on:

1   the type of social activity taking place (referred to as **field**) (linking to the function of language to represent experience);
2   the social roles and relationships between the participants (referred to as **tenor**) (linking to the interpersonal function of language, i.e. in constructing relationships between speaker/listener or writer/reader); and

Protect us

THE prisons crisis is as shameful as it is dangerous.

Thousands of hardened criminals are being freed early to make space, many returning immediately to a life of crime – some involving violence.

Overstretched warders are threatening to walk out.

Now we are told more than 60,000 prisoners were locked up in police cells last year because jails were too full to take them.

Apart from the cost – more than a room at The Ritz – this barmy stop-gap solution ties up police who should be out there protecting us from other criminals.

The public is paying dearly for 11 years of wilful refusal to prepare for a wholly predictable explosion in prisoner numbers.

We've been promised new prisons – but so far they're only talking about where to put them.

We've been promised prison ships. These could be built in months. Where are they?

This is a failure of public policy.

A government's first duty is to protect its citizens, not leave them at risk from criminals on the loose when they should and must be locked up.

(*The Sun* online 9 January 2008: http://www.thesun.co.uk/sol/homepage/news/sun_says/article244723.ece – accessed 9 January 2008).

Figure 2.7 Newspaper editorial from *The Sun*.

3   aspects of the channel of communication such as how interactive or spontaneous the text is and how close or distant in time to the event represented
(referred to as **mode**) (linking to the function of language to organise 1 and
2) in a text in a cohesive manner).

Significantly, the SFL model posits that there is a two-way relationship between
context of situation and linguistic choices. That is, the social context in terms of
its field, tenor and mode variables will affect the linguistic choices made by interactants (albeit often at an unconscious level).[1] But equally, by making certain
language choices, writers and speakers can construe their social reality. For
example, they can develop different relationships with their audience as well as
shape the degree to which their text 'sounds' written or spoken.

Table 2.1 (opposite) comprises a register analysis of the texts in Figures 2.6
and 2.7. It shows how the different language choices in the two texts shape and
are shaped by the different field, tenor and mode variables. At this point you
may not be familiar with some of the functional labelling so in brackets I have
added related (though not equivalent) traditional terms.

Although there is not the space in this chapter to conduct a comprehensive
analysis of all the language features used in the newspaper texts, Table 2.1 shows
how the writer in each text makes quite different choices and how these relate to
differences in situational variables. Thus, even though both texts can be loosely
described as belonging to a 'newspaper register' each has quite a different
purpose (reporting as opposed to arguing) and each one sets up quite different

reader–writer relations. Figure 2.7 for example, simulates a more inclusive and interactive style (e.g. through the use of the command *protect us* and the question *where are they*?). The writer is not simply reporting on events but criticising public policy and aligning the reader with his point of view. In SFL terms, the register of each text is distinct: it is to do with each text's particular configuration of field, tenor and mode variables and associated linguistic choices.

USING FUNCTIONAL LABELS TO ILLUMINATE SEMANTIC MEANING

Aside from providing a framework within which to study grammar, SFL uses functional labels of the type set out in the register analysis in Table 2.1 for a number of purposes, e.g. to shine light on how language represents the world. SFL is useful in revealing how linguistic representations imply particular points of view and values of which speakers and listeners may only be dimly conscious. (A formal analysis, i.e. one concerned with the formal properties of a text, would not reveal such phenomena.) In order to see how functional labels can provide this type of illumination, consider the following sentences.

i   Traditionally, fishermen used to catch 100,000 tons of fish per year in the North Sea.
ii The North Sea used to provide 100,000 tons of fish per year.

Above are two representations of the same 'slice' of reality, i.e. *fishing in the North Sea*. In sentence i you can see that there is an action initiated by *fishermen*, the **subject** in traditional grammar or, in functional grammatical terms, the **Actor**, i.e. the person or people doing the action. You can also see that the natural world is referred to in a prepositional phrase – *in the North Sea* (functioning as a **Circumstance** in SFL) rather than being represented by an Actor. Sentence ii, in contrast, is a representation where it is the natural world which plays the Actor role. Here the natural world is *not* relegated to the role of Circumstance and there is no human Actor.

The two sentences illustrate how grammatical choices may be related to different ways of viewing the world. Sentence i, for example, could readily be tied to a perspective where people operate on nature, where nature is somehow separate from humans. Such a perspective could help to legitimise human domination of nature, taking 'resources' from it. Nature is just a 'place' where people obtain what they need. Representations such as in sentence ii, in contrast, place nature instead of humans in a focal position and move away from the idea that humans dominate and exploit nature. With the first representation, questions may arise such as: *Why don't fishermen catch so much fish anymore? Is it something to do with the fishing industry? Are there fewer fishermen these days?* With the second representation, questions are perhaps more likely to be nature-focused rather than human-focused, for example: *What's the problem with the North Sea?*

Table 2.1 Register analysis

Register	Figure 2.6 – language choices	Figure 2.7 – language choices
Field		
Activity: Figure 2.6 – news report on government failure re. prison overcrowding Figure 2.7 – editorial opinion on what should be done re. prison overcrowding Semantic domain: prison places, crime	**Lexis** relate to prison, e.g. *jail, cells, wardens, prison offices, rehabilitate*; crime, e.g. *murder, reoffending, lags* **Processes** [verbs]: material (to do with crime control, e.g. *locked up, caught, freed*); verbal (reporting, e.g. *warned, said, admitted*) **Participants: Actors** and **Sayers** [subjects] often absent; **Goals** [objects] (e.g. *people*) are infrequent **Circumstances** [prepositional phrases/adjuncts]: mainly time (e.g. *in January, in August*)	**Lexis** relate to imprisonment, e.g. *police cells, wardens, locked up*; crime, e.g. *life of crime, violence, criminals, prisoners*; policy, e.g. *public policy, duty, citizens* **Processes** [verbs]: few material (to do with crime control), mainly relational (*is, are*) **Participants – Actors** [subjects] often absent; **Goals** [objects] often *criminals, prisoners, citizens, police* Participants in relational processes tend to be abstract, e.g. *the solution, failure, duty, crisis* **Circumstances** [prepositional phrases/adjuncts]: infrequent – time (*last year*), place (*in police cells*)
Tenor		
Relative social status (more equality between writer/readers in Figure 2.7) **Social distance** – less distance in Figure 2.7 (i.e. writer and readers are aligned as members of the public) **Speaker/writer persona** – Figure 2.6: neutral reporter Figure 2.7: authoritative opinion giver	**Pronoun use** – use of *we* restricted to quotation and refers to prison service **Speech acts** – only statements (Writer – authoritative) **Colloquial lexis:** *dodgy donations, lags* **Modality**[a] – infrequent Little use of evaluative language	**Pronoun use** – use of *we, us* refers to public at large **Speech acts** – question, command (*protect us*) Colloquial lexis: *barmy, on the loose, more than a room at the Ritz* **Modality:** deontic modals – *should, must* Overt evaluative judgments – *Overstretched, shameful, wilful, dangerous, barmy, failure*
Mode		
Spontaneity of production: Both written (edited) **Interactivity** (possibility of feedback): none, though online discussions possible re. editorial in Figure 2.7 Some simulated interactivity in Figure 2.7 **Communicative distance**: greater distance from events in Figure 2.7	**Theme – Rheme** [Text organisation]: *prisons, prison service* and *government* are foregrounded at start of sentence Absence of questions, commands	**Theme – Rheme** [Text organisation]: *the public, we* are foregrounded at start of several sentences Large font and bold print emphasise key points Use of question and command create more conversational/spoken style

Note

[a] Modality refers to the expression of a writer or speaker's judgment about the likelihood of what they are saying (e.g. How sure am I about it? – epistemic modality) or about levels of obligation (e.g. Do I have to do it? – deontic modality).

Why doesn't the North Sea yield so much fish any more? The questions show concern over the effects of the domination and consumption of nature. Different representations thus provide different orientations to the natural world (see Goatly 2004, for further discussion).

In sum, analyses of texts using SFL are designed to reveal the specific features of a text and explain these in relation to their context of situation (as in the register analysis exemplified here). In general, analysts take into account not only the relationship between a text and its immediate social context but also the wider cultural situation (see, for example, Coffin and O'Halloran 2005). They may also pay attention to the dynamic, unfolding of meaning within a single text (e.g. Macken-Horarik 2003). Such approaches distinguish text-focused, situationally oriented grammars from corpus-based grammars of the Biber *et al.* (1999) type (i.e. where situational information is light and the purpose is to characterise collections of texts rather than individual instances). Such differences in orientation and purpose need not, however, be mutually exclusive or in conflict (e.g. Coffin and O'Halloran 2006). Indeed, in Section 2.6, O'Halloran discusses how SFL theorising has itself been corpus-informed and how an orientation to multi-million word collections of texts as well as the meaning making function of specific texts in situations can enrich our understanding of both grammar and grammatics. He also considers some of the strengths and weaknesses of these approaches to describing English.

2.6 CORPUS AND FUNCTIONAL PERSPECTIVES

CONVERGENCE OF FUNCTIONAL PERSPECTIVES AND CORPUS LINGUISTICS

In line with the distinction between different linguistic levels discussed in Section 2.2, traditional grammars generally keep grammar and lexis separate. In contrast, SFL and corpus-based/driven approaches both argue that there is a tight relationship between lexis and grammar. Recent edited collections (Coffin *et al.* 2004; Thompson and Hunston 2006) detail synergies between corpus linguistics and SFL. The systemic functional linguist, Matthiessen (2006), for example, investigates how a corpus can be useful in showing the probabilities of co-occurring lexicogrammatical features. From the corpus linguistics 'end of the telescope', Hoey (2005) shows how a corpus can provide evidence for the prototypical location of words in a text, which in turn relates to their function. He uses the term 'priming' to describe the process of how habitual language use sets up expectations in the user's mind for how a word form is used. Investigation of large corpora makes it possible to reveal primings. Hoey draws on a distinction between **theme** and **rheme** that has been made in SFL. 'Theme' refers to the departure point of a clause: e.g. *The meeting* is the theme in 'The meeting has been cancelled.'; the 'rheme' is the part of a clause which is not the theme, e.g. *has been cancelled.*

Just as a word may be primed to occur (or to avoid occurring) in first or last position in a sentence, so it may also be primed to occur (or avoid occurring) in first or last position in a paragraph, a section or a text. So, for example, on the one hand, *consequence* is not only primed to favour theme, it is also primed to avoid paragraph-initial and text-initial position. The plural *consequences*, on the other hand, which is less strongly primed to occur as theme, is positively primed to be paragraph-initial, though it shares the aversion of *consequence* for being text-initial.

(Hoey 2005: 130)

This kind of analysis, based on large corpora, can enrich SFL analysis by showing where functions in a text are prototypically located and where they are not.

Having access to voluminous data in a corpus also potentially enables SFL categories to be refined, and made more delicate. Bastow (2003) notes that writers of US defence speeches are primed to place the noun phrase 'our men and women in uniform' at the end of clauses. As Hoey (2005: 130) points out, this has implications for the concept of rheme in SFL:

It is worth remarking that Bastow's claim is actually more precise than saying that *our men and women in uniform* appears in Rheme; he is specifying a quite specific position for the word sequence – final position.

Hoey agrees with Bastow that the concept of rheme is 'too big and crude a category', i.e. (everything in a clause after the theme) since corpus-based observations indicate that words are primed for more specific text locations. Corpus-based analysis can, then, show where grammatical concepts are not discriminating enough and, in turn, produce an impetus for reconceptualisation.

In SFL, language is seen as a *system* of choices (hence the term *systemic* functional linguistics) from which speakers/writers select. As an example, let us take *mood*. In the mood system, there are different clause types: declarative; interrogative; imperative. So, from the mood system, speakers/writers may select the declarative, *Aston Villa will win the Premiership*, the interrogative, *Will Aston Villa win the Premiership?* or the imperative, '*Come on Villa, win the Premiership!*'. In this 'system of choices' perspective in SFL, little focus has traditionally been given to phraseological *constraints* on choices made. Indeed, Sinclair's idiom principle, referred to in Section 2.4, would seem to indicate that there is much less choice in what speakers select than the systemic perspective in SFL implies. Is there then a tension here between SFL and corpus approaches? Consider the following sentence from Johns (1995) to which Hunston and Francis (2000: 251) refer in a critique of aspects of SFL:

The dam is costing the government 2 million dollars a month.

Hunston and Francis argue that, on the basis of corpus evidence, the sentence is used to evaluate rather than simply to describe, and can be expressed as the following pattern:

(noun = project) + is costing + (noun = organisation) + (noun = amount) + (noun = time period).

Hunston and Francis suggest that because this pattern has restrictions on noun-type and verb aspect, and carries an implied meaning of negative judgment, it is difficult to see how its realisation could be viewed in terms of a sequence of choices as SFL contends. Corpus evidence such as this does not invalidate SFL, but would seem to indicate that some corpus-driven revaluation of its theory of system choice is needed. Crucially, revaluation of the theory would not take place in relation to hundreds of words, but thousands, perhaps millions of words of textual evidence. In this way, grammatical theory building could claim credibility on quantitative grounds.

LIMITATIONS OF BOTH CORPUS AND FUNCTIONAL APPROACHES

As with any tool or perspective, there are limitations to what can be achieved by different approaches to grammar. Widdowson (2004a) highlights a number of limitations of both corpus and systemic functional linguistics. A criticism he levels at both relates to the *over*-inferring of significance from text data. Corpus data is only a textual record and so, on its own, cannot provide evidence of how, for example, words were stressed in meaning making. To see the limits here, recall Sinclair's (1991) argument from Section 2.4 on the basis of corpus frequency evidence that the prototypical usage of *of* is not prepositional. When Sinclair says, in relation to phrases such as *a bottle of juice*, that 'of Noun-2' (i.e. *of juice*) *elaborates* 'Noun-1' (*bottle*) he implies a hierarchical relationship between *bottle* and *juice*. But does such a hierarchical relationship necessarily exist in use in accordance with word stress? In other words, is Noun-1 the head noun in all uses of 'Noun-1 + of + Noun-2' just because it is the first noun? Take the following as an example: 'We drank a bottle of juice'. How one identifies the head in 'bottle of juice' could depend on where the emphasis is in this phrase in a particular situation (i.e. on phonology in a spoken text). If a speaker is communicating *how much* they drank then 'bottle' could be analysed as a head noun and 'of juice' as the 'elaborator' since 'bottle' would be stressed by a speaker. However, if the speaker were trying to communicate *what* they drank ('juice' and not 'cola') then it would be reasonable to analyse 'juice' as the head noun and 'bottle of' as the 'elaborator' since 'juice' would be stressed by the speaker. 'Headness' and what is 'elaborated' can thus be dependent on stress rather than just syntactic structure. A corpus of unannotated texts unfortunately cannot provide such information and is therefore limited in its ability to illuminate the exact relationship of *of* to what is elaborated.

SFL rarely, if at all, makes the distinction between semantics and pragmatics as traditionally defined. In not doing so, it can sometimes seem to overstate its claims about language and semantic meaning (Widdowson 2004). In relation to this, consider the following extract from a key work in SFL, Halliday and Matthiessen (2004: 29):

> It is clear that language does – as we put it – **construe** human experience. It names things, thus construing them into categories; and then, typically, goes further and construes the categories into taxonomies, often using more names for doing so. So we have *houses* and *cottages* and *garages* and *sheds*, which are all kinds of *building*; *strolling* and *stepping* and *marching and pacing*, which are all kinds of *walking*; *in*, *on*, *under*, *around* as relative locations and so on . . . More powerfully still, these elements are configured into complex grammatical patterns like *marched out of the house*; the figures can be built up into sequences related by time, cause and the like – there is no facet of human experience which cannot be transformed into meaning. In other words, language provides a **theory** of human experience . . .

'Human experience' includes a number of different phenomena, one of which is perceptual experience, e.g. what we see. This is the type of human experience which Halliday and Matthiessen seem to have taken as a starting point above, i.e. people use the semantic resources of a linguistic system, its taxonomies, how it organises time and cause, etc., to construe what they perceive. Halliday and Matthiessen's focus on human experience is at a generalised semantic level: the kinds of things, events, actions, etc. that exist or are habitual, and which are reflected in the language system (e.g. the fact that there are two human sexes is reflected in the pronoun system of English). In other words, Halliday and Matthiessen's focus is not on actual instances of language use and how they are understood by individuals in particular situations. A problem with the extract given above, however, is that human experience also includes exactly that: how people *individually understand* their perceptual experience, and how they have construed this using a linguistic system, in line with what they deem *relevant* from the particular situation, i.e. the pragmatic meanings they make. For example, if, following a marital quarrel, the husband was reporting in an email to a friend that he 'marched out of the house', the friend would probably infer that his choice of 'marched' indicated he was upset or angry.

By 'context of situation', SFL refers to aspects of the context that relate to language use and choice (see Section 2.5). In pragmatics, 'context' means those aspects of a situation, including the language use within it, which are deemed relevant by participants for communication (see Sperber and Wilson 1995). The distinction may seem trivial, but it is a significant one. This is because, from a pragmatic perspective, there is a looser link between the linguistic system and human experience than the one Halliday and Matthiessen seem to espouse. On a pragmatic account, a number of different inferences can potentially be drawn from the *same* lexis/lexicogrammatical patterns. So, other situations will lead to different inferences being generated from the utterance 'marched out of the house' in line with what is regarded as relevant for that particular human experience. From the perspective of pragmatics, a linguistic system provides generalised clues about human experience, but is hardly a theory of its immense richness, complexity and diversity.

This is not to invalidate SFL. Far from it. It does, however, help us to see very clearly where its valid zone of application lies with regard to the meaning analysis of texts. SFL is valuable as a descriptive tool in allowing systematic and delicate articulation of semantic functions in texts, something which may not otherwise be so visible. It is thus very useful, for example, for accurately seeing how a news editorial might be positioning its readers to accept particular meanings. But an SFL description of a news editorial's meaning is not the same as the reader's 'experience' of that text's meaning; in other words, by analogy with my argument above, a text does not provide a theory of a reader's experience of it. How readers take their bearings from the semantic positioning of a text in the making of pragmatic inferences will vary in accordance with situational variables other than field, tenor, mode. It will include, for instance: their own reader position, the amount of effort they invest in processing, their reading purpose, what they know and their personality. Ultimately, a comprehensive analysis of English grammar and how it achieves meaning would take into account dominant patterns of how very large numbers of English speakers actually infer pragmatic meanings from what they hear or what they read in many different situations. This is, of course, a practical impossibility.

I have been talking about the meanings that people make in particular situations when they read. But what about when they write? To what extent can corpora shed light on the meanings that an author generates as they write them down? Most corpora are made up of written texts rather than transcribed spoken texts since the latter are much more difficult to obtain. Many of the types of writing that usually make up corpora (e.g. academic English, news, fiction) are often the product of several drafts and, indeed, drafts which may have responded to critical feedback on the construction of the writer's grammar and meaning. This means that phraseologies revealed in the investigation of written corpora may be more regularised than the way in which they initially emerged in an author's mind. In other words, corpus-based written grammars are product-focused rather than process-focused. As mentioned above, phraseological meaning, on the basis of psycholinguistic evidence, is meant to have cognitive reality. However, claims about phraseological meaning and cognitive reality may be being made on the basis of product-focused corpus investigation. To see if this really is a problem, it would be useful to compare large product-focused corpora with large process-focused corpora of instantaneous and unchecked writing, e.g. informal emails, chat logs data, scribbled notes to ourselves, etc. Indeed, with process-focused corpora the possibility emerges of process-focused grammars of writing to complement product-focused ones.

This chapter began by looking at some traditional notions of grammar and some historical perspectives on grammar. It has also tried to give a sense of the intellectual excitement surrounding newer approaches to grammar – corpus linguistics and systemic functional linguistics – and suggested that the two approaches are not mutually exclusive. We pointed out more generally that different approaches to linguistic description and analysis configure 'language' in different ways (e.g. identifying distinct linguistic levels or blurring some of these distinctions) and that they also reflect different ideas about the relationship between language and the contexts within which this is produced and understood. These points will be taken up in different ways in the chapters that follow.

NOTE

1 In systemic functional linguistics, in order to display choice (or paradigmatic relations), diagrams referred to as 'system networks' are used. These allow analysts to see what interactants say or write in relation to what they could have said or written.

3

TEXTS AND PRACTICES

ANN HEWINGS AND SARAH NORTH

3.1 INTRODUCTION

This chapter focuses on the different approaches that have been taken to the analysis of texts – and the extent to which this has been regarded as part of a broader analysis of social (rather than simply linguistic) practices. It considers approaches to analysing both speech and writing, as well as the hybrid discourse associated with computer-mediated communication. The approaches we consider have arisen not only from linguistics, but also from other disciplines that share an interest in communication, particularly sociology, anthropology and philosophy. The chapter outlines issues that have been addressed in analysing texts and practices, and the methods used to do this.

An overview necessarily involves a degree of simplification. One important point to bear in mind is that the different traditions we refer to are not neatly demarcated, but arise out of a range of research projects carried out by different individuals, each of whom shares, to a greater or lesser degree, some of their goals, principles, methods and techniques with a selection of other individuals. Seminal concepts that originate in one research tradition are often picked up, applied and developed in other traditions. In the process, however, they may take on slightly different meanings, so before beginning the survey of different approaches, this chapter provides an overview of some of the concepts that are fundamental to any kind of discourse analysis, indicating the major issues that distinguish various approaches.

3.2 KEY CONCEPTS

TEXT AND DISCOURSE

A **text** can be defined as any stretch of language which forms a unified whole, whether spoken, written or electronic. In a railway carriage, for example, you might be exposed to language such as:

> Alarm. Lift flap & pull handle. That's all right, I'll just get the Met. Any tickets from Stockport? Spurs on the slide as Butt posts late winner. Between London Euston – Manchester Pi. No, I'm on the train.

Such disconnected scraps of language do not form a coherent whole and there-fore do not constitute a text. The following, by contrast, does:

I love coaching but if you ain't got good players. . . . Kanu was a great free transfer, I thought; Sol Campbell was. They cost good wages but anyone else could have taken them and I didn't see anyone else queuing up. People told me Campbell was finished but I didn't think so.

('Hair-raising goal for O'Neil', *The Times*, 15 January 2007)

The different parts of this text are linked together by the use of cohesive devices such as '*They* cost good wages' and 'I didn't think *so*'. They also hang together in terms of the coherent meaning relationships between different clauses; 'Kanu' and 'Sol Campbell', for instance, are mentioned as examples of the 'good players' referred to in the first sentence, while the whole extract works together to suggest the speaker's good judgment as a football manager.

COHESION AND COHERENCE

Cohesion refers to the linguistic features that link one part of a text to another (connections between forms).

Coherence refers more broadly to the quality of a text which makes it function within its context as a meaningful whole (connections between meanings).

Coherence, however, can be interpreted in different ways and is bound up with views about the role of context in the analysis of text. At one level, coherence involves simply the relationships between the propositions in a text (such as generalisation and example, or cause and effect, or chronological sequence). But interpreting such relationships depends on knowledge of the context in which the text was produced (in this case, a newspaper interview of a football manager) and beyond that, of relevant extralinguistic knowledge (for example, that Kanu and Campbell are footballers), and beyond that again, of the cultural practices associated with English football and sports reporting that form the wider context within which this interview can be understood.

Uses of the term **discourse** reflect these broadening views of coherence. In the narrowest sense, it refers to a linguistic unit above the level of the sentence, and it was in this sense that Zellig Harris first envisaged 'discourse analysis' as a search for grammatical patterns within a single connected text longer than a sentence, regardless of 'the meaning of the morphemes or the intent or conditions of the author' (Harris 1952: 30). Used in this way, 'discourse' is a linguistic unit, more or less equivalent to 'text'. More recent approaches, however, view 'discourse' as involving both text and context. This is the perspective, for example, commonly adopted by discourse analysts working within a sociolinguistic tradition, who focus on examining naturally occurring examples of text in use.

Discourse analysis has also been influenced by the work of philosophers and sociologists such as Michel Foucault and Pierre Bourdieu, who see language use as primarily social action. From this perspective, discourse extends beyond linguistic and situational elements to embrace 'language, action, interaction, values, beliefs, symbols, objects, tools and places' (Gee 1999). Discourse analysis thus becomes an investigation of social practices, with language use seen as always situated within a social structure and tied up with issues of identity and power. It is in this sense that linguists may talk, for example, of 'the discourse of welfare reform' or 'the discourse of masculinity'.

TEXT AND DISCOURSE

Text refers to a stretch of language which forms a unified whole. **Discourse** refers to:

1   a linguistic unit above the level of the sentence (more or less equivalent to 'text');
2   the use of language in a given context, e.g. legal discourse, classroom discourse (text + context);
3   the way language embodies ways of thinking, being and acting in the world (text + context + practice).

(cf. Swann *et al*. 2004: 83)

Along a spectrum from 'text' to 'practice', discourse analysis at one extreme would look at texts as linguistic objects without regard to their function within a social context, while at the other end it would focus on practices as social action, without relating this to any concrete linguistic data. Most analysts operate somewhere between these two extremes.

THE WIDENING CONTEXT

Context is generally defined as including both the linguistic context of a word or phrase, and also 'the social and physical world which interacts with text to create discourse' (Cook 1989: 156). Deciding what aspects of context can and should be considered when analysing discourse remains controversial. The term 'context of situation' derives from the anthropologist Bronislaw Malinowski (1923), who viewed language as a mode of action, with utterances comprehensible only in relation to the situation in which they were used within a given culture. These ideas were developed further by the British linguist J.R. Firth (1957), an influential proponent of a functional approach to language analysis in which meaning depends on the function an utterance fulfils in context. Firth categorised the relevant features of the context as the participants, the objects involved, and the effect of the verbal action. The functional approach thus contrasts with the structuralist approach predominant at the time, which focused on language as an abstract system – 'langue' (the abstract linguistic system) rather than 'parole' (its use in specific contexts).

Another linguist developing Malinowski's ideas was Roman Jakobson, a founding member of the Prague School of Linguistics, who produced a more detailed notion of the different functions of language. He suggested (1960) that any verbal communication involves six factors, each determining a different language function: context (determining the referential function); addressor (emotive function); addressee (conative function); contact between them (phatic function) and a common code (metalingual function); linguistic expression of the message (poetic function). In any particular situation, some functions will be more dominant than others, depending on the nature of the text. For instance, in poetry the 'poetic function' (where the highlighting of linguistic patterns is an end in itself) becomes the dominant one.

Function	Explanation
Referential	Refers to and conveys information about the world
Emotive	Expresses the author's attitude towards their utterance (e.g. through choice of words or tone of voice)
Conative	Influences the hearer/reader (e.g. through requests or demands)
Phatic	Makes contact rather than conveys meaning: initiating, sustaining or closing communication
Metalingual	Refers to the language code itself (e.g. to check on specific meanings)
Poetic	Focuses on the message for its own sake, emphasising the linguistic qualities of the language used

Figure 3.1 The functions of language (adapted from Jakobson 1960: 356).

ETHNOGRAPHIC APPROACHES TO RESEARCHING LANGUAGE

Ethnographic research on the use of language involves first hand participant observation within the contexts which are being studied, the recording of participants' naturally occurring talk and/or collection of written and other texts, and open-ended interviews to pursue participants' views and understandings. Recordings and other texts are analysed using some form of linguistic, discourse or conversation analysis. The interpretation of data is informed both by the analytic framework constructed by the researcher, and by the insider perspective gained through their observations and interviews.

The **ethnography of speaking** approach developed in America by Dell Hymes (1962) was also a reaction to mainstream linguistics (particularly the work of Chomsky), and addressed the issue of what speakers need to know in order to function in a particular context (their 'communicative competence'). Building on Roman Jakobson's model of language functions, Hymes (1974: 53–62) listed these variables under the mnemonic SPEAKING.

- **S**etting and scene
- **P**articipants
- **E**nds (purposes, goals and outcomes)
- **A**ct sequence (the form and order of the event)
- **K**ey (tone, manner or spirit)
- **I**nstrumentalities (forms and styles of speech)
- **N**orms (social rules governing the event)
- **G**enre (the kind of speech act or event)

From an ethnographic perspective, what is important is not simply the physical features of the situation, but the knowledge that participants draw on in order to function within it, knowledge which is developed through their socialisation into the culture (Saville-Troike 2003). This view of context underpins much work within sociolinguistics, but has been criticised for presenting an overly static view of culture as the fixed background against which a communicative event takes place, rather than recognising the role of the participants themselves in constructing the context (see, for example, Blommaert and Bulcaen 2000; Rampton 1995, 2005). Within pragmatics and speech act theory (see below), more is made of the way speaker/hearer knowledge is drawn upon as the basis for an active process of inferencing by which the hearer makes sense of any utterance. Similarly, in conversation analysis (CA – see Section 3.3 below) the interaction is seen as an active accomplishment of the participants, not simply the working out of a set of culturally-determined rules. CA is also distinct from other approaches in its refusal to make any assumptions about the context beyond those for which there is evidence in the text itself. This can be seen as a reaction to the potentially limitless elaboration of contextual variables as a means of explaining how participants make meaning, to the point where context becomes 'a convenient dumping ground for people's knowledge about the world, their own culture, etc.' (Langendoen 1968: 50).

Yet another way of carving up context is the approach taken by Halliday (himself a student of Firth), where social context and language use are related to each other through the notion of **register**, defined as the subset of a language used for a particular purpose or in a particular social setting (Halliday *et al.* 1964). In this model, the contextual variables that determine language use are:

- field (the subject matter of the discourse)
- tenor (the participants and their relationships)
- mode (the channel of communication).

However, the idea that context *determines* language use can be criticised for underestimating the active role of participants in negotiating discourse, and the term 'register' is often associated with a discredited view of language varieties as static and monolithic. Within Halliday's systemic functionalism (see Chapter 2), register remains in use to describe the level at which language interacts with the contextual variables of field, mode and tenor. Increasingly, though, systemic functional analysis has focused on 'genre' as a way of accounting for the social purpose of a text. But, like discourse and context, genre too is viewed differently from different theoretical perspectives.

GENRE

Although **genre** is a familiar term used in classifying literary or other art forms, such as sonnets or sitcoms, it has a broader application in language studies, where it identifies types of language interaction in terms of their social function. The Russian literary theorist Mikhail Bakhtin, defined 'speech genres' as emerging from the different areas of human activity: 'each sphere in which language is used develops its own relatively stable types of these utterances' (Bakhtin [1953] 1986: 60). He saw literary genres as secondary, drawing upon the primary genres that could be found in the utterances of everyday speech. Although Bakhtin's ideas were not widely known outside Russia before the 1980s, somewhat similar ideas were emerging elsewhere, based on the idea that, as members of a speech community use language to achieve particular purposes, patterns begin to emerge relating to the kind of language used, the roles of the participants and the processes involved in creating and interpreting the discourse. Genres reflect discourse expectations created by 'typified rhetorical actions based in recurrent situations' (Miller 1984: 31). In this view, genres develop rather like footpaths, emerging from the social practices of a community, but at the same time fostering the continuation of those practices.

Genre is a dual-facing concept that relates linguistic form on the one hand to social purpose on the other. Askehave and Swales (2001) talk of the need to reconcile a text-first (linguistic) approach and a context-first (ethnographic) approach, both dealing with text-in-context, though from different angles. In practice, some approaches have tended to focus more on textual features (e.g. Martin 1992; Swales 1990), while others emphasise social purposes and social action, using ethnographic rather than linguistic methods (e.g. Bazerman 1988; Miller 1984). Describing a genre in terms of its formal linguistic features runs the risk of treating genres as sets of rules that must be followed, turning genre into something static and normative rather than fluid and evolving. Ethnographic researchers would emphasise the way that individuals in a particular situation can deploy resources in order to achieve their own particular goals.

The identification of genres is not clear-cut: they are not 'out there' waiting to be labelled, but represent categories which analysts use to bring order to what is an inherently messy phenomenon. Consider, for example, the way that e-mail has developed, with a variety of conventions used in different contexts and at different times, sometimes drawing on formal genres like business letters, sometimes on informal genres such as postcards and text messages. Norman Fairclough has drawn attention to 'the productivity of texts, to how texts can transform prior texts and restructure existing conventions (genres, discourses) to generate new ones' (1992: 102). He uses the term **intertextuality** (adapted from Julia Kristeva's coining of the term, see Kristeva 1986) to refer to the way that a text incorporates other texts, for example by quoting or alluding to them, and **interdiscursivity** to refer to the way in which a text may draw upon different discourse conventions, for example, a bank leaflet which mixes the discourses of advertising and financial regulation. These transformative processes can give rise to hybrid genres, particularly in the mass media (Fairclough 1995).

MODE AND MEDIUM

One of the aspects of context discussed above was Halliday's concept of **mode**, which was glossed as 'channel of communication'. Halliday's definition of mode has varied slightly at different times, and extends beyond simply the physical means by which a message is transmitted to include whether it is spoken or written, scripted or spontaneous, monologue or dialogue. Halliday's work has highlighted the way in which these differences in mode are reflected in the linguistic features of a text. Written language, for example, typically involves **lexical density** (where meaning is packed into the individual clause through a high proportion of content words, longer noun phrases and frequent nominalisation), while spoken language typically involves **grammatical intricacy** (with shorter clauses linked together through subordination and coordination) (Halliday 1989). These differences are not, of course, absolute, and are more clearly seen as distributed along a mode continuum, with some written language exhibiting more speech-like features (e.g. postcards), and some spoken language exhibiting more writing-like features (e.g. formal speeches). Computer-mediated communication, for example, is often described as a hybrid mode (Baron 1998).

NOMINALISATION

Nominalisation refers to the forming of a noun phrase from another linguistic item such as a verb or adjective, e.g. 'The filming of the outdoor scenes took place in Kenya' rather than 'They filmed the outdoor scenes in Kenya' or 'They budgeted £15,000 for beautification of the area' rather than 'They budgeted £15,000 to make the area beautiful'.

Analysts use the terms 'mode', 'channel' and 'medium' in slightly different ways, sometimes interchangeably. Technical developments have now extended the range of modes that are amenable to analysis, and researchers have begun to explore how non-verbal elements, such as visual images or gestures, are used in multimodal texts. Gunther Kress, one of the pioneers in this field, has drawn a distinction between **mode** as a way of representing meaning by symbols, such as speech sounds, written script, hand signals, gestures or pictures, and **medium** as a way of transmitting these symbols, for example by print, phone or video. As he comments, 'If mode affects what can be said and how, medium affects who can be and is addressed and how' (Kress 2000: 87). From this perspective, research into *multimodality* involves examining the way meaning is represented in multimodal texts (defined broadly to include, for example, images with words, video, a performed play, a classroom lesson), rather than technical aspects of transmission (see also Section 3.4).

3.3 ANALYSIS OF SPOKEN DISCOURSE

SPEECH ACT THEORY AND PRAGMATICS

Nowadays it seems obvious that to investigate language use we need to look at real examples of language in use. In the case of spoken discourse, however, this has been a relatively recent development. Before the advent of tape recorders, it was impossible to preserve any more than short fragments of spoken interaction. Linguists tended to focus on decontextualised sentences, inventing their own examples to illustrate how the language system worked. Much early work on the nature of spoken interaction was carried out by philosophers of language, based on introspection rather than empirical data. Nonetheless, this work has greatly influenced the way that other researchers examine spoken data, particularly by drawing attention to the need to distinguish between the surface linguistic features of an utterance, and the functions for which it might be used in practice. Across the range of different approaches to spoken interaction, analysts share a concern to move beyond the classification of linguistic forms to identify what is going on in the interaction in terms of the purposes it serves for participants.

One influential approach emerging from the philosophy of language was **speech act theory**, which originated in the work of John Austin. The title of his book *How to Do Things with Words* (1962) signalled his move away from philosophy's preoccupation with the truth value of sentences towards an engagement with the way utterances are used in context to perform a variety of functions. Austin initially distinguished between what he called **constative** utterances, which he saw as statements of fact, and **performative** utterances such as 'I pronounce you man and wife', or 'I apologise for the delay', which cannot be evaluated as either true or false, but only in terms of whether or not they function successfully. He later collapsed this distinction, recognising that all utterances, in context, performed some kind of action such as requesting or promising or greeting, and arguing that their successful performance depended not necessarily on their truth value, but on a range of **felicity conditions**. For a felicitous request, for example, the speaker needs to ask for something which they believe the hearer can provide: you can't 'request' a friend to make you invisible, except

49

ironically. Austin distinguished between **locutionary acts** (the act of uttering – words in sequence to make meaning); **illocutionary acts** (the act performed by the speaker in producing the utterance, e.g. making a promise); and **perlocutionary acts** (the effect of the utterance on the listener, e.g. being persuaded).

ILLOCUTIONARY FUNCTION

Illocutionary function refers to what it is that a speaker *does* by virtue of producing an utterance, e.g. greeting, apologising, threatening. The terms 'illocutionary function', 'illocutionary act' and 'speech act' are often used with more or less the same meaning.

Another influential concept from the philosophy of language is the cooperative principle outlined by Paul Grice, based on the observation that 'our talk exchanges do not normally consist of a succession of disconnected remarks, and would not be rational if they did. They are characteristically, to some degree at least, co-operative efforts' (Grice 1975: 45). Grice suggests that, in order to have a conversation, participants normally cooperate with each other by observing four **conversational maxims** (1975: 45–46):

- Quantity   Make your contribution as informative as is required
                Do not make your contribution more informative than is required
- Quality   Try to make your contribution one that is true:
                Do not say what you believe to be false
                Do not say that for which you lack adequate evidence
- Relation   Be relevant.
- Manner   Be perspicuous:
                Avoid obscurity of expression
                Avoid ambiguity
                Be brief (avoid unnecessary prolixity)
                Be orderly

Conversational partners can use this cooperative principle to make sense of what the other is saying, even when the literal meaning is unclear. So, in the invented example below, B's response flouts the maxim of relation, but its apparent irrelevance leads A to infer that B believes the Browns to be at home.

A   Are the Browns home?
B   The lights are on.

B's response involves what Grice calls a 'conversational implicature', when a speaker, by saying one thing, implicates another, on the assumption that the hearer can work out what interpretation is necessary in order to make what was said consistent with the cooperative principle.

Although Grice's insight into the cooperative nature of conversation has been illuminating, the maxims themselves can be difficult to distinguish in practice, and Sperber and Wilson (1995) suggest that they can be consolidated into one overriding principle of **relevance**, based on a trade-off between cognitive effort and inferential effect. Rather than give an explanation about his lack of firm knowledge, Speaker B gives a brief answer involving minimum effort, on the assumption that A will draw the necessary inferences in order to make the response relevant. This principle of relevance, they argue, makes the other maxims unnecessary. Another challenge has come from critical analysts who question the assumption of cooperation between equal participants drawing on the same background knowledge, and highlight instead the power relations that underlie conversation (e.g. Fairclough 1989: 9–10).

Like Austin and Grice, John Searle was interested in how a speaker could say one thing and mean another. He saw the theory of language as part of a theory of action (Searle 1969: 17), but stressed its rule-governed behaviour. Taking up Austin's idea of felicity conditions, Searle specified sets of conditions for different illocutionary acts (or speech acts) in order to explicate what would be necessary for a speaker to perform them successfully. Searle's particular contribution was to show how such rules could help to explain **indirect speech acts**, where:

> the speaker communicates to the hearer more than he actually says by way of relying on their mutually shared background information, both linguistic and non-linguistic, together with the general powers of rationality and inference on the part of the hearer.
>
> (Searle 1979: 31–2)

In this later work, Searle draws on Grice's ideas about the cooperative nature of conversation and, like Grice, analyses meaning in terms of the speaker's intentions. His ideas have influenced the more cognitively-focused approach of Sperber and Wilson (e.g. Sperber and Wilson 1995), but have also contributed to developments in the functional analysis of dialogue.

Other influential work in **pragmatics** includes the **politeness theory** of Brown and Levinson (1978), which builds on Goffman's idea of **face**, i.e. a person's public self-image, which needs to be managed during an interaction. Politeness strategies can involve an orientation towards 'positive face' (a person's need to be seen as a good person) or towards 'negative face' (a person's need not to be imposed on). Positive politeness strategies include the expression of appreciation and approval and negative politeness strategies involve the avoidance of attack or intrusion, for instance through the use of indirect requests and euphemisms. Participants in social interactions each seek to satisfy their own and others' need for 'face'. The way in which a request is expressed, for example, will be influenced by the social distance between speaker and hearer, the power relations involved, and the degree of imposition involved in the request; asking your brother to lend you a pen is likely to be expressed rather differently from asking your bank manager for a large loan. This theory can also account for differences between cultures in terms of the weight they attach to either positive or negative face. It relies though on the assumption that conversational partici- pants are indeed concerned with saving each other's face and, like Grice's coop- erative principle, sees politeness as a matter of consensus, rather than deriving from unequal power relationships in society. Critical discourse analysts would paint a rather different picture, as will be discussed below.

CONVERSATION ANALYSIS

One of the key features of conversation analysis (CA) is its insistence on analysing the moment-by-moment interaction of conversation, rather than looking to the surrounding context to explain what is going on. This analytical stance derives from the ethnomethodological approach developed by the sociol- ogist Harold Garfinkel, which focuses on the production of social order through interaction at the micro-level. Garfinkel pointed out that social life is not simply a matter of following norms, because in order to follow a norm you have to be able to recognise when it applies, and different people's interpretations may vary. As a result, individuals have to coordinate their activities in any given situ- ation not only by interpreting the situation themselves, but also by recognising how other people are interpreting it. CA adopts this perspective by analysing the processes through which participants accomplish talk in interaction, and by taking as evidence only what the participants themselves show they have recognised as relevant. This approach requires close attention to the sequential structure of conversation.

Unlike much of the early work in speech act theory, conversation analysts place particular importance on using detailed transcripts of naturally occurring recorded data. Consider, for example, the following extract from a mobile phone conversation (Hutchby and Barnett 2005: 164):

```
1          ((summons))
2    SB:        Hullo?
3    Mich:      Happ::y bi::rthday:: gir:l =
4    SB:        = O: you a'right Mich?
5    Mich:   .  Yea::h what're you up to
6    SB:        Nuthing man. Ch[illing
7    Mich:                      [At home
8    SB:        Yeah (.) °Okay° (.) Are you comin' down t'day
9          (0.4)
10   Mich:      Yeah 're you gonna be in dis aft'r ↑ noon
11   SB:        Yeah
12   Mich:      A'right den i'll come an' che'k you early in da afternoo:n den
13   SB:        A'right
```

The first thing to notice is that the two speakers take turns, with no overlap between them (e.g. lines 3–4, where the symbol ' = ' indicates that one speaker follows another instantly) or very little (e.g. lines 6/7). On the basis of similar evidence from a wide range of spoken interactional data, Sacks *et al.* (1974) developed a series of rules to explain how speakers manage to coordinate their turn-taking in this way. They suggest that speakers intuitively recognise and predict **transition relevance places** where speaking turns are potentially complete (for instance, at the end of a clause or phrase, e.g. 'Happy birthday girl', or through intonation patterns, for instance high rising intonation), and where they can cut in smoothly to start talking. Another noticeable feature is the use of **adjacency pairs** (Schegloff and Sacks 1973), where the occurrence of a particular 'first pair part', such as a question, creates the expectation that a corresponding 'second pair part' will follow. Apart from several question/answer pairs in the extract above, there is also an example of a summons/answer pair, where the summons (in this case a ring tone) is answered by 'Hullo?' in line 2. In this extract, Hutchby and Barnett draw particular attention to the significance of 'At home' (spoken with a falling intonation) in line 7. They suggest that this utterance, in the sequential context of the preceding enquiry about what SB is doing, implies that for the caller 'doing nothing' is interpreted as meaning staying at home.

This sort of reasoning is characteristic of a conversation analytic approach to discourse. Avoiding any prior theoretical assumptions, the analyst attends to what the participants themselves demonstrate to be relevant to them at each point in the interaction. Contextual features are not therefore considered, unless they are demonstrably recognised by the participants. This methodological purism means that CA tends to keep to itself, and although other analysts often take over some of the methods of CA, the reverse rarely happens.

With its restricted view of context, CA is at the 'textual' end of the discourse analysis spectrum outlined in Section 3.2, as opposed to more socially-oriented approaches such as critical discourse analysis (CDA) (see below). In a critique of CDA from a CA perspective, Schegloff stresses the need for critical discourse analysts to address 'discursive events *in their import for their participants*' (1997: 184), sparking counterarguments from both Wetherell (1998) and Billig (1999). CA methodology can be criticised on the one hand for inconsistency, since by the very act of selecting what data to record the analyst is introducing some prior theoretical categories, and on the other hand for limiting its attention only to what participants demonstrate as relevant at one particular point in time, rather than in other events that may have a bearing on the current interaction. Finally, although close analysis of the detail of conversation is one of its strengths, it brings with it the danger of missing the wood for the trees, and failing to recognise the significance of larger social structures.

ETHNOGRAPHIC APPROACHES

Ethnographic approaches come out of a rather different tradition, which has its origins in anthropology, where research methods emphasise the need for analysts to immerse themselves in a culture in order to understand what is going on. Both ethnography and conversation analysis require the analyst to begin without preconceived notions of what is or is not significant for the participants, but in other respects their approaches differ. Conversation analysts tend to examine in fine detail a small amount of conversational data, whereas ethnographers aim for a 'thick description' of the participants' language practices that involves collecting large amounts of information from various sources, including interviews as well as recordings of daily interactions. And, while in CA the text is central, with features of the context used only when the text itself provides evidence of their relevance, ethnographers would not regard a text as something that can be separated from its context.

Section 3.2 outlined how Hymes pioneered the 'ethnography of communication', with its views on the crucial role of context. Hymes also set the goals for this research tradition, which aims to uncover how members of a speech community develop the communicative competence that enables them to participate appropriately in a range of speech events – an approach that has been particularly influential when applied to the pedagogy of language learning.

One of the criticisms of early ethnographies was that they adopted an 'essentialist' view of culture, in which each community was portrayed as separate, distinct and homogenous. Interactional sociolinguistics, discussed below, developed in part as a reaction to this view of culture. Recent ethnographic research, however, recognises the diversity that exists within communities and the dynamic, changing nature of cultural practice. For example, Rampton's work within urban schools in Britain (2005a, 2005b) revealed a complex relationship between ethnicity and language. The adolescents in these multicultural environments, rather than using only the language variety associated with their own ethnic group, were involved in frequent 'crossing', where they adopted the language style of a different group (see also Chapter 4, Section 4.5). His extensive interview and observational data showed that these crossings did not have one single function, but were deployed by the speakers for different purposes in different situations. The youngsters, it seemed, were making active use of a repertoire of different language styles as they constructed and negotiated their cultural identity.

Rampton's work fits within the central tradition of ethnographic research, using long-term participant observation, interviews with speakers, and analysis of recorded interaction. However, researchers in other traditions, influenced by ethnographic approaches, often employ some of the techniques of ethnography without subscribing to all of its principles. The term 'ethnographic' may be applied, for example, to research which does no more than supplement a linguistic analysis with a limited amount of interview data. While methodological cross-fertilisation may be valuable, there remains a tension between more 'ethnographic' approaches, which focus on particular situations, and avoid imposing predetermined categories on the data, and more 'linguistic' approaches, which aim for generalisation, and employ standard analytical frameworks. More recently, the term **linguistic ethnography** has been applied to research approaches which combine holistic accounts of social practice with linguistically informed analysis of participants' use of language (Rampton *et al*. 2004).

INTERACTIONAL SOCIOLINGUISTICS

Interactional sociolinguistics builds on John Gumperz' study of language and interaction (e.g. Gumperz 1982a, 1982b), drawing also on Hymes' work on the functions of language in social life (discussed above) and Goffman's sociological analysis of everyday encounters. It tends to be associated with qualitative research approaches, in contrast to the quantitative methods often used in Labovian variation studies (see Chapter 4, Section 4.4). Focusing on naturally occurring speech and its function and meaning in specific contexts, interactional sociolinguists are interested in how language is used to manage relationships between speakers, particularly in the negotiation of unequal relationships and in the context of intercultural communication. They have focused on a range of interactional features, for instance the use and effects of codeswitching between languages or language varieties (see Chapter 4, Section 4.5), different patterns of turn-taking and the use of silence (e.g. Roberts *et al*. 1992, Eades 2000; Coates 2003; Holmes 2006). Interactional sociolinguistic studies are often combined with an ethnographic approach (see above).

Goffman observed that the way we interact with each other depends on our assumptions about 'what it is that is going on', whether, for example, we are taking part in a job interview, or a seminar or a family reunion. This provides the **frame** for the interaction, affecting what we feel is appropriate to say or do (Goffman 1974). We learn these principles of social conduct through a process of socialisation, but since each individual's background and development is unique, our interpretations and expectations do not necessarily coincide. These differences in socialisation and understanding of particular frames can lead to negative consequences. Scollon and Scollon (1983) suggest, for example, that because of differences in the way native Alaskans interpreted the pre-sentencing stage of the judicial system, their behaviour made an unfavourable impression on the individuals who wrote their pre-sentence reports, leading to longer jail terms. According to Gumperz, participants' interpretations of what is going on in any particular situation depends on cues that signal the speaker's assumptions about the frame in which they are operating. These **contextualisation cues** include not only lexical and syntactic choices, but also aspects of conversational structure such as turn-taking, and paralinguistic features such as intonation, gaze and gesture (Gumperz 1982a, 1999).

We can apply the concepts of 'contextualisation cue' and 'frame' in analysing the following interaction from a paediatric examination being recorded for training purposes. Deborah Tannen points out that in this examination the paediatrician has to juggle three different frames: a medical examination of a child, a consultation with the child's mother, and a social encounter with both of them. Notice the frame shift at line 5, where the paediatrician stops teasing the child (in the social encounter frame) to give an instruction (in the examination frame), and the less successful shift at line 9 where she addresses the child in language appropriate for reporting the examination to other doctors.

1	Doctor:	Okay. All right. Now let me /?/ let me see what I can find in there. Is there peanut butter and jelly? Wait a minute.
2	Child:	No.
3	Doctor:	No peanut butter and jelly in there?
4	Child:	No.
5	Doctor:	Bend your legs up a little bit. . . . That's right.
6		Okay? Okay. Any peanut butter and jelly in here?
7	Child:	No.
8	Doctor:	No.
9		No. There's nothing in there. Is your spleen palpable over there?
10	Child:	No.

(Tannen and Wallat 1993: 66)

The language used by the paediatrician, together with her non-verbal behaviour, provides contextualisation cues to what is going on at each point (though the child herself seems to interpret line 9 as just another example of teasing). While the different frames define the nature of the activity, there are also differences in what Goffman calls **footing**, that is, the way that participants align in relation to one another. In the examination frame, the paediatrician teases the child but ignores the mother, while in the consultation frame she answers the mother's questions while keeping the child 'on hold'. Frame deals with the nature of the activity, and footing with the nature of the interaction.

Interactional sociolinguistics focuses in particular on linguistic and cultural diversity, and is often concerned with the asymmetries between participants who do not share the same interpretive backgrounds. Where contextualisation cues are interpreted differently, barriers to communication can emerge, which may help to maintain social inequalities. In examining the role of culture in shaping interaction, interactional sociolinguistics thus approaches issues tied up with the ideology of language. It does so, however, without the overt call to social action which is associated with critical discourse analysis (see below).

Sociolinguists have been interested in the role of **narrative**, or story, in interaction (e.g. Tannen 1989; Norrick 1997; Toolan 2001). Narratives, in this sense, refer not just to more formal storytelling performances but also to routine accounts of incidents and events that occur in everyday conversation. Researchers have examined the ways in which speakers use these to make a particular point and represent themselves in a certain light. William Labov (1972) argued that a fully formed conversational narrative contains the elements listed in the box below.

NARRATIVE STRUCTURE

Abstract, which summarises the events to come or offers a preliminary assessment of the significance of those events.

Orientation, which identifies the setting, characters and other background and contextual details relevant to the narrative.

Complicating action, a series of narrative clauses – the basic details of the storyline.

Evaluation(s), which indicate the point of the story, or the reason(s) why the speaker thinks the story is worth (re)telling. Such material may occur at the end, but may also be included at any point within the narrative.

Result or resolution, which resolves the story.

Coda, which signals the end of the narrative and may bridge the gap between the narrative and the present time.

(adapted from Labov 1972)

Labov distinguished between external evaluation, where a narrator steps outside the story to comment on it, and internal evaluation which included intensifiers (tone and loudness of voice, repetition), modal expressions indicating degrees of uncertainty, statements of cause or reason and reported speech. Evaluative elements may percolate right through the narrative. While Labovian analysis highlights the internal structure of conversational narratives, other researchers have emphasised the collaborative and dialogic nature of conversational story-telling. For example, in the story below about Nicole's sister's baby, Karlie invites her friend Nicole to tell a story they both know (1), then Nicole and Karlie collaboratively provide the abstract (2–3) and both contribute to the external evaluation (1, 6, 7, 8) and the coda (7–8).

1	Karlie	She did the best thing about it though, didn't she, Nicole?
2	Nicole	(*Abstract*) She didn't tell a soul, no one, that she was pregnant
3	Karlie	Until she was due, when she got into hospital, then she told them

57

4	Nicole	(*Orientation*) On Saturday night she had pains in her stomach and come the following Sunday my mum was at work and my sister come to the pub and my aunt Ella was in it and my sister went in there and said (*Complication*) 'I've got pains in my stomach' so my auntie Ella went and got my mum, and took her to hospital, and my mum asked her if she was due on and she said 'No, I've just come off' and when they got her to hospital they said (*resolution*) 'Take her to maternity'. My mum was crying!
5	Interviewer	Your mum didn't realise she was pregnant?
6	Nicole	No, and my mum slept with her when she was ill!
7	Karlie	(*Coda*) My dad said she did – Terri did the best thing about it – her sister's Terri
8	Nicole	Or if she did tell, as she's so young, she weren't allowed to have him

(adapted from Maybin 2006: 117–18)

FUNCTIONAL APPROACHES

The leading figures in the development of conversation analysis and inter-actional sociolinguistics tended to be American, at least in the early stages. In Britain, meanwhile, a different line of enquiry was developing, with the functional theories of the so-called 'London School' of Firth and Halliday (see Section 3.2) moving upcountry to re-emerge as the 'Birmingham school'. Here, John Sinclair and Malcolm Coulthard embarked upon a study of classroom discourse in which they set detailed criteria for analysis, aiming to account for the whole of their classroom data with a finite set of categories that were defined so as to allow precise identification of examples. As with conversation analysis, they focused on the evidence available in the textual data, and sought to identify general patterns, rather than simply describe the particular features of indi-vidual lessons.

Sinclair and Coulthard's model (1975) involves a hierarchy of five levels – lesson, transaction, exchange, move and act – in which a typical exchange consists of initiating (I), responding (R) and follow-up (F) (or evaluating) moves, and each move is realised by acts such as eliciting, informing, prompting, acknowledging, accepting and commenting. These acts (illocutionary acts, each fulfilling an illocutionary function, see under speech act theory above) were listed, each with a definition such as:

Accept   Realised by a closed class of items – 'yes', 'no', 'good', 'fine', and repeti-tion of pupil's reply, all with neutral low fall intonation. Its function is to indicate that the teacher has heard or seen and that the informative, reply or react was appropriate.

(Sinclair and Coulthard 1975: 43)

The flavour of this kind of analysis can be seen in the example below (1975: 67–68), where you need to read across the row to see the initiation, response and follow-up in each exchange (acts are not shown here). You will probably be able to distinguish the voice of the teacher from those of the pupils without much difficulty.

Initiating	Responding	Follow-up
What's the next one mean? You don't often see that one around here Miri	Danger falling rocks.	Danger, falling rocks. You're driving along-
Where would you be driving d'you think if you- Yes.	Round about Scotland in the mountain parts.	In the mountains. I've seen these in Wales, but I haven't driven in Scotland recently.
What about this one? This I think is a super one Isabel, can you think what it means?	Does it mean there's been an accident further along the road?	No.
	Does it mean a double bend ahead??	No.
Look at the car.	Er slippery roads?	Yes. It means 'be careful' because the road's very slippery.

Sinclair and Coulthard deliberately chose to analyse classroom interaction as they felt its overt teacher-directed structure would provide a good starting point, but it was their intention to develop an analytic framework which could be applied more generally to spoken language interaction. The three-part **IRF structure** has indeed been very influential for educational researchers such as Wells (1993) and Mercer (1995) (cf. also Mehan's (1979) three-part Initiation-Response-Evaluation structure). The problem is that an analysis designed for this very specific situation may not be suitable for other types of interaction in different contexts.

In her analysis of conversation, Deirdre Burton (1981) found that participants rarely used a follow-up move of the type found in classrooms (where the teacher traditionally has the unusual right of being able to evaluate whatever anyone else says). Instead, she suggested that an Opening move by one participant is followed by either a Supporting or Challenging move, depending on whether the next speaker supports or confronts the first speaker's propositions or proposals. This development has been carried forward by Suzanne Eggins, working within the Systemic Functional Linguistics (SFL) tradition (Eggins and Slade 1997). In general, though, discourse analysis in SFL has taken rather a different direction, with more attention given to identifying the stages of

ANN HEWINGS AND SARAH NORTH

different genres than to the close-grained detail of functional moves (see also the discussion of genre analysis in 3.4 below).

CRITICAL DISCOURSE ANALYSIS

Much of the work in genre analysis, both in SFL and in the Swales tradition (discussed in Section 3.4 below), is motivated by a concern to improve the teaching of genre, thereby helping people to gain access to discourses such as those of higher education or the professions. Interactional sociolinguistics, too, might be regarded as taking an optimistic view of linguistic and cultural diversity, with the aim of increasing cross-cultural understanding. Critical discourse analysis (CDA), however, challenges such approaches, seeing discourse as a site of struggle and calling for a change in the social structure itself. A key aspect of this approach is that 'discourse is socially constitutive as well as socially shaped' (Fairclough and Wodak 1997: 258); that, in other words, while discourse is determined by social conditions, it also reproduces and perpetuates those conditions. Critical discourse analysts may explicitly declare the political motivation for their work, for instance Norman Fairclough, a leading proponent of CDA, refers to himself as a Marxist (Fairclough 1989).

Fairclough is concerned with hegemonic power, which is maintained through the consent of those who are dominated. To explicate the way that discourse may contribute to the marginalisation of certain groups, CDA investigates the links between three levels of discourse:

• discourse-as-text: the analysis of what is said and written;
• discourse-as-discursive practice: the processes by which texts are produced, distributed, consumed and interpreted;
• discourse-as-social-practice: the social structures and practices through which discourse achieves its ideological effects.

This section considers how CDA is used in analysing spoken discourse, but CDA is also reconsidered in Section 3.4 in relation to written discourse.

Consider the following example in which a police officer interviews a witness to a robbery:

1 P   Did you get a look at the one in the car?
2 W   I saw his face, yeah
3 P   What sort of age was he?
4 W   About 45. He was wearing a . . .
5 P   And how tall?
6 W   Six foot one.
7 P   Six foot one. Hair?
8 W   Dark and curly. Is this going to take long? I've got to collect the kids from school?

9 P Not much longer, no. What about his clothes?
10 W He was a bit scruffy-looking, blue trousers, black . . .
11 P Jeans?
12 W Yeah.

(Fairclough 1989: 9)

Fairclough points out that the unequal relationship between the participants is reflected in features such as the police officer's control over the witness's contributions, the reduced form of his questions and the lack of mitigation (e.g. 'And how tall?' rather than 'Could you perhaps give me an idea of his height?'), and the lack of acknowledgement of the witness's problem with her children. The discourse reflects the nature of the relationship between the police and members of the community, and is itself part of the process by which that relationship is sustained.

CDA stresses the need for close linguistic analysis of discourse-as-text in order to explicate the way discourse can contribute to exploitation and marginalisation of certain groups. It has tended to draw on SFL for this purpose, although critical discourse analysts also turn to other analytical tools, including, for example, corpus linguistics (see Chapter 2). CDA has been criticised, however, for using linguistic analysis only in 'a supporting role' to illustrate what is essentially interpretation rather than analysis (Widdowson 1995). Similarly, Schegloff (1997) argues that critical discourse analysts tend to project their own biases into the analysis. Discussing these criticisms, Blommaert and Bulcaen (2000) suggest that a new critical paradigm is emerging, which relates micro-level analysis of text to macro-level social structures and processes, with a focus on issues such as ideology, inequality and power (see also Blommaert 2006).

3.4 ANALYSIS OF WRITTEN DISCOURSE

Unlike conversation, written discourse, whether written to be read or to be spoken, is typically pre-planned. This allows writers a greater opportunity to control the structure of their texts. Clearly, structure exists in both spoken and written texts, but it is on written texts that much of the research has been focused. Written discourse analysis has concerned itself with various levels of structure or patterning in texts from cohesive devices linking clauses and sentences, to topic organisation, to stages within genres. We begin with work that grew out of dissatisfaction with grammatical description which stopped at the level of the sentence or clause.

APPROACHES TO COHESION AND RHETORICAL STRUCTURE ANALYSIS

Analysing clauses or sentences is the work of the grammarian. Moving beyond the clause as the unit of analysis involves attending to how clauses are connected or related to each other to make a coherent text. It is a focus of work in semantics – examining how the text as a whole functions as a unit of meaning.

A coherent text relies on cohesion (see Section 3.2 above) and cohesion is a defining feature of discourse. One of the most comprehensive and influential studies of cohesion was that by Michael Halliday and Ruqaiya Hasan (Halliday's later work on systemic grammar is discussed in Chapter 2). These linguists looked at cohesion as a function of the semantic relations between sentences, that is at the discourse level: 'Where the interpretation of any item in the discourse requires making reference to some other item in the discourse, there is cohesion' (Halliday and Hasan 1976: 11). To describe the forms of cohesion they systematically analysed systems of reference, substitution, ellipsis, conjunction and lexical cohesion to identify ways in which the meanings in a text are established through the interrelations of different language resources.

FORMS OF COHESION

Reference refers to a word or phrase that links to another word or phrase and can only make sense in relation to that other meaning, e.g. Three blind mice. See how they run.

Substitution refers to the replacement of one expression in a text with another, e.g. A: Are we leaving at three? B: I think so.

Ellipsis refers to the omission of an item which can be inferred from the surrounding text, e.g. A: Am I too late? B: No, [you are] just in time.

Conjunction is indirectly cohesive as it refers to elements which presuppose the presence of other discourse components, e.g. using the words 'secondly' or 'after' implies that something was mentioned previously.

Lexical cohesion refers to cohesion achieved through the choice of vocabulary. Repetition of a word or phrase, use of a near synonym or an opposite create lexical cohesion, e.g. 'Bunny-proofing' means encasing electric *cords* in heavy-duty plastic, or blocking *cords* and outlets with furniture so the rabbit cannot reach them. It is the single most important step in preparing an indoor area for a rabbit.

Lexical cohesion can take a variety of forms. In the example:

Jan sat down to rest at the foot of a huge beech-tree. Now he was so tired that he soon fell asleep; and a leaf fell on him, and then another, and then another . . .
(Halliday and Hasan 1976: 12)

the lexical tie is between *beech-tree* and *leaf.* They are not synonyms but their proximity in the text leads us to assume that the leaves in question are beech leaves from the beech tree mentioned.

Further work on cohesion was initiated by Eugene Winter and Michael Hoey's analysis of clause relations. Winter categorised these relations as either

'Matching' – where there was a high degree of repetition as in his example 'Little boys *don't play with dolls*, girls *play with dolls*' (Winter 1994: 52) or 'Logical' – concerned with sequencing, answering questions such as 'What happened next?' 'What caused that to happen?'. He went on to look at how these combined in texts, arguing for two basic text patterns: 'Hypothetical and Real' and 'Situation and Evaluation'. 'Hypothetical and Real' texts begin with the author with-holding judgment on another's point of view. This hypothetical statement predicts a subsequent statement of what the author believes to be true or real – a denial or an affirmation, for example, 'The engineers expected *that the earth-quake would have caused damage to their underground tunnel. It did*' (Winter 1994: 64; italics in original). Letters to the editor in newspapers often take this form, as do scientific papers. 'Situation and Evaluation' texts consist of a state-ment on a topic followed by remarks on what is thought or felt about it with an optional basis or reason. This can be illustrated in relation to postcards – where the picture on the front acts as the situation and the text on the back as the eval-uation and basis for the evaluation, e.g. an Australian man writes on a postcard with a picture of a beautiful French beach: 'This is one of the best beaches here. Not a patch on our beaches in Queensland. Too much litter and pollution. Love, Mike' (Winter 1994: 58).

Hoey pursued this work in longer stretches of discourse, outlining in detail clause relations leading to patterns which he labelled problem-solution and general-particular (Hoey 1983). He exemplified the **problem-solution pattern** with the fabricated short text:

> (1) I was once a teacher of English Language. (2) One day some students came to me unable to write their names. (3) I taught them text analysis. (4) Now they all write novels.
>
> (Hoey 2001: 123)

The structure of the text is sentence (1) situation, (2) problem, (3) solution or response, and (4) result. Such a structure can be inferred by readers bringing their own cultural knowledge to bear, for example by interpreting being unable to write as problematic and therefore expecting a solution to be offered. At the linguistic level, readers are also responding to types of patterning beyond and between sentences, as identified by Halliday and Hasan. In Hoey's text this involves simple repetition of pronouns (e.g. *I*), and words (e.g. *write*). There are also more complex forms of repetition such as *teacher – taught* and *text – novels*.

At much the same time as Hoey and Winter were working on clause relations in a British context, **rhetorical structure theory** (RST) was examining some of the same issues in the United States. RST was the work of William Mann, Christian Matthiessen and Sandra Thompson and grew originally from computer-based text generation research (Mann and Thompson 1988). In order to generate comprehensible text by computer, models of how texts work needed to be robust. RST is an attempt to describe texts systematically and particularly to account for their coherence as discourse units. Like Winter, RST analysts focus on relations between clauses in a text. Of particular significance is the claim–evidence relation, though many others are also described. The RST analyst posits the different relations the reader might make between clauses as a text unfolds. More recently, the focus has shifted from the computational; RST analysts have become more expansive, seeking connections with other linguistic approaches to text and trying to describe coherence in different languages and text types (Taboada 2007).

APPROACHES TO REGISTER AND GENRE ANALYSIS

Approaches to genre and register variation have also been much in evidence in analysis of discourse. The work of Halliday and others noted in Section 3.2 applies register to the contextual variables necessary for the creation and interpretation of a text described in terms of the field, tenor and mode. The term 'register', however, has also been used in other contexts to denote different collections of features, such as those associated with the cline from formal to informal uses and those associated with particular fields of knowledge. It is frequently associated with the work of Douglas Biber and colleagues on computational analysis of texts, who have used the term broadly 'for varieties defined by their situation characteristics' (Biber *et al.* 1998: 135). Biber *et al.* have, as a central research goal, the understanding of 'how language varies when used for different purposes in different situations' (1998: 169). While being 'less theoretically precise' (Hunston 2002: 160) than the SFL use of the term, Biber's broadly defined register categories have been influential within corpus linguistics (see Chapter 2) as providing a basis for identifying and contrasting lexical, grammatical and discoursal features of texts. To investigate register variation, Biber *et al.* applied a multidimensional (MD) analysis to a corpus of different registers, quantifying variation in features such as tense and aspect markers, pronouns and pro-verbs, questions and subordination features (Biber *et al.* 1998: 145). Following statistical analysis of the correlations of these features, Biber *et al.* identified five dimensions of variation within the registers examined: 'involved' versus 'informational production'; 'narrative' versus 'non-narrative discourse'; 'elaborated' versus 'situation-dependent reference'; 'overt expression of argumentation'; 'impersonal' versus 'non-impersonal style'. This enabled registers to be compared along a scale relating to the particular dimensions. For example, in involved versus informational production, telephone and face-to-face conversations would be at the involved end of the scale, general fiction somewhere in the middle and academic prose and official documents at the informational end. In impersonal versus non-impersonal features, face-to-face conversation would be at the non-impersonal end of the scale with general fiction nearby. Academic research articles would be towards or at the impersonal end. Biber *et al.* maintain that MD analysis of registers gives a more comprehensive picture than approaches which focus on a more limited number of linguistic variables.

As noted in Section 3.2, genre analysis is the approach favoured by a variety of analysts interested in both linguistic form and social purpose. The substantial body of work on genre by John Swales has examined the typical structures of texts associated with the communicative purposes of particular discourse communities (e.g. 1981, 1990, 2004). He has focused on genres typical of university settings, particularly those encountered by students using English for academic purposes (Khine *et al.* 2003). The empirical research article (RA) is, perhaps, the most analysed of these academic genres and characteristically follows the pattern of introduction–methods–results–discussion (IMRD). Within genres, such as the RA, the descriptive unit is typically the *move*, 'a discoursal or rhetorical unit that performs a coherent communication function in a written or spoken discourse . . . a functional, not a formal, unit' (Swales 2004: 228) (compare Sinclair and Coulthard's use of the term in Section 3.3). A much researched area has been the introductions to RAs. Figure 3.2 illustrates a recent iteration by Swales of the first two moves in the Create a Research Space (CARS) model for the introductions to RAs:

Move 1   *Establishing a territory* (citations required)
                                via
            Topic generalisation of increasing specificity
                                ↓
Move 2   *Establishing a niche* (citations possible)
                                via
            Step 1A Indicating a gap
                                or
            Step 1B Adding to what is known
            Step 2 (optional) Presenting positive justification

Figure 3.2   A revised CARS model for Moves 1 and 2 (adapted from Swales 2004: 230).

Key concepts within Swales' approach – **discourse community, communicative purpose** and **genre** itself – have all come in for criticism and subsequent revision. The criticisms have largely focused on problems of defining the concepts. So, for example, there has been much debate about how to specify a discourse community. Additionally, there have been criticisms regarding the lack of analytical rigour, particularly with regard to identifying rhetorical units such as moves (Crookes 1986). Despite the problems, the approach has remained highly influential, particularly in the field of teaching academic writing.

SPEECH AND DISCOURSE COMMUNITIES

A **speech community** comprises people in habitual contact with each other through language. The term has been variously defined within linguistics. Definitions may emphasise shared language use, frequency of interaction between speakers, shared rules of speaking and interpretation, or shared attitudes and values with respect to language. Dell Hymes (1974) provides a fairly broad definition of a speech community as one whose members share 'knowledge of rules for the conduct and interpretation of speech. Such sharing comprises knowledge of at least one form of speech, and knowledge also of its patterns of use' (Hymes 1974: 51).

A **discourse community** (e.g. Swales 2004) is a grouping based on a common interest, with common goals and mechanisms for intercommunication between members. It uses participatory mechanisms to provide information and feedback, some specific lexis and genres and has a threshold level of members with relevant content and discoursal expertise.

The strength, but also the weakness, of this tradition of genre analysis is that it draws on much existing terminology, what might be referred to as 'folk taxonomies'. The research article, the grant proposal, the PhD thesis or dissertation are all recognisable to the community of academics, but their understanding of what the labels mean is likely to be coloured by their disciplinary context and experiences. There is a tendency to use these labels to classify or group texts which may have only superficial resemblances. The 'research article', for example, is a label that can be applied to very different types of texts in different disciplines. In biology, it usually refers to empirical research, whereas in fields such as mathematics and theoretical physics, where empirical research is impossible, 'theoretical' research articles are the norm. Even within a single discipline such as chemistry the ordering of sections varies, with organic chemistry favouring introduction, results and discussion, conclusion and experimental (methods), whereas physical chemistry follows the more canonical introduction, methods, results and discussion, conclusion. Such examples are a reminder that genre labels need to be treated with caution.

The approach to genre associated with SFL (see Chapter 2) also looks at generic moves or stages, but these are tied more firmly into the lexicogrammatical structures of the texts, thus responding to Crookes' criticism of Swales mentioned above. The approach is associated most closely with the work of Jim Martin and evolved from that of Michael Halliday. Working up from descriptions of typical lexical and grammatical choices, Martin (1993) and Rothery (1996) began the detailed description of typical school genres, such as the news story and the discussion, and illustrated how a genre is built up through stages – the structural elements, realised by textual and grammatical features.

Both Swales' and Martin's approaches to genre have been criticised as creating a normative and static edifice. These criticisms can be partially countered by reference to the pedagogic purpose of the descriptions. What unites both the SFL approach and that associated with Swales and the teaching of English for academic purposes, is a concern with helping students to gain understanding and mastery of the literacy conventions of their university or school subjects. This is not designed to inhibit creativity, but to provide a base on which to build. SFL genre theorists, in particular, have a more overt ideological stance, arguing for the need to teach children from disadvantaged backgrounds the type of control and ownership of genres that those from more privileged backgrounds take for granted (Kalantzis and Cope 1993).

NEW LITERACY STUDIES

The 'new' in New Literacy Studies signals a rejection, in the 1980s, of a cognitivist view of literacy based on the premise of a simple need to decode or encode written language for communication to take place. Rather than conceptualising literacy as a neutral set of individual skills and competencies, the New Literacy Studies are 'based on the view that reading and writing only make sense when studied in the context of social . . . practices of which they are but a part' (Gee 2000). This shift of focus, from literacy as technology to literacy as social practice, has highlighted the ways in which literacy is often implicated in the practices of power, and drawn attention to its uses and effects in people's everyday lives. It is the concern with the 'social' and also with the 'practice' of literacy that unites a number of different researchers (e.g. Street 1984; Gee 1990; Barton and Hamilton 2000).

The move towards a more socially situated view of literacy is illustrated by Shirley Brice Heath's concept of **literacy events**: 'occasions in which written language is integral to the nature of participants' interactions and their interpretative processes and strategies' (Brice Heath 1982: 74). Brice Heath's detailed ethnographic study of literacy events in three socio-economic communities in the southern United States relates the types of text read, the value accorded to them and the ways of making sense of them to different cultural practices at the community level. This, in turn, is related to how children progress with literacy-based activities in school. Before children ever reach school most will have been exposed to numerous literacy events and these influence their approach to school literacy practices. If the literacy practices associated with school-based work have not formed a part of the everyday literacy practices of the home, then children may start off at a disadvantage in comparison with the expected norms.

The notion of **literacy practices** draws on a sociological notion of social practice from Bourdieu, who glosses 'practice' as the routine behaviours and patterned sociocultural activities in which people engage (Bourdieu 1990). So practices emerge from the relationships between people's habitually shaped dispositions to behave in particular ways, together with their social, economic and cultural capital, within particular areas of human activity, such as the family and the classroom. The move from social practices to literacy practices is associated with the work of Brian Street (1984) and James Gee (1990).

Working as an anthropologist in Iran, Street coined the phrase 'literacy practices' as a means of focusing on the diversity in 'social practices and conceptions of reading and writing'. By foregrounding the notion of practices, he was arguing against the dominant Western view of literacy as a set of skills which are the same in all places and throughout history. Literacy practices are related to specific sociocultural contexts and are associated with power and ideology. Additionally, he argued that

> ... literacy practices are constitutive of identity and personhood ... whatever forms of reading and writing we learn and use have associated with them certain social identities, expectations about behaviour and role models.
>
> (Street 1984: 140)

Context, personhood and identity are central to Gee's idea of 'social languages', which highlights the diversity of meanings communicated through language. He focuses, in particular, on how language expresses, in the multiple contexts in which it is used, *who* we are, our identities, and *what* we are doing. Such social languages, both spoken and written, are embedded in our values and beliefs, and often tied to membership of particular social or work-based groups. They are frequently embedded in or associated with institutions and objects, including written texts. An example of the strength of the cultural embeddedness of literacy practices is provided in the context of South Africa by Catherine Kell. She describes how the conventional Western greetings and expressions of affection associated with letter writing by literacy teachers were not appropriated by their students and transferred beyond the classroom. While adult students showed themselves able to reproduce the genre in class, they resisted its use in letter writing for their own personal purposes to absent family members because it contravened 'long-standing cultural practices, including taboos or prohibitions around the use of certain terms expressing affect' (Kell 2001: 20).

The view of literacy as a cultural and contextual practice has been the subject of much research within educational settings. Mary Lea and Brian Street (1998) analysed the types of writing that students were expected to produce, the variety of views on what constituted success from academic staff, disciplinary epistemologies and the significance of writing for individual students' sense of identity. They argue that the complexity of these issues confounds the notion of 'problem' students who can't write – the so-called 'deficit' model. Rather, in order to understand the writing practices of academia it is necessary to look at the disciplinary, institutional and ideological preconceptions that underpin academic literacy practices. It is only by making these implicit expectations explicit, by unveiling the institutional practice of mystery, that students can gain the knowledge and power to enter into the powerful discourses of the academy (see also Lillis 2001). At the level of school literacy, Bloome *et al.* (2005) high-light the existence of 'classroom literacy practices' involving the use of written language associated with 'doing classroom life' (2005: 50). These are conceptu-alised as cultural practices, which draw on a more or less shared cultural model of how things are done. The roots of such practices outside the classroom have been researched by David Barton and others working in a northern English city (Barton *et al.* 2000). They draw on extensive ethnographic work involving indi-vidual interviews, family case studies, examination of writing and reading around visual texts in the local environment, and records of literacy events.

Street, Heath, Barton and Bloome all, with some variations of emphasis, see a literacy event as a social interaction which instantiates a literacy practice or practices:

> Literacy practices are the general cultural ways of utilising written language which people draw upon in their lives. . . . However practices are not observable units of behaviour since they also involve values, attitudes, feelings and social relation-ships. . . . Practices are shaped by social rules which regulate the use and distribu-tion of texts, prescribing who may produce them and have access to them. They straddle the distinction between individual and social worlds, and literacy practices are more carefully understood as existing in the relations between people, within groups and communities, rather than as a set of properties residing in individuals.
>
> (Barton and Hamilton 2000: 7–8)

Within North America the tradition of teaching rhetoric, composition and professional writing to American college students has created a body of teachers and researchers open to the insights that a more social and ethnographic approach can provide. Their contribution to New Literacy Studies is **New Rhetoric** or **American New Rhetoric** which makes use of detailed descriptions of the academic and professional contexts in which texts are situated, and includes data-gathering techniques such as participant observation, interviews, docu-ment collection and, to a lesser extent, textual analysis. Bazerman's (1988) influ-ential study of the development of the genre of the experimental article in science from its emergence in the seventeenth century to the present day, situ-ates the written products in their social and historical contexts. His work has done much to reveal the rhetorical sophistication of a form of writing which claims simply to report natural facts (Bazerman 1988: 6). While Bazerman's work was largely historically based, research into more recent scientific genres, such as the grant proposal (e.g. Myers 1990), has made full use of access to the people writing the texts explored. By such means, generic characteristics of texts are related to the social purposes of the writer and the readership.

This social turn in literacy studies has led to the cross-fertilisation of ideas between researchers with a literacy focus and those in other areas of psycholog-ical, social and cultural studies. For example, the complexity of composing text, a facet of literacy often overlooked when only the final product is analysed, has become part of the concern of literacy scholars.

When we look closely at situated composing, we do not find a smooth easy activity. Writing moves forward (and backward) in fits and starts, with pauses and flurries, discontinuities and conflicts . . . Writers are not only inscribing text. They are also repeatedly rereading text that they've written, revising text as they write as well as going back later to revise, pausing to read other texts (their own notes, texts they have written, source materials, inspirations), pausing to think and plan.

(Prior 2004: 170)

The context of production and the activities that this encompasses are seen as part of the whole practice of text production. A text is accomplished through the organisation of language resources, but its meaning relies on its relationship to other previous texts, other similar texts and to the knowledge brought to its reading by a reader. It forms one part of a system of human activity.

New Literacy Studies do not have such a close affiliation with pedagogy as the genre approaches of Systemic Functional Linguistics (SFL) and English for Academic Purposes (EAP). However, aspects of their methods have become very influential, particularly in combination with English for Academic Purposes genre approaches. Studies now frequently go beyond analysis of text and its rhetorical structure to include interviews, observations and relevant document study (e.g. Hyland 2000, Samraj 2004). Swales (1998) meshed aspects of text and genre analysis and ethnography in his 'textography' of a small university building. Each floor of the building contained different disciplines and through detailed study of the individuals, their work and their texts Swales provided a fine-grained analysis of the communicative networks of the specific discourse communities. Such combined approaches have evolved alongside the less text-focused approaches implicit in the notion of literacy practices.

CRITICAL DISCOURSE ANALYSIS REVISITED

Aspects of genre-based pedagogy, New Literacy Studies and the social turn in approaches to literacy more generally, have directed attention towards the ideo-logical dimensions of texts and their associated practices. This ideological orien-tation is particularly associated with critical approaches to discourse analysis as discussed in Section 3.3 above. Critical discourse analysis is often used to examine how values and viewpoints are represented in texts and in the case of news texts, how readers are persuaded to accept these viewpoints. Michael Stubbs provided a classic example showing how 'Blacks and Whites' involved in violence in South Africa were depicted in a British tabloid newspaper. He illus-trates how particular choices of vocabulary and grammar position people and groups in different ways:

Although the article reported violence by both Blacks and Whites, the vocabulary and the grammar used to talk about the group was distinctly different. First, the words *Black* and *White* occur with different accompanying words. Blacks act in *mobs*, *crowds*, *factions* and *groups*. They constitute *millions* who live in *townships* and *tribal* homelands. They *mass* in *thousands*, and are *followers of nationalist leaders*. But Whites (also reported as committing violence) are individuals or *extremists*: by implication different from other (normal?) Whites. Second, the grammar of the text represents Blacks and Whites differently. When Blacks are reported as committing violence, they are in subject position, and at the beginning of the clause ... However, when Whites are reported as committing violence ... [e]vents are presented in passives and nominalizations:

> a ... black ANC follower was ... killed by an unidentified white man.

> (Stubbs 1996: 95–96)

Such analyses have led to criticisms of critical approaches as fixing on linguistic features and assigning ideological significance to them without taking into account how they might actually be read:

> The analysis is bent on uncovering what is going on behind the textual scenes and pays selective attention to particular details: a word here, a grammatical form there. There is no consideration of how these features act upon each other in the text, or upon contextual conditions outside it or, in general, how the text is actually discoursally processed. There appears to be no principled theoretical motivation for picking on particular features.

> (Widdowson 2000: 167)

Responses to such criticisms have arguably created a hybrid research methodology which builds on the comprehensive lexicogrammatical analysis enabled by SFL and the extensive comparisons possible using a corpus of texts and analytical software such as concordancers, within a critical discourse analysis framework (e.g. O'Halloran and Coffin 2004).

APPROACHES TO ELECTRONIC AND MULTIMODAL TEXTS

Before concluding this section on written discourse, we turn to writing in electronic media such as mobile (cell) phones and networked computers. Electronic communication whether by e-mail, in chat groups, formal discussion forums or text messaging is claimed to blur the boundaries between speech and writing and create new genres. Studies such as those by Biber and associates (Biber *et al.* 1999), Brazil (1995), Carter and McCarthy (1995, 1997) and Halliday (1987) describe grammatical differences between spoken as opposed to written language use and this contrast has been one of the ways in which e-writing has been analysed. Baron (1998), for example, noted that first and second person pronouns, present tense and contractions, all features more commonly associated with speech, were used more frequently in e-mails than in other kinds of written discourse. In contrast, e-mails shared with writing characteristics such as relatively higher lexical and grammatical density, use of subordinate clauses and disjunctions such as 'however' and 'in contrast'. A study of chat room discourse looked at cohesion and personal reference as ways of mitigating the difficulty of negotiating interaction in discourse where adjacency pairs are disrupted and topics shift and drift (Nash 2005). However, Susan Herring (2001), in discussing computer-mediated discourse (CMD), questions whether an analysis of contrasts and overlaps with speech and writing perhaps neglects the unique features of computer-mediated communication and also its internal variety.

Approaches to analysing computer-mediated discourse focus not only on aspects of linguistic structure, as mentioned above, but also on the effect of the different electronic channels: synchronous (e.g. chat), asynchronous (e.g. e-mail), one-way (e.g. discussion lists) or two-way transmission (SMS messaging). This variety indicates the danger of generalisations when discussing computer-mediated discourse. Analysis of linguistic features in a synchronous chat environment would expect to show differences to those found in an asynchronous discussion list. Synchronicity in a one-to-many computer-mediated discourse environment, for example, can disrupt the turn-taking pattern typical of face-to-face interaction, as messages appear in the order in which they were sent, not necessarily following the message to which they are responding. One of the responses to this has been the development of 'addressivity', that is, naming the person to whom the message relates. In asynchronous environments a variety of different strategies has emerged, for example, that of pasting in or quoting the message (or part of a message) to which you are responding.

Interaction via computer-mediated discourse has developed in different electronic contexts to allow interpersonal as well as other meanings to be more easily exchanged. Analysis has focused on tools such as emoticons as a swift way of conveying attitude and emotion. An alternative is to represent physical actions and facial expressions in words, or abbreviations such as 'lol' (laugh out loud), or 'grin'. Herring (2001: 623) also discusses the use of a command in environments such as multi-user domains which attaches the status 'this is a performance or story' to the ensuing text. Thus, a series of messages can be read as telling a story, which may well involve real participants in actions in which they may or may not wish to be implicated. These participants may try to distance themselves from the narrative, but other users may decide to accept the typed messages as reality. Herring concludes that in an environment where there is little else but language, language becomes the primary resource for creating social reality.

Computer-mediated discourse can also be studied from a variety of social perspectives. The relative anonymity of the medium means that traditional sociolinguistic variables such as social class, age, gender and race may be less obvious or disguised. The use of avatars in multi-user domains such as Second Life allow interactants to assume different genders, ages and histories. In contrast, social networking sites such as Facebook and MySpace can provide very public insights into the lives of those who interact, including data on friendship groups, interests, politics and sexual orientation. So unguarded are the practices of many of the users of social networking sites that the amount of personal information disclosed has led to concerns that members may be at risk of stalking and identity fraud or that they could risk jeopardising future job opportunities as employers check sites before making new appointments. In its many forms, computer-mediated discourse illustrates the flux of both texts and practices (particularly young people's practices) which require new or adapted approaches to analysis.

Like speech and writing, computer-mediated discourse has also been subject to critical ideological analysis. The interaction facilitated by the medium is not just individual to individual but enables the building of virtual communities. Such communities may challenge or reproduce power asymmetries, such as between teachers and students or, at a global level, between those with access to computer-mediated communications and those without.

Researchers focusing on computer-mediated discourse have also felt the need to consider aspects of visual representation, such as text layout, font, colour and illustrations, thus employing a multimodal approach to analysis (e.g. Kress and van Leeuwen 2006; Jewitt forthcoming). The term **multimodality** draws on Halliday's notion of 'mode' (see above) and is used to refer to the ways in which different modes of communication (e.g. speech, writing, visual image in a print text, body movement, gesture or gaze in spoken interaction) are combined together in communication. Different meanings may be conveyed through each mode, with modes offering different 'affordances' in terms of their limitations and potential for meaning-making. Meanings conveyed in the different modes involved in an act of communication may reinforce each other or give rise to inconsistencies or contradictions.

For Jewitt and Kress, a multimodal analysis of classroom interaction includes the full repertoire of students' and teachers' meaning-making resources: 'actional, visual, spoken, gestural, written, three-dimensional, and others, depending on the domain of representation' (2003: 277) and shows how these are organised to make meaning. They use 'speech' and 'action' columns to transcribe a teacher's explanation of blood circulation in a science lesson (and also provide photographs of a diagram drawn by the teacher and a model of the upper part of the human body that he uses in his explanation):

Speech	*Action*
Now if we look at that on our	Places model on front desk
model you can actually see	stands behind model, arms in front
here	picks up heart, points at heart
the heart has four main blood	puts heart back in model
vessels okay now ...	[...]
[...]	

(Jewitt and Kress 2003: 283)

Kress and van Leeuwen argue that all communication is multimodal and they have developed a systematic approach to the analysis of different modes, drawing on semiotics and systemic functional linguistics (see Chapter 2). Kress emphasises the importance of **design** in communication, i.e. the ways in which different modes are deliberately orchestrated by speakers and writers, and brought together into textual ensembles. He argues that there is an important change currently taking place in communicative practices, with digital media replacing print and image replacing writing, as the main modes of representation, and that this has been accompanied by shifts in the authority and shaping of knowledge, and in the ways in which people engage with the social and natural world (Kress 2003). While new technologies are creating greater opportunities for multimodal text and production, it is also acknowledged that written English has always had multimodal dimensions, through its use of particular fonts and scripts and visual decoration, for instance in illuminated manuscripts (Graddol 2007).

3.5 ISSUES

The 'social turn' in linguistics has been apparent in an increasing concern to consider discourse not simply as a matter of text, but as tied up with social practices. Approaches which consider discourse from the perspective of practice are, it can be argued, better geared to handle discourse as shifting and dynamic – the more an analysis is rooted in the text, the easier it is for the text itself to become reified, treated as a finished product rather than as something emerging through a particular cluster of contextual circumstances. The concept of genre, for example, may be pulled in either a more static or a more dynamic direction. In response to criticisms of a reified view of genre, Swales (2004) has moved towards seeing it in terms of a series of metaphors, with different features of the text brought into focus depending on the metaphor chosen. The metaphor of 'genre as standard', for example, foregrounds the constraints imposed by genre norms, while the metaphor of 'genre as frame for social action' emphasises it as a starting place where people can begin to sort out their ideas, without necessarily prescribing the final form in which the ideas are presented. This latter metaphor brings Swales's work closer to approaches which emphasise social purposes and social action.

In general, views of discourse communities as self-contained, homogenous and stable have increasingly come into question, with researchers such as Rampton (2005a) and Blommaert (2005) showing how conventions are made and remade within a complex network of social relations. Similarly, Silverstein and Urban (1996) have argued for attention to 'natural histories of discourse', which investigate texts not simply in relation to the immediate situational context, but as having their own trajectories, developing out of particular resources available to particular people at particular times. The more texts are seen as situated in the particular circumstances of production, the less they are amenable to the generalisation traditionally seen as the goal of linguistic analysis.

Conversation analysis appears to stand out as resisting this move towards increasing concern with contextual variables and, although it remains influential, many linguists are uncomfortable with the narrow lens it brings to the examination of talk-in-interaction. Conversation analysis has, however, been particularly influential in discursive psychology, and is also being adopted in the study of second language acquisition (e.g. Seedhouse 2004). In both these fields, it brings the advantage of close-grained analysis of interaction, together with a concern for the 'insider' perspectives of participants.

Research in discourse analysis has tended to focus on British and North American contexts, bringing with it the danger of assuming universality for conventions that may in fact be specific to particular cultures. Wierzbicka, for example, comments on the 'astonishing ethnocentrism' of speech act theory (1991: 24), and argues that what is at issue in much of this research is 'English conversational strategies, and Anglo-Saxon cultural values' (1991: 60). While there is some research into cross-cultural pragmatics, it is often in terms of interaction between native and non-native speakers, from an 'Anglo-Saxon' viewpoint, rather than looking at English as used within other cultural contexts.

Global trends in the use of English may lead to a less ethnocentric view, though this will depend also on the extent to which the voices of academics from a wider range of countries find an international audience, and the rise of computer-mediated communication is also likely to act as a catalyst to research. The increasing use of English as a second language, and the role of Web technologies in facilitating global communication will allow wider access to the 'means of production' for English language texts. The increased speed of dissemination is likely to dissolve boundaries, both between communities and between genres, leading to even greater tendencies towards hybridisation. More and more, approaches which aim at discovering generalisable patterns in text need to be able to account for the specific and situated nature of any particular example of interaction.

Corpus technology is making available previously unimaginable amounts of data, together with tools for searching it. Although corpora can be tagged with some contextual information, they are not conducive to the sort of thick description needed for an ethnographic approach. The tension between text and practice will remain as the advantages of searching large quantities of text with little contextual information are weighed against those of studying smaller quantities of text with greater attention to the complexity of the social practices in which they are embedded.

4
FROM VARIATION TO HYBRIDITY

RAJEND MESTHRIE AND JOAN SWANN

4.1 INTRODUCTION

Chapters 2 and 3 distinguished approaches to the description and analysis of language that emphasise linguistic form, and approaches that seek to take into account the social context in which language is produced and interpreted. This chapter focuses on English (and language in more general terms) as a social phenomenon, although the approaches considered and their specific objects of enquiry are rather different from those in earlier chapters. The present chapter is concerned with processes of variation, diversity and change in English: how English varies regionally, and socially, and amongst the same speakers from one situation to another; how speakers may use such variability strategically to particular communicative effect; how English is used alongside other languages in multilingual settings; the study of new varieties of English, and the status and role of English as a global language.

In the sections that follow we try to give a sense of how such phenomena have been studied, the particular emphases of different approaches to research and how they construct 'English' as an object of enquiry. First, in the section below, some general principles of variability and change in English are discussed.

4.2 VARIATION, DIVERSITY AND CHANGE

The English language is inherently variable: so much so, that the term 'English' itself may be seen as a convenient fiction. English has changed considerably over time, so that Old English, spoken up to around 1,000 years ago, would be unintelligible to most speakers of the language nowadays. And contemporary English, the subject of this book, varies geographically and socially and continues to change so that, again, speakers of different varieties sometimes have difficulty understanding one another. The international diversity of English has led some researchers to talk of *Englishes* rather than *English* in the singular. English is also used in diverse ways, and occupies different social positions in relation to other languages in multilingual communities.

The study of such variation, diversity and change comes within the remit of **sociolinguistics**, glossed broadly as 'an orientation to the study of language that stresses the interrelationship between language and social life, rather than focusing narrowly on language structure' (Swann *et al.* 2004: 287). It is sociolinguistic approaches to language study that form the main basis of this chapter.

Sociolinguistic studies of variation and change within English have focused on different linguistic levels: variation in phonology, or the sound system of a language; grammar (syntax, or clause structure; and morphology, or word structure); and semantics, or linguistic meaning (these terms are introduced and defined in Chapter 2). The pervasiveness of sound makes this readily accessible to sociolinguistic investigation, and by far the greatest number of studies are therefore concerned with phonological variation. Studies have focused also on language and social meaning, including how language variation may be intimately bound up with the negotiation of speaker identities. Studies carried out in multilingual communities have looked at the (variable) use of English, and the status and meaning of English, in relation to other languages. This work is reflected in later sections of this chapter.

ACCENTS, DIALECTS, VARIETIES

Accents, dialects and (language) varieties refer to the speech habits that characterise a particular region or social group. Linguists tend to distinguish between **dialect** (a variety described in terms of pronunciation, grammar, semantics) and **accent** (restricted to pronunciation). In linguistics these terms do not have any evaluative associations and nor are they restricted to non-standard varieties of language: standard English in England, for instance, is regarded as a dialect of English; and **received pronunciation** *(RP)*, associated with educated middle-class and aristocratic speakers in England, is regarded as an accent. **Language variety** is a more general term that avoids having to specify whether one is concerned with an accent, dialect or, indeed, a particular language.

STANDARD ENGLISH

Standard English, like other standard languages, is usually identified as a variety that is relatively uniform, does not vary regionally, is used for a range of (usually formal) functions and is codified in dictionaries and grammars. Standard languages are formed by a process of **standardisation**, often seen as falling into four stages: the 'selection' of a regional or social variety as the basis of the standard; 'codification' of the variety; 'implementation' – the promotion and acceptance of standard norms within the community; and continuing 'elaboration' of the variety to fulfil a variety of communicative functions (Haugen 1966).

This process began in England in the fifteenth century, with the selection of a variety based on the south-east Midlands area. As James Milroy and Lesley Milroy note, '[this] was the most obvious choice because the area concerned was the most prominent politically, commercially and academically' (1999: 27; see also Leith 1997). Contemporary standard

English is still associated with educated, upper or middle class speakers. It also has certain ideological associations – e.g. standard language forms are commonly seen as 'good English', 'correct' and non-standard forms as 'incorrect'. Milroy and Milroy (1999) coined the phrase **standard language ideology** to refer to a set of prescriptive attitudes that accompany the development of a standard variety: the belief that there is only one correct way of speaking, and that non-standard varieties are undesirable or deviant.

English has also been described as a **pluricentric language** – one that has several sets of standardised or standardising norms (e.g. British, US, Australian, South African English).

Accounts of different Englishes, or varieties of English, often emphasise their distinctiveness, identifying and discussing their specific features. This perception of distinctiveness is also evident in names given to varieties – by linguists as well as ordinary speakers (Indian English, British English, Tyneside English or Geordie, distinctions drawn between standard and non-standard English). However, the identification of varieties of English is not unproblematical:

- while descriptions of varieties of English focus on their distinctive features, varieties also share many features in common;
- it is therefore not always easy to draw clear boundaries between different varieties – e.g. between standard English and a non-standard variety, or between two or more regional varieties of English;
- varieties may also encompass considerable internal variability;
- similar points apply to English and related languages – there are substantial overlaps, for instance, between 'English' and 'Scots', and whether these are regarded as separate languages is as much a political as a linguistic decision;
- descriptions of language variation tend to take a standard variety as a descriptive norm, e.g. non-standard English dialects may be described in relation to standard English (with just those features that differ from the standard identified). Similarly, 'new Englishes' such as Indian English or Nigerian English tend to be described in relation to a British (standard English) norm.

Varieties are, therefore, better regarded as idealisations than as conforming straightforwardly to linguistic facts.

4.3 DIALECTOLOGY AND REGIONAL VARIATION IN ENGLISH

The study of regional variation in English (and other languages) has been a principal concern of **dialectology**. This chapter will briefly outline the beginnings of dialectology, before looking at evidence from studies of English carried out in different contexts and at different historical periods.

TRADITIONAL DIALECTOLOGY

For a long time, linguistics was chiefly concerned with the study of written texts, with a view to establishing which languages of the world were related, and proposing laws showing the phonetic correspondences between words of those languages. A 'sound law' was intended to capture the similarities in the pronunciation of words in related languages. For instance, the equivalents of modern English 'father' are *pita* in Sanskrit, *fæder* in Old English and *pater* in Latin; the equivalents of 'foot' are *padam* in Sanskrit, *foōt* in Old English and *ped-* in Latin. These two examples (amongst many) suggest a general correspondence between the sounds *p – f – p* for whole sets of words in these languages. (Note that *æ* is the Old English symbol for the vowel in words like *cat*; the bar over the vowel 'o' indicates lengthening; while the hyphen after *ped* indicates that this is the root of the word.) Initial interest in dialectology in Europe in the nineteenth century was a result of such studies within historical linguistics, in particular the claim that such sound laws were exceptionless. Linguists eventually turned their attention to sources that would supplement written evidence and, they hoped, corroborate some of their theories. In particular they raised the possibility that dialect speech would preserve older and more regular forms than those of standard written varieties of a language. The claim that sound laws were exceptionless turned out to be false, but it did serve as an impetus to the scholarly study of dialects. Another motivation for dialect research in the nineteenth and twentieth centuries was the feeling that rural speech was being rapidly eroded by the pressures of modernisation and urbanisation, especially in Europe. The need was stressed for surveys that would record as much of traditional rural dialect as possible. Dialectology began to proceed along independent lines, rather than being necessarily linked to historical studies. The model that began to play a more significant role was that of human geography, rather than history. Dialectology is therefore sometimes labelled 'linguistic geography' or 'geolinguistics'. Harold Orton and Nathalia Wright (1974: 21), two twentieth-century British practitioners of dialectology, describe their task as follows:

> A primary aim of linguistic geography is to reveal the occurrence and distribution of speech usages, especially those characteristic of particular regions. Their diffusion can be mapped clearly and simply. Close study of the resultant maps permits significant deductions to be drawn about the movements of those usages: whether, for example they are spreading or contracting, or whether, indeed, they have been partly supplanted by other features.

The following is a brief outline of the procedures associated with traditional dialectology (based on Petyt 1980: 49–51). A preliminary investigation or pilot survey is often carried out, to gain some idea of the principal items that vary over an area and to select the kind of items that warrant close investigation. The geographical localities where the fieldwork is to be conducted are decided upon. The number of such localities and the density of coverage are constrained by

time, finances and number of fieldworkers, and possibly by the density of population in the area. A questionnaire is then compiled, comprising key items that
are believed to vary geographically (e.g. a typical question of the Survey of
English Dialects (Orton and Wright 1974) is *What do you separate two fields by?*,
which shows whether *dike* or *hedge* or some other item is used). Fieldwork is then
undertaken by one or more trained investigators, who travel to the localities
selected and make contact with people who they consider to be most suitable
informants. Questionnaires are completed in the presence of the investigator.
The invention of the tape recorder in the 1950s (and its many refinements since)
make storage relatively easy in preparation for subsequent transcription and
analysis. Data analysis is undertaken to reveal geographical patterns of distribution, usually with the aid of maps. Prior to the computer age the publication of
lists and maps was a time-consuming and expensive undertaking which often
occurred many years after the initial survey. Figure 4.1 is a map showing the
regional distribution of the terms *folk*, *folks* and *people*.

Figure 4.1 Dialect map for *folk* vs *people* (from Upton and Widdowson, *An Atlas of
English Dialects* 2006: 84–5).

In the United States a project called DARE (*The Dictionary of American Regional English* is one amongst many that aims to document regionalisms, i.e. elements of US English that are not found everywhere in the country. These include words and phrases that vary from one area to another, and are learned at home rather than at school as part of oral rather than written culture. The dictionary is a substantial project, running to five volumes (as an example see Hall 2002). DARE is based on face-to-face interviews with 2,777 people carried out in 1,002 communities throughout the country between 1965 and 1970. It also used print materials from letters, diaries, novels and newspapers. In Figure 4.2, the sample entry for *Adam's housecat* shows some of the dictionary's concerns. An example sentence illustrates the meaning of this phrase ('He wouldn't know me from Adam's house-cat'). The alternate forms for this phrase are listed (*Adam's cat, Adam's house*); the provenance of the phrase (South Atlanta; the Gulf States); the number of informants familiar with the phrase and the background of such respondents (in terms of educational level).

Adam's housecat n Also *Adam's cat, ~ house* chiefly S Atl, Gulf States See Map =Adam's off-ox 1.

1908 *DN* 3.285 eAL, wGA, *Adam's (house-)cat.* . . . "He wouldn't know me from Adam's house-cat." 1965–70 *DARE* (Qu. II26, . . "*I wouldn't know him from* _____.") 83 Infs, chiefly S Atl, Gulf States, Adam's housecat; LA25, OH90, VA69, 71, Adam's cat; AL10, Adam's house; FL48, A housecat, [corr to] Adam's housecat. [Of all Infs responding to the question, 26% had less than hs educ; of those giving these responses, 56% had less than hs educ.]

Abbreviations: S Atl: South Atlantic; eAL: East Alabama; wGA: west Georgia; Qu: Question; LA: Louisiana; OH: Ohio VA: Virginia; FL: Florida; Infs: informants; corr: corrected to; hs educ: high school educ.

Figure 4.2 Sample entry from the DARE webpage for *Adam's housecat*: http://polyglot.lss.wisc.edu/dare/dare.html.

The culmination of twentieth-century work in regional dialectology is the *The Atlas of North American English* (Labov *et al.* 2006), primarily based at the University of Pennsylvania and produced by the US sociolinguist William Labov and his team of researchers. Previously known as the *Phonological Atlas of North America*, the project has been published as a large atlas with maps and text, with an accompanying CD that provides sound samples. It is the first national survey of the USA and the first of English in North America. The project was as much concerned with change in English as with the features of individual dialects. Labov's earlier work had shown how variation in individual varieties preceded change. The accumulation of small, gradual changes in accent, vocabulary and grammar could eventually produce the vast differences that were mentioned above between Old English and present-day English. The methodology used in the *Atlas* project took the form of a telephone survey between 1992 and 1999 involving speakers born in urbanised areas with a population greater than 50,000. Interviews lasted between 30 and 45 minutes and covered everyday topics with a focus on recent developments in the respondent's city and on specific lists of words and sentences (see Labov*et al.* 2006: 28–29). The *Atlas* shows a consistent differentiation between the Northern Cities and the Southern States, each showing a different pattern of systematic vowel changes.

'The Northern Cities Shift' involves systematic changes to certain vowels. The six vowels involved are associated with another phoneme by listeners from another dialect area: *bit* may be heard as *bet*, *bet* as *bat* or *but*, *lunch* as *launch*, *talk* as *tock*, *locks* as *lax* and *Ann* as *Ian*. This shift is most advanced in northern cities like Buffalo, Rochester, Detroit and Chicago. Figure 4.3 shows the new realisations of /æ/ and the vowel in words like *Ann*, *trap*, *lax* (and similar words) in the Northern Cities. The large white circles show the cities with the greatest

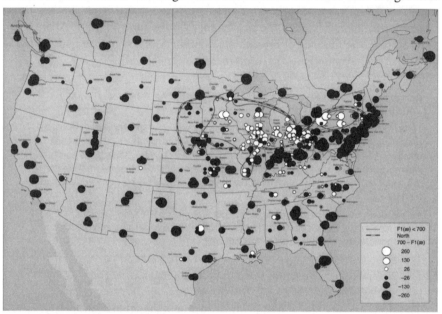

Note: the degree of change in pronunciation is measured acoustically: the legend to the map provides the range of acoustic measurements used in categorising the shift. The main point to note, however, is the cluster of white circles in the north, representing towns and cities where the vowel /æ/ is changed the most.[1]

Figure 4.3 The realisation of /æ/ (as in, for example, *lax*) in the Northern Cities compared to other dialect areas – from Labov et al. (2006: 193).

---

1 If you are interested in phonetics, note that F1 in the legend to the map stands for 'first formant', an acoustic measurement in hertz of the lowest of several frequency bands associated with vowels. Labov *et al.* take as a cut-off point a value of 700 Hz for the first formant of the /æ/ vowel. The continuous lines around areas of the map denote areas whose towns and cities have values lower than this. The circles represent the different realisations of the vowel per city or town, arrived at by the formula 700 – F1 (where 700 is the limit in hertz associated with traditional realisations of /æ/, while F1 represents the actual average value obtained per city). The white circles represent cities in which the value is greater than zero (i.e. having raised F1); the dark circles represent cities in which the value is lower than zero (having traditional low values associated with F1). The bigger the white circle, the higher the F1; the bigger the dark circle, the lower the F1.

amount of change – i.e. the vowel in *Ann* sounds like the first vowel of older pronunciations of *Ian* that still occur in other dialect areas. The largest dark circles show the cities with no such change. Intermediate degrees of change are shown by the smaller circles. The 'Southern Shift' has a different set of ongoing changes, the most salient of which is the treatment of the diphthong in words like *time* as simple vowels (or monophthongs – i.e. as if the word were *taam*).

The *Atlas* is the culmination of centuries of dialectology in many ways:

- Rather than displaying isolated and unrelated parts of language like vocabulary items or the pronunciation of individual words, it examines phonological processes and vowel systems (like the set of vowels involved in the Northern Cities Shift).
- The maps are grounded in an interest in sound change in progress, like recent developments within the Northern and Southern Shifts.
- The information conveyed in the maps has been the subject of previous intense study and scholarly debate.
- The technology of the early twenty-first century permits more precise and consistent acoustic measurements and descriptions of variants of individual vowels, and eliminates fieldworker variability to a large extent.
- The maps incorporate the production of variants as well as the perceptions of speakers.

Dialectologists are also interested in how changes like the Northern Cities Shift spread across communities in a specific geographical area. The 'gravity model' was proposed by the British sociolinguist Peter Trudgill (1974) to describe the influence of bigger centres of population on smaller ones. The analogy is taken from physics where bodies with larger mass exert a gravitational influence over smaller ones in their vicinity. In Trudgill's model, population size is analogous to mass in physics and geographical distance plays a similar role. Linguistic influence from one centre to the next is driven by proximity and population size. The equations provided by Trudgill are rather complex, and still subject to ongoing investigation. In the UK, London is one centre of influence, whose norms spread out to larger cities and from there to smaller ones. Thus a city like Sunderland in the north-east of England might be influenced by linguistic features from London, but only indirectly, since these would form a subset of forms that Sunderland shares with the neighbouring larger city, Newcastle.

The model is complicated by issues of geographical boundaries and degrees of social contact. Labov (2003), who prefers the term 'cascade model', shows how it works for the spread of new vocabulary. ('Cascade' suggests the flow of larger pools of water first into smaller ones and from there to still smaller ones.) Labov's example comes from variant terms for a sandwich made of cold cuts, cheese and garnishing on a long roll, split in half: *subway*, *hero* and *hoagie*. Drawing on advertisements in the *Yellow Pages*, Labov showed how terms could diffuse from a larger city to a smaller one. He focused particularly on the term *hoagie*, long favoured in Philadelphia. The term appears to have originated shortly after World War I, with a number of variant spellings. By 1955 the term appears well established, with its current spelling prevailing. In the neighbouring city of Pittsburgh, *hoagie* makes an appearance in the directories in the early 1960s, a time when the more established term was *sub*(*marine*). However, *hoagie* begins to take over and soon becomes the more common term. By what intermediate mechanisms do such terms spread? Labov argues that certain establishments in Philadelphia were providing the basic equipment needed to produce the sandwiches in neighbouring cities, and thus became associated with the product. The flow of influence was from the products of the bigger city to smaller ones. (Things later are made more complicated by the appearance of the *Subway* chain of stores which independently promote the term *submarine* or *sub*). The gravity model is thus intuitively plausible, but difficult to verify, since the subtleties of language change and human intentions require sustained, long-term research.

Traditional dialectology is ultimately based on the spread of populations and the consequent diversification of language over a territory. Urbanisation and migration to urban centres bring other sets of linguistic factors into play. Modern dialectologists pay attention to processes of new dialect formation arising from the establishment of new colonies (Trudgill 2004), new towns (Kerswill and Williams 2000) or the migration of peoples to urban centres (Kerswill 2006). **Dialect levelling** refers to the selection of features from an array that arises out of the contact between different dialects. Kerswill (2006) shows how children make such a selection in the new town of Milton Keynes in the south-east of England. Kerswill examined realisations of the vowel in words like *goat*, *post*, *poke*, etc., in the speech of children brought up in the new town and compared them with the norms of their caregivers. These were almost always the female parents, who had originated from different parts of the country and consequently had different realisations of the vowel. Whereas four-year-old children show fairly close correlations with the speech of their caregivers, the eight- and twelve-year-olds show a significant departure from their caregivers' norms and a greater degree of homogeneity. Kerswill argues that children are not simply adopting the regional norms of the areas surrounding Milton Keynes. They have focused on a new fronted variant, so that their pronunciation of a word like *goat* might sound more like the vowel in *gate* to outsiders. This particular change is, in fact, shared with younger speakers across the south-east of England.

4.4 SOCIAL AND STYLISTIC VARIATION

SOCIOLINGUISTIC PATTERNS

In modern sociolinguistics, dialects and social groups are central to an understanding of language variation and change. The emphasis in this tradition falls upon the finely-nuanced differences within a language according to social groupings, especially class, gender, ethnicity and region. Variation theory, as developed by William Labov (1966), studies the relationship between region of origin, age and – especially – **social class**, and characteristic ways of using language. Following this model, **variationist** sociolinguists use correlational techniques in revealing the relationship between **linguistic variables** (e.g. a vowel sound that has different *variants* that result in different accents) and **social variables** (age, gender, class, etc.).

Prior to Labov's work in the early 1960s, dialectology had scored its main successes in studies of regional differentiation. Although researchers had been aware of linguistic distinctions of a social nature within a region, they had not developed systematic ways of describing them. Earlier explanations of non-regional variation fell into one of two categories: dialect mixture and free variation. 'Dialect mixture' implies the coexistence in one locality of two or more dialects, which enables a speaker to draw on one dialect at one time and on the other dialect(s) on other occasions. 'Free variation' refers to the random use of alternate forms within a particular dialect (e.g. two pronunciations of *often* [with or without the 't' sounded]). Both views relegate variation to a position outside the language system and associate structure with homogeneity. Labov argued, instead, that language involved 'structured heterogeneity'. Labov was not the first to point to the interplay between social and linguistic determinants of certain linguistic choices. In the 1950s, working in a New England setting, John Fischer (1958) had discussed the social implications of the use of *-in* versus *-ing* pronunciations in the final syllable of words such as 'running' (whether this was pronounced *runnin* or *running*). However, Labov was the initiator of an elaborate body of work which broke new ground in understanding language in its social context, accounting for linguistic change, and broadening the goals of linguistic theory. An important motivation in his work was to understand one of the unsolved problems of historical linguistics – how changes in pronunciation are effected, as when a sound like [p] at one phase of a language may be later replaced by a sound like [f]. Labov showed that systematic variation across different groups of speakers within a community could lead to the spread of a change.

In a famous study Labov showed that, contrary to previous beliefs, the pronunciation of postvocalic *-r* in New York City was not random. 'Postvocalic *-r*' refers to the sound /r/ after a vowel in words like *nurse* or *bird*. In New York, it is pronounced on some occasions but not others. For the occurrence of postvocalic *-r* to be random there should be no way of predicting in what contexts and by whom it was pronounced, or not pronounced. By undertaking detailed interviews with a cross-section of the city's mother-tongue speakers of English, Labov was able to show a finely graded sociolinguistic patterning of /r/, represented in Figure 4.4. The two important parameters were the socio-economic class of the speaker and the level of formality of the communication. Speakers from all social groups in the 1960s tended not to pronounce postvocalic *-r* in their most casual styles, except for the upper-middle classes whose percentage score for its presence was just under 20 per cent. This feature was therefore associated with the prestige of the upper-middle classes. In more careful styles within the interview all speakers showed a higher proportion of the presence of postvocalic -*r*, and in reading out a passage and a list of words at the end of the interview the proportion increased even further.

The pronunciation of /r/ was thus sensitive to the dimension of **style**, as well as social class. This is what Labov meant by 'structured heterogeneity' in language. Under certain circumstances variation in language leads to change, as when the influence of the 'overt prestige' of middle-class usage is transferred first to the formal styles of the other social classes and then to their more casual styles.

Postvocalic -*r* is an example of a linguistic variable; and its different realisations in speech are variants (in this case whether it is pronounced or not). Labov tended to represent differences in style in a 'linear' fashion on a scale from least formal to most formal speech. He demonstrated these differences by segmenting the speech of his interviewees into a 'casual' and 'careful' style, and asking interviewees to read a short passage ('reading style' in Figure 4.4), a list of words and a list of minimal pairs at the end of the interview. ('Minimal pairs' are pairs of

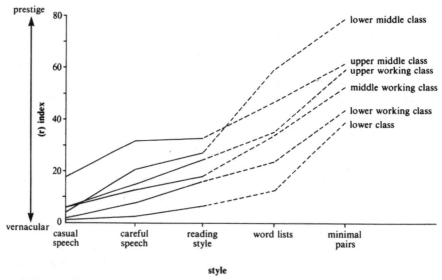

(r) index
100 = consistent pronunciation of non-prevocalic /r/
  0 = consistent lack of non-prevocalic /r/

Note: the vertical axis ((r) index) gives the frequency of pronunciation of postvocalic -*r*, expressed as a percentage score; the horizontal axis shows different speaking styles elicited during interviews; the lines represent different groups of speakers.

Figure 4.4 Social stratification of postvocalic -*r* in New York City, adapted from Labov (1972: 114).

words whose pronunciation differs by only one sound – e.g. *bat* and *pat*.) For Labov, these styles became increasingly formal, and speakers paid progressively greater attention to their speech. Labov found that the more formal the style, the greater the percentage occurrence of the variant considered more prestigious. (Labov's account of style has been critiqued and modified by later scholars, as discussed below.)

Labov drew attention to the crossing over of the line representing lower-middle class scores to go beyond that of the group immediately above (the upper-middle class) in the two most formal styles (word list and minimal pairs). He called this phenomenon 'hypercorrection', meaning that whilst lower-middle class speakers aimed to sound more like the group that is socially above them, they overshot the norms of this group in the most formal styles. Labov suggested that hypercorrection is an important mechanism through which language change occurs.

Whereas changes in the pronunciation of postvocalic -*r* are associated with overt prestige, some studies document the reverse effect in some communities – namely the 'covert prestige' or solidarity value of working class culture and speech. Although working-class speech is frequently denigrated, sometimes by speakers themselves when asked to comment on their language, the persistence of these norms calls for alternative explanations. Trudgill (1978) shows how working-class pronunciations of certain vowels (in words like *nose, road, moan*) in Norwich, in the south of England, exerted a counter influence on males who were higher up in the social scale. Women were less susceptible to the 'covert prestige' of male working-class norms. The theme of **gender differences** in the realisation of variables is, in fact, a prominent one in sociolinguistics. Gender and class appear to interact in complex ways. Likewise **ethnicity** may be an important social variable that results in differential realisation of specific linguistic variables. In Labov's New York City study, African American speakers followed the same patterns of usage for postvocalic -*r* as other speakers. But an ethnic effect could be seen in a related variable – the use of /r/ between two vowels (or 'intervocalic -*r*') in words like *Carol* and *Paris*. In this instance dropping the /r/ is an option for African American speakers, but not for other groups in the city. **Age** too is a prominent social variable.

OTHER SIGNIFICANT WORK ON SOCIOLINGUISTIC VARIATION AND CHANGE

The Labovian approach is made more concrete in a complementary approach – **social network** theory, which factors in the way speakers interact within peer and other social groups more strongly than the Labovian model. Linguistic work utilizing the social networks of speakers was pioneered by Leslie Milroy (1987). Rather than study individual speakers as part of an abstract social group defined by social class, Milroy looked at how their speech behaviour correlated with the nature of their everyday social contacts. She outlined two different types of social networks, close-knit and loose-knit ones. These are determined by two factors. First, 'density' or the number of contacts one has within the network. A maximally dense network relationship is one in which one has regular contacts with all members: one's friends' acquaintances are also one's own. A minimally dense equivalent is when one does not have much contact with one's friends' acquaintances. The second factor is whether the relationships within the network are multiplex or not. A 'multiplex' relation is one in which one interacts with another member in several roles. A neighbour might also be a friend, a co-worker and a member of the same religious group. Milroy demonstrates convincingly that close-knit networks (those characterised by relatively dense and multiplex relations) require loyalty to the local ways of speaking, whereas loose-knit networks have more diffuse norms and are more open to linguistic innovations.

Within network analysis, certain gendered patterns of work are seen to foster differences in linguistic behaviour between men and women. For example if men from a close-knit network all work at the same locale, whilst the women tend to work outside the area and are less strongly integrated into the local network, the men's speech might be more 'focused' upon a local norm, while the women's speech might be more diffuse. The strength of this analysis is that it is not gender *per se* which generates specific accents and styles of talking, but the nature of the interaction within the network. As Milroy (1987) showed, different employment patterns (say with unemployment causing more people to work outside the neighbourhood) would alter both network structure and eventually, linguistic behaviour.

Another influential study drawing on both Labovian stratificational insights and Milroyan social networks is Penelope Eckert's study at a school she named 'Belten High' (e.g. Eckert 2000). Eckert studied the bifurcation of the pupils into two primary social groups which they themselves label 'Jocks' and 'Burnouts'. These are, respectively, groups who make the school their community and hence the basis of a social identity that transcends the local environment, against those who view school as a necessary qualification for employment, but not a good social preparation for their next life stage of seeking local employment. Jocks thus invest in the ethos valued by the school (achievements in their studies, sport and school activities), while Burnouts minimise their participation in school outside classes and maximise their contacts in the local communities. This differential orientation to a large extent underlies salient differences in accent: Jocks and Burnouts participate differentially in the urban changes around them (characteristic of the Northern Cities vowel shifts – Labov, Ash and Boberg 2006). For example the vowel in *bet* sounds like older *but* (backing of the vowel) in Burnout speech; amongst Jocks it sounds like older *bat* (lowering of the vowel). On the whole it is the Burnout norm that drives the changes associated with the Northern Cities Shift: these changes show allegiance to the local urban network, whereas Jocks show greater allegiance to more widespread prestige norms.

STYLE-SHIFTING AND SPEAKER IDENTITY

Correlational studies such as those discussed above have enabled linguists to identify systematic patterns in the language used by different social groups and in different speaking contexts. However, they tend to underplay what Nikolas Coupland has referred to as 'communicative goals, the functional complexity of language in use, and issues of identity and selfhood in general' (2001a: 188). An alternative approach examines the detail of speakers' stylistic choices, including **style-shifting** – how speakers routinely shift between different speaking styles during an interaction. The focus here is on the meaning-making potential of speakers' choices: how speakers draw on particular varieties of language, in particular contexts, as a communicative resource.

A common assumption is that dialect features may acquire particular social meanings based on their association with certain social groups. In drawing on such features speakers are, therefore, indexing (calling up and foregrounding) aspects of their identity. However, the situation is actually more complex than this. In a discussion of 'indexing gender', Elinor Ochs (1992) argues that gender may be linguistically indexed directly, when a particular linguistic feature (e.g. a pronunciation, grammatical structure, word) is directly associated with masculinity or femininity. More usually, however, it is indexed indirectly, when a linguistic feature is associated with certain practices that are, in turn, perceived as gendered. This is consistent with Lesley Milroy's argument above, that language in her study was associated with patterns of interaction that were in turn associated with gender. The same principle may apply to associations between language and other aspects of identity.

Penelope Eckert, in her 'Belten High' study referred to above, identified quantitative patterns of language variation and change. However, Eckert sees these and similar patterns as reflecting speakers' local stylistic choices. Identity is not a once-for-all category, but something that is continually negotiated in interaction with others (so that a speaker may play up, or play down, a particular aspect of their identity). Eckert argues further that the social meanings associated with language varieties are not fixed: particular dialect features take on meaning through their use in context, and meanings may therefore shift or be given new inflections. Eckert sees the creation of meanings, and associated identities, as a process of *bricolage*, a term that can be roughly translated as 'do-it-yourself'. It refers to the process of making something new from whatever existing materials are to hand (Lévi-Strauss 1974; Hebdige 1984). In this case, speakers combine sets of linguistic resources with existing meanings to create new meanings, or new twists on meanings (Eckert 2000, 2004). For instance, a British speaker may switch from a local accent to something nearer RP to index expertise while also introducing a note of irony or self-parody. Eckert emphasises the collaborative nature of such meaning and identity construction: styles are developed in **communities of practice**, as speakers 'jointly interpret the social landscape and jointly carve out a place for themselves within that land-scape' (2000: 215).

COMMUNITIES OF PRACTICE

A community of practice is 'an aggregate of people who come together around mutual engagement in some common endeavour' (Eckert and McConnell-Ginet 1992: 490). The term differs from other words used to identify groups of speakers (e.g. 'speech community', 'discourse commu-nity', defined in Chapter 3) in that the emphasis is on activities or practices jointly engaged in by speakers: the claim is that ways of speaking derive from such activities/practices. Speakers are likely to be members of several communities of practice. Examples include work colleagues, members of a religious group, a friendship group.

Nikolas Coupland, similarly, has analysed dialect style as a form of 'persona management', illustrated in a now classic study of the pronunciation features adopted by a radio DJ in Cardiff (Coupland 1985, 2001). In this case, the DJ drew mainly on local Cardiff pronunciations of English but also adopted more standard pronunciations and some pronunciations from other dialects (e.g. Cockney and what to British ears sounded like American speech). Coupland argues that style is multidimensional rather than running along a single dimen-sion such as formal–informal as argued earlier by Labov: speakers may draw on a range of linguistic features to foreground different identities or personae. The specific meanings of speakers' choices are however context-dependant: the use of Cardiff pronunciations by the radio DJ may index local solidarity but also sometimes humour when the DJ jokes about his own incompetence; and 'American' pronunciations are, here, a form of mimicry, parodying 'slick DJ patter'. Coupland invokes the concept of 'micro-contexts' to account for local shifts in the DJ's talk, but notes that context is not simply an external factor that affects someone's talk: shifts in style themselves index particular contexts. Rather than adopting certain ways of speaking as a response to contexts, there-fore, Coupland sees the DJ as a creative 'orchestrator of contexts'.

Such work takes the study of variation and change in English closer to the concerns of **interactional sociolinguistics**, the socially-oriented and contextu-alised study of language in interaction. Researchers such as Eckert have also incorporated an **ethnographic approach** in their work. (Interactional socio-linguistics and ethnographic approaches to language study are also discussed in Chapter 3, Section 3.3.) This contrasts in several ways with correlational studies of language variation and change:

• The focus is not on the establishment of general patterns (the quantitative distribution of linguistic variants across different contexts and speaking styles) but on what Eckert terms stylistic practice – looking at how speakers draw on particular features in interaction with others: the moment-by-moment playing out of speaker choices.

- There is also a focus on speaker creativity – speaker choices are seen as motivated, and as producing certain effects, rather than simply as responses to a certain context; style is also seen as playing a part in the construction of contexts.
- Style is seen as multidimensional, with respect to the range of linguistic features speakers draw on and the interplay of meanings to which this gives rise.
- Meanings are relatively complex and heavily context-dependent.
- Methodologically, studies rely on qualitative, often ethnographic, evidence.

There are, however, also potential links between the study of local, contextualised behaviour and large-scale correlational studies. Coupland comments:

> Individuals within what we conventionally recognize to be meaningful social categories enact dialect personas with sufficient uniformity for survey researchers to detect numerical patterns of stratification. [. . .] It is in relation to group norms that stylistic variation becomes meaningful; it is through individual linguistic choices that group norms are produced and reproduced.
>
> (2001a: 198)

Eckert's own work has included the quantitative identification of patterns of variation and the local, qualitative exploration of speaker choices. And the New Zealand linguist Janet Holmes (1996) has argued more explicitly that quantitative and qualitative approaches may complement one another: for instance, the identification of general patterns in language use (the association of certain features with certain groups) may help in attributing meanings to speakers' local, contextualised linguistic choices.

Evidence from qualitative studies of style-shifting is compatible with influential explanations of speaker variation that would see this as primarily a response to an audience. These include, most notably, **accommodation theory** developed by the social psychologist Howard Giles and other researchers (Giles and Powesland 1975; Giles *et al*. 1991) and **audience design**, developed by the sociolinguist Allan Bell (Bell 1984, 2001). In each case, speakers are seen as continually designing, and redesigning, their speech in relation to their immediate audience or other reference groups.

Such research is also compatible with contemporary postmodern theories of language, and identity. Indeed, Coupland's (2001a) discussion of style is intended to show how sociolinguistics, rather than being self-contained, can engage productively with 'current social theorising about language, discourse, social relationships and selfhood' (186). Within such current theorising, identity is seen not as something that one has, and that may be reflected in language, but as something that one does in specific contexts – a routine and continuing interactional achievement. Researchers have also emphasised the plurality of speaker identities, and the fact that these may be taken up in different ways – specific identities may be emphasised or played down, negotiated, contested or subverted, linguistically and by other means. With respect to language, there is greater emphasis on the complex and highly contextualised nature of language meaning – not only on how utterances take on meanings in particular contexts but also bring with them the 'taste' of previous contexts of utterance (Bakhtin [1935] 1981). Such ideas form part of what has sometimes been termed the 'postmodern turn' (Cameron 2005) or 'shift' (Swann 2002) in relation to studies of language and identity.

4.5 MULTILINGUAL LANGUAGE CHOICE AND CODESWITCHING

PATTERNS OF LANGUAGE USE IN MULTILINGUAL CONTEXTS

In almost every country in which it exists, English occurs as part of a larger bilingual or multilingual situation. In the United States, for example, indigenous languages survive despite the threats of endangerment over the past two centuries. Spanish was a precursor to English in some parts of the south-west, and remains a significant second language of the country. In most territories where English has a sizeable portion of speakers, a hierarchical kind of multilingualism often exists, that has been labelled **diglossia**. The term 'diglossia' was coined by Charles Ferguson (1959) to refer to situations where 'high' and 'low' forms of a language co-exist in a society, each associated with different domains of use. An example cited by Ferguson was the use of classical and colloquial Arabic in Egypt. This concept was extended by Joshua Fishman (1967) to cover bi- or multilingual contexts, in which different languages had 'high' and 'low' functions. In a diglossic situation languages are somewhat compartmentalised according to domains like the home, religion, the neighbourhood, education, the media, government and so forth. In some societies, e.g. Nigeria, indigenous languages predominate in the first three domains, English in the latter three. In the classic diglossic relationship, like that between colloquial and classical Arabic in Egypt, the language varieties do not overlap in specific domains. This requirement is less true of post-colonial societies, where some degree of give-and-take between the former colonial language and the local languages is possible. In multilingual countries an important determinant not applicable to the homogeneous Arabic society studied by Ferguson, is the make-up of the audience. In Nigeria, for example, it is conceivable that a politician might use English in national broadcasting, but Yoruba if speaking to an audience that understands this major local language. Furthermore, strategic switching is possible between languages within the same situation to achieve effects that go beyond those associated with monolingualism in the domain. Such 'codeswitching' is considered in more depth below.

Linguists have sometimes used survey evidence to study particular patterns of language use in multilingual communities. For instance, Carol Myers-Scotton (1993) reports on evidence from earlier surveys she carried out in Kenya. In this case, the most common pattern is trilingual: speakers need to choose between their mother tongue, Swahili and English. Most urban Kenyans use their mother tongues at home or with others in the community from their own ethnic group. The mother tongue is important as a means of maintaining ethnic identity and in securing certain material advantages (for example, help from other members of the group in obtaining employment or other benefits). People at the top of the socioeconomic scale also use some English at home, particularly with their children to help them to do better at school. In Nairobi, speakers sometimes switch between their mother tongue, Swahili and English. This is particularly prevalent among children and young people, and a slang variety called Sheng has grown up in certain areas – a mix of Swahili and English.

At work, speakers may use their mother tongue with people from the same ethnic group, or Swahili with people from other groups. English is used particularly in white-collar occupations. It may be used when communicating with superiors as an indicator of education and authority. And its use among speakers who share a mother tongue may mark out a relationship as one of the workplace. Outside work, Swahili and English are used with people from other ethnic groups. The use of English and other languages is therefore associated with certain locations (e.g. work and home). Language choice also varies between different speakers. And it is associated with particular interlocutors, and particular interactional purposes. Importantly, language choice is not simply a response to a particular context: English and other languages may be used strategically, for example, in the negotiation of relations between people, and to convey aspects of the speaker's identity.

LANGUAGE MAINTENANCE, SHIFT AND DEATH

Although patterns and regularities may be identified in language use, these are not necessarily stable. For instance, the association of English with global technologies and higher education leads to its ascendancy in the more formal and technical forms of communication. A consequence of this axis of power and prestige is that many societies and subgroups within them find it increasingly difficult to maintain local or regional languages. The dilemmas involved in maintaining a language in the face of competition from more powerful regional or global languages has been an important topic in sociolinguistics since the 1960s. The study of **language death** and the possibility of reviving endangered languages has become a major area of research since the 1980s. The term **language shift** was first used by Uriel Weinreich (1953: 68) to denote 'the change from the habitual use of one language to that of another'. The opposite term **language maintenance** was proposed by Joshua Fishman (1964) to denote the continuing use of a language in the face of competition from a regionally and socially more powerful language. Whereas 'language shift' denotes the replacement of one language by another as the primary means of communication and socialisation within a community, 'language death' is used when that community is the last one (in the world) to use that language. The spread of English first via colonisation and now via global technologies has resulted directly or indirectly in the endangerment or death of many indigenous languages. Likewise, non-English immigrants into a country in which English is dominant find it difficult to transmit their home language to children and grandchildren born in the new environment. This has been a recurrent pattern in the United States with migrants from Europe, who have found it hard to resist the melting pot effect of the US, with languages like German, Italian and Norwegian seldom being transmitted in families beyond two generations. In a study of language shift in the UK, Li Wei (1998) identified differences in the extent to which speakers maintained their home languages, and related this to social networks. Li Wei studied groups of British-born Chinese people living in the north-east of England, the children of those who had migrated to the region from the early 1960s. He found that, while there was a general shift from Chinese to English-dominant bilingualism across generations, patterns of language use amongst British-born speakers varied depending on the family's region of origin. One group of speakers – those whose families came from Ap Chau, a small island near Hong Kong – seemed to have maintained their use of Chinese to a greater extent than those from other regions. Li Wei notes that families from Ap Chau have a relatively high level of contact with others from the island. A major focus for such contact is the local evangelical church which provides opportunities for several social and cultural activities, including Chinese language lessons for British-born children.

For indigenous languages of Australia and the Americas, the causes of shift and death are clear. Once-viable and autonomous speech communities were either destroyed or deprived of their traditional land and resettled with other groups who did not always share the same language. Eventual reorientation to a new, westernised society further weakened traditional forms of the surviving languages among the young. Nettle and Romaine (2000) propose that, where an indigenous group retains control of its traditional habitat and way of life, language maintenance is likely. Thus, the areas where languages are most abundant are in the tropics, where small-scale economies can be built around a rich, local ecosystem. The reality, however, is that the world's indigenous peoples and their languages are dying out or being assimilated into modern civilization because their habitats are being destroyed (2000: 47–48). The authors cite the European settlement of different parts of the world as the intrusion of a whole ecosystem into the domain of another. By contrast, where local communities have control over local resources, they are much more likely to conserve them.

This is not because traditional peoples have some mysterious essence that keeps them in harmony with nature [. . .] as some romantic portrayals of indigenous people imply. It is for the more practical reason that it is the traditional people who will have to stay around in the environment and make their living there [rather than outside developers].

(Nettle and Romaine 2000: 160)

Turning to other situations involving urbanisation and 'internal' migration, the cause of shift is more complex. It is one of the few points of agreement in studies of minority and immigrant languages that there is no single set of factors that can be used to predict the outcome of language-maintenance efforts. Causes of shift are generally multiple and interrelated. Kloss (1966) has pointed out that many of the factors may even cut both ways. Most discussions centre around Giles *et al.*'s (1977) identification of factors like status (economic, social, socio-historical and language status); demography (relative sizes of speaker sub-populations) and institutional support for the different languages (in education, administration, the media, etc.). How to safeguard the local languages while learning more prestigious and powerful languages associated with a wider economy is the challenge facing many communities today (e.g. Welsh in relation to its powerful neighbour English). Fishman's (1991) model of **reversing language shift** proposes that stable diglossia has to be achieved (with the local languages maintaining their place in the home and primary education), before harder battles in more formal and technical domains can be waged.

CODESWITCHING

It was suggested above that multilingual speakers may switch between the languages at their disposal as one of their strategies of language choice. Such **codeswitching** between English and other languages has also been the object of sociolinguistic study. It is one of the concerns of interactional sociolinguistics, and many studies also have an ethnographic component (see also Chapter 3, Section 3.3).

CODESWITCHING

Codeswitching refers to instances where speakers switch between codes (languages or language varieties) during a conversation. Codeswitching may also occur in writing, but most research has been done on speech. Codeswitching may involve different amounts of speech and different linguistic units: from several consecutive utterances to individual words and morphemes. The example below, from Li Wei's study of codeswitching between Chinese and English in the north-east of England, is an example of this latter type of switching:

Yeo hou do yeo CONTACT.
Have very many have contact
'We have many contacts.'

(Li Wei 1998: 165)

Note that Li Wei gives first a literal translation of the utterance (here in italics), then a more idiomatic version in quotation marks.

In the literature, a range of terms is found for different types of switching. A distinction is sometimes made between 'intra-sentential code-switching', as in the example above, and 'inter-sentential codeswitching', or switching at the end of a sentence. The term **code-mixing** is also found, particularly for intra-sentential switching. When switching between languages is the norm in a community, the resulting mix of languages may be referred to as a **mixed code**. A mixed code is usually thought of as a new language variety, but there is no straight cut-off point between codeswitching and the development of a mixed code.

Codeswitching is a similar linguistic behaviour to style-shifting (see Section 4.4) and, in fact, the term codeswitching may also be used for switches between styles. More usually, however, studies of codeswitching focus on switches between relatively distinct varieties or languages.

Codeswitching, like style-shifting, is bound up with speaker identity. Where languages are associated with different identities, switching between languages allows speakers to manage these identities. Studies of codeswitching between English and other languages have often focused on the different identities associated with English (as a postcolonial or global language) and local or regional languages.

Suresh Canagarajah, for instance, provides the following example of switching between English and Tamil in an English lesson in a school in Jaffna, Sri Lanka:

TEACHER: What did I give for homework yesterday?
STUDENT 1:   Page forty.
TEACHER: Okay, take them out, I want to correct your work first. (Goes towards Student 2)
STUDENT 2:   **Naan ceiya marantuTTan**, Miss.
              'I forgot to do it'
              (Teacher continues in English)
                   (Canagarajah 2000: 204; English in plain text, Tamil in bold)

A great deal of contextual information is needed to understand this switch. English is the official language of such English lessons (it is the language that teachers say is used). Tamil is, however, also used, both by teachers (for non-pedagogical matters – e.g. encouragement and compliments) and students (for making excuses, and for 'under the desk' talk with other students). In this case, the student is seeking to establish solidarity with the teacher, appealing to her identity as a fellow Tamil speaker. The teacher rejects this, upholding institutional norms by continuing in English. There is, however, a broader ideological clash between Tamil and English. As part of their struggle for independence, the Liberation Tigers of Tamil Eelam (Tamil Tigers), who were in control of most of the Jaffna peninsula, imposed a Tamil-only policy for public communication. This was a response to the dominant Sinhalese community, but also to elite Tamil–English bilinguals in Jaffna. However, English language classrooms maintained an English-only ideology consistent with international English teaching practices. Canagarajah comments:

> The wider political agendas that motivate these language policies are quite different: while English-only policies in small postcolonial communities contribute to the integration of English teachers and their students into global ELT networks dominated by Anglo-American agencies and thereby ultimately contribute to the imposition of centre hegemony, local language-only policies are calculated to achieve cultural and political autonomy from the forces of globalization, especially those from the West.
>
> (2000: 201)

Canagarajah argues that speakers use codeswitching to negotiate their way between these competing positions, in effect constructing hybrid postcolonial identities in the classroom and in other contexts (194).

As was discussed in the previous section, in multilingual settings English is often associated with certain high-status domains of use – education, professional employment, high-level administration, international activity. The specific meanings attributed to English, however, and the identities it is used to construct, will vary across different linguistic, cultural and political contexts. For examples of three contrasting studies, see Monica Heller's research on English and French in Canada (Heller 1992); Carol Myers-Scotton's research on English, Swahili and other African languages in Africa (mainly Kenya – Myers-Scotton 1993a); and Niko Besnier's research on English and Tongan amongst transgendered speakers in Tonga (2003).

Some interesting recent work on codeswitching involving English has focused on a phenomenon termed **language crossing**: the adoption, by speakers, of languages or varieties that are not generally thought to 'belong' to the speaker (Rampton 1998, 1995). This has also been referred to as **styling the other**. A related term, borrowed from the Russian literary theorist Bakhtin, is **stylisation**. This last is defined by Nikolas Coupland as the 'knowing deployment of culturally familiar styles and identities that are marked as deviating from those predictably associated with the current speaking contexts' (2001b: 345).

Ben Rampton's classic ethnographic study of crossing was based on a study of multi-ethnic adolescent friendship groups in the South Midlands of England. Different types of crossing were evident amongst these speakers: the use of Panjabi by speakers of Anglo and African Caribbean descent; the use of Creole by speakers of Anglo and south Asian descent; and the use of what he termed stylised Asian English by all three groups. In using these varieties, speakers were not actually claiming membership of particular ethnic groups (e.g. a white Anglo speaker using Creole was not laying claim to an African Caribbean identity), and nor were speakers actively deconstructing ethnic boundaries. However, Rampton argues that, in foregrounding inherited ethnicity, crossing at least partly destabilised this.

Rampton comments that his informants had differing alignments with the varieties they used. For instance:

> Creole was much more extensively integrated into multiracial peer group recreation than either stylised Asian English or Panjabi . . . it was used much more by members of ethnic out-groups [i.e. other ethnic groups]. Creole symbolised an excitement and an excellence in youth culture that many adolescents aspired to, and it was even referred to as 'future language'.
>
> (1998: 304–5).

Stylised Asian English, by contrast, was associated with limited linguistic and cultural competence. It represented 'a stage of historical transition that most adolescents felt they were leaving behind, and in one way or another [Asian English] consisently symbolised distance from the main currents of adolescent life' (1998: 305). Stylised Asian English was often used, not in relation to the speaker's own identity, but in relation to an identity attributed to the person addressed.

This latter point is illustrated in the interaction below, between teenage boys of Indian descent. Here, Sukhbir uses his normal vernacular in telling off some younger pupils as they run past the school bike sheds. When this has no effect, his friend Mohan switches to stylised Asian English. Rampton argues that the use of Asian English here attributes reduced competence, and perhaps irresponsibility, to the younger pupils.

SUKHBIR:	STOP RUNNING AROUND YOU GAYS (.)
SUKHBIR:	[((laughs))
MOHAN:	((using a strong Indian accent for the words in bold:))
	[EH (.) THIS IS NOT MIDD(LE SCHOOL) no more (1.0) this is a respective (2.0)
ANON:	(school)
MOHAN:	school (.) yes (.) took the words out of my mouth (4.5)

(adapted from Rampton 1998: 297)

Note the following transcription conventions:

Square brackets mark the beginning of overlapping speech;
(school) – an uncertain transcription
((laughs)) – 'stage directions' or comments
CAPITALS – loud enunciation
bold – instance of language crossing
(.) – pause of less than one second
(1.0) – timed pause (approximate length of pause in seconds).

As the alternative terms 'styling' and 'stylisation' suggest, while we have considered crossing as a particular type of codeswitching, Mohan's switch into Indian English may equally be seen as a form of style-shifting. The Cardiff DJ studied by Coupland (see Section 4.4) engages in similar behaviour in adopting features of Cockney or Americanised speech. As mentioned above, the term 'codeswitching' tends to be used for alternation between different languages, or language varieties that are fairly readily distinguishable. In some cases it would be possible for a speaker to combine codeswitching between languages and style-shifting within one or more of these languages. However, the two also refer to similar types of linguistic activity, and the distinction between them is not clear-cut.

4.6 THE STUDY OF NEW VARIETIES OF ENGLISH

The term **language spread** is used to denote the process whereby the uses or users of a language increase (Cooper 1982) often via territorial expansion of people speaking the language or its acquisition by people from adjacent areas. In modern times both forces have applied in the spread of English, French, Swahili, Russian, Spanish and so forth. Language spread is often associated with political imposition, creating new linguistic relations in particular territories. While the era of colonisation of most of Africa and Asia by European powers ended in the mid-twentieth century, their linguistic effects are still felt in the now-independent territories. With the redrawing of group borders after independence came a new sense of nationhood between groups of people who previously had little substantial contact with each other. Dilemmas of choosing a national language in postcolonial contexts often resulted in the retention of colonial languages like French, Portuguese or English.

The comparative study of English in these colonial and postcolonial contexts and in areas affected intensely by globalisation is termed **World Englishes**. Kachru (1992) uses this term to cover the sum total of Englishes on the planet, and conceptualises them as belonging to one of three circles: the **Inner Circle** of territories where English is the dominant mother tongue (the UK, USA, Canada, Australia, etc.), the **Outer Circle** of territories to which the language spread via colonialism (e.g. India, Nigeria, Malaysia) and the **Expanding Circle** to which the language has spread via globalisation, without there being significant numbers of English-speaking settlers (e.g. China, Thailand). In linguistic terms, Kachru characterises the Inner Circle as 'norm-providing', since it exerts influences on the other circles via teaching resources and literary materials. He sees the Outer Circle as 'norm-developing', i.e. different territories are in the process of developing and gradually accepting some of their own linguistic norms. He characterises the Expanding Circle as 'norm-dependent', since English is usually used for external communication with other nations, and there is no tradition of using English for literary purposes. For the Expanding Circle there has been no one defining encounter with British or American rule. English is restricted to being a subject studied in the classroom and an important means of international communication, and interaction with tourists. Kachru's terminology has been widely used, though there are some difficulties in drawing exact borders between the three types. In colonial times there was an intermediate category of 'protectorates' (e.g. Egypt), which were not formally colonised but fell under the British sphere of influence. They appear to be intermediate between the Outer and Expanding Circle. Another difficulty is that a monolithic term like Inner or Outer Circle masks a great range of variability within specific countries. In the ex-colonies there is a vast difference between the more 'elite' varieties of English and the more 'popular' forms. Finally, Mesthrie and Bhatt (2008) suggest that the spread of English in Europe also cuts across the Outer Circle–Expanding Circle divide, as the socio-political conditions of contact are different. English in a country like Holland seems more like an Outer Circle variety, rather than the Expanding Circle to which it belongs. Globalisation generally appears to be bringing the circles closer to each other.

More traditional terminology often used in the Applied Linguistic study of English are **ESL (English as a Second Language)** and **EFL (English as a Foreign Language)**. These terms attest to the significance of English in different parts of the world. English has continued to play an important (if sometimes controversial) role in 'new' nations after they gained their independence from the British empire. In these countries, English is frequently used in government, administration and education, sometimes together with other indigenous languages. Apart from such formal usage, English may also be used for internal communication among people who do not share a common language (especially among an educated elite). This is the situation in countries like India, Sri Lanka, the Philippines, Nigeria and Ghana. The category 'ESL' is used by linguists in reference to such territories, even though some speakers might speak English from a young age. It contrasts with the category 'EFL', where English plays a more restricted role internally and is not generally a medium of instruction in schools. Furthermore, while ESL countries typically have a distinct body of literature in English, EFL countries do not. ESL and EFL, therefore, correspond roughly to Kachru's Outer and Expanding Circles.

Outer Circle (or ESL) varieties are also termed **New Englishes**. Platt *et al.* 1984 used the term for a variety that satisfies the following criteria:

- It has developed in an area where English is not spoken as a first language by a large number of people.
- It has developed through the education system rather than being acquired initially as a language of the home.
- It is used for a range of functions (e.g. as an inter-group language, in parliament, in official communication, in the media).
- It has become 'indigenised' by adopting words from local culture and 'nativised' by stabilising some structural features associated with local languages and/or the language-learning process.

There are some problems with this characterisation, notably in its narrowness. The definition excludes, for example, the English of Aboriginal Australians on the grounds that there is a majority of first-language speakers of English in the country. Mesthrie and Bhatt (2008) refer to Platt's usage as 'narrow ESL' as opposed to a broader conception that includes varieties like Aboriginal English as 'New Englishes', irrespective of the proportions between them and the dominant variety of English in the territory.

Platt *et al.* (1984) also argued that New Englishes exist as a broad class with a well-defined set of sociohistorical and linguistic characteristics. They cite similarities that are widespread in the New Englishes, like the frequent use of 'copy pronouns' in topic-comment constructions (e.g. Fiji English: *Most Indians, they know English*; Singapore English: *But the grandson, he knows to speak Malay*). In this construction, the first noun phrase of the clause is repeated (or 'copied') as a pronoun, especially where some sense of contrast or emphasis is intended. Although pronoun copying is a regular feature of colloquial L1 English, it is believed to be used more frequently and in a wider range of contexts in the New Englishes. (**L1** is the abbreviation linguists use for a person's first language; **L2** for a person's second language, and so on.)

Another common feature of New Englishes is the use of 'invariant tags': the addition of a tag question (like *isn't it*) which has a clearly defined grammatical relationship with the subject and verb phrase of the main clause. The following examples are from Platt *et al.* (1984: 129):

West African English: He loves you, **isn't it**/He loves you, **not so**?
Sri Lanka: Upili returned the book, **isn't it**?
India: He is going there, **isn't it**?

In these examples *isn't it* replaces a whole array of possibilities from standard English (*doesn't she, won't he, is she, isn't he, will it*) Such an innovation was probably devised by the first generation of learners of English in individual colonies and passed on to succeeding generations, thus becoming the norm. It is a simpler rule than the standard form which changes the form of the auxiliary verb (frequently adding a form of the verb *do*), changes the positive form of the main clause to negative in the tag or vice versa; and repeats the subject as a pronoun with the right marking for gender, number and case. In some cases there is reinforcement from the indigenous languages which have invariant tags, e.g. Hindi *na*.

Not all New English features involve the stabilisation of strategies used in learning English as a second language. Each variety shows specific indigenisation in its features of vocabulary and accent. By retaining (and thus sharing) some features from the indigenous languages of the territory, New Englishes blend into their sociocultural context. Individual New Englishes also show specific pragmatic differences in the way material from English can be recast to express new nuances – like politeness. In Indian English (and some other New

Englishes) *aunty* may be used as a title of respect, but usually for non-kin members. For kin members an indigenous term would be retained, even when using English. Thus *Kay aunty* is respectful use for an outsider; *aunty Kay* an informal and more 'modern' version; *aunt Kay* is formal and literary (not spoken); and *Kay maasi* is informal usage for an actual aunt (here one's mother's sister in Gujarati, differentiating her from a paternal aunt – 'father's sister'). On a scale of intimacy to formality we thus have: *Kay maasi – Kay aunty – aunty Kay – aunt Kay*. As with codeswitching, patterns of 'New English' usage show linguistic hybridity and the strategic deployment of linguistic forms to achieve and sustain complex relationships between speakers.

As English becomes more widespread and used by an elite who are well-versed in local and global norms, the distinction between a **native speaker** and a **non-native speaker** of the language has become blurred. Traditionally, a native speaker is assumed to be one who has learned a language from birth without formal instruction. By contrast, a non-native speaker of a language has learned it as a second (or later) language some time after being initiated into his/her native language and does not display the same automatic fluency in the non-native language as in the native language. Paradis (1998: 207) describes a speaker's native language as 'the dialect acquired from the crib . . . acquired incidentally, stored implicitly, and available for automatic use'. Several commentators (notably Singh 1998) have pointed out that such definitions of a native speaker seem to be premised on the norms of monolingual societies, whereas in fact the world is largely multilingual. For many New English speakers monolingualism is the marked case, a special case outside of the multilingual prototype. In some multilingual societies a child may be said to have several native languages, with the order of acquisition not being an indicator of ability, but of a complementary functional relationship.

PIDGINS AND CREOLES

Pidgins have always had a special fascination within sociolinguistics: as varieties that originate and grow in the spaces between previously established languages. They are thus a special outcome of **language contact**, a term that encompasses the changes that languages undergo and the new forms that arise under multilingualism. Pidgins arise as a means of communication in new multilingual situations between speakers of different languages who would otherwise be unable to communicate. They initially draw on a small vocabulary adopted from whatever resources speakers can marshal from around them, slotted into elementary grammatical structure and often aided by gestures. If and as communicative needs become more sustained and significant, the pidgin will grow more complex and less dependent on pragmatic means (including gestures). Pidgins tend to draw on the dominant language in the contact situation for their vocabulary, but not for the grammar, which comes from other sources. In the era of colonisation and slavery this dominant language was often a European one, which supplied the bulk of the vocabulary, but not the grammar. English pidgins include Nigerian Pidgin English, which arose in the era of slavery and has direct links with pidgins and Creoles of the Caribbean and other parts of West Africa. Nigerian Pidgin English is, in fact, the language with the greatest number of speakers in Nigeria and the largest pidgin/Creole worldwide (Faraclas 2004: 828). Another famous pidgin, which has grown into a national language is Tok Pisin of Papua New Guinea, which has its roots in a South Pacific pidgin of the eighteenth century. Tok Pisin stabilised in the mid-nineteenth century as a solution to the need for communication between speakers on this large and very multilingual island once they were drawn out of their traditional villages into colonial plantations. Tok Pisin enabled both 'horizontal' communication among speakers of different indigenous languages, as well as 'vertical' communication between European employers and indigenous employees. It is important to recognise (despite popular misconceptions) that existing languages do not 'degenerate' into pidgins. Rather, pidgins are new mediums for inter-ethnic communication (Baker 1995: 12). The differences between **pidginisation** (the formation of a pidgin) and second language acquisition are instructive. In the second case there is a 'target language' to which speakers have enough access to identify and have an expectation of being able to master. Development and correction of early learned forms takes place in the direction of this target language. A pidgin in comparison is more 'off-track', and target language speakers are few and not readily available to provide models of speech. The need for quick communication across different groups initially for purposes of labour makes the pidgin grow without significant access to the language of power. Many Tok Pisin examples show the use of lexical items taken from English but refashioned into a new grammar: *-pela* (deriving from English *fellow*) marks numerals, adjectives and demonstratives (*dispela* = 'this'; *bigpela* = 'big' *mitupela* = 'exclusive dual' – i.e. 'we, excluding you'). Likewise *belong* is refashioned from the verb of English to a marker of possession (rather like a suffix or preposition 'of'): e.g. *haus belong em* = 'his/her house'. In other situations a pidgin could be based on the vocabulary of an indigenous language, with English and other European language speakers performing the bricolage (in the sense of the term explained above, Section 4.4). Thus, in Fiji and South Africa indigenous pidgins (lexically based on Fijian and Zulu respectively) arose in response to the immediate communicative needs. Speakers of the dominant language contribute to this process by the use of 'foreigner talk' – i.e. simplifying one's own language when conversing with others who are not fluent in it ('foreigners').

The most important characteristic of a pidgin is that it is no one's home language and each group using it often associates it with the 'other' party. However a pidgin can develop into a 'full' language, complex in structure and widespread in function (beyond labouring contexts into the social domain). If in time people transmit this expanded variety to their children as a primary language, then the pidgin is said to have become a **Creole** (or to have creolised).

A Creole, in this account, is not a pidgin, but 'an ex-pidgin', much more complex and stable and evincing the properties of other primary languages. **Creolisation** in the linguistic sense is thus different from its sociological sense, where it usually means mixing of cultures and – sometimes – mixing of people. There are many lively debates within Pidgin and Creole Studies about the processes of creolisation and their relation to pidginisation. One concerns whether Creoles can be formed without a prior pidgin stage. Thomason and Kaufman (1988) label such languages 'abrupt Creoles' – languages which do not derive from any one predecessor but instead show vocabulary and grammar coming from different sources. Some abrupt Creoles may have formed in parts of the Caribbean, where historical research has yet to uncover earlier pidgin varieties. However, 'gradualists' believe that the growth from pidgin into Creole is incremental and imperceptible, rather than 'instantaneous' (i.e. showing a disjuncture once the variety becomes a primary language). By close and persistent archival work, scholars like Arends (1993), Baker (1995) and Singler (1996) have shown the gradual unfolding of pidgin and Creole grammar in specific territories (Suriname, Mauritius and Haiti respectively). In the Pacific, Tok Pisin is creolising (i.e. becoming a language of some homes and the first language of some children), without showing any major disjuncture in the process (Jourdan 1991). Still other scholars ('anti-exceptionalists' like Mufwene 2001 and DeGraff 2003) believe that the differences between pidgins and Creoles from 'other' languages tend to be exaggerated, and that the labels are unwarranted, since the two types are part of the broader phenomena of language contact, rather than exceptions to human languages that have to be specially explained. As with the construct of the native speaker – above – we are witness to a postmodern questioning of what the nature of linguistic norms are, and whose perspectives they embody.

4.7 ENGLISH AS A GLOBAL LANGUAGE

Accounts of English as a **global language** emphasise the vast numbers of people across the world who use English, and the increasing numbers who use English as an additional language. Robert McCrum *et al.*, for instance, comment:

> Today, English is used by at least 750 million people, and barely half of those speak it as a mother tongue. Some estimates have put that figure closer to one billion. Whatever the total, English at the end of the twentieth century is more widely scattered, more widely spoken and written, than any other language has ever been. It has become the language of the planet, the first truly global language.
>
> (McCrum *et al.*, 2002: 9–10)

And Randolph Quirk famously referred to English as 'a language – the language – on which the sun does not set, whose users never sleep' (1985: 1). A note of triumphalism often creeps into such attempts to represent the global status of English. The status of English as a global language is, however, controversial.

Section 4.5 on multilingual language choice and codeswitching discussed the association of English with high social status, and its use in many multilingual contexts as a language of education and white-collar employment. English is therefore often seen as a language of opportunity and personal advancement. Furthermore, its use as a **lingua franca** facilitates international and intra-national communication, often between L2 speakers. However, it is also seen as a language of exclusion, and as something that threatens local cultures and languages, leading in this last case to language shift and death. These tensions surrounding the status and use of English are well documented and discussed in accounts of English as a global language such as Crystal (2003). One of the fiercest critics of the international spread of English, and English language teaching, is Robert Phillipson (1992), who discusses this in terms of **linguistic imperialism**: for Phillipson, English linguistic imperialism is associated with other forms of imperialism (e.g. cultural, economic) that systematically assert the dominance of 'western' countries and their cultures. Different positions on the role of English as a global language are discussed critically by Alastair Pennycook (see Chapter 5) and, more specifically in relation to African contexts, by Busi Makoni and Sinfree Makoni (see Chapter 17).

More complex discussions of the position of English as a global language see English as intricately embedded within processes of **globalisation** (also discussed further by Pennycook). 'Globalisation' refers, broadly, to an increasing level of interconnectedness between different parts of the world. This is bound up with economic change, as processes of production and consumption increasingly operate on a global level (with, for instance, companies employing workers and targeting consumers in different national contexts); with technological developments, which allow rapid communication across the world so that time and space come to be seen as compressed; and also with culture and identity, as cultural practices are disseminated across the world and national, social and personal identities may be redefined in relation to larger global processes. While globalisation is sometimes associated with increasing homogeneity, this is not straightforwardly the case: for instance, international companies may tailor products to different local groups of consumers. Globalisation may also give rise to attempts to maintain a range of local practices and identities, sometimes referred to as **localisation**. Language is embedded in all these processes, and many studies have focused on changing forms and uses of English, as well as changes in the status of the language that are both a response and a contribution to globalisation/localisation. For instance, Canagarajah, in his study of English and Tamil switching in English language teaching (ELT) classrooms (see Section 4.5 above) interpreted this in relation to the global hegemony of Anglo-American ELT practices and local Tamil language policies.

In a discussion of the potential future of English, David Graddol (1997/2000, 2006) argues that the global position of English may change as English becomes part of a 'new world order of languages' (2006: 22). First, other languages are providing regional challenges to the dominance of English, with Mandarin

Chinese and Spanish increasingly influential (respectively, in Asia and South America). But also, the use of English as a language of wider communication within national contexts (such as India) and internationally need not rely on 'native-speaker' models. Alternative varieties, including regional varieties, may be preferred. The spread of English, therefore, does not necessarily confer an advantage on monolingual native speakers of the language.

Studies of language and globalisation often draw on the concept of '(cultural) flow' to discuss the origins of linguistic forms and meanings and their appropriation by speakers in other contexts. This may be exemplified in research on hip-hop, a well-known (and well-studied) global language practice. In a study of Nigerian hip-hop, for instance, Tope Omoniyi (2006) argues that Nigerian hip-hop artists have re-appropriated forms from African American hip-hop artists, in turn derived from African roots, and combined these with local Nigerian forms to produce a hybrid 'glocal' identity.

Alastair Pennycook (2003) emphasises the complexity of global practices such as hip-hop, drawing on lyrics such as the following from the Japanese rappers Rip Slyme:

Lyrics	Transliteration and translation
Yo Bringing That. Yo Bring Your Style 人類最後のフリーキーサイド	Yo Bringing That. Yo Bring Your Style Jinrui saigo no furiikiisaido
	Yo Bringing That, Yo Bring Your Style The last freaky side of the human race

(Pennycook 2003a: 515)

Pennycook points to the use of *Yo*, a term often found in hip-hop, originating in African-American English: he sees the first (English) line of the lyrics as an example of crossing, or styling the other. The following line, in Japanese, is itself mixed, using three different scripts: Kanji, Katakana (often used for the transcription of non-Japanese words) and Hiragana (used for Japanese morphemes and grammatical items). *Furiikiisaido* ('freaky side') is a switch from English, adopting Japanese morphology.

Pennycook argues that influential views of English as a world language (whether this is seen, relatively neutrally, as a language for international communication, or as contributing to linguistic imperialism and the homogenisation of world culture, or whether the plurality of 'world Englishes' is emphasised) cannot account for this and similar examples. While there is not a recognised variety of 'Japanese English', English here is part of speakers' identity repertoires: 'Japanese rap, in English, is part of Japanese language and culture' (2003: 517). Pennycook sees identity here not as a fixed attribute, but as something that is performed, refashioned and re-invented in specific contexts. This is consistent with contemporary models of identity now prevalent in sociolinguistic research – see earlier discussion of 'style' and 'stylisation' in Sections 4.4 and 4.5.

In terms of cultural flows, Pennycook suggests that these can be understood as 'occurring both within inequitable relations of language, culture, power and money, and at the same time as always potentially reworkable' (2003b: 525). While ideas, stylistic innovations, etc. tend to travel from the USA to different parts of the world and not vice versa, hip-hop may be used locally in different ways, including to index resistance to western hegemony. Nor do ideas flow only from the USA – Pennycook refers to influences within the Pacific Islands and New Zealand that have given rise to a pan-Pacific hip-hop network.

The idea of 'flow' provides an image of language, and languages, as 'on the move': as processes rather than fixed entities. A similar metaphor can be found in Thomas's (2007) conception of 'vagues linguistiques', or linguistic waves, discussed initially in relation to French in post-colonial contexts but re-applied by Makoni and Makoni (this volume) to English in Africa. In Section 4.2 on 'Variation, diversity and change' it was noted that 'English', and varieties of English, are idealisations. Languages are not really neat, bounded entities: there are no clear boundaries between varieties, and varieties are also constantly changing. Concepts such as 'flow' or 'waves' are an attempt to capture such instability. It is, however, difficult to discuss language entirely in terms of process. Partly, we lack an appropriate conceptual vocabulary: as Makoni and Makoni point out, even terms such as 'hybridity', designed to account for variability and change, presuppose discrete linguistic entities that are recombined. Also, however, languages do not rush along like running water. Change is fairly slow, and it is therefore possible, and reasonable enough, to provide snapshots – accounts, albeit temporary and idealised, of how things stand now. This 'temporary stasis' is evident in accounts of English grammar in Chapter 2, but also in studies of processes such as codeswitching, stylisation and language change in progress discussed in this chapter.

PART I: FURTHER READING

HISTORY

While this Companion focuses on contemporary English language studies, the following provide accounts of the history of English for those who would like to follow up this topic. Baugh and Cable is a classic discussion of the history of English, now in its fifth edition. Crystal is a more popular account that also covers contemporary language. Leith and Milroy and Milroy provide a stronger emphasis on social and political issues, with Milroy and Milroy focusing particularly on standardisation both historically and in the present day. Mugglestone is a substantial edited collection, bringing together contributions from a range of scholars and including a final chapter on the twenty-first century. Singh is a more introductory volume.

Baugh, A. and Cable, T. (2002 5th edition) *A History of the English Language*, London: Routledge.
Crystal, D. (2004) *The Stories of English*, London: Penguin.
Leith, D. (1997 2nd edition) *A Social History of English*, London: Routledge.
Milroy, J. and Milroy, L. (1999 3rd edition) *Authority in Language: Investigating Standard English*, London: Routledge.
Mugglestone, L. (2006) *The Oxford History of English*, Oxford: Oxford University Press.
Singh, I. (2005) *The History of English: A Students' Guide*, London: Hodder Arnold.
Strang, B.M.H. (1970) *A History of English*, London, Methuen.

CHAPTER 2 DESCRIBING ENGLISH

In the list below, Nunan provides an introduction to linguistic description, drawing mainly on traditional concepts and categories. Coffin, Donohue and North, and O'Halloran and Coffin provide introductions that incorporate a functional perspective. Bloor and Bloor and Thompson focus more specifically on functional approaches to grammar, and Coffin, Hewings and O'Halloran combine functional and corpus approaches.

Bloor, T. and Bloor, M. (2004 2nd edition) *The Functional Analysis of English: A Hallidayan Approach*, London: Hodder Arnold.
Coffin, C., Hewings, A. and O'Halloran, K.A (eds) (2004) *Applying English Grammar: Functional and Corpus Approaches*, London: Hodder-Arnold.
Coffin, C., Donohue, J. and North, S.P. (forthcoming 2009) *Exploring English Grammar: From Traditional to Functional Grammar*, London: Routledge.

Nunan, D. (2007) *What is This Thing Called Language?* Basingstoke, Hants: Palgrave Macmillan.

O'Halloran, K.A. and Coffin, C. (eds) (2006) *Getting Started. Describing the Grammar of Speech and Writing*, Milton Keynes: The Open University.

Thompson, G. (2004 2nd edition) *Introducing Functional Grammar*, London: Hodder Arnold.

CHAPTER 3 TEXTS AND PRACTICES

There are a number of introductory student handbooks on discourse analysis, for example Cameron and Lillis and McKinney. Gee presents a social approach to discourse analysis, Fairclough introduces critical discourse analysis, Blommaert examines theories and methods in this area and Biber, Connor and Upton combine discourse and corpus analysis. Jaworski and Coupland introduce a range of classic articles, Shriffrin gives a general overview of different approaches and Maybin, Mercer and Hewings present contexualised approaches to studying texts and practices in English.

Biber, D., Connor, U. and Upton, T.A. (2007) *Discourse on the Move: Using Corpus Analysis to Describe Discourse Structure*, Amsterdam: John Benjamins.

Blommaert, J. (2005) *Discourse: A Critical Introduction*, New York: Cambridge University Press.

Cameron, D. (2001) *Working with Spoken Discourse*, London: Sage.

Fairclough, N. (2003) *Analysing Discourse: Textual Analysis for Social Research*, London: Routledge.

Gee, J.P. (2005) *An Introduction to Discourse Analysis*, London: Routledge.

Jaworski, A. and Coupland, N. (eds) (2005) *The Discourse Reader*, London: Routledge.

Lillis, T. and McKinney, C. (2003) *Analysing Language in Context: A Student Workbook*, Stoke on Trent: Trentham Books.

Maybin, J., Mercer, N. and Hewings, A. (eds) (2nd edition 2006) *Using English*, London: Routledge.

Schiffrin, D. (1994) *Approaches to Discourse*, Malden, MA: Blackwell.

CHAPTER 4 FROM VARIATION TO HYBRIDITY

Several sociolinguistics textbooks provide more detail on the topics discussed in Chapter 4 – examples include Holmes and Mesthrie *et al.* Coupland gives a more specific sociolinguistic account of contemporary ideas on speakers' variable language use. Several books provide accounts of English with a focus on its position as a global language – as examples we list below Crystal, Graddol *et al.* (this also includes historical chapters) and McArthur. Pennycook discusses contemporary ideas about English and globalisation, with specific reference to hip-hop.

Coupland, N. (2007) *Style: Language Variation and Identity*, Cambridge: Cambridge University Press.

Crystal, D. (2003 2nd edition) *English as a Global Language*, Cambridge: Cambridge University Press.

Graddol, D., Leith, D., Swann, J., Rhys, M. and Gillen, J. (eds) (2007) *Changing English*, Abingdon/New York: Routledge.

Holmes, J. (2008, 3rd edition) *An Introduction to Sociolinguistics*, Harlow, Essex: Pearson Education.

McArthur, T. (2002) *The Oxford Guide to World English*, Oxford: Oxford University Press.

Mesthrie, R., Swann, J., Deumert, A. and Leap, W. (2009 2nd edition) *Introducing Sociolinguistics*, Edinburgh: Edinburgh University Press.

Pennycook, A. (2007) *Global Englishes and Transcultural Flows*, London: Routledge.

DICTIONARIES AND ENCYCLOPEDIAS

For those who would like to check concise reference works that explain key terms and concepts, Crystal's 'Dictionary' provides one of the best known dictionaries of linguistics, Swann *et al.* focus on sociolinguistics and Wales on stylistics, particularly the study of literary language. Crystal's 'Encyclopedia' is a substantial but popular reference work on language and Mesthrie, despite the title, is a comprehensive reference work, focusing on sociolinguistics and bringing together the work of a wide range of scholars.

Crystal, D. (2003 5th edition) *A Dictionary of Linguistics and Phonetics*, Oxford: Blackwell.

—— (2003 2nd edition) *The Cambridge Encyclopedia of the English Language*, Cambridge: Cambridge University Press.

Mesthrie, R. (ed.) (2001) *Concise Encyclopedia of Sociolinguistics*, Oxford: Elsevier.

Swann, J., Deumert, A., Lillis, T. and Mesthrie, R. (2004) *A Dictionary of Sociolinguistics*, Edinburgh: Edinburgh University Press.

Wales, K. (2001 2nd edition) *A Dictionary of Stylistics*, Harlow, Essex: Pearson Education.

Part II
Current issues and debates

5

ENGLISH AND GLOBALIZATION

ALASTAIR PENNYCOOK

It is not difficult to make a case that English is intimately tied up with globalization. From its wide use in many domains across the world and the massive efforts in both state and private educational sectors to provide access to the language, to its role in global media, international forums, business, finance, politics and diplomacy, it is evident not only that English is widely used across the globe but also that it is part of those processes we call globalization. What this means for English, other languages and cultures, and processes of global change, however, is much harder to determine. In order to tackle such a question, we need first of all to think through very carefully what is meant by globalization. In this first section, therefore, I shall sketch out some of the major concerns around globalization in an attempt to clarify how I am using the term in this context. The following sections will then look on the one hand, at ways in which English is tied up with processes of globalization (questions of English and various media, development, inequality and religion), and on the other, at different ways of thinking about English as a global language (as a threat to other languages, as lingua franca, as a collection of world Englishes). The chapter ends with a discussion of potential new ways of thinking about global Englishes.

GLOBALIZATION AND ENGLISH

Vast amounts have been written about globalization. Lacking space or reason to try to cover this burgeoning literature, I shall instead draw attention to certain themes that have implications for discussions of English. First, globalization is not only about economic processes, but political, technological and cultural processes as well. Kumaravadivelu (2008: 32), for example, sees globalization in terms of new 'interconnections and flows among nations, economies and peoples. It results in the transformation of contemporary social life in all its economic, political, cultural, technological, ecological, and individual dimensions'. To view all aspects of globalization as flowing from the role of international capital is to overlook several concerns. While globalization is, of course, interlinked with international capital, it is by no means reductively determined by it. Capitalism remains a driving force in the world, yet it is not clear that we live in an era of capitalism so much as corporatism (Graham *et al.* 2007; Pennycook 2007), where a particular set of neoliberal ideologies predominates, turning publicly-owned sectors into privately-run corporations and emphasizing a free market to which large corporations should have access. While global inequalities of poverty, health and education remain primary concerns, it is more useful to see globalization as complexly related to these than as synonymous with their cause. International relations of trade, commerce, pollution, interaction and intervention are fundamentally inequitable, but it is not useful to reduce globalization only to a term that reflects such inequities.

Second, therefore, to suggest that globalization is *only* a process of US or Western domination of the world is to take a narrow and ultimately unproductive view of global relations. Likewise, to view culture and language in terms only of reflections of the economic is to miss the point that new technologies and communications are enabling immense and complex flows of people, signs, sounds and images across multiple borders in multiple directions. The very point about globalization is that it is global, and thus inevitably caught up in multiple influences. Indian and Philippino call centres, indigenous education conferences, global migrations of workers, Japanese animated cartoons, anti-globalization networks, fashion trends, salsa classes, gay and lesbian travel organizations and the ubiquity and similarity of urban graffiti, are all part of globalization. Globalization may be better understood as a compression of time and space, an intensification of social, economic, cultural and political relations and a series of global linkages that render events in one location of potential and immediate importance in other, quite distant locations (Giddens 1999). Education is a good example of this, with students moving in increasing numbers to take up educational possibilities elsewhere (Singh and Doherty, 2004), resulting in changing practices in the new 'educational contact zones', and new flows of knowledges across borders. This diversity of concerns can be captured in part by Appadurai's (1996) formulation of 'scapes' – ethnoscapes (the new mobility of tourists, migrants and refugees), technoscapes (new technologies), financescapes (flows of capital), mediascapes (global media), and ideoscapes (ideas and values) – and the various additions that have been made to them, including sacriscapes (religion) (Waters 1995), eduscapes (global educational movements), and of interest to the theme of this chapter, global linguascapes (languages) (Pennycook 2007).

Third, globalization is both old and new. By this I mean that we need to understand both its historical precedents and its contemporary particularity. While Steger (2003) suggests that globalization can be mapped more or less against the entirety of human history, others, such as Robertson (2003), describe successive waves of globalization starting with the era of European expansionism. For Mignolo (2000: 236), although the scope and speed of current globalization is without precedent, it is 'the most recent configuration of a process that can be traced back to the 1500s, with the beginning of transatlantic exploration and the consolidation of Western hegemony'. Such perspectives that render globalization the latest manifestation of European imperialism have been critiqued for failing to account for 'the novelty of the structures and logics of power that order the contemporary world. Empire is not a weak echo of modern imperialisms but a fundamentally new form of rule' (Hardt and Negri

2000: 146). Unlike the old imperialism(s), which were centred around the economic and political structures and exchanges of the nation state (indeed, the two were in many ways mutually constitutive), globalization represents a fundamentally new set of relations. A view of globalization as the historical continuation of European imperialism may also suffer from a Eurocentrism that overlooks the role of other empires (Ottoman, Chinese, Japanese to name a few) and global forces. It is nevertheless not so hard to reconcile these two arguments. On the one hand, if we lose sight of the historical precedents of the current state of globalization, we lose a crucial understanding of how current global conditions have come into being; on the other, if we focus too much on continuity, we fail to see that the forces of globalization demand new ways of thinking and new solutions to new problems.

So, finally, globalization demands that we think differently. The rapid and extensive changes brought about by globalization cannot be conceptualized through pre-globalization lenses. There is an important distinction between an understanding of globalization as a realist position that focuses on the state of the world under late capitalism, and an alternative position that focuses on the ways in which globalization undermines our modernist modes of thought. This way of thinking is in part captured by Radhakrishnan's (2007: 313) explanation of *worldliness* as acknowledging 'that the very one-ness of the world can only be understood on the basis of an irreducible perspectival heterogeneity'. Not only does globalization thus invoke new forms of localization but it also changes them. As Edwards and Usher (2008: 24) explain, 'the integration of the globe reconfigures rather than supplants diversity, in the process introducing new forms of economic, social and cultural creolisation'. Central here is not only the concern as to whether globalization is a process of homogenization or heterogenization (increasing similarity or increasing diversity) (Kumaravadivelu 2008; Pennycook 2003a) but also what new forms of language, culture and knowledge it brings about and what new ways of thinking about these it makes possible.

It is evident, therefore, that while we cannot deal with English without also dealing with globalization, we need to consider very carefully how we understand globalization in order to understand global English. Certainly a historical perspective tells one story: from a minor language isolated to an island off the north coast of Europe in the sixteenth century, it was the expansion of British colonialism, as people moved to colonize newly invaded territories (North America, Australia) and to work within newly colonized states (India, Nigeria), that led to its first wave of expansion in the eighteenth and nineteenth centuries. The subsequent emergence of the United States of America as a dominant global player in the twentieth century played a major role in the current dominance of English. English is now embedded in many parts of the global system. One need only map it against a list of 'scapes' (finance, media, tourist, religion and knowledge production) to see its global significance. At the very least, we need to understand how English operates in an uneven world (see Radhakrishnan 2003), how English is involved in global flows of culture and knowledge, and how English is used and appropriated by users of English around the world, from popular culture to unpopular politics, from international capital to local transaction, from diplomacy to peace-keeping, from religious proselytizing to secular resistance. Yet the very conditions of globalization and the role of global English also demand that we rethink what we mean by language, language spread, native speakers or multilingualism. Indeed, globalization requires us to consider whether we should continue to think of languages as separate, distinguishable, countable entities. I shall return to these concerns at the end of this chapter after looking in greater depth at the social, cultural and political roles played by English, and the changes that English has undergone.

ENGLISH IN AN UNEVEN WORLD

The first set of concerns about English and globalization are questions of the sociology of English and its relation to globalization. It is common in language studies and English language teaching to talk in terms of English as the 'language of international communication' rather than a language embedded in processes of globalization. English is all too often assumed to be a language that holds out promise of social and economic development to all those who learn it, a language of equal opportunity, a language that the world needs in order to be able to communicate. Yet any critical analysis suggests that it is also an exclusionary class dialect, favouring particular people, countries, cultures, forms of knowledge and possibilities of development; it is a language which creates barriers as much as it presents possibilities. As Tollefson (2000: 8) warns, 'At a time when English is widely seen as a key to the economic success of nations and the economic well-being of individuals, the spread of English also contributes to significant social, political, and economic inequalities'.

Bruthiaux (2002a: 292–93) argues convincingly that, for many of the world's poor, English language education is 'an outlandish irrelevance', and 'talk of a role for English language education in facilitating the process of poverty reduction and a major allocation of public resources to that end is likely to prove misguided and wasteful'. Bringing a sophisticated economic analysis to the question of global English, Lysandrou and Lysandrou (2003: 230) argue that 'the embrace of the English language is to the detriment of the majorities of communities the world over insofar as it contributes to their systematic dispossession'.[1] Thus we need to distinguish very clearly between individually-oriented access arguments about escape from poverty, and class-oriented arguments about large-scale poverty reduction. 'For those who already speak English,' suggests Tollefson (2000: 9):

> the economic value of the language translates directly into greater opportunities in education, business, and employment. For those who must learn English, however, particularly those who do not have access to high-quality English language education, the spread of English presents a formidable obstacle to education, employment, and other activities requiring English proficiency.

As Ramanathan's (2005: 112) study of English and vernacular medium education in India shows, English is a deeply divisive language, denigrating vernacular languages, cultures, and ways of learning and teaching on the one hand, and dovetailing 'with the values and aspirations of the elite Indian middle class' (112) on the other. While English opens doors to some, it is simultaneously a barrier to learning, development and employment for others.

Some of the harshest critiques of the global role of English have come from Robert Phillipson's (1992, 1999, 2003) description of linguistic imperialism, a term he uses to show how English has been incessantly promoted over other languages (leading to inequitable relations between languages and threats to the continuing sustainability of minority languages and cultures) and how English is also connected to wider processes of globalization: an uncritical endorsement of capitalism, a narrow vision of modernization, the homogenization of world culture, and so on (1999: 274). While Phillipson thus quite appropriately locates English within inequitable relations of globalization, and shows that, rather than an accidental process, the global spread of English has been very deliberate policy, his vision of globalization is also a narrow 'homogenization' perspective (Pennycook 2003a; Kumaravadivelu 2008) that allows for little understanding of the complexity of global flows and resistances, and which does not adequately account for the ways in which the spread of English has also been a result of people's active learning of the language (Brutt-Griffler 2002b). While we ignore Phillipson's warnings at our peril, it is also crucial to understand the ways in which English is resisted and appropriated, how English users 'may find ways to negotiate, alter and oppose political structures, and reconstruct their languages, cultures and identities to their advantage. The intention is not to *reject* English, but to *reconstitute* it in more inclusive, ethical, and democratic terms' (Canagarajah 1999: 2).

There are many other domains in which the role of English in processes of globalization is worth examination. For some, English is part of '*the homogenization of world culture* . . . spearheaded by films, pop culture, CNN and fast-food chains' (Phillipson and Skutnabb-Kangas 1996: 439; italics in original). More detailed analyses of popular culture, the complex global circuits of flow of culture and language, and the ways in which languages are borrowed and used, however, suggest both that we need to operate with a more open attitude to forms and flows of popular culture, and that the local use of English in different contexts cannot be so simply reduced to the erosion of difference (Pennycook 2007). Another area of significance is the way in which English learners' 'language desires' are produced in the global marketplaces of English, where 'English emerges as a powerful tool to construct a gendered identity and to gain access to the romanticized West' (Piller and Takahashi 2006: 69). Karmani's (2005: 262) discussion of the relations between English and Islam also points to the urgency of understanding how English is implicated in global relations: 'As the "war on terror" rages on military, political, and media fronts, a crucial much-forgotten battle is also being contested on the linguistic front: between "Islam and English'". The promotion, use and teaching of English in such contexts cannot be understood without an appreciation of the control of oil, current concerns about terrorism, and the recent increase in global battles over religious affiliation. Attention has also been drawn recently to the connections between English language teaching and Christian missionary activity (Pennycook and Coutand-Marin 2003; Varghese and Johnston 2007). In many domains, therefore, we need critical analyses of the ways in which English is linked to inequitable global relations while at the same time it is used, changed and appropriated for local purposes.

ENGLISH AS THREAT, LINGUA FRANCA OR CENTRIFUGAL FORCE

A focus on the ways in which English and other languages are affected by this global role produces several competing frameworks for analysis. One set of concerns is that English is taking over from other languages. 'If inaction on language policy in Europe continues, at the national and supranational levels,' Phillipson (2003: 192) warns, 'we may be heading for an American English-only Europe'. While this homogenization threat needs to be taken quite seriously, the measures taken to oppose it also need to be considered with caution. Arguing for the need to safeguard diversity through the support of other European languages, particularly French, Hagège (2006: 37; my translation) argues that 'to defend a culture is also to defend the language in which it is expressed'. To defend diversity in terms of bolstering national languages, however, is to operate with a view that the nation state and its attendant languages are a guarantor of diversity, a view that runs counter to the broader image of diversity put forward, for example, by proponents of creolization, which valorizes mixing and hybridity over the purisms of national languages (Bernabé et al. 1993). More broadly, this concern over the threat to other languages posed by English has become part of the wider debate over linguistic human rights, and whether linguistic diversity can be guaranteed through international legislation (Skutnabb-Kangas 2000). Widely debated in terms of its practicality, whether the focus should be on linguistic or cultural diversity, and how linguistic and minority rights are related (May 2001), this 'willingness to use the language of human rights on the global level to frame local linguistic demands vis-à-vis global English' (Sonntag 2003: 25) may also fall into the trap of continuing to promote the very ways of thinking about language and diversity that are part of the problem. A language rights perspective thus promotes the defence of linguistic diversity in terms of less powerful languages being accorded equal rights with dominant languages, and does so within a political perspective on human rights that promotes global solutions to local problems.

A different concern is that the widespread use of English leads to impoverished communication. Again, Phillipson (2003: 176) warns that the use of English across Europe is leading to 'a simplified, pidginized but unstable "Euro-English" that inhibits creativity and expressiveness, whether English is used as a mother tongue or as a foreign language, a language that is spoken with so much imprecision that communication difficulties and breakdowns multiply'. Addressing the trend in applied linguistic circles to adopt a laissez-faire attitude towards heterogenization, Jenkins (2006b: 36) expresses a concern that

> if a policy of pluricentricity is pursued unchecked, in effect a situation of 'anything goes,' . . . there is a danger that their accents will move further and further apart until a stage is reached where pronunciation presents a serious problem to lingua franca communication.

One way of countering these centrifugal language forces has been an attempt to describe a core of English as a Lingua Franca (ELF) pronunciation – or a lexico-grammatical core in the work of Seidlhofer (2001) – based on the actual negotiated use of non-native speakers of English. This approach to global English, therefore, rejects the claims of 'native speaker varieties' of English (American, British, Australian) in favour of descriptions of actual English use in different areas of the world (particularly Europe and Asia).

This focus on English as a lingua franca has engendered considerable debate. Of particular concern is whether such work remains only at the descriptive level or whether such descriptions of English could also be translated into syllabi for teaching. The concern here is that to teach what are seen as 'reduced' versions of English may be detrimental to learners' possibilities. The ELF approach has also been critiqued from the World Englishes perspective on the grounds that it falls into the camp of those approaches to English that 'idealize a monolithic entity called "English" and neglect the inclusive and plural character of the world-wide phenomenon' (Kachru and Nelson 2006: 2). Also rejecting the dominance of native speaker ('inner circle') varieties of English, a focus on World Englishes has taken up a strong focus on heterogeny by looking at 'implications of pluricentricity . . . the new and emerging norms of performance, and the bilingual's creativity as a manifestation of the contextual and formal hybridity of Englishes' (Kachru 1997: 66). The central focus has been on descriptions of those varieties of English that have developed in former British colonies where English has an internal role within the country (Singaporean, Indian, Philippine amongst other Englishes). Many detailed accounts of how such 'outer circle' varieties of English differ at all levels – phonological, syntactic, lexical, semantic, pragmatic – from inner circle varieties have been produced, alongside the argument that such varieties need to be established as the local norms by which standards of correctness are judged. The 'expanding circle' of all other English users (from China to Brazil) has received less attention, yet there are significant debates emerging over the status that should be accorded to local varieties in this expanding circle, and whether the sometimes derogatory terms such as 'Chinglish', 'Japlish' and so forth should be reclaimed to describe valid local English variants.

While a world Englishes perspective has been influential in making its case for a diversity of Englishes, it has also been critiqued on various grounds. Along with its focus on hybridity at the expense of a more critical analysis of English in the world, and the descriptive and analytic inconsistencies of the three circles, is the problem that the locus of analysis is on national varieties of English. Overlooking diversity within regions and the scope of change within globalization, therefore, the world Englishes framework has been described as 'a twentieth century construct that has outlived its usefulness' (Bruthiaux 2003: 161). Just as a language rights perspective maintains a twentieth-century model of international relations, so a world Englishes perspective maintains a focus on national Englishes. Neither raises the question of whether we need to reconsider what languages are in more fundamental terms. It is also less than clear whether the world Englishes focus on diversity is in fact so different from a lingua franca approach as its proponents claim. Thus, when Braj Kachru focuses on 'educated South Asian English' rather than 'Broken English' (2005: 39) he is surely open to the same critiques that he levels at the purveyors of ELF. As Parakrama (1995: 25–26) points out, 'The smoothing out of struggle within and without language is replicated in the homogenizing of the varieties of English on the basis of "upper-class" forms. Kachru is thus able to theorize on the nature of a monolithic Indian English'. Similarly, Canagarajah (1999: 180) observes that in Kachru's

> attempt to systematize the periphery variants, he has to standardize the language himself, leaving out many eccentric, hybrid forms of local Englishes as too unsystematic. In this, the Kachruvian paradigm follows the logic of the prescriptive and elitist tendencies of the center linguists.

On one level all these approaches to global English share a similar interest in promoting diversity. While the world Englishes model places its hopes in a plurality of Englishes, the language rights perspective discussed earlier puts its faith in the defence of languages other than English (Skutnabb-Kangas 2000). Both treat a relation between language, culture and nation as the lynchpin of diversity. For the ELF approach, the question is whether it will focus predominantly on regional cores of English – albeit decentred from the former loci of correctness and recentred in new canons of intelligible usage – or whether it will focus on the diversity of language uses that are tied neither to native nor to nativized varieties (Kirkpatrick 2006; Rubdy and Saraceni 2006) in order to capture how 'postcolonial speakers of English creatively negotiate the place of English in their lives' (Canagarajah 2006c: 200). While other approaches have been suggested, such as Schneider's (2007: 19) Dynamic Model which suggests that 'the evolution of language follows principles of its own' and that there is therefore a 'common core' behind the processes of localization, it is clear that, as Tupas (2006) observes, none of these models of English spread will have much relevance for English users unless they also take into account the dynamics of English in an uneven world.

CONCLUSION: NEW LANGUAGES FOR NEW TIMES

Several times in this chapter we have encountered the critique that discussions of the global role of English have failed to engage with the injunction to think differently. These approaches to global English – whether linguistic imperialism and language rights, or world Englishes and English as a lingua franca – remain stuck within twentieth-century frameworks of languages and nations. The central concern that the debates between these rival conceptualizations leave uncontested is how we can understand diversity outside those very frameworks that are part of the problem. Neither a defence of national languages and cultures, nor a description of a core of English as a lingua franca, nor even a focus on plural Englishes adequately addresses questions of diversity under new conditions of globalization. A focus on the worldliness of English (Pennycook 1994; 2007), however, demands in Radhakrishnan's (2007) terms, that the very one-ness of English can only be understood on the basis of local perspectives of difference. This is not a question of pluralizing Englishes but of understanding the way different language ideologies construct English locally. Questioning the ways in which we have come to think about languages within colonialism and modernity, and regarding the grand narratives of imperialism, language rights, linguae francae or world Englishes with suspicion, this perspective looks towards local, situated, contextual and contingent ways of understanding languages and language policies.

This suggests the need to think about English and globalization outside the nationalist frameworks that gave rise to twentieth-century models of the world. In dealing with English in an uneven world, we do need to understand its historical formation within forms of nationalism and imperialism, and its contemporary roles in the inequitable distribution of resources, in the promotion of certain ideas over others, in the threat it may pose to other languages, cultures and ways of being. And yet we need simultaneously to appreciate, not only its appropriation and relocalization by diverse users, but also its reconfiguration as something different. Perhaps it is time to question the very notions that underpin our assumptions about languages (Jacquemet 2005; Makoni and Pennycook 2007), to ask whether the ways we name and describe languages as separate entities and the ways we view bi- and multilingualism, are based on twentieth-century epistemologies that can no longer be used to describe the use of languages in a globalizing world. If it is clear that the ways we think about language are inevitably products of particular historical contexts, then an age of globalization suggests that we need both to reflect on how and why we look at languages as separate, countable, describable entities in the way we do, and to consider that languages may be undergoing such forms of transition as to require new ways of conceptualization in terms of local activities, resources or practices.

NOTE

1 This does not imply, however, that the solution lies in opposing the spread of English since it is 'the realm of economic policy, not that of language policy, that one should look to for redress' (Lysandrou and Lysandrou 2003: 230).

6

ENGLISH AND CREATIVITY

ROB POPE

Creativity from a Western point of view can be defined as the ability to produce work that is novel and appropriate.

(Lubart, Todd 'Creativity across Cultures' in Sternberg (ed.) 1999: 339)

Something relevant may be said about creativity, provided it is realised that whatever we say it is, there is also something more and something different.

(Bohm, David and Peat, David, *Science, Order and Creativity*, Routledge, 2nd edn, 2000: 226)

No one man's English is all English [. . .] It is not today what it was a century ago, still less what it will be a century hence. [. . .] And there is absolutely no defining line in any direction: the circle of the English language has a well-defined centre but no discernible circumference.

(from the *General Explanations to the New English Dictionary on Historical Principles* (subsequently Oxford English Dictionary), 1933: xxi–xxii)

These three epigraphs help to set the scene. They also sound some notes of caution. 'Creativity' as commonly understood nowadays, the first quotation warns, may be a specifically *Western* – and, one may add, a specifically *modern* Western – concept. Such is the current preoccupation with the 'novel' and the 'new' (at the expense of the 'old' and the 'traditional'), while a question quite rightly lingers over 'appropriate' (for whom and what?). At the same time, as the second quotation suggests, any 'creativity' worthy of the name is likely to exceed attempts to limit it to a single, once-and-for-all definition; it may always turn out to be 'something more and different'. Finally, the quotation from an early edition of the *OED* puts the whole matter of what can be meant by 'English' (whose it is, when and where?) up for interrogation. This prompts some vigorous updating and a provocative re-reading shortly.

Taken together, all the above quotations also confirm that the nouns 'creativity' and 'English' are singularly abstract shorthand for what in fact are ceaselessly changing, complex and often contentious phenomena. From the outset, then, we might be inclined to shift both into the plural: to recognise that just as it is sometimes preferable to speak of 'Englishes' and 'literatures in English' (so as to register the massive linguistic and generic differences between, say, a riddle in Anglo-Saxon, a poem in modern South Africa and a conversation amongst students in Wales, as we do later in this chapter); so it may sometimes be better to think of 'Creativities' depending on the perceptual modes and technological media in play, verbal and otherwise. To anticipate another example, a song performed live by Bob Dylan may subsequently be recorded in a studio and, much later, lead to an illustrated book and to a contemporary multi-media website. But for all the interconnections, the kinds of creativity the above media represent are substantially incomparable. So, while we may be quite happy – if unsettled – as to what 'English/es' can refer to, we may still be more than a little anxious about what 'creativity' – even if pluralised as 'creativities' – might really mean, in theory or in practice. And justifiably so.

The fact is that the abstract noun 'creativity' has only been around in English for less than 150 years. This comes as a big surprise to most people. The first reference to creativity in the *OED* is in 1875 and the term only becomes widespread during the 1920s, when it refers almost exclusively to a secular and pervasively natural or generally human capacity rather than a religious and specifically divine or narrowly artistic one. The Anglo-American philosopher and educationist A.N. Whitehead, strongly influenced by Bergson's *Creative Evolution* (1911), sets the tone by identifying '[t]he creativity whereby the actual world has its temporal passage to novelty' (1926: 90). In this respect, crucially, modern 'creativity' may be distinguished from the archaic notion of 'creation', (a term employed in English since the fourteenth century), which was primarily associated with '*the* Creation' in the Biblical Genesis by 'God the Creator' and then, from the late sixteenth century onwards, selectively extended to include more or less special people such as poets and artists. As we shall see, the 'creation/ creativity' distinction can still prove serviceable. But it easily gets blurred by the fact that the verb 'create' and the adjective 'creative' can refer to a vague mix of exclusively divine, narrowly artistic or broadly human capacities.

We still, however, need to establish a fuller and more flexible sense of what may be meant by – and equally importantly done with – the other item in the title: 'English'. For the fact is that this is a piece of writing *in* English *about* English and, like most academic work in the area, it is therefore a kind of 'meta-English'. This presents peculiar, often overlooked opportunities, especially if we take 'creativity' as a subject to be participated in and played around with, not just observed and worked out as an object. By way of demonstration as well as refined definition, what follows is a rewrite of the above extract from the 'Historical Explanation' of the 1933 edition of the *New English Dictionary on Historical Principles*. Here is how it might be re-cast now, in the early years of the twenty-first century, so as to highlight changes in the nature, status and perception of English since (the changes are highlighted in italics):

No one man's *or woman's or child's or machine's* English is all English. *Perhaps we had better talk of Englishes or processes of Englishing* [. . .] It is *indeed* not today what it was a century ago, still less what it will be a century hence. [. . .] And there is absolutely no defining line in any direction; the circle of the English language *perhaps had* a well-defined centre *but now it has many centres and intersecting spheres of influence (American and Australian and Caribbean, for instance, as well as those of the global media) and* no discernible circumference – *because this geometrical metaphor may need to be replaced by another (based on, say, open systems and evolving networks . . .).*

(from the General Explanations to the New English Dictionary on Historical Principles (subsequently Oxford English Dictionary),
1933: xxi–xxii as rewritten 2008)

The point of this rewrite is not in any way to suggest that the editors of the early edition of the *OED* were unusually prejudiced or lacking in prescience. Indeed, their words have a remarkably modern, almost 'postmodern' ring to them. Rather, the purpose is to explore, through experiment, a number of intricately interrelated issues: that what counts as 'English' may be differently conceived and conceptualised; that direct critique (critical-creative rewriting) can expose these issues differently, and in some respects more strikingly, than critical analysis alone (ideally one does both); and that therefore writing *in* English *on* English ('meta-English') presents creative opportunities as well as further grounds for critical reflection. The same applies to the theoretical interlude that follows.

5 RE-, 4 TRANS-, 3 INTER-, A COUPLE OF CO-, AND AN -ING!

This subheading started out as an alternative, slightly bizarre title for the chapter as a whole. Those bits of words are presented in this way so as to explore, as well as explain, how the topic of 'English and creativity' can be grasped in both active and analytical ways. In fact, it is the 'productive' or 'generative' – and in that sense 'creative' – capacity of those prefixes and that suffix that is being highlighted here. They stick out strangely: we usually meet them as 'bound' morphemes attached to a wide variety of word stems, some of which will be featured below. What's more, all these items are further 'foregrounded' by being ordered in a palpably playful, descending series: from an uncompromisingly numerical '5 Re-' through the casual colloquialism of 'a couple of Co-' to a singularly odd '-ing'. Each will be considered in turn, bearing in mind that all throw light on the nature of language in general and English in particular, as well as contributing to a working model of creativity.

RE- *is for repetition with difference.* It signals an iterative process in which things are done *afresh* not just again. The 5 Re- words featured here are: *Repetition* itself, which initially carried a core sense of re-petitioning, 'asking again', and balances *Response*, which still carries the sense of 'answering back' (and in the process perhaps prompting a further response in return). *Re-cognition* and *Re-vision* are another closely related pair, here hyphenated so as to highlight the possibilities of 're-thinking' and 're-seeing' what was first thought and seen otherwise. In the terms of a Russian Formalist such as Shklovsky or a German dramatist such as Brecht, their function is to 'defamiliarise' and 'make strange'. *Re . . . creation* is the fifth and fundamental term that underpins the others. It is a key concept here because it offers a frame for thinking of creativity as 'creation from something else' not 'creation from nothing' (*ex nihilo*). The suspension dots within the word are a graphic device designed to draw attention to the crucial gap that must be bridged, filled or fallen into – always afresh, never again – when seeking to move from what already is to what comes to be; from the old to the new; from what in some sense was already created to what will in some different sense be created otherwise. (For a related, somewhat different argument, see Pope 2005a: 84–90, 191–92, 278–79.)

TRANS- *means getting across*. 'Across' is what the Latin prefix means; its Greek equivalent is *Dia-*, as in dialogue ('across-word', of which more shortly). The first three of the 4 Trans-words featured here are: *Transition*, which focuses on the point of movement or development from one state or stage to another; *Transformation*, which emphasises change of form and, by extension, substance, metamorphosis (linguistically, it is associated with transformational-generative grammar and the name of Chomsky); and *Transaction*, which draws attention to the exchange, usually entailing some kind of change, involved in any sustained process of action and reaction (in conversation analysis it refers to what gets 'done' through a series of exchanges). The final and, again, foundational term in the present context is *Translation*. This refers not only to movement across distinct language barriers (e.g. English to Chinese, or vice versa – *inter*lingual translation) but also shifts and switches between different historical stages and different stylistic varieties of notionally 'the same language' (*intra*lingual translation; e.g. from Old to Modern English or from the discourses of a 1960s pop song to those of modern environmentalism, as discussed below). At its most capacious we can speak of 'translation' (including adaptation) between media: e.g. novel to film, song into book and exhibition (also examined below). Many of these dimensions of 'translation' are also embraced by *Dialogue* ('across-word', *dia-logos*), especially the Bakhtinian concept of 'dialogism'.[1]

INTER- *operates in the spaces between*. Whereas trans- emphasises 'across-ness', inter- emphasises 'between-ness' or 'among-ness'. There is a subtle yet significant difference. Of the many inter- words that might usefully be featured here, I shall concentrate on three: interplay, intertextuality and intervention. *Interplay* draws attention to the spaces for play between and among elements (words, people, objects, events): the 'room for manoeuvre' in flexing, stretching, bending – even breaking and re-making – the rules of whatever 'game' is perceived to be in play (see Cook 2000). *Intertextuality* operates in the spaces between texts. It depends on the fact that texts, like words, make sense in relation to one another (and two another and three another . . .). This means that a text, even a single word or part of a word (a prefix, for example), has many possible places and potential values – not just one – in whatever universe of discourse (or multiverse of discourses) are reckoned to be relevant and worth citing (sighting, siting). It goes *with* saying, then, that language is slippery stuff.

Intervention is the term offered here (and elsewhere) to designate the kind of deliberate invention that 'comes between' something as initially 'found' (a word, text or other object) so as to make it into something similar yet different: to see and say it 'otherwise'. It is where active reading may turn into textual transformation (see Pope 1995; Knights and Thurgar-Dawson 2006). Intervention is what might be called 'interplay with attitude' and, as far as texts are concerned, a kind of 'active intertextuality'. An example is the above updating and rewriting of the passage from the *OED*.

[A] couple of CO- is, I must admit, a frankly opportunist attempt to mention some of the many relevant words beginning with co- while observing a descending order from 5 to 1. For there are numerous terms sporting the prefix co- (including com- and con-, all of which derive from Latin *cum* meaning 'with', 'together') that might be featured here. *Co-operation* is the first of the pair. The hyphen is there by design: it emphasises 'operating *with*' and may or may not involve cooperation (usually without a hyphen) in the general sense of 'getting on with', 'agreeing to do'. Co-operation, in the present sense, recognises both positive and negative dimensions of 'operating with' someone or something else: *con*flict as well as *con*sensus; *com*petition and even *co*ercion (so you can attach it to whatever stem seems appropriate at the time). It therefore entails argument as well as agreement, power as well as pleasure, expressions of being 'with' and 'together' that may still carry traces of repression and oppression, kinds and degrees of inclusion that may still beg the question of who or what is still being excluded. For the fact is that creating something invariably involves un- and re-creating something else and, if not destroying it entirely, then at least de- and re-constructing it otherwise. These processes are reciprocally defining and ceaselessly ongoing. All of which finally bring us to . . .

-ING! This looks especially odd on its own but is remarkably productive when attached to all manner of stems (as in the penultimate two sentences in the paragraph above). It is the continuous/progressive participle and suggests ongoing and potentially open-ended process. When it comes to reconceptualising and reconfiguring notions of creativity (there go another two, along with a couple of re- and con- for good measure) the -ing is crucial. Crea*ting* emphasises the sense of process, of being in on the activity as it unfolds. It also leaves open the possibility of who or what may be the agent responsible at what stage, and can be used as a noun too (e.g. 'Creating is difficult'). All these grammatically versatile and conceptually volatile qualities of 'creating' are absolutely crucial when it comes to challenging and changing widespread assumptions about 'creativity'. As an uncompromisingly abstract noun, the latter tends to emphasise both the 'thing-ness' and the ideal generality of what it refers to. It cannot be used as a verb and, therefore, tends to suppress complications of agency, process and history. In this respect 'creativity' is like 'language' and 'literature' (both also abstract nouns), which are significantly different from such dynamic and complementary pairings as 'speaking/listening' and 'writing/reading'. The possibility of 'Englishing' as a productive alternative to 'English' is developed later in this chapter.

Con-verse-ation?

The fundamental distinction – and potential connection – between a modern, secular and inclusive conception of *creativity* and a traditional, religious, artistic and selective conception of *creation* is writ large in two significant and symptomatic studies that came out in the same year (2004): Ronald Carter's *Language and Creativity: The Art of Common Talk* and Derek Attridge's *The Singularity of Literature*. The first is concerned with conversation; the second with literature, chiefly poetry. Taken together, in how they differ as well as converge, they help to establish the dynamic for a kind of dialogue ('con-verse-ation'?) between linguistic creativity and literary creation.

Carter's *Language and Creativity*, as its subtitle suggests, offers an essentially 'common' conception of creativity grounded in everyday conversation: 'the art of talk'. It is premised on the proposition that 'linguistic creativity is not simply a property of exceptional people but an exceptional property of all people.' The emphasis is upon speakers – potentially all speakers – as 'language makers and not simply language users' (Carter 2004a: 13, 212). Above all, for Carter, the regular strategies of conversation are to do with kinds of interpersonal and topic-based 'convergence and divergence' and, formally, with 'pattern forming and re-forming'. These are recognised as 'creative' insofar as the conversation tends towards 'relationship building' and is expressed through the 'refreshing and transforming' of verbal resources.

An extended example of 'the art of common talk' (which we can only catch a flavour of here) is a long and involved conversation among three female students in shared accommodation in Wales (Carter 2004a: 6–9, 102–8). They are getting together over tea on a Sunday evening and there is much convivial talk about which cake or chocolate bar to have ('Speaker 2: Oh it's a toss up between the Cherry Bakewell . . . /Speaker 1 [laughs]/Speaker 2: . . . and the Mars bar isn't it'); about putting on weight ('S2: Miss paranoid about weight here. /S3 (from distance) Yeah. But you know. /S2: You're not fat Sue.'); and a particularly lively and humorous series of exchanges about the 'dangly bit' of an earring that appears to have 'fallen apart a bit' and so turned into 'Mobile earrings!'. The underlying creativity of this conversation, Carter maintains, is not just to do with the presence of figures of speech and play on words; these are the more obviously 'artful', potentially 'literary' aspects of language use which Carter prefers to see on a continuous 'cline of literariness' rather than as the property of some exclusive activity called 'literature'. Rather, what is fundamentally creative is the way in which the speakers deploy and share – in the present terms 'co-operate' through – these resources, and thereby reinforce and refresh their relationship. In short, the creativity is of a primarily interpersonal, dialogic and social kind. The analytical and theoretical apparatus that Carter brings to bear is selected accordingly: from conversation and discourse analysis, social psychology and anthropology in general and creativity research in particular (which tends to be framed by those working in social and cognitive psychology and education).

Such, then, is linguistic creativity in its 'common', especially conversational form.

Attridge's *The Singularity of Literature*, as its title suggests, takes a quite different tack, and over only partly overlapping verbal terrain. His focus is upon what makes responses to 'literature' (here chiefly poems and novels) 'singular', and his emphasis is upon 'creation' as a primarily aesthetic and ethical activity. How is it that notionally 'the same text' may keep on generating not just different reactions but freshly 'performed' responses, each of which is in some sense 'original' and therefore 'creative'. In this respect Attridge's book is itself a creative response to and continuation of what the author hails as the Kantian project of 'exemplary originality': the recognition that enduring work (in effect 'great literature') is perennially inspiring to others (Attridge 2004: 35–41). Attridge's key terms are 'event', 'performance', 'singularity' and 'alterity' ('otherness', dynamised as 'othering'); and his primary references are to contemporary literary and critical theory, especially aesthetics and ethics.

The substantial differences, as well as some subtle connections, between Carter's view of 'common' creativity in conversation and Attridge's view of 'singular' creation in literature can be illustrated by the latter's analysis of a single poem (Attridge 2004: 111–18). The poem in question is 'The Actual Dialogue' by the black South African writer Mongane Wally Serote, and it is built round a situation in which a black man hails a white man at night, in the darkest days of apartheid. This is how the poem begins (Serote 1974: 24):

Do not fear, Baas.
It's just that I appeared
And our faces met
In this black night that's like me.

What Attridge does is, in effect, 'stage' and 'perform' a critical reading which is alert to his own 'upbringing as a white male South African' and sensitive to the poem's haunting realisation of a potentially threatening yet also strangely heartening encounter. Both the dramatic power of the poem and the subtlety of the critical response turn on the fact that, from the first, the reader is put in the position of the white 'Boss' (Afrikaans 'Baas') who is being addressed out of the darkness on the road. He is – and by extension we are – told not to be afraid ('Do not fear, Baas') and yet he is – we are – also constantly reminded that this open reassurance (or veiled threat) is being issued 'In the night that's black like me' (a line that is repeated as a kind of refrain). The overall complexity of effect depends upon a number of dramatic, narrative and stylistic features often associated with more challenging kinds of literature: the dramatic indeterminacy of the initial situation; it is framing so as to offer the reader a privileged yet pressured subject position; the choice of identifying with the (black) 'I' who speaks, the (white) 'you' spoken to, or both; the power of figurative language (here simile, 'the night that's black like me') to generate ambiguity and atmosphere;

and the capacity of the repeated line to say the same thing but accumulate different meanings. In all these ways, a close and sensitive reading of Serote's poem confirms both the singularly 'creative' resources of the poem itself and, one may add, those of the person reading it.

Taken together, then, Carter's 'common' approach to conversational *creativity* and Attridge's 'singular' approach to literary *creation* give us a good sense of the main terms and issues in play. What they demonstrate, at the very least, is that, for anything like a full grasp of the present subject, we need to locate ourselves and our objects of study on a whole range of intersecting continua. In fact, we need a subtle and searching con-verse-ation across language–literature and reading–writing as complementary and reciprocally defining processes. We must also be alert to arts and poetics that extend beyond 'art' and 'poetry' narrowly conceived, and be prepared to recognise the points of difference as well as areas of overlap between traditional visions of creation and modern models of creativity. Further, I would add, we ought to grasp – actively and analytically – the richly critical–creative resources of our own academic and educational practices of reading and writing: to re-cognise the fact that we write *in* as well as *about* English, and that every occasion of (re)reading is also an opportunity for (re)writing. That brings us to the theory-in-practice of . . .

ENGLISHING CREATIVITIES, RE-CREATING ENGLISHES

This section heading is also offered by way of a provocation. It sounds sufficiently odd for some people to find grotesquely offensive and for others to find quirkily suggestive. Either way, in its defence it might be pointed out that 'Englishing' has been periodically available as a verb and noun for over 500 years, while 'englishes' (lower case and plural) has been a bone of contention for some 40 and the plural 'creativities' (usually tied in with 'multiple intelligences' – verbal, visual, kinetic, spatio-temporal and so on) has been around for somewhat longer. At any rate, it is hoped that this final section will help further to ground an approach to English and Creativity that is itself creative as well as critical: verbally dynamic and irreducibly heterogeneous. Theoretical and practical, too; for the commentaries draw liberally on the '5 Re-, 4 Trans-, 3 Inter-, a couple of Co-, and an -ing', and include questions as well as suggestions for further rewriting and response. In the course of reading you may come up with entirely different questions and suggestions.

OLD ENGLISH RIDDLE AND A MODERN ENGLISH TRANSLATION

Ic seah wrætlice   wuhte feower
samed siþian   swearte wæran lastas
swaþu swiþe blacu.   Swift wæs on fore
fuglum framra   fleag on lyfte
deaf under yþe.   Dreag unstille

winnende wiga   se him wegas tæcneþ
ofer fæted gold   feower eallum.

A marvel! I saw four figures
travelling together: their tracks were dark
the way very bright. One of them sped ahead:
lighter on the wing, it flew in the air
dived under the wave. Restlessly the leader
drew on and showed the way
over the ornamented gold to all four.

This is an Old English riddle in a tenth-century manuscript from Exeter cathe-dral (based on Mitchell and Robinson 2001: 238; the translation is mine). As this is a riddle, the first thing is to ask: what might it be? (For the usual solution, see note.[2]) A second question might be: how far does recognition of what is being referred to depend upon a re-cognition (re-thinking) of the tools and materials of writing at the time? More generally, is some measure of re-vision (seeing afresh, 'making strange') common to all texts we might call 'creative' (playful, imaginative) and do they always require an active response? Yet further ques-tions are naturally occasioned by the intertextual relations between these two texts and others: the second is just one of many possible translations – and there-fore transformations – of the former (e.g. *blacu* in the third line is a crux: it could mean a 'black' or 'bright' way; I chose the latter); the Anglo-Saxon riddle is itself an adaptation of a Latin riddle and therefore an intervention in the sense of being something both 'found' and deliberately '(re-)made'. Meanwhile, we are presented with the fact that the metrical resources of Old English verse featured heavy alliteration and stress, organised in more or less formulaic half-lines. The present translation catches a little of the flavour of this, but is otherwise (as is common in Modern English poetry) in free verse. These are issues that require us to engage in the interplay of – 'old-new' creativities as well as Englishes.

Re . . . creation. How would you make a riddle about, say, e-mailing, texting or blogging nowadays? What kinds and forms of English might it use, what clues might it give, and how might it prompt your reader/viewer/listener to re-cognise and re-vise their sense of the medium and the message?

ANSWERING BACK, CARRYING FORWARD . . .

Here are the opening lines of two poems both called 'This Be The Verse', the first by Philip Larkin (1974: 30) and the second a response to it by Carol Rumens (2007: 9):

They fuck you up, your mum and dad.
They may not mean to, but they do.

Not everybody's/Childhood sucked:
There are some kiddies/Not up-fucked.

Taken together, these two snippets of text represent a snatch of poetic dialogue between a man and a woman across time – a kind of 'con-verse-ation'. There are at least two closely interrelated things we can do with and to these texts, as with and to any texts:

1 *We can analyse and reflect* on the kinds of English and creative resources in play: the shock, for some people, of 'fuck . . . up' in Larkin's poem about children and parents; the witty inversion of 'Not up-fucked' in the response by Rumens; the differently balanced lines and rhymes of both; and so forth.
2 *We can also respond, critically and creatively*, with a couple of lines of our own: with our own reflections on childhood, parents and poetry; picking up and turning over some of these words as we see fit. Two such responses recently offered by my students began 'They fuck you up, your children . . . ' (Chris Thompson) and 'Why should people swear in verse/and sometimes worse?' (Katie Noah).

(Both poems in full – and many paired poems by other writers – can be found in Duffy 2007.)

Here are some lines from the last verse of Bob Dylan's 'A Hard Rain's A-Gonna Fall' (2007 [1963]: 10–13):

Oh, what'll you do now, my blue-eyed son?
Oh, what'll you do now, my darling young one?
I'm a-goin back out 'fore the rain starts a fallin',
I'll walk to the depths of the deepest black forest,
Where the people are many and their hands are all empty [. . .]
And I'll tell it and think it and speak it and breathe it [. . .]
And it's a hard, it's a hard, it's a hard, it's a hard,
It's a hard rain's a-gonna fall.

Analysing this for the kinds of English in play and creativity displayed requires recognition not only of the textual trace of 'the words' as such (dramatic structure, metaphorical density, alliteration, parallelism) but also of the highly distinctive qualities of Dylan's singing voice and solo acoustic guitar. A fuller understanding in terms of the context and moment of composition might then take into account the fact that, as Dylan recalled in an interview three years later, he wrote these words at the time of the Cuban Missile Crisis in 1962, partly in response to the threat of seemingly imminent annihilation by nuclear war between the USA and the Soviet Union; and perhaps especially the fact that 'The words came fast – very fast . . . Line after line, trying to capture the feeling of nothingness'.

Activating this for the kinds of English in play and creativity displayed through and in response to the text could take a quite different line – even while crossing with that (and those) above. It might, for instance, pick up on Dylan's observation that 'it doesn't really matter where a song comes from. It just matters where it takes you'. Most immediately and spectacularly, where that could take us now is to the book, exhibition and website called *Hard Rain: Our Headlong Collision with Nature* (Mark Edwards, lyric by Bob Dylan, London: Still Pictures Moving Words 2007; quotations are from here: 10–13; also see www.hardrainproject.com). This provides an image for each line of Dylan's song, a series of essays on contemporary global politics and ecology, an open forum and an ongoing programme for action.

Going yet further could be different again. It might involve choosing a song or piece of music that fascinates you and putting images and ideas, or other words and music, to it; co-operating with others in putting on a performance event or designing a website with links; or perhaps developing the whole thing along other lines entirely . . .

The implications of the texts and activities featured above obviously extend as far, and in as many directions and dimensions, as we care to push them. One possible conclusion, writ small in the earlier prefixes and their accompanying suffix, is that creativity in language involves many and constantly varying kinds of re . . . creation, translation, intervention and co-operation; it also means attending to – and preferably participating in – ongoing processes: -ing! Another possible conclusion, drawing on the review of work by Carter and Attridge, is that creating in language is at once an extremely 'ordinary' and 'extraordinary' matter – as 'common' as conversation and as 'singular' as literature. The precise emphasis may still depend on whether we prefer to talk of 'creativity' in broadly social and more or less inclusive terms or of 'creation' in specifically aesthetic and more or less exclusive ones.

Meanwhile, the subjects called 'English' span 'Language' and 'Literature' (often embracing Cultural Studies and Critical Theory) and continue to construct their objects of study very differently and through very different apparatuses. To take a couple of extremes: on one side, through Linguistics, English may claim to be an empirical social science; on another side, through Creative Writing, English may claim to be a practice-based art. And yet, ultimately – for all their differences of object, aim and methodology – both deal with language experientially as well as experimentally, and both engage in kinds of discovery and invention (see Currie 2002; Cook 2005; Wandor 2008). That is, in the terms of the present piece, they are intensely involved in 'recreating english' in their own images and discourses and, more often than not, 'englishing creativity' too (even if in the names of criticism)! So are we all, each in our own way. Each in our own way. The trick is to fully grasp we are doing it, to draw on all the resources at our disposal, and to engage with them (and one another) in a spirit of *serious play*. English *as* Creativity, for example.

NOTE

1 In Bakhtin's view, language is fundamentally dialogic: it always involves 'another's words in one's own language' and 'the utterance that is suspended between the speech that was and the speech that will be'. Because essentially dialogic, language requires a

high degree of 'response-ability/responsibility' in both speakers and listeners: the pun is central to Bakhtin's use of Russian *otvetsvenost* too, sometimes translated as 'answer-ability'. (For further discussion, see Maybin and Swann 2006: 418–24, 435–41 and Goodman and O'Halloran 2006: 436–37.)

2 A quill pen between two fingers and a thumb (hence 'four in all'), dipping in ink and writing in an illuminated manuscript.

7

'HEARTS AND MINDS'

PERSUASIVE LANGUAGE IN ANCIENT AND MODERN PUBLIC DEBATE

GUY COOK

This chapter will deal with persuasive language in contemporary public life, but begins with the past. The intention is first to establish broad categories, and second to see whether there is anything new about persuasive language in our own times.

Shakespeare's *Julius Caesar* was written over 400 years ago about events 1,00 years earlier, but its central event dramatises two approaches to persuasion still highly relevant today. The situation is as follows. Caesar's personal power has grown, and he is seen as a threat to Roman republicanism and democracy. (Similar concerns have been levelled in our day at leaders from Moscow to Harare and Islamabad.) A combination of public motives and private jealousies leads a group of senators to conspire against Caesar. They take decisive action and assassinate him, but do not plan fully for the aftermath of that violent action. (Again, there are plenty of modern parallels, such as the chaos which followed the 2003 invasion of Iraq.) They are unprepared for the power vacuum which follows Caesar's death, and the key role in it of persuasive language (or, as we might say, 'spin'). After the assassination, a 'multitude' gathers, 'beside themselves with fear'. The conspirators need to woo this 'plebeian' (i.e. public) opinion.

Two speeches to the crowd decide the course of events. The first is by Brutus, the most respected and influential of the conspirators, a man who would have had high ratings for trustworthiness in Roman opinion polls, had they existed. His support has been energetically canvassed by the other conspirators to give their plot credibility and he has apparently acted out of genuine concern for the public interest rather than jealousy or personal interest.

Brutus adopts a particular strategy to win over the crowd. His speech is calm, balanced and factual. He lists Caesar's vices, but also his virtues. He gives reasons for and against the murder, explaining why, when he weighed them up, he decided regretfully to join the conspiracy.

> As Caesar loved me, I weep for him; as he was fortunate, I rejoice at it; as he was valiant, I honour him: but, as he was ambitious, I slew him. There is tears for his love; joy for his fortune; honour for his valour; and death for his ambition.

The crowd listen respectfully to this measured prose, and seem reassured, though there is a gasp when Caesar's protégé Mark Antony appears during Brutus' speech bearing Caesar's bloody corpse.

The second speech is by Mark Antony, left alone with the crowd. Brutus has given permission for this out of a sense of fair play, on condition only that Antony shall not 'blame us', but this proves a fatal mistake. He adopts a quite different approach, and his speech is presented in resonant rhythmic verse. He begins with the famous, apparently democratic opening of 'Friends, Romans, countrymen, lend me your ears', professes understanding of the killers' motives, and praises Brutus as 'an honourable man'. But he is also apparently distraught, so overcome with grief for Caesar that he breaks off at one point to weep.

> Bear with me,
> My heart is in the coffin there with Caesar,
> And I must pause till it come back to me.

Then, gradually, skilfully, eloquently, with vivid and emotive imagery, he turns both his meaning and the crowd around, while at the same time denying his intention to do so, talking, as modern politicians do, about influencing 'hearts and minds': a phrase now used in the wars 'against terrorism' and in Iraq.

> O masters, if I were disposed to stir
> Your hearts and minds to mutiny and rage,
> I should do Brutus wrong, and Cassius wrong,
> Who, you all know, are honourable men:
> I will not do them wrong; I rather choose
> To wrong the dead, to wrong myself and you,
> Than I will wrong such honourable men.

Thus 'honourable' comes to mean the opposite of what it did, and the word here lends itself to a heavily sarcastic intonation. Antony has agreed with Brutus not to blame the conspirators for what has happened – and he sticks, literally, cunningly, to the letter of this agreement.

Antony has more than words in his persuasive armoury however; his tactics are visual as well as verbal – 'multimodal' as we would call them in English Studies today. He makes good use of his props: his own grief-stricken appearance, Caesar's bleeding body, and lastly a mysterious document which he waves at the crowd (rather as Chamberlain did after meeting Hitler in Munich) but without actually showing anybody what it contains. It is supposedly Caesar's will, making lavish legacies to the people of Rome. By adding this appeal to greed, he has the crowd now completely in his hands. Brutus and his accomplices are forced to flee. Antony and his allies take power. The persuasive power of emotion has triumphed over reason. We cannot tell whether Antony's tears for Caesar are sincere or not, but from the point of view of successful persuasion, this matters less than how they are used.

These two speeches encapsulate two opposite approaches to persuasion and two ways of relating to an audience. One strategy is to set out, as clearly and objectively as possible, the evidence and the reasons for holding a point of view, but to let the audience decide. It implies an optimistic, respectful view of public opinion, though it can be open to charges of smugness and political naivety. The other strategy is an appeal to emotion and self-interest, clouding the listeners' judgment and reason, and skilfully manipulating them into agreement, while all the time professing the opposite,

> O judgment! thou art fled to brutish beasts,
> And men have lost their reason.

and denying its own artistry

> I am no orator, as Brutus is,
> But as you know me all a plain blunt man

This second strategy implies a lack of respect and a low opinion of its audience, seeing them as ignorant, uncritical, and easily swayed, but can be presented by its proponents as realistic and necessary.

The contrast of these two speeches reflects categorisations of rhetoric which were widely accepted in both Caesar's and Shakespeare's time. Aristotle's *Art of Rhetoric* distinguishes three strategies of persuasion: reasoned proof (*logos*), emotional appeal (*pathos*) and appeal to the good reputation of the speaker (*ethos*). He speaks also of three styles of rhetoric: the grand, the middle and the plain; and of three purposes: to judge past events (as in law courts), to decide future events (as in government) or for ceremony (as in, for example, speeches at weddings and funerals). These categories are well illustrated by Brutus and Antony. Both seek to influence the opinion and behaviour of the crowd and both rely on their own good reputations. Brutus, however, attempts reasoned proof, while Antony appeals to emotion. While Brutus speaks in a grand style, Antony affects that of a 'plain, blunt man' – though his speech is in fact very carefully crafted. Brutus deliberates on what has happened, and urges the crowd to support him. Antony appears to be speaking only ceremonially, but turns his funeral oration into an incitement.

These events in the Roman forum provide a particularly clear model of political debate: two rival points of view, two related styles of oratory, an audience which chooses between them, and immediate consequences. We can use this Brutus/Antony dichotomy, and the categories of classical rhetoric they illustrate, as a model to describe contemporary persuasion, showing how any actual instance draws upon one or the other, identifying different elements with one style or another. We can also ask whether techniques of persuasion have changed, and whether there is anything distinctive about them in our own time.

The forms of contemporary persuasion are many and various and – superficially at least – very different from those of the past. They have adopted new media as they have appeared – photography, film, computers, Internet, mobile technologies – and appear in very different contexts from the Roman market-place. There seems little in common indeed between the speeches of a Brutus or an Antony and such modern acts of persuasion as an Internet pop-up seeking our credit card for an online purchase, a glossy university brochure with sunny lawns and smiling pretty faces, or the styled ways in which service personnel in retail outlets and call centres talk as though they had no greater concern in life than our welfare and well-being. Professional persuasion is probably more prevalent than ever before, and increasing – inevitably so in societies where political and market power depends upon popular choice. The study of rhetoric and persuasion is still thus very much alive, and has benefited from the insights of contemporary linguistics into how the systems of language (sounds, words, grammar) interact with each other and with the context of their use to achieve rhetorical effects. Thus, in recent decades, there has been a wealth of linguistic analysis of prominent persuasive genres. These include advertising (Leech 1966; Vestergaard and Schrøder 1985; Cook 1992, 2001, 2007; Myers 1994, 1999; Forceville 1996; Goddard 1998; Simões Lucas Freitas 2008), public relations (Swales and Rogers 1995; Mautner 2005) political rhetoric and media language (Fairclough 2000; Silberstein 2002; Koller 2004) and 'service speak' (Cameron 2000).

It is not possible in this short chapter to cover all of these areas – the reader is advised to follow up the references above. What the rest of this chapter does, however, is to look at persuasion around one very particular topic – namely food.[1] Though this may seem an odd choice, it is one which neatly focuses the issues in the study of contemporary rhetoric, for those whose business is to persuade us what to eat use both the most contemporary media and the most ancient of techniques. Food, moreover, is a topic prominently treated across different discourses, from marketing, to politics, journalism and science. Of these, marketing is our first focus, as it has been said with some justification (Fairclough 1993) that in contemporary society, everything – from political ideology to education to health to relationships to 'success' and happiness – is treated as an item for sale.

So let us move forward now 2000 years to an apparently very different forum: food packaging in a modern supermarket. Here too are voices with strong points of view, setting out to influence the opinion and behaviour of the populace, and they do so with a host of arguments. Save money! Be healthy! Lose weight! Indulge yourself! Impress your friends! Promote fair trade! Be kind to animals! Protect the environment! There are obvious differences between packages and speeches of course, which may make this comparison appear initially ridiculous. This is trade rather than politics, the domain of the Shakespearean clown rather than hero, and the subject matter is altogether more every day: literally the price of eggs rather than the future of an empire. Also, the mode is writing, rather than speech, so there is no recourse to the cadence of the voice or gestures of the speaker; conversely, there are aspects of packages, as tangible and visible objects, which are unavailable in speech: pictures, colouring, texture, layout, fonts and position in the store.

The mundanity of food as a topic is only apparent however. Food production, distribution and retail is humanity's biggest activity, and decisions about it are of immense consequence in every dimension of our lives, affecting not only our environment, health, and cultural identity, but also our political processes. On contemporary food issues there is a division of opinion, quite as sharp as traditional political distinctions between democracy and autocracy, or left and right. On the one hand are those who favour intensive chemical-aided production and a globalised distribution system, claiming that this is the only realistic way to feed the world; on the other hand are those who favour more localised and less industrialised production, arguing that this is fairer, more practical, and environmentally and socially beneficial. Both sides adduce powerful, apparently reasonable, arguments; both can appeal to our emotions and self-interest. Significantly for our analysis, they also need to have public support, and therefore, like Brutus and Antony, to carry public opinion with them. Indeed, persuasion is an intrinsic part of democracy, and it is no coincidence that rhetoric and democracy both originated in the same period of Greek history (Vickers 1988). Yet the sphere of public influence is perhaps shifting away from traditional political institutions. With food, as with many of the most significant developments in contemporary human life, what happens is the sum of individual choices and actions, rather than grand decisions by those in power, and the sum of our individual shopping choices may have more effect on the future, than the way we vote in elections (Tormey 2007) – making developments in Walmart, Tesco or LeClerc more significant than those in the White House, Westminster or Versailles.

Let us look then at how those with an interest in promoting one food policy or another pursue their aims.

PATHOS: POETRY AND STORIES, IMAGES AND INTIMACY

On the small surface of a food package, many different discourses are brought together – law, retail, health, nutrition and gastronomy – all or any of which may influence the potential purchaser. There is obligatory factual information about weight, ingredients, nutrition, expiry, storage, place of origin, manufacturer and – optionally – preparation. These factual descriptions tend, however, to be smaller and less prominent than the flamboyant appeals to the consumer which accompany the product description, using poetic and emotive language and appealing to the purchasers' self-interest. (I use the word 'poetic' here, following Jakobson 1960, to refer to any language use which focuses attention on the form of the message.) This tends to be the case across the range of available foods. Thus, though there may be sharp division in the politics of food, there is little difference in the way rival agricultures are marketed – rather as there is little difference in the rhetoric of opposed political parties, or the advertising campaigns of rival products.

Take, for example, the description of *Waitrose Organic 12 English Pork Chipolatas*. The packet is pastel grey with line drawings of happy pigs among oak leaves and acorns. On the front, we read:

> Waitrose organic Chipolatas are made from selected cuts of belly and shoulder of pork from organically reared, English pigs. The pork is coarsely chopped and blended with herbs and spices to produce succulent and full flavoured chipolatas. Our organic pigs are reared outside with freedom to root and roam on selected farms in Norfolk and Lincolnshire.

and on the back

> James Keith supplies Waitrose exclusively, with pigs from his farm in Norfolk. The pigs are reared outdoors throughout their lives in small family groups and fed on a balanced cereal diet with vitamins and minerals. Warm shelters and straw bedding protect them from winter, while mud baths keep them cool in summer. James' expertise, care and commitment to the more extensive nature of organic farming ensures we deliver consistently high quality and traceable sausages.

Though this is factual (and correct) information, it is phrased and presented in a way to appeal to readers' emotions, with intimations of exclusivity (*selected* (twice), *exclusively*), culinary expertise (*coarsely chopped and blended*), self-indulgence (*succulent and full flavoured*), nationalism (*English, Norfolk, Lincolnshire*). The language is extravagant, with alliterative phrasing (*full flavoured, root and roam, care and commitment*) and sensual tactile imagery (*mud baths, warm shelters*). In addition, the accountability of the supermarket (*we deliver consistently high quality and traceable sausages*) is complemented by the personal touch of the small business run by a named individual in which animals are treated almost as humans (*family groups, bedding* and *baths*). In addition, the narrative alternates between impersonal third person (*Waitrose organic Chipolatas are made from*) and more intimate first person (*our organic pigs, we deliver*) as though the reader were engaged face to face in a friendly chat with the retailer, as they might be in a local shop or market stall. The whole creates a friendly but powerful message, a bucolic image of a rural idyll, calculated to appeal to an urban market.

Nor is the persuasive technique only verbal. Like Antony, the writers of such packages know how to exploit all available modes. When questioned in interviews, they are much less preoccupied with language than with such matters as colour schemes, the feel of the packet, the visibility of the product through a cellophane panel or the positioning in store (Cook *et al.* 2007). This is not just language, but language as part of an embodied experience (Scollon and Scollon 2003).

In marketing of this kind, the tone and language is personal, poetic, vague, narrative, emotional and sensual. In these ways marketing, like political rhetoric, seeks to present a one-sided view and to omit or downplay any counterarguments. Packages do not mention the disadvantages of their contents unless obliged to do so (*SMOKING KILLS*, or *can aid slimming only as part of a calorie controlled diet*). Politicians do not express any doubts about their policies, or discuss problems to which they do not have a sure-fire solution. Even where manufacturers are bound by law to list harmful ingredients, for example, they may find ways to fulfil the letter of this obligation, while simultaneously dishonouring its spirit – rather as Antony honoured his promise not to blame the conspirators for their action. Thus, children's sweets containing harmful additives (such as Aspartame, Quinoline Yellow, Sunset Yellow FCF, Ponceau 4R) often name them only by their European codes (E951, E110, E104, E124), print them in tiny letters against transparent wrapping cluttered among translations into several languages and fold this part of the label inwards – making them difficult to find, or if found to read or, if read, to interpret.

The partisan, poetic, emotive and factually selective approach to persuasion is not only the province of commercial marketing. It permeates public relations (PR) in our society, and is embraced by non-commercial as well as commercial organisations (Moloney 2006). In an age where marketing assumptions dominate even the PR materials of universities supposedly committed to rational evidence-based enquiry (Mautner 2005), it is tempting to believe that there is perhaps nothing which falls outside this general approach to promotion – nothing which belongs, as it were, to Brutus rather than to Antony. There are, however, exceptions to this general tendency: discourses which aspire to avoid subjective bias, to present evidence on both sides as clearly and precisely as possible, to put their audience in the best position possible to consider and verify any claims. Certain approaches to journalism are of this kind, though by no means all, and even those with most integrity can never eliminate bias completely. So too are legal processes, in aspiration if not always in actuality. Even party politics is in principle an institution allowing the balanced presentation of two sides of a case for consideration by an electorate. The pre-eminent instance of aspiring to disinterested and dispassionate rational consideration of evidence, however, is science. Indeed, according to the philosopher Karl Popper (Popper 1972), 'good' science should test itself, as Brutus did, by constantly trying to overturn its own claims – something quite alien to advertising, marketing, PR or political propaganda.

Such at least is the principle. In practice, the distinction between partisan and disinterested discourse is more complex. Let us turn now to how science is used in contemporary persuasion.

APPEALS TO *LOGOS*: SCIENTIFIC EVIDENCE

The prestige of science is frequently enlisted in contemporary persuasion, for example, by politicians, journalists and advertisers and, as such, deserves special mention. This too can be well illustrated from food promotion where promotional material for certain product types regularly uses scientific facts and evidence. A packet of *Kellogg's Special K* cereal, for example, reports a scientific study conducted by 'a leading university' to see if eating this cereal twice a day would reduce participants' weight:

> 94 volunteers took part. All 5 body parts were significantly reduced, with the greatest reduction from the waist. 35% lost greater than 1 inch from the waist. Waist: hip ratio was reduced by 1.4%.

A pictured group of smiling women seem to testify to this success. But though science is used here, it is alluded to rather than presented in a way which can be assessed. In addition, there is some tension between the use of language in science and the chatty style of cereal packaging. The phrase *significantly reduced* which has a particular meaning in statistics, or *all 5 body parts*, which has a particular meaning in anatomy, are likely to be interpreted conversationally in quite a different way.

Such 'scientific' claims, however, especially where they relate to health, are tightly regulated by law. For this reason all those using them for persuasion must tread very carefully indeed. This is why, in the case of food, copywriters may prefer to focus upon subjective qualities such as 'succulence', and conclusions are often left to be inferred rather than directly stated – whether the women in the picture, for example, are the ones who took part in the experiment.

An illustration of the deployment of science in persuasion is provided by the debate over GM crops and food. Two major issues in this debate are matters for scientific enquiry: whether GM crops are dangerous for wildlife and the environment (Defra 2003; Firbank *et al.* 2003) and whether GM food poses any hazard for human health (Smith 2003). Yet the debate also raises ethical, political, philosophical, cultural and aesthetic issues not susceptible to scientific analysis: the implications of globalisation for political processes (both within and between countries), the relation of humanity to the natural world, the social and psychological impact of technological change, the religious and philosophical implications of new scientific knowledge, the growing power of corporations and the safeguarding of traditional farming and cuisine. As such, it brought a variety of interested parties into conflict, each with their own incommensurable discourses and ideas. Yet, despite this variety, as the conflict intensified, both sides in the debate sought to present it as wholly scientific and to claim that the evidence was on their side.

In a speech on British Science, for example, the (then) British Prime Minister, Tony Blair, used his own peculiarly personalised narrative style to recount how

> [t]he idea of making this speech has been in my mind for some time. The final prompt for it came, curiously enough, when I was in Bangalore in January. I met a group of academics, who were also in business in the biotech field. They said to me bluntly: Europe has gone soft on science; we are going to leapfrog you and you will

miss out. They regarded the debate on GM here and elsewhere in Europe as utterly astonishing. They saw us as completely overrun by protestors and pressure groups who used emotion to drive out reason. And they didn't think we had the political will to stand up for proper science.

(Blair 2002)

But although these words purport *to stand up for proper science*, they have, in our taxonomy of persuasive rhetoric, far more of the Antony about them than the Brutus, more *pathos* than reasoned proof. The argument is personalised and attributed to unnamed informants (thus skilfully making the argument someone else's rather than his own). And many things are left deliberately vague in a way quite alien to scientific precision. It is not clear who these informants are, nor why they are regarded as so authoritative, nor to whom exactly the 'we' they criticise refers or why opponents of GM in Britain are somehow outsiders. (Within the COBUILD corpus,[2] the word *overrun* usually collocates with enemy armies or pests.) There are classic poetic uses of rhetorical language too, such as the alliterative *soft on science, protestors and pressure groups*, and the 'triplet' structure 'They said . . . They regarded. . . . They saw' broken by 'And they didn't think. . . . '. We may wonder who exactly it is who uses 'emotion to drive out reason'.

This example illustrates how the invocation of science in contemporary persuasion is not necessarily as rational and disinterested as it may claim. (For more detailed discussion see Cook 2004.) Such developments should raise concerns about the role of persuasive language in a democracy and the need to protect discourses in which balanced and disinterested debate is institutionalised – but constantly threatened. Just as law can become politicised in Stalinist or McCarthyite show trials, or the press suborned when owned by politically partisan media magnates, so science can be perverted when enlisted in a particular commercial or political 'cause'.

ETHOS: CELEBRITY, PERSONALITIES AND POLICIES

The GM debate also illustrates two common features endemic in contemporary politics. The first is a loss of trust in those – such as scientists, business leaders and elected politicians – who should be able to speak with authority (Cook *et al.* 2006). The second problem is that many key issues in contemporary policy (e.g. nuclear power, stem cell research, nanotechnology, genetic screening and DNA evidence) involve technical arguments which not everyone is capable of assessing. These are major, and growing, problems for contemporary democracies.

When arguments cannot be trusted or followed, the audience may revert to making a judgment of the source. Assessment focuses less on the *message* and more on the *messenger*. In daily life, this is not an unreasonable strategy. We cannot verify everything for ourselves. We *believe* something because we *believe in* the person who tells us of it.

This reasonable tactic, however, is very easily exploited. Advertisers frequently put their words in the mouths of trustworthy characters who speak on their behalf (a tactic Tony Blair used too, we may note!). Classic advert characters are dentists, grandmothers, honest yokels, friendly neighbours, forthright friends, who may vouch for the merits of toothpastes, pasta sauces, loaves, washing powders, deodorants and so on (Cook 2001: 94). One variety of this shift from message to speaker as a source of persuasion in advertising is the use of celebrity endorsements – where it little matters what the speaker says, provided they are someone the hearer trusts, or wishes to emulate. (This seems to work, though not much acumen is required to realise that the celebrity probably does not use the product and only says they do for money.) This trust of celebrities extends beyond advertising too, and may be indicative of a need for authority figures to fill a vacuum in public life.

The effect of such individual authority can be found in another British debate over food (this time over the quality of school meals), and the intervention into this debate of celebrity chef Jamie Oliver. In a series of only four TV programmes Jamie Oliver was shown lambasting current policy, while taking over and improving the catering in a primary school, within a tight budget. So successful were these programmes, that within weeks the reform lobby was in the ascendant, government policy and provision were radically reformed, and school food quality improved throughout the nation. Where an army of nutritionists, academics, educationalists and parent groups had failed, a relatively uneducated 30-year-old chef had succeeded. This was, in other words, an outstanding example of successful persuasion. How did it work?

Like Antony ('I am no orator, as Brutus is, / But as you know me all, a plain blunt man'), Jamie Oliver denies his own persuasive skills and presents himself as a man of the people, saying for example:

> I was . . . secretly I was quite stressed about it, oh, the last two weeks.
> Haven't been sleeping properly the last week just . . .
> didn't know what the kids would be like,
> didn't know what the head mistress was going to be like,
> didn't know what Nora was going to be like.
> So now lovely, got my bit, now I can get on with it, I can be a normal
>   bloke.

His language too, including frequent swearing, reinforces the same image, and he talks to his audience with the grammar and diction of a colloquial harangue. His is the plain style, in Aristotelian terms, and he frequently asserts his own lack of education:

> why the bloody hell does the government not see it like that? . . . Even if a
> raving idiot (which I was at school) does the sums you can see that putting
> money in NOW is the way forward. . . .

Yet his use of language is in fact anything but unskilled: as shown by the rhetorical triplet with its rhythm and parallelism in the first of these quotations ('didn't know what . . . ' X 3). And just as this multimillionaire superstar is very far from being the 'normal bloke' of his persona, so his rhetorical style is far from the artless spontaneity it claims for itself. His authority derives partly from his reputation as a cook, but also relies on a charismatic presence in which everything about him – manner, appearance, humour – marks him out as an alternative to established authority.

His success is a classic example of *ethos*, the third type of rhetoric in Aristotle's tripartite scheme, in which persuasion is achieved through the character and credibility of the speaker.

CONCLUSION AND AN EVALUATION

This chapter has explored opposite tendencies in contemporary persuasion. On the one hand, it has illustrated continuity with the past, showing how the rhetorical features identified by Aristotle and dramatised by Shakespeare are still very much with us today. On the other hand, it has hinted at some new departures, or at least new emphases, which make contemporary rhetoric distinctive.

In pursuit of continuity, we have looked in particular at: argument by appeal to emotion (*pathos*), argument which uses – or appears to use – reason (*logos*), and argument by appeal to personality (*ethos*). Typically, arguments by *pathos* use vague and poetic language, storytelling and imagery, and rely, at the same time, heavily upon modes of communication other than words – such as gesture, props and voice quality in speech; pictures, colour and texture on objects such as packaging. Though there is nothing intrinsically wrong with such uses of language – indeed they are positive qualities in genres such as poetry, song and storytelling – there are reasons to be concerned when they influence personal or political decision-making about matters of consequence, such as the choice between democracy and autocracy in Ancient Rome, or public opinion on crime or health or the environment – or the choice of food (and its production and distribution) – in our own time. The issue is not one of absolute value but of confusion of genre and purpose, as when the techniques of poetry are used to persuade rather than to delight. Exploitation of such confusion is further illustrated by the merger of factual evidence and reason (*logos*) – of the kind offered by science – with both emotional argument and persuasive intent. Interwoven with these techniques, whether in packages, political speeches or TV programmes, is argument by *ethos*, and the affectation of a plain 'man of the people' style, most notably in the role of celebrity in contemporary persuasion. Perhaps our own time would benefit from greater awareness of the clear categories of classical rhetorical theory as a safeguard against such insidious confusion. Yet, as Antony's speech illustrates, there is nothing new about the persuasive merger of genre boundaries in the manipulation of a gullible audience.

NOTES

1 The analysis draws upon a series of research projects on persuasion in debates over food policy (Cook 2004; Cook *et al*. 2004, 2006, 2007, 2008).
2 COBUILD sampler www.collins.co.uk/Corpus/Corpus Search.aspx accessed 11 July 2008.

8

COMPUTER-MEDIATED ENGLISH

BRENDA DANET

Internet technologies have generated a variety of relatively new textual means of communication, many of which have become an integral part of everyday life for hundreds of millions, and which are challenging the literacy practices of print culture. These new modes include asynchronous, person-to-person, private e-mail and one-to-many postings to Listservs, discussion forums, Usenet, and blogs (weblogs), as well as synchronous text-based chat (e.g. Internet Relay Chat), instant messaging (ICQ, Yahoo! Instant Messenger), and graphical modes incorporating typed asynchronous and synchronous text (Second Life, Active Worlds).[1] These new modes of writing have spawned an academic specialty among linguists, sociologists, anthropologists, and communication researchers of 'interactive written discourse' (Ferrara *et al.* 1991), 'electronic language' (Collot and Belmore 1996), 'Netspeak' (Crystal 2006), or, most commonly, *computer-mediated communication* (CMC).[2]

Compared to speech and to pre-digital writing, digital writing is, paradoxically, *both doubly attenuated* (diminished) *and doubly enhanced* (Figure 8.1).[3] Digital text is attenuated because it lacks materiality. Printing of digital files is optional. E-book devices like Amazon's Kindle challenge our deep-seated attachment to the physical attributes of books (Danet 1997). Because online textual communication is dynamic, interactive, and ephemeral, we often experience it as speech-like. Yet, compared to speech, it is also attenuated, since the non-verbal and paralinguistic cues that accompany speech are missing.

At the same time, online writing is also doubly enhanced. Unlike speech, it leaves traces, which can be reread and studied, as long as the file is open. In real-time modes online writing is enhanced, compared to material-based writing, since it restores the presence of one's interlocutor, absent or even long dead, in the case of manuscript and print texts.[4]

Many researchers who have written about computer-mediated 'communication' were, in fact, writing about computer-mediated *English*. Authors whose native language is English published in English about communication online in English by participants who were generally native speakers. Exceptions are books by Naomi Baron (2000, 2008) and David Crystal (2006), both of whom

	"speech"	"writing"
Attenuated	absence of non-verbal cues	loss of text as object
Enhanced	ability to re-examine utterance	restoration of presence of interlocutor

Figure 8.1 The paradoxical nature of digital communication (from Danet 2001: 12).

explicitly contextualize English-based online linguistic phenomena within the history of the English language.

English is the de facto lingua franca of the Internet, not only because of American political hegemony and the dominance of world English in science, business, and diplomacy, but also because the technologies that make the Internet possible were invented in the 1960s and 1970s in the United States (Hafner and Lyon 1996). At the same time, as these technologies have spread around the world, and have become more advanced, the Internet has become heavily multilingual. Among 1.2 billion people online since 2006 (Almanac 2007) – a remarkable one-sixth of the world's population – hundreds of millions are communicating in languages other than English, or in non-native varieties of English, or both (Danet and Herring 2003, 2007a, 2007b; Wright 2004). By fall 2004, native speakers of English constituted only a little over one-third of world Internet users (Figure 8.2). In this chapter, I will discuss computer-mediated English of both native and non-native speakers.

Total: 801.4 million

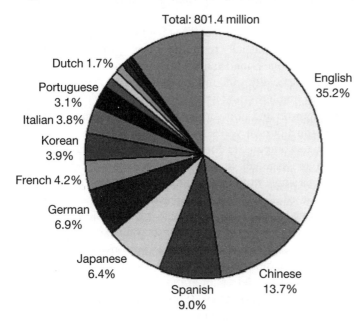

Figure 8.2 Online language populations, September 2004. Source: Global Internet Statistics (by language), http://www.glreach.com/globstats/index.php3 (accessed 1 April, 2008).

DISTINCTIVE FEATURES OF COMPUTER-MEDIATED ENGLISH

An extensive body of research has identified many distinctive linguistic and discourse-level features of computer-mediated English, only some of which can be discussed in this brief, introductory overview. Table 8.1 lists some of the most commonly noted features, together with examples. This list reflects the fact that

Table 8.1 Some common features of computer-mediated English

Feature	Examples
Multiple punctuation	Type back soon!!!!!!
Eccentric, non-standard spelling	Type back sooooon!!!!!! Warez (wares)
All capital letters	I'M REALLY ANGRY AT YOU!
All lower-case	he told me that mary is coming for christmas.
Acronyms, abbreviations	BRB (be right back); TTYL (talk to you later); bf (boyfriend)
Descriptions of actions	*grins* <grins>
Emoticons	:-) (smile) ;-) (wink) :-((frown)
Rebus writing	CUl8tr (see you later)
Asterisks for emphasis	I'm *really* angry at you!
Written-out laughter	hahahaha

CMC has a strong tendency to be informal and *playful*: typists play with spelling, typography, and identity. As in real-world playful performance, CMC tends to invite special attention to the form of the message (Bauman 1992). This is especially true of chat modes, which partially resemble forms of oral performance, but even sometimes of one-to-one e-mail and postings to asynchronous groups.[5]

Multiple punctuation, especially exclamation points, the use of asterisks framing selected words for emphasis, and written-out laughter heighten expressivity, mimicking paralinguistic and non-verbal features of speech. Comic-like descriptions of actions, third-person verbs or nouns bracketed in asterisks or angle brackets, attempt to compensate for visual information lacking in the written text. Writing a message all in capitals is generally understood as shouting, though marking a single word in all capitals just emphasizes it. A norm discouraging extensive use of all capitals crystallized in early hacker culture, long before communicating online became a mass phenomenon (Raymond 1996).[6] The converse, all lower-case, occurs in contexts where speed of typing is the thing, though for younger generations, lower-case and non-standard spelling are a form of playful transgression (Sebba 2003a), signaling membership in online culture. Rebus writing, using letters or graphic symbols to indicate words or syllables, as in 'CU' for 'see you', is not new. It too combines considerations of efficiency with signaling in-group membership.

Perhaps the best known feature of CMC is emoticons ('emotion icons') or 'smileys'. Viewed with the head tilted toward one's left shoulder, these clusters of typographic symbols mimic smiles, winks, frowns, and other facial and full-body expressions.

:-) (smile)   ;-) (wink)   :-((frown)

The basic idea was proposed by Scott Fahlman (n.d.) in 1982. While entire compilations exist (Godin 1993), only a very few are actually in use, notably the basic smile, frequently used in chat and instant messaging.

E-MAIL

Specific modes of computer-mediated English have distinctive structural or discourse-level features. The memo-like structure of e-mail (private e-mail, postings to groups) was inspired by the intra-organizational printed memorandum, a late nineteenth century/early twentieth century development (Yates 1989: 95). Anglo-American tradition distinguishes between the templates of the business letter and the informal or personal letter. There are countervailing forces in today's e-mail. Its ostensibly formal memo-like structure may seem strange, at least to initiates, if one is just telling a sibling about grandma's visit. At the same time, the general tendency toward informality and playfulness invites deviation from the business letter template (Danet 2001: Chap. 2; Gimenez 2000). Messages are often knowingly or unknowingly unedited, not only for spelling or typography but also for syntax (Baron 1998). Even in business or professional communication there is considerable variability in e-mail openings and closings, ranging from the conventionally formal to the most informal, or their omission.

A distinctive feature of e-mail is the tendency to cite all or part of a previous message, or even a series of messages. In many e-mail programs, hitting the reply button replicates the entire message received. The main function of citations is to provide context for the current message, since one may not remember the contents of a previous message to the sender (Eklundh and Macdonald 1994). Citations are common in international business communication (Gimenez 2006) and in one-to-many communication, where multiple topics or 'threads' are discussed. While citations may sometimes prevent misunderstanding and flaming,[7] sudden intense conflict (Tanskanen 2001), in other contexts rapidly proliferating multiple citations are an indication of escalating conflict (Danet forthcoming).

INSTANT MESSAGING

Instant messaging (IM) is synchronous, permitting instant communication with a person who is also online.[8] This technology blossomed in the late 1990s. A 2004 survey found that more than four in ten online Americans used IM (Shiu and Lenhart 2004). By 2005 half of UK online consumers used IM; usage was ubiquitous among young consumers (van Kruijsdijk 2005), as in the United States. Moreover, it is increasingly used in the workplace too.

Research on the language of IM thus far has produced conflicting findings. In a study of workplace IM, messages were informal, and used relaxed grammar and spelling (Nardi *et al.* 2000). Yet Baron (2008) found that misspellings and abbreviations were largely absent in IM messages sent by American college students. She concluded that, despite certain resemblances of messages to speech, this generation largely transferred writing habits learned in school-based literacy to IM. Lewis and Fabos (2005) reached a partially similar conclusion in a case study of the IM practices of seven American teenagers.

Abbreviations were lacking, and there was concern for standard spelling. The researchers claim that message features demonstrate digital literacy – cultivation of narrative strategies to generate interesting, flowing conversation, and creative uses of language. Canadian IM users thought of the IM window as a space for slang, and were aware of switching to an informal register when doing so (Spatafora 2008). Similarly, American teenagers apparently do not perceive online communication as 'writing' (Lenhart *et al.* 2008).

In recent years IM and SMS (short message service on mobile phones), also known as text messaging or texting, have begun to converge. Teens tend to use both (Lenhart *et al.* 2007). It is increasingly possible to receive IM messages on a cell phone, and to send an SMS message online. SMS, however, is asynchronous. To what extent do these relatively short, one-to-one messages resemble each other?

While it is possible to send relatively long messages in IM, generally in 'chunked' serial transmissions (Baron 2008: 55), SMS messages may contain only up to 160 characters, including spaces. Despite this difference, the features of SMS apparently resemble those of IM. In a study of UK teens' SMS (Thurlow and Brown 2003), three sociolinguistic maxims guided choices: brevity and speed, paralinguistic restitution, and phonological approximation, including for non-standard pronunciation. Abbreviations and emoticons were again less common than popularly thought.

In the first systematic comparison of SMS and IM among American college students (Baron 2008: 151–60; Ling and Baron 2007), emoticons and acronyms were rare in both. SMS messages were longer, probably because IM messages were broken up into short chunks, and contained more abbreviations, though even in those abbreviations were relatively rare. Sentence-final punctuation was more prevalent in IM, probably because of greater ease of input, made not just with thumbs.

CHAT

Playful performance flourishes in text-based synchronous chat. Participants play with identity, often composing nicknames with clever use of spelling and typography (Bechar-Israeli 1995; Danet 1998; Turkle 1995). In an improvisational sequence on IRC (Internet Relay Chat; Figure 8.3), participants simulated smoking marihuana, using the letters and symbols on the computer keyboard. Players nicknamed <Thunder> and <Kang> mobilize some of the features discussed above, including descriptions of action (*passes joint to kang*; *puff* *hold*; *gurble gurble gurble*), typed simulation of laughter (hehehe), and smiley icons. <Kang> uses an unusual one: >:-) – when commenting about what they are accomplishing (lines 130, 436).[9] That they are pleased with their performance is indicated by 'yea!' (line 366) and <Thunder>'s 'wow' (line 375).

The most striking feature of this sequence is one not mentioned in Figure 8.3,

Example #1:
    Line 126 <Thunder>sssssssssssssss *passes joint to kang*
    ....
    <Kang> thanx dude *puff* *hold*
    ....
    >:-)
    ....
    138 <Thunder> kang exhale . . . you will die :-)
    <Kang> *exhale*
    <Kang> ;)
Example #2:
    Line 340 <BlueAdept> <gives first bong rip to Thunder . . .
    ....
    <Thunder> *gurble gurble gurble*
    365   ssssssssssssssssssssss
    <Kang> yea!
    ....
    <Thunder> sssssssssssssssss
    370 <Thunder> ssssssssssssssssss
    <Thunder> ssss
    <Thunder> ss
    <Thunder> s
    <Thunder>
    375 <Thunder> wow
Example #3:
    Line 419 <Kang< :|
    <Kang> :|
    <Kang> :\
    <Thunder> heheheh
    <Thunder> heheheheheh
    <Thunder> that was great
    425 <Kang> :/
    <Kang> :)
    <Thunder> hehehehehhe
    <Kang> *exhale*
    <Kang> :0
    430 <Thunder> :| :| :\sssss :)
    <Kang> hheeeheee
    <Thunder> :-Q :| :| :\sssss :)
    <Thunder> heheheh
    435 ....
    >:-) cute

Figure 8.3 A textual and typographic simulation of smoking marihuana
           (from Danet 2001: Figure 3.3).

exploitation of the graphic shape and sound of the letter *s*, beginning in line 126, in which the long series of *s*'s simulates the sound of sucking in the smoke. In lines 369–74 the decreasing number of *s*'s simulates the disappearing smoke visually. The climax of this textual charade is line 432, in which <Thunder> encapsulates the entire sequence in one line of text – taking the joint (indicated by the tail of the *Q* in the letter *Q*) in one's mouth, inhaling, exhaling, seeing the smoke disappear, and experiencing pleasure.

<Thunder> :-*Q* :| :| :\sssss :)

In the 1990s the inherently dramatic nature of text-based chat inspired theatre professionals to experiment with virtual theatre. Various groups organized online productions in which the players were dispersed geographically. Scripted performances left room for last-minute typed improvisation, as in the case of the Hamnet Players, who mounted clever parodies of Shakespearean plays (Danet 2001: Chap. 3; Danet *et al.* 1995). In early work, the Plaintext Players used previously prepared scenarios but no scripts, leaving it to actors to improvise their roles online (LaFarge 1995). The Plaintext Players now incorporate real-world as well as online actors in their productions, anchored in a physical venue (LaFarge and Allen 2005). Purely textual virtual theater has receded today, because of the attractiveness and increased availability of multimedia technologies.

WRITING SYSTEMS AND THE DOMINANCE OF ENGLISH

English has had a historical advantage on the Internet. The American designers of early technologies worked with the ASCII[10] character set, containing 95 usable graphical characters, based on the Roman alphabet and the English language (Figure 8.4). While they did not intentionally discriminate against speakers of other languages, their choices made it difficult, if not impossible, to communicate in languages other than English. Speakers of languages with other alphabets, such as Greek or Russian, and especially those needing a right-to-left interface (Arabic, Hebrew), were at a serious disadvantage. For many, romanization was common. 'Greeklish', romanized Greek, is a prominent example (Tseliga 2007). Romanization of languages other than English still occurs sometimes, even when it is possible to incorporate characters from one's native language (Lee 2007; Palfreyman and Al Khalil 2003).[11]

Today, with the advent of Unicode,[12] a major technical development which can potentially accommodate all the world's written languages, multilingual communication online is increasingly common. Speakers of many languages can spend their online day in their native language. For instance, the Japanese

```
  ! " # $ % & ' ( ) * + , - . /
0 1 2 3 4 5 6 7 8 9 : ; < = > ?
@ A B C D E F G H I J K L M N O
P Q R S T U V W X Y Z [ \ ] ^ _
` a b c d e f g h i j k l m n o
p q r s t u v w x y z { | } ~
```

Figure 8.4 The ASCII character set, source: http://www.cs.tut.fi/~jkorpela/chars. html#ascii, accessed 7 April 2008.

presence online is extensive (Gerrard and Nakamura 2004). However, at the time of writing, e-mail addresses, domain names on the Web (URLs), and HTML (the markup language for Web pages) continue to be based on the original ASCII code, and if users want to reach out globally, inevitably they encounter the Roman alphabet and English.

PATTERNS OF USAGE BY NON-NATIVE SPEAKERS

Studies of the influence of the linguistic/cultural background of non-native speakers of English on their online choices in English-only settings are relatively rare, except among specialists in second language learning. In Bjørge's (2007) study of e-mails to professors by students in Norway, non-native speakers from countries stressing hierarchical differences were more formal than those from countries of relatively egalitarian values. Bloch (2004) argues that native speakers of Chinese in an English-based discussion in the Usenet newsgroup *soc.culture.china* incorporated Chinese rhetorical strategies in their arguments. In a study of e-mails to American professors by American and international (Asian) students

> the American students ... displayed greater initiative than the international students in their virtual e-mail consultation with their professor by setting up face-to-face appointments, addressing substantive issues and obtaining input, and by their ability to collapse a potentially lengthy e-mail exchange into one effective message.... issues of culture and second language ability account for this difference: international students are unfamiliar with general values and norms in North American universities, and the cultural values they bring with them are often in contrast with those they encounter in the American setting; ... as non-native speakers of English, the sociopragmatic and pragmalinguistic resources of international students are more limited than those of native-speaking peers.
>
> (Biesenbach-Lucas 2005: 40–41)

LANGUAGE CHOICE

Non-native speakers of English sometimes use it online because they have no choice, because of the technical difficulties outlined above. However, there are many national, regional, and global situations in which they do have a choice, yet they prefer English. Egyptian professionals preferred English for professional communication even with other Egyptians, and romanized Arabic for personal e-mail (Warschauer *et al*. 2002). On a discussion list for Swiss medical students English became the de facto lingua franca within a few years' time, evidently because in multilingual Switzerland it was no one's native language (Durham 2003).

However, English is not always the dominant Internet language in multilingual contexts, and sometimes there is resistance to its dominance. In Uzbekistan, Russian, English, and Uzbek compete for use online, and there is resistance to globalization, Western influence, and the dominance of English (Wei and Kolko 2005). Nearly all survey respondents reported use of Russian online. Seventy percent did so for English, though only one-third said they used English most often. At present, use of Uzbek is hampered by the relative paucity of Uzbek material online.

In a 2001–4 online discussion forum of the European Union, more than 90 percent of threads introduced in English were conducted only in English, although participants were free to write in any language (Wodak and Wright 2007), reflecting the fact that English is widely accepted as a lingua franca. Axelsson *et al.* (2003) studied language choice in a multilingual, international, graphical chat context. Again, despite the possibility of using other languages, English was the default language, except in themed settings. Non-native English speakers were willing to change to English even in situations where the majority were not native speakers.

CODE-MIXING, CODE-SWITCHING

In bilingual or multilingual online contexts, inter-sentential code-switching and intra-sentential code-mixing are extremely common. Female students in Dubai code-switch and even script-switch from English to Arabic in IM (Palfreyman and Al Khalil 2003). Code-switching and lexical borrowing between Cantonese and English, common in Hong Kong conversation, recur in IM and chat online. Romanized Cantonese sentence-final particles are frequent (Fung and Carter 2007; Lee 2007), as in

> yes **ar** . . . just set up my computer **ar**
> hahahhahaha!! That's true **ga**!
> sorry again **lor**[13]

The instigator of a flame event on an English-based Listserv for Israelis introduced romanized Hebrew strategically, to neutralize his offensive behavior (Danet forthcoming). In a study of code-switching between Jamaican Creole (Patois) and English, English dominated in e-mails and discussion forums, but the proportion of Patois words in discussion forums was double that for e-mails. Forum participants were mainly abroad, whereas most e-mailers were in Jamaica, suggesting that it was more important to those abroad to express emotional attachment to Patois (Hinrichs 2006).

THE FUTURE OF ENGLISH ONLINE

The study of computer-mediated English and of CMC generally is daunting because of rapid changes in technology. In this brief overview I have been able to discuss only the three most popular modes and a fraction of the issues studied by CMC researchers (see Herring 2004). Of necessity I have omitted blogs, which are proliferating rapidly, and whose linguistic features are only beginning to be studied (Crystal 2006: 238–47; Gurak *et al*. 2004). A new research question is: to what extent does online communication in languages other than English resemble communication in English (Danet and Herring 2003, 2007b)? Are there distinctive patterns for specific linguistic/cultural groups?

In this age of tremendous technological change there is great uncertainty as to the appropriateness of linguistic choices in digital writing (Baron 2000: Chap. 9; Crystal 2006: 104–12; Danet 2001: Chap. 2). As we have seen, non-native speakers of English have a double burden: deciphering what is culturally appropriate in English, while contending with the same puzzlement as native speakers regarding how to respond to the affordances and constraints of new media.

It would be a mistake to attribute changing linguistic patterns to technological factors alone. The trend toward greater informality was already recognized in the early 1980s, before personal computers became common. Robin Lakoff (1982) noted that written documents of all kinds were becoming more speech-like. The Plain Language movement in the USA and the UK pursued the reform of bureaucratic and legal language to make it, in effect, more like speech (Redish 1985). Naomi Baron (2000) showed that ideological change regarding the teaching of writing fostered a more oral style.

It is often claimed in the popular media that the Internet is destroying language. Professional linguists generally reject this view. David Crystal (2006: 270–6) believes that CME is greatly enriching our communicative options, though Naomi Baron (2008: 169) worries about 'whateverism' – 'a marked indifference to the need for consistency in linguistic usage'. Some research suggests that the influence of the new media on writing is less extensive than is popularly believed – *at least thus far* – and that young people can learn to differentiate between different genres of writing, as, indeed, they learned to do in the pre-digital past (Spatafora 2008). Lenhart *et al*. (2008: 21) concluded that

> [y]oung adults generally do not believe that technology negatively influences the quality of their writing, but they do acknowledge that the informal styles of writing that mark the use of these text-based technologies for many teens do occasionally bleed into their school work.

Will English be the lingua franca of the Internet in the future? Online linguistic diversity is generally growing, though it is far from reflecting real-world linguistic diversity (Paolillo 2007). Many languages are not represented on the Internet, nor will they ever be, because of the lack of infrastructure and resources in poor countries, because they lack scripts, and because in many multilingual countries there are too many minority languages to accommodate.

While many language groups are rapidly growing online, the primary contender for first place is Chinese. In one estimate, by 2050 there will be 1.384 billion native speakers of Chinese, compared with 508 million native English speakers (Graddol 1997/2000: 21, Table 7). In Figure 8.2 we saw that by 2004, while native English speakers constituted the largest group within the online population (35 percent), the second largest language represented (14 percent) was already Chinese. By December 2007, in mainland China there were 210 million users online.[14]

China's economic ascendancy, huge, proliferating population, and rapid expansion of the Internet suggest the possibility that Chinese might overtake English as lingua franca. However, the complexities of logographic Chinese script and other features of the language, as well as the challenge of inputting it online (see Su 2003) make it unlikely that Chinese will replace English (Bruthiaux 2002b). Also, the Chinese are rapidly learning English (Yajun 2003). For the foreseeable future, English will probably remain the lingua franca of the Internet, though scholars will continue to debate this issue (Crystal 2003; Graddol 2006).

NOTES

1 This list of technologies is not exhaustive. For more details on these and related technologies, see Baron (2008).
2 See Crystal (2006); Danet (2001); Herring (1996, 2001); Herring *et al.* (forthcoming).
3 This discussion draws on Danet (2001: 11–12).
4 For a more comprehensive discussion of the features of speech and writing and how they pertain to CMC, see Crystal (2006: 26–52); Baron (2008), Chap. 4.
5 See Danet (2001), Chapters 2 and 3.
6 On the origins of play with language and typography generally, see Raymond (1996) or the online version, *The Jargon File*, www.ccil.org/jargon/jargon.html, accessed 2 April 2008.
7 'Flaming' is originally a hackers' term (Raymond 1996), and is now widely used by CMC researchers. See Avgerinakou (2003); Danet (forthcoming); O'Sullivan and Flanagin (2003).
8 Some IM software supports group chat, not just one-to-one messages.
9 This emoticon, with the optional hyphen omitted – >:) – means 'devilish', according to a smiley dictionary at www.smileyworld.com/emoticons/emoticonresults.asp, accessed 7 April 2008.
10 ASCII stands for 'American Standard Code for Information Interchange.'
11 Online papers by Palfreyman and Al Khalil, as well as by Su, Durham, Warschauer *et al.*, and Axelsson *et al.*, cited later, are also available in Danet and Herring (2007b).
12 See http://unicode.org, accessed 7 April 2008 (Anderson 2004).
13 Examples from Lee (2007).
14 Source: ChinaTechnews.com 18 January 2008, www.chinatechnews.com/2008/01/17/6302-chinese-mainlands-internet-population-tops-200-million, accessed 11 April 2008.

9

ENGLISH LANGUAGE TEACHING IN THE OUTER AND EXPANDING CIRCLES

SURESH CANAGARAJAH AND SELIM BEN SAID

Enlightened policy on the teaching of English outside the traditional 'native speaker' communities has been considerably influenced by Braj Kachru's (1986) notion of World Englishes. Kachru should be credited for pluralizing the English language by showing the rule-governed nature of the new varieties that have emerged in postcolonial communities. His well-known three circles model charts the historical spread and functional differences of the language by developing a sensitivity to the *expanding circle* (where English was beginning to be used as a foreign language – EFL), the *outer circle* (with its own well-established varieties since colonial times, where English was a second language – ESL) and the *inner circle* (where ownership of English was claimed and norms originated). Kachru called these communities norm-dependent, norm-developing and norm-providing, respectively, to indicate their relative status. Based on this model, teachers have assumed that the language norms and pedagogical models for EFL in the expanding circle come from US or British speech communities, while they have been more tolerant of local norms and practices in ESL teaching in the outer circle.

However, recent forms of globalization have generated new forms and functions for English language, complicating distinctions like ESL and EFL. They raise new pedagogical imperatives for teachers and the need to redefine scholarly constructs that explain language learning. After we outline the social and communicative changes underway, we will consider how these developments complicate policy, pedagogy and scholarship in English language teaching (ELT). Then we move on to consider briefly how diverse communities cope with these changes. We treat Tunisia as an example of a multilingual community grappling with the emergence of English, re-evaluating the place of the other more established languages, Arabic and French, in the community and schools.

THE CONTEXT

The new social and technological forces unleashed by the forms of globalization in late modernity have generated a new relationship between communities. Diaspora groups, the Internet, transnational production and economic relationships, and the compression of time and space through travel, media and communication account for what Hall (1997) calls *postmodern globalization*. This social context is marked by traits that differ from the centre/periphery stratification that accompanied colonization and have been with us until recently in what Hall calls *modernist globalization* (see Canagarajah 2006b). The new social context can be described as follows:

1 the interaction between communities is multilateral (i.e. international involvement at diverse levels is needed in today's economic and production enterprises);
2 national boundaries have become porous as people, goods and ideas flow across borders;
3 languages, communities and cultures have become hybrid, shaped by this fluid flow of social and economic relationships.

English enables and is in turn shaped by these 'transcultural flows' (to use Appadurai's (1996) terminology). The conditions featuring postmodern globalization complicate some of the assumptions behind the Kachruvian model:

i English varieties have started to leak outside their national borders. The foundation on which Kachru's model stands – that outer circle norms are justified in terms of the communities which have nativized them for their own use – is shaken. All communities need proficiencies in varieties outside their own. Indian English is no longer relevant only for Indians. Personnel from the outsourced companies in Madras or Bangalore use their variety of English when they conduct business with people from other countries. More importantly, even British or American nationals cannot be satisfied with their prestigious varieties anymore. Americans now have to transact many important types of domestic and personal business with companies outside their border. Indian English is now necessary for Americans as well. They should at least have receptive skills in World Englishes to transact business with outsourced companies.
ii Speakers in the expanding circle do not use English only for extra-community relations. For countries like China, Vietnam, The Phillipines and Brazil, English performs many important functions within their own borders. International news, popular culture and advanced education in local contexts involve English. Hip-hop music in English has been appropriated and recreated in a wide range of communities – such as Belgium, Japan, Holland – for consumption locally (see Mitchell 2001; Pennycook 2003b). Such considerations demand that we take account of the increasing currency of English in expanding circle countries.
iii With increasing currency of English in their local contexts, expanding circle communities are developing local varieties similar to the outer circle varieties. For example, scholars from Mexico (Clemente and Higgins 2008) and Germany (Erling 2002) argue for the presence of Mexican and German English, respectively. When we realize that expanding circle communities

may be developing their local varieties, we cannot treat them only as 'norm dependent' as Kachru labelled them.

iv   More importantly, we are learning that expanding and outer circle communities are developing new norms as they use English for lingua franca communication. Multilingual speakers do not seem to defer to inner circle norms when they communicate with each other in English (see Seidlhofer 2004; Jenkins 2006a). Researchers into English as a Lingua Franca (ELF) point out that, when speakers in the outer and expanding circles speak to each other, they are able to negotiate their differences in their own terms, and accomplish their communicative needs effectively, developing new norms (Jenkins 2006a; Seidlhofer 2004). The search is on for the lingua franca core (Seidlhofer 2004), a possible grammar that does not belong to any national variety, but facilitates communication when speakers step outside their communities. Some researchers point out that these ELF norms are constructed inter-subjectively and instantaneously between subjects for their particular communication in each specific situation (House 2003; Meierkord 2004).

v   If there is still a grudging acceptance in the Kachruvian model that the inner circle countries enjoy ownership over English, the spread of English questions this assumption. The oft-cited statistics by Graddol (1999) and Crystal (1997) show that the speakers outside the inner circle are now greater in number. In terms of the currency and usage of the language, there is even clearer evidence that English is used more in multinational contexts by multilingual speakers than in homogeneous contexts of monolingual speakers (see Graddol 1999). These considerations raise questions about the 'periphery' status of the outer and expanding circles in the Kachruvian model. The latter communities are quite central to the character and currency of English today.

These developments demand a reconceptualization of the relationship between the diverse varieties of English (see Canagarajah 2006b). We must move closer to the position that English is a heterogeneous language with multiple norms and diverse grammars. We must start working with Crystal's (2004: 49) notion of English as 'a family of languages' or McArthur's (1987) egalitarian model where the different varieties relate to each other on a single level (and not hierarchically as in Kachru's). The new relationship between English varieties complicates our notions of norms and proficiency that are so important in pedagogical contexts. What does it mean to be a proficient speaker of English today? Which community's norms should teachers treat as their target for acquisition in their classrooms?

NORMS AND PROFICIENCY

In a context where we have constantly to shuttle between different varieties and communities, one has to be multidialectal. This does not mean one needs production skills in all the varieties of English. One needs the capacity to negotiate diverse varieties to facilitate communication. The passive competence to understand new varieties is part of this multidialectal competence. In this sense, the argument whether local standards or inner circle standards matter in a specific pedagogical context becomes irrelevant (see Davies 2002 and Pakir 2005 for this debate). We need both – and more (i.e. the ability to negotiate the emerging lingua franca norms, and the norms of other outer and expanding circle communities). Not only are norms relative, variable and heterogeneous, they are also changing. A proficient speaker of English in the postmodern world needs the capacity to negotiate diverse varieties. He or she should be able to shuttle between different norms, recognizing the systematic and legitimate status of different varieties of English in this diverse 'family of languages'.

All this leads to the view of English as a heterogeneous language with multiple norms, each norm coming into play at different levels of social interaction. While lingua franca norms come into play in multilingual contexts, the local norm may have to be used in clearly demarcated contexts of inner circle or outer circle usage. In extremely formal institutional contexts, where inner circle norms are conventional (such as academic communication), one has to adopt the established norms. Proficiency in the world of postmodern globalization requires the ability to negotiate this variability. We have to address the fact that there are different norms that come into play at different levels of social interaction.

This multilayering of norms doesn't have to be as confusing as it sounds. Though pedagogy and assessment are still largely focused on unitary norms, research into the everyday communication of multilingual students and adults shows that they draw on intuitive resources and skills to negotiate diversity effectively. Students adapt to the varieties of neighbouring communities for symbolic and affective reasons outside the classroom. Harris *et al.* (2002) show how a Bengali student in London picks up Rastafarian English from the Jamaican communities in his neighbourhood in order to communicate with them. Ibrahim (1999) finds that Somali students in Toronto adopt hip-hop English for certain contexts, adopting Afro-Canadian identity and cultural features to develop a more urbane and local identity. Lam (2000) finds that a Chinese-American student, who is defined as 'limited English proficient' in the classroom, negotiates diverse varieties with his Internet 'buddies' from other countries as they successfully discuss topics in pop and teen culture. Such untutored strategies of negotiation develop in social practice as multilingual people engage with speakers of other languages in their linguistically diverse environments. According to the South Asian perspective on identity and community articulated by Khubchandani (1997), such strategies are 'native' to outer and expanding circle communities because of their multilingual history.

PEDAGOGICAL IMPLICATIONS

The ability to negotiate English in diverse transnational contexts in postmodern communication requires us to move beyond proficiency in single varieties of English and to develop broader competencies that enable students to deal with the multifarious Englishes they may meet in their everyday life. Here are the set of competencies we have to develop in classrooms:

1 **Language awareness**: the need to engage with multiple English varieties, and even other languages, is so great in postmodern globalization that it is unwise to develop competence in only one language system. It is more important to develop the cognitive abilities to negotiate multiple codes as one shuttles between communities. Scholars in English lingua franca research put it aptly when they say that the needs of international negotiations in English imply that we have to move from 'teaching languages' to 'teaching Language' (Seidlhofer 2004: 227). We would articulate this shift as moving from 'teaching English' to 'teaching Language.' One should be able inductively to process the underlying system in the varieties one encounters in social interactions. One should draw on intuitive skills to develop relative communicative competence in new varieties according to one's needs. Therefore, pedagogy should develop a student's ability to discern the structure, pattern or rules from the available data of a given language. Part of this language awareness is the lingua franca core. Speakers have to know that in contexts clearly marked as multilingual, certain sounds and grammatical structures may not affect communication and, in many cases actually facilitate communication (see Seidlhofer 2004 for a review of the features available from research so far).

2 **Sociolinguistic sensitivity**: one's awareness of dialect differences, identity considerations, contextual constraints and cultural sensitivity is important as one shuttles between diverse communities in the postmodern context. McKay (2005) argues that this sensitivity should recognize different pragmatic norms for different contexts of communication. So, outer circle speakers have to recognize that there are well-established pragmatic conventions for English communication in inner circle communities that are different from their own; however, in their own local community they should feel free to adopt the pragmatic strategies from the local languages and cultures that now shape English as well; and yet, in lingua franca communication with multilingual speakers, they might have to draw on negotiation strategies (which are not culture- or community-specific) to interact with speakers who lack common communicative conventions.

3 **Negotiation skills**: we have to devise more interactive and collaborative pedagogical formats for developing one's proficiency in strategies of language negotiation. Such a proficiency might involve the following:

- codeswitching, crossing (Rampton 1995);
- speech accommodation (Giles 1984);
- interpersonal strategies, e.g. repair, rephrasing, clarification, gestures, topic change, consensus-oriented, mutually supportive (Firth 1996; Gumperz 1982a);
- attitudinal resources, i.e. patience, tolerance and humility to negotiate differences (see Higgins 2003).

In effect, we have to shift our emphases from language-as-a-system to language-as-social-practice, from grammar to pragmatics, from competence to performance, in our attitude to proficiency. The bias in language teaching and testing circles is still very much on the first construct in each pair. Defining language use as *performative* involves placing an emphasis on the second construct in each pair, and considering how language diversity is actively negotiated in acts of communication under changing contextual conditions. In other words, it is not what we know, so much as the versatility with which we do things with English that defines proficiency.

A suitable pedagogy for ELT should not only enable students to negotiate the variability in norms in English worldwide, but also to participate in such processes of appropriation by using the language with creativity and agency. We can summarize the shifts in teaching practice as shown in Figure 9.1.

It is important to realize that, rather than focusing on a single language or dialect as the target of learning, teachers have to develop in students competence in a repertoire of codes to manage postmodern communication. While joining a new speech community was the objective of traditional language learning, now we have to train students to shuttle between communities by deploying the relevant codes. Furthermore, in a context of diverse norms and conventions in the system of English language, it is important to understand the relativity of notions of correctness. If what is non-standard in one community could be standard in another, it is more important to teach students how to negotiate appropriate usage for the different contexts. It is even possible to bring local norms into international communication with appropriate ways of

From:	*To:*
'target language'	repertoire
text/lang. as homogeneous	text/lang. as hybrid
joining a community	shuttling between communities
focus on rules/conventions	focus on strategies
correctness	negotiation
language/discourse as static	language/discourse as changing
language as context-bound	language as context-transforming
mastery of grammar rules	meta-linguistic awareness
text/lang. as transparent/instrumental	text/lang. as representational
L1 or C1 as problem	L1 or C1 as resource

Figure 9.1 Shifts in pedagogical practice.

flagging one's intention to represent one's identity or special rhetorical purposes. For such purposes of voice and agency, we have now to focus more on strategies of communication rather than on grammatical rules. With effective discourse strategies, speakers/writers may employ features of their sociolect, or even personal coinages, for special rhetorical purposes. It is possible for certain vernacular or non-standard items to become mainstreamed over time as they gain wider social acceptance – as we see in many examples in the history of the English language. From this perspective, we have to teach language as changing rather than static. But, too often, the underlying assumption of language teaching is conservative and prescriptive. Other matters of pedagogical common sense, like the context-bound nature of language, have to be modified by the realization that effective discourse strategies can be instrumental in changing the context of communication. Such pedagogical shifts are important at a time when the notion of language as transparent has been challenged by the aware-ness that speakers and communities represent their identities, values and cultural practices through this rich semiotic system. In this endeavour, the first language or culture of a speaker may not be a hindrance, but a resource.

The changing pedagogical priorities suggest that *testing* too must go through significant changes to assess one's ability to negotiate the complex communica-tive needs of multilingual and contact situations. As we realize that norms are heterogeneous, variable, changing and, therefore, interactively established in each context, we have to move away from a reliance on discrete-item tests of formal grammatical competence and develop instruments that are more sensi-tive to performance and pragmatics. Assessment would focus on one's strategies of negotiation, situated performance, communicative repertoire, and language awareness. To this end, we must develop new instruments with imagination and creativity (see Canagarajah 2006a).

To sustain these new pedagogical practices, we are seeing the development of macro-educational changes in the professional discourse relating to ELT. The micro-level changes in day-to-day classroom practice must be complemented by suitable research and scholarship informed by a revised set of priorities. This is a shift from a hierarchical approach in professional structuring to a more collab-orative approach between diverse communities, as illustrated in Figure 9.2.

While the superiority of 'native' varieties has led to a dichotomized approach to language teaching (where professional expertise from the inner circle is treated as authoritative), the pluralized approach to English language will encourage multilateral knowledge flow. Local knowledge from the many outer and expanding circle communities can offer valid contributions to pedagogical practice. Also, the insights of practitioners – especially in communities distant from research and scholarly centres – should be given an important place in knowledge formation in the field. The role of language consultants will also change. Traditionally, personnel from cultural and educational institutions in the inner circle assumed the right to travel to other countries to initiate curric-ulum change. After only a few months of observation, they enjoyed the power to

SURESH CANAGARAJAH AND SELIM BEN SAID

	From:	To:
expertise:	established knowledge unilateral knowledge flow researcher-/scholar-generated	local knowledge multilateral knowledge flow practitioner-generated collaborative
curriculum:	innovation/change top-down	continuity ground-up
pedagogy:	methods-dominated skills-based	post-method practices project-based
materials:	authenticity published in the centre	relevance locally generated

Figure 9.2 Shifts in professional discourse and structure.

dictate changes in a top-down manner, often influenced by the pedagogical fashions of the centre. In the revised approach, we have to consider negotiating with existing curricular traditions to generate changes ground-up. This would involve active partnership between donors and local agents in educational development. As for authoritative methods, thankfully, recent pedagogical literature articulates a 'post-method' consciousness (see Kumaravadivelu 1994; Prabhu 1990). It is now recognised that there is no 'best method' that assures successful learning; the validity of the concept of methods is itself challenged, as pedagogical practices are eclectic, contextual, and contingent. This reorientation can empower local teachers to focus on the learning strategies that work for their own students in the light of the purposes and objectives that define their teaching. The reality of multiliteracies and postmodern work conditions, which encourage shuttling between different discourses according to the shifting domains of work, has also challenged the traditional compartmentalization of skills. In the place of skills-based teaching, many are moving to project-based pedagogies which focus more on carrying out specific communicative objectives, acquiring the discourses and skills relevant to the project in the process of accomplishing it (Warschauer 2000; Cole and Zuengler 2003). In the case of teaching materials, again, the current emphasis on authenticity is misdirected. Authentic materials are typically composed of a corpus of language features characteristic of inner circle communication. These materials come from centre publishers for the pragmatic reason that they have the resources to mass-produce textbooks for other communities. But if authenticity is defined in terms of the shifting purposes and identities of the speakers, it has to be contextually negotiated. Teachers are adopting many strategies to collect texts that are locally meaningful, e.g. students' bilingual journals, recordings/transcriptions of local communication, documentation of oral histories and collection of interview and narrative data from families by student ethnographers. Through these activities, many teachers have developed teaching materials that are relevant to the local community (see Auerbach *et al.* 1996).

REVISING SCHOLARLY CONSTRUCTS

In the light of the empirical and theoretical developments articulated above on the changing face of English, we have to reconsider some of the important linguistic constructs that have informed English language teaching. The main ones are detailed below.

ESL/EFL/L1 PEDAGOGIES

In the light of the common challenge that all communities (including inner circle communities) face in having to negotiate multiple varieties of English, it makes no sense to separate pedagogies into ESL and EFL. Pedagogical wisdom has favoured separating language minority students in inner circle communities where English has to be learnt as an active second language according to inner circle norms (ESL), outer circle students who have to learn local varieties for active local communication (ESL) and expanding circle students who are supposed to learn 'native' English varieties for international communication (EFL). Speakers of all communities have to negotiate a range of Englishes in their local and non-local contexts as the global and the multilingual have interpenetrated all social domains. Ironically, some inner circle scholars, such as Horner and Trimbur (2002), have questioned the wisdom of teaching only standard American English in writing programmes designed primarily for Anglo-American students. We are approaching a situation when pedagogies for L1 students won't be dissimilar from pedagogies for L2 learning.

NATIVE/NON-NATIVE SPEAKER

Many assumptions make us critique this distinction: multilinguals speak English as one of the languages of their active everyday communication with native proficiency; many multilinguals acquire English at the same time as the language of their family or their local community, enjoying two or more native languages; some are natives of a locally developed variety of English (e.g. natives of Indian English). We realize that language identities are hybrid, relational and multiple in postmodern contexts of diaspora, migration and intercultural contact (see Braine 1999). Identities are relative to affiliation (an individual may wish to express allegiance to a language he/she does not speak well), expertise (one may have more fluency in English than in the language of one's family) and birth (one may prefer to use and identify more with a language that is not the language of one's birth). Rampton (1990) has indeed proposed that we distinguish speakers according to birth, affiliation and expertise. However, this nuanced perspective doesn't provide neat labels for use. Though Jenkins (2003) has proposed the labels Monolingual English Speaker of English (MES), Bilingual English Speaker (BES) and Non-Bilingual English Speaker (NBES), it is difficult to define bilingual competence in a situation where many who use English for functions in specific domains (pop music, rap, the Internet) may not be proficient in other contexts. There is no universal standard of proficiency we can use to categorize a person and the search for appropriate labels continues. For now, the labels *expert* and *novice* will help to bring out some nuances. They help to make a distinction between speakers based on expertise (rather than geographical location, race or birth). They also affirm the notion that expertise is gained through social practice, and that all of us are relative experts or novices in different varieties of English.

INTERLANGUAGE

Traditional wisdom held that, as learners move towards the target language, they form incorrect versions of the system which could become fossilized and remain permanent. These incorrect approximations of the target were labelled *interlanguage* and teachers specialized in strategies to move learners toward the target (see Selinker 1972). However, in the context of recognizing language diversity, we have new questions about interlanguage. How do we define an error in the context where English norms are relative – e.g. when what is correct for one community may be incorrect for another? How do we define an error when global speakers are appropriating English according to their values and needs to fashion new norms for local communication? What does interlanguage mean when each speaker is using English creatively with new variations to represent his/her identity? Would hybrid forms of English (featuring a mixture of languages) be treated as interlanguage when scholars recognize these mixed forms as legitimate uses for multilingual speakers? Is what we see as an incorrect approximation actually an indigenously appropriated form of local English? When a language is appropriated by a whole community to suit its own interests and values, developing unique grammars and conventions in the process, we cannot treat speakers of that variety as displaying an interlanguage. The term *macro-acquisition* has been used to understand how a community appropriates another language and develops proficiency in endonormative terms (Brutt-Griffler 2002a). We have to develop ways to map the micro-acquisition of learners within the macro-acquisition of the communities of which they are a part.

SECOND LANGUAGE COMPETENCE

The above questions raise concerns about the dominant models that explain second language competence. In the past, language competence was measured in terms of native speaker competence. From this perspective, an individual was incompetent if he/she failed to match the native speaker's proficiency and usage. This assumption has many limitations: a second language learner may not want to speak like a native speaker (e.g. he/she may hold a different ideal in order to represent his/her multilingual and multicultural identity); the process of acquisition might also be different as the second language learner develops a competence relating to his/her first and other languages, not separated from them. In other words, the competence of a multilingual is qualitatively different from that of the monolingual and, therefore, it might be unfair to use the 'native speaker' ideal to measure a multilingual's competence. Also, multilingual competence does not constitute separate competencies in each language, which are then put together, but an integrated whole that accommodates parallel workings in multiple languages (see Canagarajah 2007). Vivian Cook (1999) has coined the label *multicompetence* to reflect the distinct nature of competence of a second language speaker.

An underlying problem in many of the dominant ELT pedagogical constructs is that they are ridden by what Cook (1999) calls the *comparative fallacy*. The haste to judge language performance by using limited and unfair norms has affected ELT. The treatment of a putative native speaker of English functioning in a homogeneous speech community as the norm is one manifestation of this comparative fallacy. Multilingual speakers do not treat the speakers of inner circle varieties as their frame of reference. Julianne House (2003) reminds us that the yardstick for measuring second language learners should be an expert multilingual speaker functioning under comparable socio-cultural and historical conditions of use, and comparable goals for interaction (573). Such proposals show that we are moving towards a paradigm shift in ELT. When the power of the native speaker of the inner circle is challenged, many of our pedagogical and linguistic assumptions fall flat, and we are forced to develop new constructs that explain the language acquisition and use of multilinguals.

POLICY AND PRACTICE IN DIVERSE COMMUNITIES

Since English has been a language of a restricted elite since colonization, the challenge for many outer circle communities in South Asia and Africa is to democratize the acquisition of English (Ferguson 2006). Its status as linguistic capital even now only exacerbates the competition for proficiency. However, for those who were denied access to the language, the association of English with colonization poses attitudinal conflicts. Furthermore, with limited teachers and few resources, local authorities are unable to teach English to all the possible learners in the community. With large classrooms and few textbooks, teachers have to resort to traditional teacher-fronted pedagogies that are not fully effective in developing communicative competence (Ferguson 2006; Bruthiaux 2002a; Bunyi 2005; Brock-Utne 2005).

The challenge for expanding circle communities is different. Rather than resting on their colonial inheritance, these communities are keen to catch up with the benefits of globalization through learning English. There is also no colonial baggage in these countries, and speakers treat English as a neutral new language that is beneficial to them (Nunan 2003). The level at which English teaching is started has been progressively altered to lower and earlier levels. There is considerable governmental interest in sponsoring English language teaching. However, the teaching approaches and linguistic norms of the inner circle are unthinkingly promoted in these countries. Nunan (2003) discusses the way in which many countries like China, Vietnam, South Korean and Japan treat communicative language teaching as the preferred pedagogy. The pedagogy is a failure as it is not well-integrated into the local teaching traditions and learning needs, and teachers are not trained adequately to adopt these imported methods and materials (Nunan 2003; Tsui 2003; Hu 2002). There are paralyzing inconsistencies between policy and practice in outer and expanding circle communities as they struggle to fashion a pedagogy that addresses the increasing local demand and unique educational challenges.

ELT IN TUNISIA

Tunisia is an interesting case that illustrates the trends in both outer and expanding circle communities. It is, additionally, a test case of a colony of another European language (French) now weathering the challenges from a rival colonial language (English) within a multilingual community. Although French was dominant in the past in the aftermath of French colonization, it is losing ground in the context of intense Arabization and Islamization at the policy level. More recently, the importance of English as a foreign language (EFL) in Tunisia has been rising steadily and challenging the dominance of French as a second language in education.

Despite the prevalent multilingualism found in the Maghreb in general and in Tunisia in particular, the adoption of Arabic as the main official language is primarily explained by the strong tie that exists between Islam, the main religion in these countries, and the Arabic language. The policy of Arabization, which was initiated by Algeria, subsequently extended to the rest of the Maghreb (i.e. Morocco and Tunisia) and has imposed itself as 'the only politically acceptable solution' (Battenburg 1997: 281) in these countries. Tunisia's official language, as stipulated by the national constitution, is Modern Standard Arabic (MSA) and this is the dominant language in education. French is also a very visible language in the country, yet its influences in society and education are slowly fading out as a result of the strong policy of Arabization and the rising influence of English. The case of Tunisia is symptomatic of former North African protectorates and colonies, which are now slowly distancing themselves from dependence on the French language and turning to English as a tool for development.

Although the influence of the French language in Tunisia is slowly diminishing, it is, however, still maintained to some extent by France's influence over her former colonies. French 'political' resistance to American-led initiatives in Africa and the Middle-East is the outcome of fears about the loss of French influence in these areas of the world and loss of the accompanying economic benefits. In Tunisia, France's fear of threats to its interests is outwardly manifested in the discrepancy in funds provided by foreign governments to support second language cultural and educational activities. In 1996, funds provided were respectively ($400,000) from the UK, ($600,000) from the USA and ($20 million) from France (Battenburg 1997: 287).Yet, external financial contributions alone will not determine the linguistic future of Tunisia, and the development of private English language institutions as well as English for Specific Purposes (ESP) courses offered by the British Council and Amideast[1] suggests that Tunisians are increasingly aware of their need for the English language in diverse areas such as the military, medicine, engineering, tourism and secretarial services. It is clear that the English language is occupying a larger space in the Tunisian educational system and progressively replacing and challenging the position of French in a variety of key sectors.

The development of ELT in Tunisia, which has gradually increased in the past half century following the country's independence in 1956, is motivated by a number of factors which make English currently the privileged choice for second language learners. Most importantly, English in Tunisia constitutes a language of symbolic power and economic opportunities which is essential for the internal development of the country. The prestige formerly associated with French is now related to the English language, especially in an age of globalization where English is an index of economic growth and a means to access an international wider market. In this context, while the government is starting to implement new policies for the teaching of English earlier on in the curriculum, teachers and educators express concern that more means for sustained linguistic training in English should be devoted at all levels of education (Battenburg 1997: 286).

According to Daoud (2001), despite the considerable advances in ELT/ESP in Tunisia, teacher training, assessment and evaluation are all areas which need more attention in the future. The author identifies a number of strengths and weaknesses in the ELT profession in Tunisia. With respect to the strengths, there is a high demand for general English courses at all levels of education and a rising interest is noted, particularly in the area of English for Specific Purposes (ESP), especially since Tunisia has a highly developed tourism industry where English can be encountered in many contexts. In addition, more departments of English are offering pre-service teacher training to provide ELT practitioners with better pedagogical tools in order to optimize their teaching. One of the important limitations in the domain of English teaching in Tunisia relates to the lack of coordinated feedback, from practitioners and stakeholders in the ELT profession, about English teaching and learning practices, either among peers or to curriculum designers and policy makers. This lack of coordinated effort and bottom-up feedback has resulted in a number of gaps in the ELT domain, for instance a lack of curriculum or assessment structure, inadequate teacher preparation, particularly with respect to testing practices, and a lack of systematic evaluation of pedagogical programmes.

CONCLUSION

In the context of the changes in ELT discussed in this article, Tunisia and other communities face a common pedagogical challenge. They have to devise policy and expertise in terms of local knowledge and community needs. This is especially pressing as these countries depart from the norms and expertise borrowed from inner circle communities and develop their own pedagogical practices and professional expertise. As Adrian Holliday (2003) puts it, we have moved from an 'us/them' distinction (between the inner circle and the rest of the world, or native speakers and non-native speakers), to a 'we' (or 'we are all in this together') position where all English-speaking communities have to negotiate their norms on equal footing. Rather than looking at communities and classrooms through professional spectacles, we see them for what they are as we design specific approaches to suit them. Treating this as a fundamental 'change in attitude,' Henry Widdowson explains that 'local contexts of actual practice are to be seen not as constraints to be overcome but conditions to be satisfied' (2004b: 369). Such an ecological approach additionally has the advantage of keeping all the variables and contextual richness intact, as we teach or research English in diverse contexts.

NOTE

1 America and the Middle East (Amideast) is a cultural agency which promotes the teaching of American English and provides funds for academic exchange programmes, such as the Fulbright Scholarship.

10

ENGLISH AT SCHOOL IN ENGLAND

RICHARD ANDREWS

INTRODUCTION

'English at school' is a significant title for this chapter. As Goodson and Medway state in their introduction to *Bringing English to Order* (1990), 'attempts to control and define the subject move beyond the subject community because changing English is changing schooling' (vii). They go on to say that it is not only schooling that is changed; the British state shows a particular interest in changing – or stopping changes in – English as a curriculum subject. Ownership of the curriculum space that is termed 'English' is seen as a battleground for certain sets of values, notions of heritage and conceptions and practices in education more generally. Add to this contested space the practice of inductive thinking (i.e. thinking that is generated from texts 'upwards' towards concepts, as opposed to deductive thinking which works from a general theory to specific instances) that English tends to encourage, and there is tension and electricity in the air. Snyder's recent book about this political and curricular space as it manifests itself in Australia, *The Literacy Wars* (2008), proves that the topic remains alive.

The present chapter focuses on English, as it has developed as a subject within England over the past 50 or so years. There are obvious limitations to such a focus but, at the same time, the development of the subject within England is an interesting case. The education system and the so-called *National* Curriculum in England are different from those in Wales and Northern Ireland, and even more so from those in Scotland. There are complexities and confusions around the terms *English* as a language, *English* as school subject, *English* as a university subject and *England* as a country. While it is not the function of this chapter to explore those distinctions, it is at least valuable to be aware of them.

Although there is a rich history of English as a school subject in the post-war period from 1945 to the mid-1960s (see Goodson and Medway 1990; Hardcastle and Medway 2008), much of it is still to be written. There is a general assumption that the surge of interest during the 1960s in the creative dimensions of English, and the celebration of experience through fiction, poetry and drama, took place in reaction to a stultifying English curriculum in which form mattered more than content, and adherence to the styles of a limited set of genres/text-types mattered more than expression. Indeed, as far as we can tell from textbooks and personal accounts of the period, the late 1950s and early 1960s were characterized by continuity in the subject from the end of the Second World

War and before. According to Medway (1990), 'English was simply the sum of its well-established parts: literature, composition, instruction and exercises in written language and (less universally) speech training' (5). In other words, this was a subject that had been initially shaped in the Renaissance (and in turn from classical Greece and Rome), with emphasis on *progymnasmata* or written rhetorical exercises, the reproduction of written models and speech training. Although there were key differences in the English curriculum between the grammar schools and secondary moderns, the Leavisite tradition of elitism in literary studies percolated into schools where one aspect of 'the core of English, in this view, was the reading of literature as an active, creative and essentially moral pursuit through which the degeneracy of contemporary mass society might be combated' (5). What is striking about Medway's account of English in 1958 is how conventional the subject was. With certain exceptions – emerging practices that were a precursor of English a decade later – it sat happily within the relatively safe and limited world view of adults for young people in the 1950s, and its values and practices were coincident with those of the school as a whole. Readers are recommended to look at Medway's chapter for an in-depth analysis of the changes taking place within English between 1958 and 1968.

The present chapter concentrates on the period from the mid-1960s onwards, following the Dartmouth conference of 1966[1] and the publication of Dixon's *Growth through English* (Dixon 1967, 1969). It moves through a brief consideration of some of the issues and key turning points in the period between that seminal conference in 1966 and the present. The three main phases of change in English studies in schools during this period could be defined as follows.

First, from the mid-1960s to the early 1980s, in which there was more emphasis on expressiveness and the emergence of a personal 'voice', in relation to a 'personal growth' model of English teaching. The second phase – from the 1980s to the early 2000s – marked a greater understanding of the processes of writing, a recognition of the importance of spoken English and the beginning of the use of computers in classrooms. In the third of these phases, from the mid-1990s to the present, there has been a tension between the functions of the uses of English in wider society and those in schooling and assessment.

We now look at each of these periods, via a selective lens in each case. The method is to summarise the main trends, but to focus on one or two less well-known or less accessible texts in order to illustrate the character of the period.

THE MID-1960S TO THE EARLY 1980S

The emergence of a personal voice in English in the 1960s manifested itself in a number of ways. Following critique of classroom discourse in Barnes' chapter in *Language, the Learner and the School* (Barnes *et al.* 1969), in effect suggesting that teachers talked for most of time and that there was little in the way of open or unloaded discussion between pupils, there was a gradual and patchy growth in pupil talk in classrooms. The speech genres moved away from formal debate and oral presentation (rehearsed readings, performances, etc.) to small-group discussions without the immediate supervision of the teacher, a more questioning approach from pupils, and a greater range of speech genres within a single lesson – a movement that spawned the term 'oracy' in the 1960s. Pupils' voices were heard more on school councils and in the sometimes tentative exploration of issues in the classroom, sometimes arising from literary and other texts and, at other times, from social and political issues that would be generated from documentary texts and/or contemporary events. Throughout this period, the growing power of the voice made itself a presence in the English classroom.

Another way in which 'voice' manifested itself was in the late Romantic recognition of a singular, distinctive imprint in pupils' writing. Although full establishment of this principle had to wait for the work of Donald Graves and others in the USA in the 1980s, the seeds were sown in the 1960s and 1970s through celebration of individualism in expression, acknowledgement of the status of dialect and idiolect, and the presence of a more vernacular feel in written language. Graves captured the spirit of the movement in the following words about process writing: 'Divorcing voice from process [writing] is like omitting salt from stew, love from sex, or sun from gardening' (Graves 1983: 227). The sentimental, slightly prurient tone, however, was indicative of a movement in its latter stages. What was important about the increased emphasis on voice in writing in this period was recognition of the importance of personal experience, its linking to wider political and conceptual matters, and the closer links between speaking and writing that had been established as far back as 1958 in Gurrey's *Teaching the Mother Tongue in Secondary Schools*; and in Britton's *Talking and Writing: A Handbook for English Teachers* (1967) and *Language and Learning* (1972), both of which concentrated on the importance of linking speech to writing, of their centrality in learning to think, and the development and nurturing of language as opposed to literature.

One of the most influential books of the periods, but one which has had less recognition than others, is Summerfield's *Topics in English for the Secondary School* (1965) – and the subsequent anthologies, *Voices* (1968), *Junior Voices* (1970) and *Worlds* (1979).

Topics in English for the Secondary School was written and published in the wake of existing topic work which Marshall (1964) had criticized for being uninspiring and largely based on factual work. Her main criticism, accepted by Summerfield, was that children were often left to 'get on with it' by themselves without much guidance or inspiration from the teacher. The results, in most cases, were dry and disappointing to teachers and learners alike. Summerfield recommended a more engaged, rounded, imaginative exploration of topics in English, connecting these to personal as well as social and political experience. His emphasis was on content as a core element of an English curriculum, and he espoused the belief that almost any topic (e.g. the study of the Eddystone lighthouse) could provide a focal point for intellectual exploration in a variety of modes and genres.

A criticism might be levelled that the list of topics was arbitrary: 'snakes and reptiles' sat alongside 'Christmas'; 'horses and donkeys' next to science fiction and the American civil war next to motorcycles. But such a cornucopia of topics was not only a personal one, as Summerfield admits in the introduction; it was also one that reflected the surprising and sometimes absurd congruities of everyday life and experience. The book is influential because it marked a shift away from a preoccupation with the systems of language to the uses of language, as well as to the integration of language with experience, memory and the imagination. While these three qualities were not absent in earlier conceptions of the subject, they were less central.

Voices, an anthology, was the subject of a 40-year retrospective on BBC Radio 4 in 2008. Its mixture of riddles, lists, children's work, poems from different cultures (especially contemporary American and eastern European – the latter partly inspired by Ted Hughes and Daniel Weissbort's work on *Modern Poetry in Translation*), folk tales and fragments, collectively mined a rich vein in late 1960s culture. Combined with arresting photographs and images from the history of art, it provided a gritty, accessible, colourful anthology for schools.

Other notable and landmark books in the period were Dixon's *Growth through English* (1969), Moffett's *Teaching the Universe of Discourse* (1969), and Britton's *Language and Learning* (1972). Dixon established the case for a personal growth model of English, arising from discussions at the Dartmouth seminar of 1966 – a model which held sway for much of the rest of the century. In the 1990s, Goodwyn (see Goodwyn and Findlay 1999) undertook two surveys of English teachers' views of the principal models for their practice and values, and found the personal growth model by far the dominant one, placing heritage, media studies or functional skills models very much in a subsidiary position. Moffett's contribution was manifold. The main elements were a reinvigoration and realignment of rhetorical categories, lending greater emphasis to narrative and to the dialogic principles underpinning much of spoken and written discourse that formed the backbone of the language, arts and English curriculum. Britton's work, both in his early 1970s work on speech and learning (1972) and in the mid-1970s project on the development of writing abilities (Britton *et al*. 1975), laid emphasis on expressive talk and writing as the well-spring of the formation of identity and learning practices, diversifying into 'poetic' and 'transactional' functions of language use.

THE 1980S TO THE EARLY 2000S

In many ways, the 1980s saw a further development of work which had commenced in the 1970s. For instance, the government-sponsored National Writing Project (1985–88) encouraged teachers to build on students' existing skills and personal experience in developing their competence and individual growth in writing on a variety of topics for a range of audiences; and the National

Oracy Project (1987–90) aimed to enhance the role of speech in the learning of students aged five to sixteen, across the curriculum. There were a number of key developments from about 1980 – developments which have continued to resonate in the practice and theory of English teaching in primary and secondary schools until recently. Their influence has waned in the past few years, mostly because of the dominance and increasing stranglehold of assessment-driven models of learning. In short, these key developments are: the emergence of drafting and editing in the practice of writing; the ubiquity of narrative as a principal mode of expression, even to the point of being a 'human paradigm'; the identification of need for better teaching in argument and argumentation, first flagged in studies by Freedman and Pringle in Ontario; the influence of the Certificate of Secondary Education (CSE) on the formation and establishment of the General Certificate in Secondary Education (GCSE) in 1986, in particular on coursework and the rise of spoken English in the classroom; increasing understanding of the processes of writing; and the advent of the computer in classrooms from about 1980, with its attendant influence on writing and reading through word-processing and other software programs.

Again, this section will focus on some of the less well-known but nonetheless influential publications of the period. First, however, Graves' *Writing: Teachers and Children at Work* must be mentioned as capturing the early 1980s interest in drafting and redrafting. The principal tenets of Graves' work were that classrooms needed to be shaped and organized to create a suitable climate for writing; that topics should be chosen and shaped by the emerging writers themselves; that drafting and redrafting was a core practice to be encouraged; and that 'conferencing' (i.e. discussing a draft) in a small group and/or teacher/ pupil interaction was essential to the development of writers. Such a move at primary or elementary school level transformed writing practices in classrooms from a cruder, more time-limited 'rough to best' approach, where the focus on the final version would be on surface accuracy and presentation. It also made the connection between writing and talking-about-writing, so that composition seemed more of an organic, integrated activity. Graves has had his disciples (e.g. Calkins 1994) and those disciples have had their critics (e.g. Harwayne 2001), especially where the emphasis on drafting and provisionality has been reified into a fixed process or set of practices in the classroom.

The two publications I will concentrate on as indicative of the period are Rosen (1987) and Brown *et al.* (1990).

Harold Rosen's *Stories and Meanings* is a short, persuasive account of the power of stories. It brings together oral and written stories, validating the claim that the two are more closely connected than any other meta-genre or mode of linguistic discourse. At one end of the spectrum are told stories from a variety of contexts and cultures, including the anecdotes and tales told as part of the everyday fabric of human discourse; at the other end are novels like *Ulysses* and *War and Peace*. The concentration on narratology (the study of narrative, which attained central ground in literary and discourse studies in the 1970s) and narrative (an interest in story, which reached similar ground in English educa-tion and as a 'human paradigm' in the 1980s) is intense and illuminative. It is not only the ubiquity and pleasure of stories in themselves, but the power of narra-tive to arrange experience and memory, and to act as a communicative link and bond in societies, that is celebrated. For other studies in the 1980s on narrative, see Dixon and Stratta's *Writing Narrative – and Beyond* (1986) and Andrews' *Narrative and Argument* (1989).

The other strand of 1980s English that I wish to highlight is the result of a project undertaken by the University of Leeds School of Education and The Training Agency – at that time, the sub-department within the government concerned with the preparation of the potential labour force for employment. Whereas much of the discourse on language for employment is reductive in that it sees language as 'functional' and concerned with 'basic skills', the 'Developing English for TVEI'[2] project (Brown *et al.* 1990) was innovative and radical in that it dug deeper into the kinds of language that might be generated through engagement with the workplace and with the 'real world' outside the classroom. It thus sought to build a bridge between 'vocational English' on the one hand, and a liberal arts version on the other. Its mission was not to replace personal, expressive and literary English with a version that was colder, more official and probably less imaginative and exciting. Rather, it wished to bring together 'versions of English' (the title of a 1984 book by Barnes, Barnes and Clarke), both to extend the conventional notions of English and to reveal the fact that workplace language was more fascinating and richer than had been assumed. Examples from the project included the commissioning of a report by a school librarian from 14–16-year-olds in which she pledged to implement their recom-mendations (and which resulted in changes in the library's subscriptions, making the library a much more visited and well-used resource within the school); and work with a centre for adults with learning difficulties that helped 14–16-year-olds to understand human nature in more depth and thus to appreciate literature – in one case, *Macbeth* – more deeply.

MID-1990S TO THE PRESENT

The third period is characterized by increasing tension between curricular and assessment demands, and continuing development in the understanding of the importance of the visual, of multimodality, of rhetoric; as well as of the evolving relationship between new technologies and English.

The curricular and assessment demands of English are well accounted for, though not critiqued, in successive versions of the National Curriculum for England, and in more recent and reflective publications like Stannard and Huxford's *The Literacy Game* (2007) which gives the most comprehensive account of the National Literacy Strategy and subsequent national primary and secondary strategies (from 1996 to 2006). Andrews (2008) provides a timetable of developments with regard to the strategies, and a critique of the initiative. In this section, I will give a brief overview of key works, but will also use a less readily available source to act as a focal point for the section as a whole.

A good example of a key work in this period – not so much for its coherence as its influence – is the version of English in the National Curriculum (DfEE/ QCA 1999) within the overall third revision of the curriculum, known as 'Curriculum 2000'. Historically, there had been initial publication of statutory provision for the various National Curriculum subjects between 1998 and 1990, followed by a simplifying and scaling down of the 'orders' in the Dearing Review of 1993.[3] Curriculum 2000 represents the third version of the National Curriculum. The curriculum sets down the statutory requirements of teachers, but does not specify how these should be met; the strategies are much more specific about how to 'deliver' the curriculum.

In many ways, Curriculum 2000 represents a well-honed, balanced and enlightened curriculum for English at primary and secondary school levels. The overemphasis on personal and narrative writing and on the literary genres of the first two versions is tempered. There is a better balance between expressive, personal autobiographical writing and reading in one corner of the English curriculum, and informational and argumentational writing and reading in the other corners. The development of argumentation, in particular, is given space at both primary and secondary levels in a way that would have been unthinkable a decade earlier, as evidenced by the near total absence of this kind of discourse in the first two versions of the National Curriculum. There is reference to drafting and editing, to experiencing a wide range of texts, and to integrating drama activities within English.

But there are many points at which the 2000 curriculum represents a back-ward-looking framework for the development of language skills and capabilities. The school literary canon, for example, is Anglocentric and predominantly literary (mirroring the narrowly 'national' aspiration of the curriculum) rele-gating other writers to the peripheries ('writers from different cultures and traditions'), even though some of those writers were born, grew up or have made their home in England. Information and communication technologies (ICT) are seen as marginal, as are media and moving image texts. Multimodality (see, for example, Kress and van Leeuwen 2002) (i.e. the study of how the individual modes of speech, image, the printed word, gesture and so on are combined together within social semiotic communication) and the place of language study and development within a multimodal perspective, are hardly mentioned. The compartmentalization of the language curriculum into types of writing and reading that must be covered ignores the fact that many examples of genres and text-types are hybrid. And there is a renewed emphasis on what can be done in class, rather than broaching the walls of the classroom and school to see how the language curriculum could be enlivened by engaging with real world issues, contexts and audiences.

Furthermore, despite research evidence to the contrary, there is continued and renewed belief, enshrined in the 'orders', that the decontextualized teaching of formal grammar and of language awareness will be of direct benefit to pupils' writing and reading development (see Andrews *et al.* 2006).

We now appear to be approaching the end of a period during which there has been overemphasis on targets and levels in English and across the curriculum in both primary and secondary school sectors. The National Literacy Strategy and subsequent primary and secondary national strategies, mentioned above, are evidence of further centralization and control over not only what is taught, but how. Concentration on the assessment of English, Maths and Science at key stages 2, 3 and 4 (in the latter, through the reporting of school performance in terms of those achieving five A–C grades at GCSE and including English and Maths within that figure), and more recent proposals for twice-yearly assessments as part of a more personalized learning trajectory, indicate a narrowing of aperture in the curriculum, more 'teaching to the test', and less space and time for sustained writing and reading, talking and listening. In effect, we are currently in a phase that began in the late 1980s of US-based marketing/management culture resulting in the commodification of learning. As content and process get squeezed even further, there will come a turning point when such reduction of the learning process will become unsustainable – either through disaffection, with young people's lives ever-distancing themselves from curricular and assessment regimes; and/or through a genuine reduction in the quality of performance.

ENGLISH NOW – AND THE WAY FORWARD

The year 2015 has been set by *English 21* (QCA 2008) as one to work towards for a full-scale review of the English curriculum. Between then and now, in the medium-term, what can be done to ensure that children and young people aged 5–16 improve their writing, are engaged by their reading, become articulate in spoken language and are equipped for further study and/or work after 16? What new conceptions of English as a subject may emerge, linked to what models of language? The *English 21* project and consultation itself has produced a series of responses that have influenced the present state of the subject in schools.

Responses to the original consultation suggested that speaking and listening needed to be given more prominence; that the literary heritage was important but not static; that technology must support learning but not lead it; that creativity was important to English; that the art and craft of the subject needed input from literary, biographical and travel writers; and that the language of work needed to be addressed. The responses to the consultation were distilled by the Qualifications and Curriculum Authority (QCA) (see QCA 2005) into four interwoven concepts:

- competence in using language effectively in a range of situations;
- creativity in exploiting linguistic resources, experiences and imagination to make new meanings;

- cultural appreciation of the best in language and literature; and
- critical skills in looking at all forms of media and communication, in addition to literary texts.

These aspirations and principles are in the tradition of the personal growth and literary heritage models of English, but do reveal that the core strands of English remain unchanged, and the layering of traditions and approaches mentioned in the introduction to this chapter create a bedrock of shared values that underpin the subject.

It appears, though, that the conservatism brought about by a combination of unreconstructed Leavisite values and 'national literary heritage' on the one hand, and personal growth and 'relevance' on the other, continue to make for a subject that – while popular and assured of its centrality to the primary and secondary curriculum, as well as in advanced study at college and university level – is increasingly anachronistic. Although it attempts to bring cultural studies (e.g. film, gaming) closer to the heart of the subject, it does so by keeping them at arm's length – as a topic for the honing of critical skills rather than a field in which works might be made as well as critiqued. The subject feels like a twentieth century creation that is in need of more radical reform in the present century than QCA suggests.

The persistent literariness of the English curriculum in schools makes it difficult to say that the subject is underpinned by any one model of language. At times in the past fifty years, various models or movements in relation to language have influenced teaching in the subject, and, to a lesser extent, the curriculum. These include, in roughly chronological order: psycholinguistics; Chomskian linguistics; sociolinguistics, language in use, language as social practice; language as discourse and as part of contemporary rhetoric; and verbal language as one mode within a multimodal conception of communication. The trend is one from smaller units of language to larger ones; and from a preoccupation with language as a system to language within a larger communication and social context.

English is a subject in which *composition* plays a central role. In order to decide which modes and media were suitable for a particular communication, knowledge about the affordances of those modes and media need to be developed, as well as competence and capability in the use of the modes and media. Motivation and engagement in composition of this kind would mean extending the genres to those used out of school as well as within school, so that the English curriculum was relevant to young people's lives. Such embracing of the so-called functional genres need not mean an impoverished, dry mimicking of reports, memoranda, mission statements and other text types from the world of work. It can mean that projects undertaken from the classroom could take on real world issues, like the creation of a zebra crossing outside school, a campaign for an arts centre or youth centre; or the setting up of a council or forum for a particular purpose (e.g. green issues, raising funds for the developing world, other voluntary activities). The combination of such forms of engagement with work experience can provide situations in which communication is essential and in which composition and reading are learnt in the course of doing something else. It must be acknowledged, too – in the spirit of the report *All Our Futures* (DfEE/DCMS 1999) – that creativity is not confined to literary genres, autobiographies and travel writing, but can manifest itself in (usually multimodal) compositions like brochures, blogs, manuals, 'how to' guides and other informational and persuasive genres.

Finally, it is important to recognize that speaking, writing, viewing, reading and listening are inter-related and that exploitation of their connections can enhance understanding and production. In some versions of literacy, where reading is often seen as the marker of competence, it is surprising that writing and viewing are not accorded the same status or centrality. It is even more surprising that speaking and listening are not seen as central to the business of developing capability in English. Speaking and listening can be used as a rehearsal for writing or reading; and they can also follow engagement with printed or online texts. But they also need to be seen as forms of communication and composition in their own right. Such a plea for the significance of speaking and listening has been a consistent one in relation to learning from the 1960s to the present; what is new, and yet to be fully realized in practice, is that speech may become – perhaps by 2015 or thereafter – the principal mode of composition, alongside the visual, from which written forms can be generated and read. Such a shift is a logical development from the work of Barnes *et al.* in the 1960s, cited earlier; and would sit neatly within a model of English language development which is based in social and political contexts. Furthermore, the economy of communicative choices in the real world makes it likely that the selection undertaken by the curriculum – and which is labelled 'English' – will continue to be contestable.

NOTES

1 'The Anglo-American Conference, held at Dartmouth College in the summer of 1966, was designed to improve the teaching of English and the cooperation between scholars and teachers in Great Britain, Canada, and the United States' (abstract to the conference proceedings). It is often cited as a key influence on the replacement of a transmission model of English teaching, with a model of personal growth.
2 The Technical and Vocational Education Initiative.
3 The Dearing Review was set up in response to a feeling that the first version of the National Curriculum in England and Wales was overcrowded and put too much pressure on subjects and on teachers within the curriculum.

11

INSTITUTIONAL DISCOURSE

CELIA ROBERTS

WHAT COUNTS AS 'INSTITUTIONAL DISCOURSE'?

Institutions are held together by talk and texts but are also sites of struggle and exclusion. The study of institutional discourses sheds light on how organisations work, how 'lay' people and experts interact and how knowledge and power circulate within the routines, systems and common-sense practices of work-related settings. However, the concept of 'institutional discourse' is not an easy one to define, since both words are highly contested.

A fundamental notion of the institutional derives from a social constructivist view of reality in which all institutions are made up of shared habitual practices. So, rather than seeing institutions as particular types of fixed settings that have an effect on language use, language and interaction construct the institution in dynamic ways. Stable and enduring features of talk and text are assembled through particular social settings: 'insitutionalisation occurs wherever there is a reciprocal typification of habitualised actions by types of actors' (Berger and Luckmann 1967).

So the institution is brought about by the gradual sedimentation of repeated actions, which provide a common stock of cultural knowledge. Those 'in the know' are the professionals, experts and bureaucratic officials who assess people and problems according to this shared cultural knowledge. Most of the studies discussed in this chapter take a broadly social constructivist perspective, but what counts as 'institutional' depends upon disciplinary backgrounds and epistemological stance.

For example, in their wide-ranging overview of talk and interaction at work, Drew and Heritage (1992) describe 'institutional interaction' as task-oriented and involving at least one participant who represents a formal organisation:

> talk-in-interaction is the principal means through which lay persons pursue various practical goals and the central medium through which the daily working activities of many professionals and organisational representatives are conducted. We will use the term 'institutional interaction' to refer to talk of this kind.
>
> (Drew and Heritage 1992: 3)

This definition stems from the sociological tradition of Conversation Analysis (CA) which focuses on the detailed interactional processes of specific activities such as service encounters or proceedings in court. By contrast, the feminist ethnographer, Dorothy Smith, takes a more critical stance in which work outside formal contexts is also seen as institutional. Her notion of 'institutional ethnography' encompasses the everyday world of women's work in supporting the home and family where this 'world' is 'organised by and sustains the institutional process' (Smith 1987: 166). So, 'institutional' may refer to specific activities and the interactions of representatives of organisations or, more widely, to everyday practices which are affected by and feed into such institutions as family, law or medicine.

There are even more differences of stance over the meaning and scope of what constitutes 'discourse' (see Chapter 3 in this volume). Discussions of this concept as they relate to institutional and organisational studies revolve around a dichotomy: first, discourse as empirical analysis of regularities in organisational activities (e.g. how do doctors and patients accomplish a consultation together) and, second, in a larger and more abstract sense, as a resource for identification and knowledge construction within relations of power. Some of these differences are exaggerated by the disciplinary regimes within which research is done. For example, organisational discourse analysis based on sociolinguistic, pragmatic and CA theory uses technical linguistic analysis to look at how talk and text produce organisational life. By contrast, organisational discourse studies have emerged from management and organisational theory and focus on discourse as a resource for people as social-organisational beings to manage and challenge the complexity and unpredictability of working life (Grant and Iedema 2005). Although there is very little cross-referencing between these two approaches, both, at least in certain aspects, draw on critical and post-structuralist theories, particularly the work of Michel Foucault. They both include some of the same analytic approaches, such as narrative and metaphor analysis and, within both, there are researchers who are concerned with practical relevance and contributing to change. So, discourse stretches from the micro-phenomena of pauses and prosody to the orders and relations which are part of the 'ruling apparatus' (Smith 1987: 160).

Faced with such an elastic concept as 'discourse' and such a wide-ranging definition of 'institutional', it is hard to set boundaries around what we can usefully count as 'institutional discourse'. In this chapter, we will limit the discussion to certain approaches and methodologies and certain types of interaction, drawing on sociolinguistic, pragmatic, discourse and conversation analytic, ethnographic and micro-ethnographic methodologies from both descriptive and critical perspectives. The focus will be on specific activities where there is at least one institutional/organisational representative but we will also include studies where the analysis is informed by an understanding of the wider discourses that construct and control social and institutional life.

INSTITUTIONAL AND PROFESSIONAL SETTINGS AND DISCOURSES

Most of the studies of institutional and workplace life involve professionals and the two terms 'institutional' and 'professional' are often used interchangeably.

However, there are useful distinctions to be made between institutional and professional discourse (Sarangi and Roberts 1999). The latter is acquired by professionals as they become teachers, doctors, human resource personnel and so on. Institutional discourse, following Weber (1947) and the critical theorist Habermas (1979), is characterised by rational, legitimate accounting practices which are authoritatively backed up by a set of rules and regulations governing an institution. So, for example, in the medical setting, the diagnosis and agreed course of action or the clinicians' working up of narratives into a case are professional discourses but the gatekeeping functions of selection, assessment and training rely on institutional discourse.

However, in most settings, professionals are using both types of discourses. For example, Cicourel (1981) shows that the recoding of patient information into abstract categories relates both to clinical treatment and also, institutionally, to the systematic organisation of patient care. At this level, the more abstract categories feed into the accounting practices and rules which construct the institution. Record-keeping in medical (Cicourel 1981; Iedema 2003), educational (Mehan 1993) and legal settings (Cicourel 1968) and other bureaucratic encounters (Sarangi and Slembrouck 1996) is an obvious site where professional knowledge is recontextualised into a form where it can be institutionally managed.

The distinction between professional and institutional discourse is also apparent in some of the 'frontstage' and 'backstage' work of professionals. Erving Goffman made the distinction between the frontstage 'performance' aspect of social life and the 'backstage' where this performance is rehearsed and sometimes knowingly contradicted (Goffman 1959). In institutional settings, much of the front-stage work is between the expert and the lay client or applicant in service encounters in healthcare (Fisher and Todd 1983; West 1984; Heritage and Maynard 2006) social work (Hall 1997) or other bureaucratic settings (Collins 1987). Other frontstage work is even more clearly a performance, as in educational settings (Sinclair and Coulthard 1975; Mehan 1979) or in legal settings (Atkinson and Drew 1979). The backstage is where professional knowledge is produced and circulated but also where staff and professional groups do the institutional work. This is where, for example, care plans and records are discussed and made accountable, where decisions are ratified and the initial professional frontstage work is not so much contradicted, in Goffman's terms, but reshaped and reframed to fit into institutional categories (Agar 1985; Zimmerman 1992).

CROSS-CUTTING THEMES

Despite the varied settings which have been the focus of institutional and workplace discourse and interaction over the past 30 years, there are themes which are common to many of them.

GOAL-ORIENTED ENCOUNTERS

In comparing institutional talk to ordinary conversation, Drew and Heritage (1992: 21–24) suggest that its defining characteristic is that it is goal-oriented and that this, in turn, involves particular constraints on what is allowable, and special aspects of reasoning or inference. These goals may be more or less explicitly defined but they all have some element of what Agar calls 'diagnosis' (Agar 1985). For example, in emergency calls (Zimmerman 1992), the participants are clearly oriented to an urgent task but, at the opening of a doctor–patient encounter, the routine is for the doctor to elicit some display of symptoms from the patient, so the goal is clear but the way in which the consultation will then develop will depend upon local contingencies (Heath 1981). Home visits by a health visitor consist of several less well-defined goals (Heritage and Sefi 1992) and the purpose of the encounter is jointly negotiated over the course of the interaction.

Similarly, the constraints on contributions, while generally giving an interaction its institutional character, vary depending on the overall function of the event. Courtroom interaction (Atkinson and Drew 1979), news-interviews (Greatbatch 1988) police interrogations (Heydon 2005) and cautions (Rock 2007) and job interviews (see below) clearly contain ritual and formal components, which constrain turn-taking and what are allowable contributions. Two examples from legal settings illustrate this well. In their study of interpreter-mediated courtrooms, Mason and Stewart quote from the O.J. Simpson case where a Spanish speaking witness is asked how long they have been resident in the USA. The interpreter's rendition of the Spanish is 'I came in 69, you figure it out'. This is greeted with laughter in the court since it is not pragmatically appropriate for a witness to tell the attorney what to do (Mason and Stewart 2001). In the somewhat less public and dramaturgical setting of suspect interrogation in the police station, the constraints on what is allowable can be as coercive, although more subtle. Police formulations of a suspect's story or explanation, reworking the response to fit the goals of the enquiry, are routinely unchallenged by suspects, with the result that their version of events is removed from the final report (Heydon 2005).

Each institutional encounter also entails 'special inferences' (Levinson 1992) drawn from both background knowledge and from the structural properties of the activity. Levinson illustrates this with some particularly telling examples from courtroom testimony of a rape victim. The incident had occurred on a cold winter's night. After establishing that the victim had been wearing make-up, the defence lawyer apparently suddenly changes topic from make-up to health.

Example 1

D: You had had bronchitis had you not?
V: Yes
D: You have mentioned in the course of your evidence about wearing a coat?

v: Yes

d: It was not really a coat at all, was it?

v: Well it is sort of a coat-dress and I bought it with trousers, as a trouser suit.

d: That is it down there isn't it, the red one?

v: Yes

d: If we call that a dress, if we call that a dress you had no coat on at all had you?

v: No

(Levinson 1992: 83)

Levinson makes the point that it is the juxtaposition of these different topics, in other words the sequencing of the questions, which builds up a set of inferences to make what appears a natural argument for the jury. The inferences are that a girl in poor health had put on make-up and gone out dancing on a cold night without even a coat on and was, in effect, looking for sexual adventures. As readers of this transcript, we can make these inferences because of what we know about the nature of rape cases and about the goals of the defendant's lawyer in establishing that alleged rape victims are loose women who are 'asking for it'. The fact that the professional has control over what topics are initiated and over the turn-taking system, and that the young woman is positioned by these structural constraints means that she has little or no opportunity to challenge or rework the argument.

GATEKEEPING AND LABELLING

Most institutional and workplace encounters involve some sort of labelling and sorting process where people are checked through an invisible gate. In service encounters, 'the institutional representative uses his/her control to fit the client into the organisational ways of thinking about the problem' (Agar 1985: 153) and this may happen both frontstage and backstage. In studies of workplace settings, the labelling and sorting of people, information and arguments is distributed across many different groupings so that the decision-making process is hard to pin down to one event or encounter, as Deidre Boden discusses in her ethnomethodological study (Boden 1994).

The notion of gatekeeping implies the 'objective' assessment of applicants with a view to making decisions about scarce resources. These may be jobs, educational or training opportunities, housing and other social benefits and so on. Weber's arguments for efficient, objective and rational forms of work control influenced the development of bureaucracy and the formal modes of assessment and selection that are central to institutions (Weber 1947). Ironically, these 'objective' procedures were in part a response to an increasingly ethnically and linguistically diverse society and yet studies of institutional discourse have shown how these very procedures tend to reproduce inequality:

(G)atekeeping encounters are not a neutral and 'objective' meritocratic sorting process. On the contrary, our analysis suggests that the game is rigged, albeit not deliberately, in favour of those individuals whose communication style and social background are most similar to those of the interviewer with whom they talk.

(Erickson and Shultz 1982:193)

In their seminal study of educational counselling interviews, Erickson and Shultz show how decisions about students depend upon judgments of their 'performed social identity' (Erickson and Shultz 1982) as they are played out through the social and cultural organisation of the interaction. They identified two factors that were crucial in determining whether the counsellor's advice offered or closed down educational opportunities for students: one related to solidarity through shared membership of a group or community – co-member-ship – and the other to the interactional performance, in particular the rhythmic co-ordination of the interview. Lack of co-membership and conversational arhythmia led to less helpful and optimistic advice for students.

Together with the work of John Gumperz (discussed below) this micro-ethnographic study explores the relationship between language and the socio-cultural order. Organisations have their own cultural practices, as the previous section has shown, and the gatekeepers tend to align with these ways of inter-acting since their own socio-cultural norms and styles of communicating are similar. There is a fit between their own ways of understanding and doing and the distinctive interests of the institution. However, where the lay participant brings to the interview different linguistic behaviour and socio-cultural knowl-edge, there is no easy fit and the social evaluation of the applicant is based on the uncomfortable moments and lack of alignment experienced by both sides. This can lead to less good advice or failure to secure a job or, in encounters involving even higher stakes such as in asylum-seeker interviews, deportation from a safe country to a dangerous one (Maryns 2006).

Example 2

In this next example, an Afro-Caribbean student has just told a white counsellor that he wants to be a counsellor too.

C: essentially what you need
first of all you're gonna need
state certification state
teacher certification (..) in
other words you're gonna have to be
(S begins slight head nodding)
certified to teach in some area (..)
English or history or
whatever happens to be your bag (..)
(slight head nodding by student)

S: mhm (and more accented head nodding)
(Erickson and Shultz 1982: 134–6 (simplified transcription,
C = counsellor, S = student))

The counsellor's reply is punctuated by rhythmically organised pauses where he expects an active listening response. Erickson and Shultz argue that both sides misread the other's culturally influenced organisation of the interaction so that the student's slight head nods are ignored. The counsellor continues his explanation with increasingly lower levels of abstraction, 'talking down' to the student on the assumption that he did not understand 'state teacher certification' until the student, with the vocalised response 'mhm' and more accented head nodding, is seen to have responded appropriately. In the viewing session afterwards, the student stopped the video at this point and commented that the counsellor 'was trying to knock me down' (1982: 137). These moments of arhythmia and consequent 'hyperexplanation' create uncomfortable moments which feed into the gatekeeper's judgment of students and the decisions about their future educational careers.

Gatekeeping decisions are interactionally produced but they are also the product of what Mehan calls the 'politics of representation'. This is the means by which various interested groups compete with each other over what is the correct, appropriate or preferred way of representing the particular slice of the world which is within the institutional gaze:

> Proponents of various positions in conflicts waged in and through discourse attempt to capture or dominate modes of representation. They do so in a variety of ways, including inviting or persuading others to join their side, or silencing opponents by attacking their position. If successful, a hierarchy is formed, in which one mode of representing the world . . . gains primacy over others, transforming modes of representation from an array on a horizontal plane to a ranking on a vertical plane.
>
> (Mehan 1993: 241)

These modes of representation include the technical jargon of institutions, the means of classifying and coding events and people, and the way in which an institutional representative speaks for the institution, for example, the use of 'we' rather than 'I' in patient healthcare professional consultations. Linked to the notion of how lay stories can be fitted into institutional criteria, Mehan is interested in how categorical 'facts' and categories such as 'intelligence', 'special needs', 'deviance' emerge from the ambiguity of everday life. Whereas many of the studies of institutional encounters focus on the formal face-to-face encounter, Mehan's ethnographic study of how children are considered for placement in special education programmes included observations and video recordings of frontstage settings (classrooms, testing rooms) and backstage ones such as teachers' lounges, referral committee meetings and also interviews with parents and gatekeepers and reviews of student records.

With these different data types, Mehan illustrates how a general call for help from a classroom teacher becomes transformed into the more abstract and distant language of institutional discourse: from a schoolchild who 'needs help' into a 'learning disabled child'. Rick Iedema (2003) draws on Habermas' distinction between the lifeworld (the everyday world of conversations, informality and feelings) and the systems world (of rationality, formality and accountability) in discussing this transformation. Iedema calls this process part of the new linguistic technologies in which power is simultaneously hidden and reinforced. Texts and modes of talking which are increasingly distant from active doing and saying become timeless and taken for granted. Power inheres in these increasingly abstract forms since only those in the know can fully understand their meanings. This depersonalised and distant institutional language is summed up by the critical anthropologist and social theorist Pierre Bourdieu as: 'impartiality, symmetry, balance, propriety, decency and discretion' (Bourdieu 1991: 130) and by his notion of 'euphemisation' in which uncomfortable judgments are masked by discreet language. This next example is a short extract from a speech pathology progress report on a six-year-old boy, Francis, who is perceived as having fluency problems:

Example 3

> Clinicians attempted to elicit conversation from the children while they were completing a craft. This was a more challenging environment for the children since they were required to do two things at once (i.e. speak and make a craft). By the end of the term, the activities focused on requiring the children to interact with one another, while involved in manipulating objects. Clinicians verbally reinforced easy messages sent by the children. When the activity allowed for spontaneous conversation and interaction, Francis was able to remain fairly fluent. However, when asked a question, he became dysfluent. The dysfluencies consisted of hard starts, interjections, prolongations and/or repetitions. It was noted that Francis was less attentive when the parents joined the group. It was observed that he had difficulty sitting still and diverted his attention toward his mother relying on her to answer for him.
>
> (Stillar 1998: 175)

The institutional discourse of this text, Stillar argues, combining scientific (interjections and prolongations) and more lifeworld (fairly fluent) vocabulary, masks its attitudinal and persuasive function. The classificationary system of observation and assessment euphemises the label of poor speaker given to Francis and underplays the formal assessment setting in which he has to perform. The report appears impartial and discreet, balancing Francis's fluency and dysfluency and glossing over the differences between the highly technical assessment of his language and the general evaluation of his behaviour. The institutional discourse of the report both reflects and reproduces institutional authority.

In a referral committee, as with the clinician's report in Example 3, where children become labelled in institutionally appropriate terms, it is the psychologist's means of representation that prevail. The psychological language in which the child is represented is accepted without question whereas the lay descriptions and evaluations from teachers and parents are constantly challenged. The psychologist's report is accepted *because* it is produced in institutional language which lay participants cannot understand. As the 'legitimate speaker' (Bourdieu 1991) with the authority to represent ambiguous accounts with institutional certainty, the psychologist's role in labelling the child and deciding on what action to take overrides the more contextual accounts from teachers and parents. So both the modes of representation and the interactional constraints imposed in such meetings ensure that institutional categories dominate and, in making decisions about ordinary people, the institution also looks after itself.

SOCIAL RELATIONS, ASYMMETRY AND 'FACE'

Although many of the interactional features of institutional encounters display the power and authority of institutional representatives, as the gatekeeping interviews and meetings discussed above show, in such encounters both sides also have to manage the social relations and alignments required in the moral conduct of face-to-face activities (Goffman 1959). Goffman's notion of 'footing' captures in its metaphor some of the delicate interactional footwork that has to be done by participants if they are to manage their professional or client identities, their roles and the moment-to-moment ways of relating to the other. For institutional representatives, their reputation, how they save 'face' and are sensitive to potential face loss in others, has to be managed within what is widely recognised as asymmetrical relations in most institutional interaction.

Although there is no simple contrast between symmetrical conversation and asymmetrical institutional discourse, most studies of the latter recognise its asymmetrical character. Some aspects of this asymmetry have already been mentioned: the degree of control over the content of talk, the allocation of turns, the special inferencing to which experts have access, the differential distribution of participation rights and the very different impact that decisions have for the client or applicant (Drew and Heritage 1992; Thornborrow 2002). The asymmetrical nature of medical consultations has been widely studied to show these inequalities (Fisher and Todd 1983; West 1984; Mishler 1984).

Although these studies show how patients are interrupted (Frankel 1984), rarely challenge the health professional's decision or manage their explanations with the doctor's expertise in mind (Gill and Maynard 2006), the professional rarely exerts any raw power. The exercise of power and authority is laminated over with language and bodily conduct which is sensitive to issues of face and politeness. The critical linguist Norman Fairclough describes the 'conversational' mode of institutional talk where equality is simulated and covert mechanisms of control are substituted for overt markings of power (Fairclough 1992).

Talk becomes euphemised (as do the types of written institutional texts illustrated in Example 3) and cautious – the 'little chat' describes a high-stakes gatekeeping interview – and professional elicitations are embedded in casual social conversation.

Institutional talk takes on a special kind of asymmetry when both sides do not share the same grounds for negotiating understanding (see below), as is often the case with linguistic and socio-cultural differences between lay and expert participants. The face-saving social chat of the medical consultation evaporates when the patient cannot align to the doctor's footing. In this next example, a mother (whose first language is Twi, a language of Ghana) has come to have her eight-week-old baby checked at the baby clinic. The GP already knows that she has three daughters. The GP punctuates the silence of the physical examination with brief sequences such as the following:

Example 4

1   D   so your three daughters must <u>love</u> having little babies

2   P   (1)

3   D   your other children (.) the girls do they help you with =

4   P   = yeah the first one help me

5   D   I bet

6   D   ((you're very lucky having all those sisters (..) yes))

      ((D turns to address the baby))

D then continues to examine the baby

(Roberts and Sarangi 2005)

The doctor's comment at line one may function as social chat to fill the silence or as an elicitation of how the mother is managing at home with four young children, or both. There are plenty of what the interactional sociolinguist, John Gumperz, calls 'contextualisation cues' (Gumperz 1982a) which trigger inferences about the intention of the utterance as a moment of social chat: the initiating 'so', the switch to a more intimate register with the words 'must love', with emphasis on the word 'love', and the falling final tone which suggests a comment rather than a doctorly elicitation question. However, the mother's lack of uptake of the doctor's comment (at line 2 where there is a one second pause) leads to a reformulation into a much more direct question (line 3). The social face of the institution is sacrificed to the strictly professional business of checking up on the home.

METHODOLOGIES AND ANALYTIC FRAMEWORKS

Most of the studies within the scope of this chapter share a common methodological interest. They reflect a social constructivist perspective in which small-scale routines and habits of institutional life are seen as feeding into wider social structures. They are also grounded in the observations, recordings and textual data of institutional activities, giving primacy to the fine-grained detail of these activities. However, they range in stance from the descriptive accounts of talk-in-interaction to more critical debates about how such events come to be produced within relations of power.

ETHNOGRAPHIC STUDIES

Some of the early ethnographies of the workplace stem from the tradition of the Chicago school, where the focus on the observation of socially and culturally bounded worlds drew on methods of participant observation and interviews. Long periods spent within institutions provided insights not only into how they functioned as workplaces but also into the perspective of those who were regulated by them. Goffman's study of asylums is a classic account of what he called 'total institutions' (Goffman 1961). More recent ethnographic work has combined detailed recordings of talk with a more traditional ethnography in educational settings (see the discussion above of Mehan 1993) and medical settings (Cicourel 1992; Mishler 1984; Atkinson 1995).

SOCIOLINGUISTIC STUDIES

Early sociolinguistic studies were concerned with the relationship between language and context and how certain variables explain the nature of institutional interaction; for example, West's work on the relationship between interruptions and gender (West 1984). However, increasingly, sociolinguists have drawn on ethnographic methods and on conceptual frameworks informed by social and critical theory, notably Foucault and Bourdieu (for example, Heller in French Canadian educational contexts, 2006 and Gumperz in gatekeeping contexts, 1992). Interactional Sociolinguistics (IS), drawing on the ethnography of communication, pragmatics and Conversation Analysis (CA) (see below) has made gatekeeping encounters in linguistically diverse settings a special focus of interest (Gumperz 1982a, 1992). Gumperz and his associates (Gumperz 1982b) link the CA methods of interactional analysis with a sociolinguistic understanding of a variety of communicative styles and relate situated interpretive processes to wider ideological discourses. Some aspects of the IS method are illustrated in the final section of this chapter.

CONVERSATION ANALYSIS

The most extensive and methodologically coherent studies of institutional talk are within CA. Drawing on Harvey Sack's plea for an aesthetic of 'smallness and slowness' (Silverman 1999), the orthodox CA position is that the *how* of talk-in-interaction discovered through technical analysis must come before the *why*, and that the participants' orientation to what is happening should take priority over the analyst's. The interpretation of data depends on how participants display their understanding of the interaction rather than on any outside contextual information. Two edited collections (Drew and Heritage 1992, which includes a range of workplace settings, and Heritage and Maynard 2006, which focuses on medical care) represent CA methodology well.

DISCOURSE ANALYSIS AND CRITICAL DISCOURSE ANALYSIS

Early discourse analysis (DA) used speech act theory to try to formulate rules for coherent discourse in institutional settings (Sinclair and Coulthard 1975 in the classroom and Labov and Fanshel 1977 in a therapeutic interview). However, the emphasis on rules for well-formed discourse underplayed the mutual negotiation of understanding and the active context-creating function of interaction, which is the focus of CA and IS research. While critical discourse analysis (CDA) maintains the focus on the detailed analysis of talk and text, it takes a radically different stance from the earlier studies and from CA. Detailed linguistic analysis is integrated with critical theory, drawing on Habermas, Foucault and Bourdieu to understand how institutional discourse serves to both reflect and construct unequal power relations. This understanding, in turn, can contribute to social change (Fairclough 1992; Caldas-Coulthard and Coulthard 1996; Sarangi and Slembrouck 1996; Wodak 1996; and Iedema and Wodak 1999).

JOB INTERVIEWS: A CASE STUDY OF INSTITUTIONAL DISCOURSE

This final section takes the particular activity of the job interview to draw together and illustrate several of the themes referred to in this chapter. As a high-stakes gatekeeping activity, it is an obvious target for research, even though naturally-occurring job interviews are not easy to record and some studies have had to rely on simulations. The studies referred to here are from both the English-speaking world and from Germany, the Netherlands and Scandinavia and draw, specifically, on two British studies on selection interviews for low-paid and junior management posts. Most of this research takes a critical stance, influenced by Gumperz's position that there is a communicative dimension to discrimination (Gumperz 1982a and b, 1992) in which language and socio-cultural knowledge interact to produce and reproduce inequality.

The British research, focusing on minority ethnic groups in job interviews, shows that it is not ethnicity per se that disadvantages minority ethnic groups in job interviews, but a lack of socialisation into the norms and assumptions of this activity, since it is those candidates who were born overseas that fair less well (Roberts and Campbell 2005). The authors argue that a 'linguistic penalty' is experienced by this group. This penalty is faced by anyone who has not developed the 'linguistic capital' of the particular institutional sub-field of the job interview (Bourdieu 1991). The discourses required and the ability to move between and blend them into a convincing synthetic whole, interactionally construct the ideal candidate. The fact that this 'linguistic capital' is taken for granted by employers as a matter of individual competence or merely a question of adequate preparation masks its power in reproducing structural inequalities. Failed candidates 'just don't have the skills'. In the following example, Ire, a Nigerian candidate is being interviewed for a low-paid delivery job:

Example 5

Ire: Nigerian, Candidate born abroad, Borderline Successful

I: right what would you tell me is the advantage of a repetitive job (1)
C: advantage of a
I: repetitive job (1)
C: er I mean the advantage of a repetitive job is that er:m it makes you it it keeps you going, er it doesn't make you bored, you don't feel bored you keep on going and, I mean I me-a – and also it it puts a smile on your face you come in it puts a smile on your face you feel happy to come to the job the job will (trust) you
I: you don't get to know it better
C: sorry
I: you don't get to know it better
C: yeah we get to know the job better we I mean we learn new ideas lots of new ideas as well
I: right what is the disadvantage of a repetitive job
C: well, disadvantage er:m, er disadvantages (1) you may you may f-offend customers you may f-offend our customers in there that's a disadvantage of it
I: you don't find it boring
C: yeah it could also be boring, to be boring and you- and you, yet by being bored you may offend the customers
I: how how would you offend them by being bored
C: by not putting a smile on your face

(Roberts and Campbell 2005: 39)

This short extract exemplifies many of the themes of the selection interview. First, the hidden assumptions of the interviewers serve to construct inequality when there is no shared definition of the interview. Shared inferential processes depend upon 'socially constructed knowledge of what the interview is about' (Gumperz 1992: 303) but there are few explicit clues to this or what candidates' roles and modes of communicating should be. The question in line 1 is designed to elicit a particular competence that relates to self-management. British interviews are now routinely constructed around a competency framework that also includes competencies such as team working, communications, customer focus, adaptability and flexibility. These reflect the discourses of the 'new work order' (Gee *et al.* 1996) in which workers, however low their status in the workplace, are expected to buy into a corporate ideology. Flattened hierarchies require individuals to be autonomous and self-regulating. So the competency questions at lines 1 and 14 are based on a set of conventionalised expectations that repetitive jobs are boring, but that enterprising, self-managing candidates will recognise this and find ways of dealing with the boredom which will maintain their identity as motivated workers. The candidate's requests for clarification, the perturbation phenomena in lines 4 and 5 and the interviewer's rebuttals of his responses in lines 9 and 18 show that he has not cued into the special line of inferencing embedded in this new work order ideology and into the fabric of the interview. So, despite attempts to make interviews culturally and ideologically neutral, current workplace ideologies leak into the interview at all points, as studies in other contexts have also identified (Birkner 2004; Auer and Kern 2000).

The interview also contains other inherent contradictions in its presentation as an objective sorting process (Linell and Thunquist 2003) since, as a social encounter, it is shot through with subjectivities. Issues of personality, social class or ethnicity remain 'unmentionables' and only conveyed implicitly (Komter 1991; Birkner 2004: 298) and yet personal liking and co-membership (Erickson and Shultz 1982) are at the hidden heart of decision-making. Despite Ire's best attempts to interpret the interviewer's questions, he remains a borderline candidate since the misunderstandings displayed create uncomfortable moments that feed into doubts about his acceptability for the job.

The sequential organisation of the interview illustrates its fundamentally asymmetrical character and the role of the interviewer in the final decision-making. Candidates are routinely blamed for what is a joint production (Campbell and Roberts 2007). The interview is controlled almost entirely by the interviewers who govern the interactional norms, allocation of turns and speaking roles (Komter 1991; Birkner 2004). In this extract, the interviewer has a script which she drives through and in which only certain answers are allowable and institutionally processable. So, the interview is not only a site for individual selection and the reproduction of inequality, it is also a site for the production and maintenance of institutional and social order (Auer and Kern 2000; Makitalo and Saljo 2002).

TRANSCRIPTION CONVENTIONS

Based on Jefferson, G. 'A Technique for Transcribing Laughter and its Subsequent Acceptance/Declination' in Psathas, G. (ed.) 1979 *Everyday Language: Studies in Ethnomethodology*, New York: Ervington, 79–96 and Gumperz, J. and Berenz, N. 'Transcribing Conversational Exchanges' in J. Edwards and M. Lampert (eds) 1993 *Transcription and Coding Methods for Language Research*, Hillsdale, NJ: Lawrence Earlbaum Associates, Inc.

() talk too obscure to transcribe

[overlapping talk begins

] overlapping talk ends

(1) silence timed in seconds or pause of less than half a second (.) or more than half a second (..)

: lengthening of a sound

Becau- cut off, interruption of a sound

<u>He</u> says. Emphasis, i.e. perceived stress based on pitch change and/or increased volume

= latching, i.e. no silence at all between sounds

(()) non verbal communication, anonymised data or other comments

\ low falling tone

/ rising tone

12

USING ENGLISH IN THE LEGAL PROCESS

DIANA EADES

INTRODUCTION

I wonder if I might uplift from Your Honour the documentation? might seem a rather strange way for a lawyer to ask a judge if he can take back a piece of paper. Legal English is an occupational register, which includes specialised vocabulary and many formal sentence constructions. It is well known that legal documents, such as wills and contracts, are characterised by this specialised register, known in ordinary English as 'legalese'. To a lesser extent, specialised vocabulary and formal sentence constructions are also found in spoken legal contexts, such as the opening example above from a courtroom hearing.

So, you might speak English, but can you understand what goes on in court? Actually, it is likely that many people will understand most, if not all, of the talk that is addressed directly *to* them (and note that, in the opening example, a lawyer is talking to a judge, not to a witness). In spoken legal contexts the legal vocabulary and sentence structures typically occur in talk between lawyers and judges: it is a kind of 'insiders' language', similar to the way in which computer technicians might discuss your computer problems, in their specialised register, in front of you.

But there is more to specialised legal language than vocabulary and grammar. This chapter will focus on features of pragmatics – how language is used in social contexts – which are specific to legal contexts, in particular to the criminal justice process in common law systems (used in countries such as the UK, Australia and the USA). The ways in which English is used in the legal process have been investigated by sociolinguists in several different legal contexts. For example, Rock's (2007) study of police interviews with suspects investigated the ways in which 'rights texts' – such as advising detainees of the right to have a lawyer present – are presented and explained, and how detainees respond. Her analysis found that there is much more going on in this part of the police interview than simply the explanation of the suspect's rights: police officers and detainees can also be variously engaged in reassuring, persuading, making suggestions, empathising, learning, presenting identity and showing affiliation. Sociolinguists have also researched the use of English in interviews with lawyers, examining the ways in which lawyers take the stories of their clients and transform them so that they 'work' in the legal process (e.g. Trinch 2003).

COURTROOM TALK

As research data is much easier to access in courtroom hearings than in other legal contexts, this is where most of the research has been focused. In court, there are strict constraints on who can talk to whom about what and when. Witnesses are not permitted to ask any questions, unless it is to request clarification of the immediately preceding question which they have been asked. And they are not permitted to avoid answering questions, except under very limited conditions. Within this highly constrained discourse structure of courtroom hearings, sociolinguistic microanalysis has examined the specific linguistic mechanisms used by lawyers and judges to exercise control over witnesses. The earliest of this work, in the 1980s, was particularly interested in how the syntactic form of questions can control the participation of witnesses. For example, many more yes/no questions are found in cross-examination than in examination-in-chief. In examination-in-chief, lawyers question their own witnesses, and one of the main goals is to facilitate the witnesses' telling their own stories in the most favourable light, and without saying anything that will damage their case. Thus, the lawyer decides how a witness's evidence will be presented, what topics will be covered, in what order and in what way. This usually means that the lawyer steers the witness through their story in quite small fragments, in answer to specific questions, such as *And who did you see then? Did this person do anything at that time? How did [this person] leave the park?* In cross-examination on the other hand, witnesses are questioned by lawyers from the opposing side, whose aim is to show that they are inconsistent in some details of their story, or are unreliable, untrustworthy or not to be believed. The major linguistic strategy for achieving this cross-examination goal is presenting questions to which the witness can only answer *yes* or *no*. The propositions of these questions typically point to inconsistencies in the answers, or between these answers on the one hand, and, on the other hand, earlier answers in court (e.g. during examination-in-chief), or an earlier version of the witness's story, such as that told during a police interview. The interest in the power of questions to control witnesses' answers led to a number of linguists producing hierarchies of question types, from most controlling (declarative plus tag, e.g. *You were there, weren't you?*) to least controlling (broad 'WH-questions', that is *what?, why?* and *how?* questions). These hierarchies differ slightly with regard to the ways in which linguists assess degrees of control. Examples can be found in Woodbury 1984 and Gibbons 2003: 103–5.

But a number of studies have pointed out that it can be problematic to assume that particular linguistic forms (such as question types) always function in the same way. In my (Eades 2000) study, I showed how a question type which is generally considered by linguists to be quite controlling – declarative yes/no question, such as *You go out of your way to avoid the Smiths?* – can be used by witnesses as an invitation to provide explanations. There are a number of other features of courtroom interaction which affect the way in which question forms are understood and replied to, such as immediate legal context (for example, whether examination-in-chief or cross-examination), relationships between questioner and witness, intonation, and the content of preceding questions and answers.

As linguists and sociolinguists have learnt more about the complexities of courtroom talk, they have broadened their unit of analysis beyond individual question–answer pairs, and have examined a number of other ways in which power and control are exercised over witnesses. Other concerns include the ways in which witnesses' participation is so constrained that there is little chance for negotiation, and ways in which witnesses' descriptions of events, people and situations are reformulated in order to create a different reality from that being presented by witnesses. For example, a number of sociolinguists have examined language use in rape trials, showing how witnesses' presentations of what happened to them are rephrased in order to change the claim of forced sex to one of consensual sex. This legal strategy often involves tricky linguistic mechanisms for shifting blame or for removing responsibility or agency for particular actions. For example, Ehrlich (2001) analysed the linguistic means used to attribute non-agency to a defendant, including the use of unaccusative constructions (where an action is presented as simply happening), and the nominalisation of actions (using an abstract noun instead of a verb). These two grammatical strategies are powerful in removing agency, as we see in one of the questions that the complainant was asked by the defendant's lawyer: 'Well, your shirt came off first as a result of fondling of the breasts, right?' (Ehrlich 2001: 53). In this question, no-one is responsible for either of the actions referred to: it is the agentless 'fondling' (a nominalisation) which is responsible for the complainant's shirt coming off (in an unaccusative construction). Such a question could be asked differently in order to attribute agency to the defendant, for example 'Well, when he was fondling your breasts, he took off your shirt, right?'.

Another linguistic examination of the power of word choice in the courtroom is found in Cotterill's (2003) analysis of lawyers' opening statements in the famous O.J. Simpson trial. Opening statements are supposed to be a neutral summary of the case, a 'road map' by which the lawyer for the prosecution and the lawyer for the defence explain to the jury how they will organise the evidence to be presented. But Cotterill argues that since '*overt* evaluation and persuasion are banned in opening statements, lawyers must achieve a persuasive effect in their opening statements through the subtle use of language' (2003: 64, emphasis in original). So, for example, the defence counsel used the word *incident* to refer to alleged assaults by Simpson on his wife over several years leading up to her death. Cotterill found that in the 450 million word Bank of English corpus, this word 'collocates strongly with a series of words which convey singularity and randomness' (81). And, as incidents often collocate in the Bank of English corpus with the intransitive verb *occur*, the use of this word *incident* enables the defence to talk about the alleged domestic violence predating the murders, without attributing agency to the defendant (or to anyone else).

Linguistic and sociolinguistic research, such as the studies referred to above, are shedding some light on how and why it is difficult for witnesses to participate in courtroom hearings. Witnesses with the greatest experience in linguistic manipulation and negotiation are probably at the greatest advantage in court-room hearings. And witnesses who do not speak Standard English may be at the greatest disadvantage. While non-English speaking witnesses should have access to interpreting services (see Berk-Seligson 2002), people who speak a nonstandard dialect of English typically are given no recognition of the possibility of miscommunication due to subtle dialectal differences, which can have significant consequences.

SPEAKERS OF AUSTRALIAN ABORIGINAL ENGLISH

This is a matter of considerable importance in Australia, where most Aboriginal people speak a dialect of English, known as Aboriginal English, in their dealings with the law. And it is not just researchers who are interested in this: Australian Aboriginal people are greatly over-represented in police custody and prisons, at more than ten times the rate of non-Aboriginal people. There are many complex factors involved in this over-representation, and differences in the use of English comprise one of these factors.

There is considerable variation in the varieties of Aboriginal English spoken throughout the country, with the heaviest varieties (those furthest from General Australian English) being most widely spoken in the more remote areas, and the lightest (or closest to General Australian English) in urban and metropolitan areas.[1] Communication with speakers of heavy Aboriginal English can be affected at the levels of phonology, grammar, semantics and pragmatics. For example, Koch (1985: 180) reports a witness giving evidence at a land claim hearing who said 'Charcoal Jack – properly his father'. This was understood by the court as the witness being unsure of the family relationship in question, consistent with it being recorded in the official transcription as 'Charcoal Jack – probably his father'. But this was a misunderstanding, in which several features of heavy Aboriginal English were ignored, including the interchangeability of /b/ and /p/, and the use of the word *properly* to mean 'real'. So, we can see that a subtle but important misunderstanding arose because of phonological and semantic differences, combined with a cultural difference, namely the usage of the term *father* in Aboriginal English to refer to a person's biological father as well as any of this biological father's brothers (thus the qualification *properly* is used to specify a person's 'real' or biological father, as opposed to a man who would be called *uncle* in other varieties of English). The witness was not expressing lack of certainty about the relationship. On the contrary, he was being specific about what kind of father-relationship was involved.

There is much less scope for miscommunication in terms of phonology, grammar and semantics with speakers of light Aboriginal English. But my work over two decades has shown has shown that, even where such differences between Aboriginal English and other varieties of Australian English are not great, there are significant pragmatic differences, which have implications for intercultural communication (e.g. Eades 1991).

SOME PRAGMATIC FEATURES OF ABORIGINAL ENGLISH

Elsewhere (e.g. Eades 1991, 2007), I have written about differences between Aboriginal English and General Australian English in the ways in which information is sought. These differences are not just dialectal differences, but they involve cultural differences as well. While the legal process relies heavily on interviews, and indeed interviews are widespread speech events in western societies, they have not been part of the experience of Aboriginal societies until the past couple of decades. For many Aboriginal societies within Australia, information- seeking is typically much less direct, more time-consuming and involves much more reciprocality than one-sided interviews. So, there is a major problem with the participation of Aboriginal people in the legal process, which results from the disjunction between interviews on the one hand, and typical Aboriginal ways of finding out information on the other. Compounding this disjunction is an important difference in the way in which silence is used, interpreted and evaluated.

Silence sounds the same in any language or dialect, but that does not necessarily mean that it always has the same meaning. In many Aboriginal interactions silence is important and positively valued. It often indicates a participant's desire to think, or simply to enjoy the presence of others in a non-verbal way.[2] This is a difficult concept for most non-Aboriginal people to recognise and learn because, in western societies, silence is often negatively valued in conversations. Indeed, many Conversation Analysis studies of English conversations in western societies support Jefferson's (1989) finding that the 'standard maximum tolerance for silence' is less than one second. Between people who are not close friends or family, silence in conversations or interviews is frequently an indication of some kind of communication breakdown. This difference has serious implications for police and lawyers and in courtroom interviews of Aboriginal people. Aboriginal silence in these settings can easily be interpreted as evasion, ignorance, confusion, insolence or even guilt. According to law, silence should not be taken as admission of guilt, but it can be difficult for police officers, legal professionals or jurors to set aside strong cultural intuitions about the meaning of silence, especially when they are not aware of cultural differences in the use and interpretation of silence. Further, a misunderstanding of Aboriginal ways of using silence can lead lawyers to interrupt an Aboriginal person's answer. Of course, we customarily define interruption as involving a second person starting to talk before the first speaker has finished talking. But, if we accept that the first part of an Aboriginal answer often starts with silence, then to start the next question before the Aboriginal interviewee has had time to speak is, in effect, to interrupt the first part of the answer.

INTERCULTURAL COMMUNICATION AWARENESS

From the early 1990s, there was some recognition both of sociolinguistic differences in ways of communicating – including the use and interpretation of silence – and of the need to educate legal professionals about them. In 1992, the Queensland Law Society published a handbook for lawyers about communicating with speakers of Aboriginal English (Eades 1992). This lawyers' handbook is widely used in law schools and by lawyers who work with Aboriginal clients. It has also been cited in judgments,[3] excerpted in other handbooks, and extensively drawn on by the Queensland Criminal Justice Commission in its report on Aboriginal witnesses in criminal courts (CJC 1996). There are also a number of workshops and similar initiatives aimed at increasing intercultural awareness in members of the legal profession and the judiciary.

The importance of intercultural communication with Aboriginal people in the legal process was highlighted in the year following the publication of the lawyers' handbook in the *R.* v. *Kina* case. In this case (see Eades 1996), lawyers who were unaware of Aboriginal ways of using English, had been unable to adequately represent an Aboriginal woman in her murder trial in 1988. As a result, the jury never heard about the horrific abuse suffered by Kina which would have been relevant to issues such as provocation and self-defence. In her 1993 appeal, the lawyers' lack of awareness of Aboriginal ways of using English was one of the factors which resulted in the decision to quash her murder conviction. For example, not recognising that Aboriginal answers to questions often begin with considerable silence, the lawyers had been unsuccessful in their attempts to elicit her story. They reported that she had been very difficult to communicate with, and she reported that they had asked her questions, and not waited for the answers. Discussing the implications of Kina's case on the day following this decision, the state Attorney-General spoke about 'the need for the legal system to have knowledge of the problem of cross-cultural communication and be sensitive to it' (*7.30 Report* ABC television, 30 November 1993).

But, is the apparent increase in awareness of Aboriginal ways of communicating resulting in more successful and equitable participation by Aboriginal people in the legal process? The answer to this question requires much more research, but we can already glimpse some developments which suggest that the answer might be summarised as 'only sometimes'.

THE MAPLETOWN STUDY

In the mid-1990s, I carried out research in the District (intermediate) Court of a country town in New South Wales, referred to by the pseudonym of Mapletown (Eades 2000). Aboriginal people in this area speak a very light variety of Aboriginal English, and the study found few instances of miscommunication which could be attributed to dialectal differences in phonology, grammar, semantics or pragmatics. What was striking about the Aboriginal evidence in these cases was both how little was said by the witnesses, and the ways in which they were silenced in examination-in-chief.

The study found that some lawyers seemed to have a good understanding of some Aboriginal ways of communicating. For example, some lawyers used their knowledge of the positive Aboriginal use of silence to the advantage of their clients. The example below (Eades 2000: 172) comes from a sentencing hearing in the case of an Aboriginal defendant who had pleaded guilty to assault. In answering questions which could help to establish grounds for minimising the severity of his sentence, he was invited by his lawyer (defence counsel, DC) to show remorse for his actions to the judge (the duration of the silence is shown in parentheses).[4]

Example 1

DC: And do you tell His Honour that you know you shouldn't – and that you're sorry for having done that?

WITNESS: Uh well– yeah – I am – sorry (6.7) when we're not – oh sorry – when we're not drinkin' you know –we don't even fight or nothin' – you know – when we're drinking it's a bit of a problem –it's one of them things – drinking.

The witness answered with a formulaic apology, and the very long (6.7-second) silence which followed would not be allowed by many lawyers. But the power of the witness's silence, which was not interrupted by the lawyer (or judge), was evident, as it was followed by a personal, honest-sounding explanation which can be helpful to a typical defence strategy of suggesting that the most appropriate sentencing should include alcohol rehabilitation rather than a prison sentence.

But, the Mapletown study also found a number of instances in which Aboriginal witnesses were not allowed to tell their story by their own lawyer, and in some cases by the judge. This silencing of witnesses was brought about sometimes by interruption of the witness, and at other times by metalinguistic comments about how to answer a particular question, such as 'I don't think it's an answer to the question'. An important finding of this study related to the central role of Aboriginal culture in communication, as the silencing of Aboriginal witnesses appeared to occur particularly in situations where legal professionals (whether lawyer or judge) were seriously ignorant about fundamental aspects of the everyday cultural values and practices of Aboriginal people. Readers are referred to Eades (2000) for discussion and examples which illustrate this point.

THE PINKENBA CASE

But what about the use of English in the cross-examination of Aboriginal witnesses (by lawyers for the opposing side)? While there has been little research that has addressed this question, serious concerns have been raised by a 1995 Queensland case, known as the Pinkenba case (*Crawford* v. *Venardos & Ors* 1995 Unreported, Brisbane Magistrates' Court, 24 February). Before discussing Aboriginal English in this case, we need a summary of the incident involved.

Three young teenage Aboriginal boys were approached by six armed police officers late one night when they were walking around a shopping mall in Brisbane. The police officers told the boys to get into three separate police vehicles and they drove them 14 kilometres out of town to an industrial wasteland in Pinkenba, where they abandoned them. As a result of complaints by the boys and their families, an investigation was conducted into the incident, which resulted in the police officers being charged with unlawful deprivation of liberty. Although each boy had a criminal record for such offences as stealing, they were not charged with any offence that night, and they were not taken to any police station. According to police, the boys had been 'taken down to Pinkenba to reflect on their misdemeanours' (ABC *Four Corners*, 8 March 1996).

The first stage in the trial process against the police officers was the committal hearing in the magistrates' court. Most of the four-day hearing consisted of evidence from the three boys, which included lengthy cross-examination by each of the two defence counsel who represented three of the police officers. The case centred on the issue of whether or not the boys had got into and travelled in the police cars against their will: no doubt was ever raised that they were approached and told to get into the police cars, and that they were taken to the industrial wasteland and abandoned there. The defence case was that the boys 'gave up their liberty' and that 'there's no offence of allowing a person to give up his liberty'.[5] So, this was a very serious and strongly- contested hearing, in which the only evidence against the police officers was that of the three Aboriginal boys, the victim–witnesses in the case. Although they were legally children, they had no protection or support such as is offered in Children's Court, because they were not defendants, but witnesses in an adult court. The cross-examination of the boys was devastating: these three young Aboriginal part-time street kids, with minimal successful participation in mainstream Australian institutions, such as education, were cross-examined by the two most highly paid and experienced criminal barristers in the state. It is hardly surprising that the boys were unable to maintain a consistent story under the barrage of cross-examination, which involved so much shouting at times that many legal professionals in the public gallery were amazed that the lawyers were not restrained or disallowed from using this haranguing behaviour.

Elsewhere (e.g. Eades 2006, 2008), I have written about the linguistic strategies used by these two defence counsel to manipulate and misconstrue the evidence of the three boys. These strategies succeeded in persuading the magistrate to accept defence counsels' construction of these victim–witnesses as criminals with 'no regard for the community', and the reinterpretation of the alleged abduction as the boys voluntarily giving up their liberty while the police took them for a ride.[6] As a result, the charges against the police officers were dropped.

The manipulation of Aboriginal ways of using English was central to this defence strategy, and one aspect of this related to silence. In some instances, defence counsel allowed little time between asking an initial question and following it up with pressured, often shouting, repetition. In such situations the witness was given little chance to think about the question, or to use the lengthy silence which characterises many Aboriginal conversations, and particularly interviews with Aboriginal people. But there are a number of silences throughout the hearing. Consistent with the widespread Aboriginal use of silence at the beginning of an answer, we find silences of more than one second prefacing many of the answers of all three of the witnesses. But a number of other witness silences in answer to questions in these examples are not followed by witness answers. While these occurrences of silence might perhaps be seen as evidence that the legal system is accommodating Aboriginal ways of speaking, both defence counsel made sure, in two ways, that this is not how these silences would be interpreted.

First, such silences were invariably followed by some form of harassment, as we see in Example 2.

Example 2

DC2:   The only thing that was <u>said</u> was this one thing was it? (1.5) (by) one police officer – hop in the car (0.8) mm? (1.5) that's the only thing you can remember being said (1.2) right? (1.8) is that right Albert? (2.7) Albert?

This question came after considerable skilful work by the defence counsel in constructing 13-year-old Albert as someone who has no consistent or reliable account of the Pinkenba event (Chapter 8 of Eades (2008) provides a detailed examination of the combination of linguistic strategies used). Albert had been getting increasingly frustrated, as evidenced in answers such as *Told you there were six of them* [police officers], and *No, I'm not silly* (just before this extract). But the question in this extract went to the heart of the boys' complaint that they were *forced* to go in the police cars, and the defence argument that, on the contrary, the police simply said *hop in the car* and the boys knew they had the right *not to go with the police*. It is hardly surprising then, that Albert was taking his time to answer the question that *the only thing that was* said was *hop in the car*. But defence counsel was not willing to allow him to use silence, and pressured him with tag questions *right?* and *is that right?*, and by calling his name, *Albert*. Interestingly, Albert did give a very soft reply, which seemed not to be heard by defence counsel, saying *Nuh you tell lies.* Defence counsel simply continued with the same line of questioning.

Second, on several occasions defence counsel drew attention to the silences, with overt implications that are at odds with the way in which silence is used and interpreted by Aboriginal people. Example 3 below, like much of the cross-examination of all three boys in this case, was not about the night they were taken for a ride by the police, but rather about the witness's criminal behaviour. Thirteen- year- old David may well have been wondering why he had to answer so many questions about his own past trouble, which had already been addressed by the criminal justice system. His 2.7-second silence in answer to the question about whether he was *going to commit more offences*, was interpreted by defence counsel as a suggestion that he *probably will*. Rather than interpreting this silence in terms of the pragmatics of Aboriginal ways of using English, the defence counsel took the opportunity to suggest that the child victim–witness would become a habitual criminal.

Example 3

1 DC1:	(1.8) I see well now you've – you agree that you've got these convictions back in 1993 don't you?
2 DAVID:	(0.6) Yes.
3 DC1:	Are you going to commit more offences?
4 DAVID:	(2.7) No.
5 DC1:	(0.6) **You <u>paused</u> a while before that** – what's the answer – probably you will?
6 DAVID:	(2.2) I dunno.

The linguistic strategies of the cross-examining lawyers, which included the exploitation of Aboriginal English ways of communicating, such as silence, were overt and very effective. In deciding to drop the charges against the police officers, the magistrate's decision primarily amounted to a criticism of the boys, including the statement that they 'have no regard for members of the community, their property or even the justice system'. This criticism was largely based on their minimal answers to the cross-examination questions, many of which were haranguing, as illustrated in Eades (2008). The magistrate's decision caused a public outcry: it seemed to give the support of the legal system to the police removal of Aboriginal young people who were not charged with any crime and thus not under arrest. As a result of the appeal by the boys' families against the magistrate's decision, a judicial review was held: a judge read all of the evidence and decided that the magistrate's decision should be upheld. Indeed, the legal process did give legitimacy to the right of the police to remove Aboriginal young people in circumstances which were undeniably intimidatory, and a denial of liberty in ordinary terms, if not in legal terms.

In this legitimisation of police removal of Aboriginal young people, the exploitation of Aboriginal English ways of communicating played a key role, as the examples above demonstrate. It was disturbing to find that the two defence counsel had at the Bar table a copy of the handbook for lawyers (Eades 1992). The handbook had been written to assist lawyers to communicate more effectively with Aboriginal witnesses. But, in the Pinkenba case, it appears to have been used upside-down, as it were. The provision of intercultural awareness for lawyers seems to have been used to make things worse in terms of intercultural communication. An understanding of Aboriginal ways of using English, such as the use and interpretation of silence, appeared to provide the defence counsel with a powerful tool in the manipulation of the evidence of the Aboriginal boys. In my (Eades 2008) book, I situate this case within the ongoing societal struggle over the rights of police officers to remove Aboriginal people from public places, which began in the colonial period. Criminologists such as Cunneen (2001) have argued that the state continues to exercise neo-colonial control over the movements of Aboriginal people. The Pinkenba case exemplifies this control, and the struggle over it, as well as the central role of language practices in this process.

CONCLUSION: APPLYING SOCIOLINGUISTICS IN THE LEGAL PROCESS

There are many ways in which English is used differently in the legal process than in other contexts, and readers can pursue this topic in Cotterill (2003) and Gibbons (2003). Sociolinguistic research can shed light on how these differences can affect the delivery of justice, and in this way can contribute to sociolegal work (see Conley and O'Barr 1998).

Sometimes sociolinguists become involved in the practical applications of their work to the legal process. For example, Rock's (2007) work on police interviews resulted in a number of recommendations, starting with broad 'social measures to ensure that people who find themselves in contact with any aspects of the legal system already have a fair understanding of that system' (252). She also made a number of specific recommendations about changes to the ways in which police advise suspects of their rights. Her work with a police sergeant in redesigning a written brochure provides a salutary lesson on the practical applications of sociolinguistic research. Their uncluttered and clearly written brochure was subject to further revision without their input, and the resulting text includes unclear and clumsy expressions, redundancies and proofing errors. As Rock concludes about applying sociolinguistic research, the 'sociolinguist can observe and even participate in language debates in institutions but ultimately those institutions and their parts mediate those efforts' (261).

My work on intercultural communication with Australian Aboriginal people has provided another insight into the complexities of applying sociolinguistic research in the legal process. The lawyers' handbook was intended to address some of the disadvantage experienced by Aboriginal people because of subtle but significant pragmatic differences, for example in the ways in which silence is used, interpreted and evaluated. But understanding linguistic and sociolinguistic differences between language varieties, as well as related cultural differences, is not necessarily sufficient to explain communication issues affecting Aboriginal people in the legal system: historical, social and political struggles are also involved. The Pinkenba case highlights the role of societal power relationships in what happens in courtroom talk. At the same time, it shows how linguistic strategies, such as exploitation of Aboriginal ways of using and interpreting silence, have effects which are far more wide-reaching than just the courtroom interaction. They are central to the functioning of the criminal justice system, which legitimises neo-colonial control over Aboriginal people.

Sociolinguists need to develop understandings about how our research can be adopted for specific legal purposes, and about the social and political processes that interact with language use and sociolinguistic research.

NOTES

1 Australian linguists generally follow speakers' labels using 'heavy' instead of 'basilectal' and 'light' instead of 'acrolectal', because of the perceived value judgments inherent in these linguistic labels.
2 Some similarities can be noted with the use of silence in Native American societies (e.g. Basso 1970, Philips 1993, Gumperz 2001).
3 A judgment is often also referred to as a decision. It is the (usually written) report given by a judge or magistrate at the end of a case, in which the final decision is both given and explained, often with reference to decisions in some specific earlier cases.
4 The following standard transcription conventions are used:

- underlining indicates utterance emphasis;
- a number in parentheses indicates the length of a pause in seconds, e.g. (3.2);
- a dash – indicates a very short untimed pause within an utterance;
- **bold** type indicates a particular part of the transcript being highlighted in my analysis;
- DC is the abbreviation for defence counsel;
- the names of the witnesses are pseudonyms.

5 I was in court observing most of the hearing. Quotations are from my transcription of the official tape-recording.
6 In Eades (2008) I show how the boys were not only taken for a ride by the police that night (literally) but, following this, they were taken for a ride by the justice system (metaphorically).

13

LANGUAGE, GENDER AND SEXUALITY

DEBORAH CAMERON

INTRODUCTION

Since the early 1990s, the theme of men and women metaphorically 'speaking different languages' has become ubiquitous in popular culture. According to books like *Men are from Mars, Women are from Venus* (Gray 1992), women love to talk, whereas men prefer action to words. Women view talking as a way of connecting with others emotionally, whereas men treat conversation either as a practical tool or a competitive sport. Women are good at listening, building rapport with others and avoiding or defusing conflict; men confront each other more directly, and are less attuned to either their own or others' feelings. More recently, a new wave of popular science writing has linked these observations to differences in the way male and female brains work (e.g. Baron-Cohen 2003; Brizendine 2006). One study of Australian schoolchildren's attitudes to foreign language learning (Carr and Pauwels 2006) found that pupils as young as 12 knew all the 'Mars and Venus' clichés. 'Girls can do languages – that's how their brains are', said one boy. Another commented: 'Girls enjoy talk: it's what they do, what they're good at'. And most of the girls agreed that 'boys are hopeless communicators!'.

But when you embark on the academic study of language and gender, you will quickly notice how different it is in its assumptions, questions, methods and conclusions. Academic researchers, unlike popular writers, do not equate studying *gender* with cataloguing *differences* between men and women. The more that evidence has accumulated from studying men and women in a range of communities and contexts, the clearer it has become that generalizations along the lines of 'men use language like this and women use it like that' oversimplify what is really a much more complicated picture. Accordingly, this chapter will not be structured as a series of general statements about the way men and women use English. Instead, it will explore the complexity of the relationship between language and gender. It will explain why male–female differences do exist, but are difficult to generalize about, and also why the influence of gender on language does not show up *only* in male–female differences. And in the process, I hope, it will dispel a few popular myths.

WHY GENDER MAKES A DIFFERENCE

It is not just a myth that gender influences language-use – but that is not simply because men and women are 'naturally' different kinds of people. Rather, gender influences linguistic behaviour because of its impact on other things that influence linguistic behaviour more directly. We know from a large body of sociolinguistic research that the way people use language can be related to, among other things, the social networks they belong to, their habitual activities, their identities as particular kinds of people and their status relative to others. Each of these things is potentially affected by the gender divisions which are characteristic of our society.

- *The way someone uses language is influenced by their social network.* Most people's social networks include a core group of close friends: although there are exceptions, the closest and longest established of our friendships are usually with people of our own gender. Because we spend so much time with them, and because we care what they think of us, these same-gender peers become a 'reference group' for us: the norms, beliefs and habits of the group exert a strong influence on many aspects of our behaviour, including our ways of speaking.
- *The way someone uses language is influenced by their involvement in particular activities and social situations.* For most people, the nature of this involvement will reflect, to a greater or lesser degree, opportunities and preferences which are linked to gender. For instance, girls are more likely than boys to spend time shopping together; boys are more likely than girls to spend time playing computer games or team sports together. Adult women are more likely than men to be found in some occupations (e.g. cleaning, nursing and clerical work), while adult men are more likely than women to be found in others (e.g. construction, firefighting and senior management jobs). If these differing activities are associated with different ways of talking, then the fact that men and women tend to do different things will also produce differences in their ways of speaking.
- *The way someone uses language is influenced by their sense of identity – who they think of themselves as being.* Language communicates information not only about the world (e.g. 'it's raining'), but also about what sort of person the language-user is or wants to be seen as: who s/he feels s/he is like and who s/he feels s/he is different from. Almost everyone considers their gender to be an important aspect of their identity and, as such, it is among the things their way of speaking communicates information about.
- *The way someone uses language is influenced by their power and status relative to others.* Despite the significant social changes that have occurred over the past 50 years, there is still a strong relationship between gender and power/status: women remain on many measures the 'second sex', and this may have a bearing on the language used by men and women in any given situation.

Given these observations, it would be surprising if we did *not* observe gender-related variation in linguistic behaviour. But, equally, it would be surprising if that variation were a simple matter of men speaking one way and women another – because the relationship between gender and language-use is not a simple matter of one directly 'causing' the other. Let us look more closely at that point, and its implications.

WHY GENDER DIFFERENCES ARE COMPLICATED

The influence gender exerts on language is typically not direct, but *mediated* by other variables. For instance, language-use is influenced by the activities people habitually undertake, and their activities in turn may be linked to their gender. The more direct link is between activity and language, not gender and language. As an illustration, consider the register of language which used to be called 'motherese', because it is prototypically used by mothers to babies and young children. Today, it is more often referred to using gender-neutral labels like 'child-directed speech' and 'caretaker speech', in recognition of the fact that men (and other non-mothers) also use it when they are taking care of young children. What explains its use is not the gender of the speaker but their involvement in a particular activity. If women use it more frequently than men, it is only because more women than men are intensively involved in caring for infants. Women who have no contact with infants are less likely to use caretaker speech than men who have regular contact with infants.

The relationship between ways of speaking and the activities speakers are engaged in is also illustrated by studies of language and gender in the historically male-dominated 'public sphere' of work, politics and religion (e.g. Baxter 2005; Holmes 2006; Walsh 2001). When women enter traditionally male institutions, it is often suggested that their distinctive ways of communicating will change the institutional culture. For instance, when a large number of women were elected to the British Parliament in 1997, many commentators predicted that women's more co-operative, consensus-building style of interaction would help to make debates more 'civilized'. However, research conducted by Sylvia Shaw a few years later suggested that this had not happened: women had for the most part adopted the adversarial style (Shaw 2005). Bonnie McElhinny (1995), who studied the speech of women police officers in the US city of Pittsburgh following an initiative to recruit more officers from under-represented groups, also found that the women had accommodated their speech to the norms that existed before, for instance by adopting a very unemotional style of interacting.

Of course, it might be argued that these women were not using their 'natural' or preferred style of speech – that they felt compelled to behave like the men in order to be accepted. But, even if that were so, it would not change the finding that, in practice, the women's speech was more strongly influenced by their professional role than by their gender. And, in fact, the women police officers denied that they were imitating men; they said they were simply adopting the style which was appropriate for police work. It is not hard to follow their logic: police officers deal with highly-charged and potentially dangerous situations where it is helpful to come across as calm and in control. For historical and cultural reasons these qualities are conventionally seen as 'masculine' rather than 'feminine'; but it does not follow that women cannot communicate them when the situation demands it. Styles of speaking are not integral personal characteristics, like eye colour or blood group, which people carry with them wherever they go and whatever they do. The evidence from sociolinguistics shows that we all vary our linguistic behaviour in different situations.

But the influence of activity or situation on language-use does not operate in isolation from other influences, such as the influence of power/status. Even when men and women are participating in the same activity, they may not be accorded equal status as participants, and that too may affect their linguistic behaviour. This is a particular problem for women in the public sphere where, until quite recently, they were excluded from participation, and where they are still viewed by some people as illegitimate or inferior participants. All speakers, in all situations, have to consider how their stylistic choices may cause others to perceive them, and for women in many contexts these calculations must take account of sexist prejudices and double standards. The US politician Hillary Clinton came up against these during her campaign to become the Democratic candidate in the 2008 presidential election. When she presented herself verbally as authoritative and capable (presumably to counter the common prejudice that women cannot be strong leaders) she was criticized as 'cold' and 'strident'; but when she adopted a more 'feminine' persona, speaking personally, showing emotion and shedding tears, she was criticized as weak and manipulative.

What about the influence of identity and group membership? In sociolinguistics, it is a truism that speaking is an 'act of identity' or, in other words, that our linguistic choices communicate what kind of person we are or want to be seen as. It is obvious that gender is a basic component of identity, and that for most of us it is conceptualized as fixed and stable: we have a clear sense of ourselves as either men or women (not as neither or as a bit of both), and this does not change depending who we are with or what we are doing. So, it might seem that the influence of gender on our linguistic acts of identity is straightforward, a matter of using language to signal either that we are men or that we are women. But in reality things are not that simple.

THE COMPLEXITY OF GENDER IDENTITY

Below I reproduce several comments from actual conversational exchanges which I have recently participated in or overheard. They are all descriptions of people, of the kind that could have been produced in response to the question: 'What kind of person is X?'

1   he's 19 and a real lad
2   he's, like, your typical ex-public schoolboy
3   he's a white south African, you know, a great hulking brute, really loud
4   I think he must be one of those sensitive metrosexual types
5   he was what Dad would have called a bit light on his feet

These are all descriptions of men, as we can tell from numerous linguistic clues (most obviously the pronoun *he* which appears in all of them), but none of them contains the generic word *man*. The terms which denote or imply masculinity (e.g. 'lad', 'schoolboy', 'brute', 'metrosexual') are much more specific. And that captures an important insight: gender may be a basic component of everyone's identity but, on its own, it does not define anyone's identity. No one would answer the question 'what kind of person is X?' by saying simply, 'he's a man', or 'she's a woman'; no one thinks of him- or herself as just a generic 'man' or 'woman'. We think of ourselves and others as particular *kinds* of men and women, whose masculinity or femininity both inflects and is inflected by all the other attributes that shape our identities: for instance age (example 1 above), social class (2), ethnicity and nationality (3), lifestyle and social attitudes (1, 4), and sexuality (5 – participants in this conversation knew that the expression 'a bit light on his feet' was the speaker's father's euphemism for 'gay').

In each of the descriptions I have quoted, the meaning of the masculine category-term chosen by the speaker derives less from the contrast between masculinity and femininity, and more from an implicit contrast between different varieties of masculinity. When you describe a man as a 'typical ex-public schoolboy', the point is not to distinguish him from wealthy white upper-class women who were educated at public schools, it is to distinguish him from other men who do not share his privileged social background. The 'real lad' is not being contrasted with his female counterpart, the 'ladette', but with men like the 'metrosexual' who represent an opposing style of masculinity. Among women, similarly, 'tomboys' contrast with 'girly girls', refined 'ladies' with raucous 'ladettes' and ambitious 'career women' with domesticated 'mums'. These differences among men, or among women, are no less significant for our sense of identity than the difference between the two genders. And that also means they are no less significant for our linguistic (and other) *acts* of identity. The effects of gender-identity on linguistic behaviour are not simple and uniform, because gender identities themselves are not simple and uniform. Arguably, indeed, it is the distinctions between different kinds of femininity or masculinity which we are likely to be most attentive to when making stylistic choices. Most of us do not regard gender itself as something we have a choice about, but we do have choices about what kinds of men or women we want to be – and, just as importantly, what kinds of men and women we do *not* want to be.

The linguist Mary Bucholtz (1999) studied a group of self-identified 'nerd girls' in an American high school, and found that their style of speaking differentiated them sharply from other girls of the same age, class and ethnicity. The nerd girls actively wanted to be different: they rejected the mainstream teenage obsession with being 'cool', and instead based their identities on the rather 'uncool' principle of valuing and displaying intellectual achievement. To symbolize that, they spoke in a very 'correct' and formal standard English, doing their best to avoid informal speech variants (e.g. they carefully did not 'drop their gs' at the end of words like 'tripping'); they used learned vocabulary while avoiding teenage slang and steered clear of the African-American expressions which many white teenagers used to symbolize coolness. They also avoided the overtly feminine or 'sexy' self-presentation cultivated by mainstream girls, preferring something more androgynous. Nerd girl style was not just different from mainstream or cool girl style, it was defined explicitly in opposition to it.

But, if we examine the actual linguistic features whose adoption or avoidance signify the contrast between cool girl and nerd girl identities, it becomes evident that they are not just arbitrary choices. Simply by being noticeably different from the other girls' style, the nerd girls' style conveys the general meaning 'we are not mainstream'; but, in addition, the particular features which are used to mark the difference convey something more specific about nerds as a distinctive subcategory of non-mainstream students. The combination of careful pronunciation, highly literate, formal vocabulary and prescriptively correct grammar is readily understandable as a metaphor for the serious intellectual values which are central to nerd identity.

This illustrates a more general point about language-using as an act of identity. When a person or group of people constructs a style, what they are doing is making choices from an array of linguistic options which have symbolic value. Creativity is displayed in the way people put different options together to produce a style whose meaning is specific to them; but this is only possible because the various elements already carry some kind of meaning. In relation to gender, therefore, we might ask: are there features of language which symbolically carry meanings of masculinity and femininity, enabling real speakers to pick and choose from them as they construct their own more specific gendered identities?

One way of approaching this question is to look at the advice on language-use given to a group of people who have an unusually strong investment in gender as a 'generic' identity, and who often receive explicit instruction in how to communicate that identity. The people I mean are transsexual or transgendered: individuals who are brought up as members of one gender group, but who identify with the other one so strongly that in later life they seek to become members of it. This involves not only the bodily transformations brought about by taking hormones and perhaps undergoing surgery, but also a transformation of the individual's everyday behaviour – how someone dresses, how they move and, of course, how they use language.

Here are two extracts from advice literature written for male-to-female transsexuals (MTFs) on the art of speaking like a woman:

> The student learns to let her voice rise and fall as she speaks . . . A man might say, in a near monotone, 'that's a nice dress', but a woman, allowing her vocal pitch to soar, would say, 'you look gorgeous!' . . . Another good tip is to let your sentences end on an up note, almost as a question.
>
> (Vera 1997: 131–2)

When women talk, they move their mouths more than men; here again, smiling comes into play. . . . The more facial expression, the more smiles, the more you look and listen, the better feminine conversationalist you will be.

(Stevens 1990: 76–7)

What, you might ask, is this advice based on? Is it, for instance, based on research showing that the various features mentioned (wide pitch range, high rising intonation contours, high-affect words like 'gorgeous' and frequent smiling) were consistently used by some representative sample of women speaking in some everyday situation? The short answer to that is 'no': what we have here is not an empirical description of *women's* speech, but an ideological representation of *feminine* speech. The features just listed do not acquire their gendered associations from the frequency with which they occur in actual women's speech, but from their aptness as linguistic symbols of certain qualities which, in our culture at least, are considered archetypally 'feminine'. For instance, pitch variation and words like 'gorgeous' connote the emotional expressiveness our culture both attributes to and approves of in women, whereas the 'near monotone' in which men are said to utter the much more moderate assessment 'you look nice' connotes the approved 'masculine' opposite, emotional control. Smiling and gazing intently at interlocutors connotes eager-ness to please them – a charming quality in the subordinate sex, but at odds with the authoritative demeanour we expect from the dominant one.

Clearly, no actual speaker is obliged to incorporate these symbols of gender into his or her real-life behaviour (women police officers in McElhinny's study deliberately avoided smiling; 'gorgeous' is probably not a vocabulary item favoured by Bucholtz's nerd girls). Representations of 'masculine' and 'femi-nine' speech are not behavioural templates that men and women copy, they are more imaginary reference points against which people understand that their behaviour will be measured. For instance, if it is part of our cultural knowledge that the stereotypical 'feminine conversationalist' smiles all the time, real-life variations in the frequency and intensity of smiling will be meaningful in relation to that imaginary norm. If a woman smiles frequently she may come across as emphasizing her femininity, whereas if she smiles infrequently she may come across as playing it down. Such contrasts can be exploited by speakers to produce particular effects (though exactly what those effects are will depend on the specifics of the context): for instance, continuous smiling might be part of a style which is designed to communicate 'I'm a woman and I'm flirting with you', whereas no smiling at all might be part of a style which is intended to communi-cate 'I'm a police officer and I'm about to arrest you'.

It is possible that some recipients of the advice I have quoted do treat it as a template to be copied, since they have a particular motivation for embracing gender stereotypes: behaving in a stereotypical manner reduces the risk that others will find your gender ambiguous, and avoiding gender ambiguity is some-thing many trans people are understandably anxious about. Once again, though, we should not assume that all members of a group – even such a small minority group as trans people – construct their identities in exactly the same way. One MTF, Kate Bornstein (1993), has explained that she rejected the advice completely, on the grounds that it was only applicable if you were planning to be a heterosexual woman. Bornstein herself was planning to be a lesbian, and she regarded the speech-style her teachers recommended as incompatible with that identity. This raises questions about the intersection of gendered with sexual identities, and whether the latter have a bearing on linguistic behaviour.

GENDER AND SEXUALITY

You might think that Kate Bornstein's reasoning is simple: a 'feminine' speech style is inappropriate for a lesbian because lesbians are women who act like men (while gay men are their inverse, men who act like women). Historically, that understanding of homosexuality as essentially gender deviance or 'inversion', was commonplace (in some societies it remains the prevailing view), and it still provides one resource which language-users can draw on, for instance by adopting 'feminine' behaviour as part of a flamboyantly 'camp' gay male style, or 'masculine' behaviour as part of a 'butch' lesbian style. However, it is a mistake simply to equate 'gay' with 'camp' or 'lesbian' with 'butch', since many other gay and lesbian styles exist. Some gay male styles are not effeminate but hyper-masculine (while others combine elements of both). Lesbian styles range from the traditional masculine 'butch' through the dungaree-clad radical feminist to the glamorous 'lipstick lesbian'. Like gender identities, sexual identities are specific rather than generic; and, once again, that means there can be no single, generic 'gay' or 'lesbian' way of speaking. Since the 1970s there have been various attempts to delineate a distinctively gay male speech style (e.g. Hayes 1981; Leap 1996) – though there have been far fewer attempts to do the same for lesbians – but these have generally failed for the same reason that early attempts to identify a distinctive 'women's language' failed: because there is too much variation within the group, and too much overlap between it and other groups, for large-scale generalizations to hold (for a summary and critical assessment of this line of research, see Kulick 2000).

But, in any case, Kate Bornstein's remarks on the 'heterosexual' quality of advice to MTF transsexuals are unlikely to reflect her commitment to the idea that lesbians are, linguistically speaking, honorary men. Bornstein herself grew up as a man: if she saw no difference between lesbian speech and masculine speech, why would she have needed voice lessons at all? In western societies nowadays, there is a conceptual distinction between gender identity (being a man or a woman) and sexual preference (desiring either same-gender or other-gender partners). Bornstein clearly recognizes that distinction, since she identi-fies *both* as transgendered (her gender identity does not match the sex of the body she was born with) *and* as homosexual (her preference is for sexual part-ners who share her gender identity). So, the question remains: why does she link the 'feminine' style taught in voice lessons to a specifically heterosexual female identity? And is there, in fact, a link?

Many researchers would agree that there is a special relationship between gender and heterosexuality. The two do not just interact in the way that gender interacts with other social variables like ethnicity and class; their relationship is more one of mutual constitution, meaning that each requires the other and is defined in terms of the other. Heterosexuality obviously requires gender difference: it is defined as an orientation towards partners of the 'other' gender. But, perhaps less obviously, this orientation shapes our conventional definitions of masculinity and femininity, which are imagined not just as different, but as the proverbial 'opposites that attract'. (It is not a coincidence that when I wanted to give an example of a context in which a woman might actually approximate the generic 'feminine' style presented in advice literature for transsexuals, the example I came up with was 'flirting' – in other words, a context where gender is communicated to solicit sexual interest.)

We do not think and talk about other social divisions in this way: no one would describe being French as the 'opposite' of being British, or say that a construction worker belongs to the 'opposite class' from a city financier. For one thing, nationality and class are not binary oppositions – there are more than two possibilities. But also, our societies are not based on the expectation that every French person should pair off with a British person (and every construction worker with a financier) to form a household and raise a family. In the case of men and women, by contrast, that *is* the default expectation. Consequently, masculinity and femininity tend to be defined very much in terms of the opposing and complementary qualities which are meant to equip men and women for life as members of that basic social unit, the heterosexual couple.

The construction of gender in heteronormative terms (i.e. on the assumption that heterosexuality is the norm) is a process that begins well before most people become sexually active. Researchers like Penelope Eckert (1996) and Janet Maybin (2002) have described the way in which pre-adolescent children start to construct masculinities or femininities which reference adult heterosexual behaviour. Boys, for instance, exchange dirty jokes and casual remarks about women's bodies; girls stop using their bodies physically in similar ways to boys and spend more time adorning and comparing notes on them. As Eckert points out, what is driving the process at this stage is not an active interest in sex or courtship, but rather the 'developmental imperative' whereby children's status among their peers depends on displaying age-appropriate behaviour: the greatest sin is to be 'immature' or 'babyish'. For pre-adolescents, a heterosexual self-presentation symbolizes maturity and thus social acceptability. In adulthood, verbal displays of heterosexual identity no longer obey this particular imperative, but they do retain their usefulness as a bonding device among same-gender friends (see e.g. Kiesling 2002) and as a way of making oneself socially acceptable by claiming the status of an 'ordinary' or 'normal' person (see

Kitzinger 2006, who points out that gay men and lesbians cannot use casual references to their sexuality in the same way).

All this helps to explain why someone like Kate Bornstein might seek alternatives to the generic 'feminine' speech-style. If 'feminine' speech is defined in terms of the qualities that are supposed to attract men to women, it is unlikely to appeal to a woman who describes herself as both a lesbian and a 'gender outlaw'. Bornstein does not want to be a 'normal' woman – but that does not mean she wants to be a man (if she did, she could just have stayed one). As a product of the 'queer' politics of the 1990s ('queer' meaning 'anti-heteronormative' rather than just 'not heterosexual'), what she wants to communicate is neither conventional femininity nor conventional masculinity, but a critical or subversive attitude to conventional gender distinctions (for more discussion of 'queer' styles of language-use, see Livia and Hall 1997).

This, though, is a relatively unusual ambition. While recent research has underlined the complexity and diversity of gendered linguistic behaviour, it also suggests that most people are not 'gender outlaws'. In this discussion, I have emphasized the choices individual speakers make, but it is also important to remember that choice is not exercised in a social vacuum: it is constrained rather than completely free, and will typically be affected by considerations such as the desire to be acceptable to peers, the demands of the context and the need to avoid the prejudicial (sexist or homophobic) judgments which are one manifestation of the continuing inequality of our society. Studying linguistic variation means studying the interaction of choice and constraint: it is the interplay between them that produces both the diversity of people's behaviour and the patterns sociolinguists find in it.

CONCLUSION

In this chapter I have argued that the relationship of language to gender and sexuality is a complex and multifaceted one. But I should acknowledge that this brief discussion does not convey its full complexity: there are many areas of research and debate which I have not had space to touch on. Fortunately, there are book-length surveys which give a more comprehensive account of recent work on both language and gender (Eckert and McConnell-Ginet 2003) and language and sexuality (Cameron and Kulick 2003). But 'comprehensive' does not mean 'definitive': this is a field of inquiry where there are lively debates among scholars, where many questions remain to be investigated, and where new questions are emerging all the time.

14

PERSPECTIVES ON CHILDREN LEARNING ENGLISH

FROM STRUCTURES TO PRACTICES

BARBARA MAYOR

INTRODUCTION

Interest in how children acquire language has a long history, with links to, amongst other disciplines, biology, neuroscience, anthropology and philosophy, as well as the perhaps more obvious linguistics, psychology and sociology. The different research traditions of these disciplines tend to emphasise different aspects of the learning process, rely on different kinds of evidence for their validity, and lead to different theoretical interpretations of what may be happening as children try to make sense of their spoken environment. (For over-views of the field at different points in time, see Gleason and Weintraub 1978: 171–83; Ochs 1979; Nicholls and Wells 1985: 2–7; Mitchell and Myles 1998; Sealey 2000; Oates and Grayson 2004.) I have chosen to cluster the various traditions into three broad perspectives and, for the sake of clarity, I emphasise the differences rather than the commonalities between them, although in prac-tice there is considerable overlap and the proponents of each have built on each other's insights, as well as occasionally challenging what has gone before.

According to the *nativist perspective* (which has links with biology, neurology, cognitive psychology, theoretical linguistics and philosophy), language is an innate human ability which follows a predictable developmental path.

According to the *empiricist perspective* (which has links with cognitive neuro-science, developmental psychology and education), language learning is a complex cognitive activity related to learning in general, and is dependent on the learner's individual experiences.

According to the *social perspective* (which has links with social psychology, anthropology, cultural studies and applied linguistics, especially pragmatics), language is essentially an accompaniment to social interaction, and can only be acquired in the context of performing socially meaningful acts with other speakers.

I will go on to say more about each of the three perspectives and the different kinds of insights each has yielded, as well as some of the limitations of each, stressing in particular the challenges that are often posed to received wisdom by the observation of bilingual acquisition. Despite the fact that most English speakers today acquire, in the words of Canadian researcher Merrill Swain

(1972) 'bilingualism as a first language', bilingualism/biculturalism still tends to challenge conventional assumptions about both the neurological organisation of languages and links between languages and cultures. (For overviews of this vast topic, see for example, Grosjean 1982, Romaine 1995 and Li Wei 2000.)

THE NATIVIST PERSPECTIVE

Prior to the 1960s it had been thought, in line with the dominant behaviourist theories of the time, that children learn to speak largely by imitation of the models in the environment around them. So-called nativist approaches, pioneered by US theoretical linguist Noam Chomsky (1980, 1986), on the other hand, see language as an innate human ability. They treat language learning as a cognitive process activated by maturation, which follows a predictable developmental path regardless of the nature or quality of the linguistic input – although some minimal input is required to trigger the process. According to Chomsky, language is a genetically determined faculty controlled by a language acquisition device [LAD], 'an innate component of the human mind that yields a particular language through interaction with presented experience' (1986: 3). Individual languages are mapped onto an underlying Universal Grammar (UG) system, or what Chomsky (1986: 25) describes as an initial state of readiness for learning human language. Chomsky's UG theory makes a distinction between the *universal principles* that are shared by the grammars of all natural languages and the *parameters of variation* that need to be set differently for each language. Researchers within this tradition (Brown 1973: 198; Radford 1990: 5) have therefore been at pains to point out that innateness should not simply be conflated with universality.

As described by Rosamond Mitchell and Florence Myles,

> children would . . . know, rather than have to work it out, that sentences are made of phrases which consist of [a predictable set of elements]. However, they would not know the precise ordering of these elements which is found in their own language . . . they would have to set the . . . parameter on the basis of language input.
>
> (1998: 59–60)

According to US psycholinguist, Stephen Pinker (1994: 268), the telegraphic utterances of young learners 'already reflect the language being acquired: in 95 per cent of them, the words are properly ordered'. In other words, children don't perversely opt for word orders that are not permitted in the language spoken around them and, where there is some flexibility allowed, may consistently favour one order over another (Pinker 1994: 282).

Evidence from the small number of children tragically isolated from social contact in their early years supports both the claim that there is a critical period for language acquisition and the argument that at least some language input is needed during that period to act as a trigger, since such children neither spontaneously develop language in isolation nor do they go on to develop normal language competence beyond a certain stage of maturation. Obviously no baby is pre-programmed to speak English or any other language, but it has been observed (through experiments involving sucking or preferential gaze) that babies are primed, even from within the womb, to attend to the particular melody of the language that surrounds them. Their early experimentation with babbling soon differentiates those sounds which are meaningful in their linguistic community from those which are not. Babies can identify English by its particular melody, with the stress on the first syllable of words, and 'may use word stress to help them segment the stream of speech' (Wells 1985c: 27). Research with babies growing up bilingual suggests that they start to distinguish the sound systems and vocabularies of their languages earlier than the grammars, but the evidence varies according to the context of acquisition and the languages involved, and this is still an area of ongoing research (see, for example, Romaine 1995, Deuchar and Quay 1998, Genesee 2000).

According to the nativist perspective, the developmental trajectory of a monolingual English-speaking child is seen as predictable and natural. It is claimed that the stages and order of acquisition are constant, even though an individual's rate of progress and linguistic output will differ. The cumulative evidence from a range of studies, both observational and experimental, has produced a range of standard inventories of what constitutes 'normal' monolingual development. Thus there are standard charts of the order of acquisition of the phonemes of English (for example, Sanders 1961, adapted by Aldridge 1991, reproduced in Bancroft 2007: 13), and of the mean length of utterance (MLU), measured by number of words at various ages (for example, Brown 1973: 56, reproduced in Plunkett and Wood 2006: 175). Although the original research on which these were based may have been tentative in its claims, the charts take on a life of their own and are reproduced widely in truncated form.

In terms of morphological development in English, it is claimed that children gradually replace simple imitation (as in *she held two mice*) by internalising and applying a set of rules (as in *she hold-ed two mouse-s*), before finally settling on the unique mix of rules and special cases that constitute their local variety of English. Most children's early mistakes in generalising rules are thus indicative of creative minds at play, rather than the mere parroting of adult speech. Pinker (1994: 416) remarks that 'A child who echoed back a parent's sentences verbatim would be called autistic, not a powerful learner'. He quotes a child who says *I don't want to go to your ami* (meaning *I don't want to go to Miami*) (1994: 267). This is clearly not an utterance that the child has ever heard spoken, but rather evidence of independent analysis and rule generation.

A large-scale developmental study by British educationalist Gordon Wells (see Wells 1981 and 1985a) provided evidence for the nativist argument that it is the intrinsic semantic and syntactic complexity of utterances that influences the order of their production by young learners of English, rather than the frequency of environmental input: 'Models provided by others are only of use when children have reached the stage of being able to assimilate them to their own developing systems' (1985c: 32). Moreover, research with children acquiring English as a second language (see Dulay *et al*. 1982: 102–3) lends support to the idea that this natural order of acquisition within English may apply regardless of the child's first language. For example, Roar Ravem (1974) found that his Norwegian-speaking son and daughter, like monolingual English-speaking children, used reduced structures like *Where Daddy go?* and faulty analogies like *Where Daddy is going?* before they produced the mature form *Where is Daddy going?* According to Ravem, this did not reflect interference from Norwegian, which would probably have led to a form like *Where go Daddy?*

A distinction is also drawn by nativists between the child's active linguistic *performance* and their underlying knowledge of the system, or linguistic *competence*. A child may, thus, be sensitive to a distinction between their own developing phonology or grammar and those of an adult, even though unable to reproduce the latter in normal speech. British psycholinguist Jean Aitchison (1994: 183–84) quotes a girl called Nicola who called herself 'Dicola', and Pinker (1995: 119) describes a child who objects forcibly when her father mimics her own use of the past tense 'readed'. The argument here is that children have an abstract model of the English language in their minds (their linguistic competence) which may differ from their current state of ability to produce the language. It has been noted in particular that children appear to hold in memory certain salient items from what they hear, producing what is sometimes termed 'telegraphic' or 'holophrastic' speech. Such speech usually consists of content words only; it appears that function words are normally acquired relatively late in sequence. Wells (1985c: 27) attributes this to the stress patterns of English, observing that 'in stressed languages generally, it is the unstressed items that are omitted in early utterances'.

Children's telegraphic utterances are, of course, open to diverse interpretation, and each may have several potential grammatical expansions, depending on contextual clues like intonation and gesture. Rather than focusing exclusively on linguistic *form*, therefore, pioneer US researcher into child language Roger Brown (1973) made one of the first attempts to classify the range of *meanings* he observed young children trying to express. Brown identified the eight most basic semantic relations, including Agent-Action (as in *mail come*), Action-Object (*want more*) and Agent-Object (*mommy sandwich*) (1973: 114, 173). When these relations are combined into more complex sequences, he argued that word order in English is largely fixed in the sequence Agent – Action – Recipient/ Object – Location (as in *Adam put it box*) (1973: 203–5).

This focus on meaning-making points towards the territory of the empiricist perspective, which deals with language as a reflection of children's developing understanding of the world. Before moving on, however, I will first consider some of the limitations that have been identified with the nativist perspective, from both within and beyond the discipline of cognitive psychology.

SOME CRITIQUES OF NATIVISM

- Work in the nativist tradition, with its quantitative approach to the acquisition of features, has tended to foreground the surface *forms* of language. As British applied linguist Alison Sealey (2000: 76) has observed, the focus of Universal Grammar theory is on language as a *system* and children merely as the instrument.

- Supporting examples have often been drawn from the researcher's own intuitions. Brown ironically commented that 'The linguistic scientist typically does not rely on some corpus of *mere speech production* in constructing his grammatical descriptions' (1973: 161, my emphasis). Such intuition has been shown by corpus linguists to be an unreliable window on actual language practices (Sinclair 1991: 4) and certainly cannot claim universal validity. They are also what Radford (1990: 3) has termed 'adultocentric'.

- There is an over-reliance on non-naturalistic data collection, including the use of experimental methods and/or a laboratory setting, with the aim of controlling social factors in order to test particular hypotheses. Use of such methods to investigate naturally-occurring phenomena is thought to be unreliable because it distorts human behaviour and thus tends to bias results. Furthermore, as Australian linguist Clare Painter has pointed out, 'children . . . in their first year or two of life . . . make very unsatisfactory laboratory subjects' (1984: 37).

- Despite the appearance of scientific objectivity, much is still left to the interpretation of the researcher in recording and categorising evidence. For example, the transcription of babies' early utterances may entail assigning recognisable English phonemes or words to what are effectively indeterminate sounds. Similarly, the expansion of children's telegraphic speech relies on conjecture about their intended meaning, and some data may be artificially forced into pre-existing categories. Ochs, whose notion of 'transcription as theory' has been very influential, stresses that 'context is critical to an intelligible transcript' of children's speech (1979: 10).

- Developmental charts are often reproduced uncritically, thus appearing to reify the learning process and leading to what Aitchison has termed 'preordained path theories' (1994: 182). There is a risk that idealised models of language acquisition, assuming a fixed developmental progression, ignore individual or group differences (e.g. between different varieties of English) and hence make overgeneralised claims. It has been argued that such models can only ever represent 'probabilistic tendencies, not categorical certainties' (Sealey 2000: 132). In practice, it may be individual differences which account for the major part of variation, and the acquisition of a feature does not necessarily proceed in a linear fashion.

- Nativist approaches tend towards an analytic rather than a holistic approach to language, focusing on individual words, rather than whole phrases with social meaning. British psycholinguist Alison Wray has observed that 'although we have tremendous capacity for grammatical processing, this is not our only, nor even our preferred, way of coping with language ... much of our entirely regular input and output is not processed analytically, even though it could be', but rather in formulaic, socially contextualised chunks (2002: 10). This poses a serious challenge to the concept of MLU measured in words.

- Nativist theories tend to rely on evidence from the English language and from monolinguals to make claims about language acquisition in general. There are significant structural differences between human languages, particularly in terms of the relative role of inflection as opposed to word order, and the ways in which syntactic roles are indicated (see Pinker 1994: 232–33), which pose a challenge to even the most familiar English-language concepts like 'word' and 'sentence', as well as claims about the order of acquisition of grammatical features. What does all this mean for the *principle* of calculating vocabulary size or MLU; still more their application to bilingual children?

THE EMPIRICIST PERSPECTIVE

A strict nativist position would argue that 'Language is no more a cultural invention than is upright posture' (Pinker 1994: 18) and that relative poverty of input makes little or no difference to a child's potential to acquire language, provided exposure occurs at the right developmental stage. Nativist models thus tend to underplay individual or cultural differences in experience. Empiricist approaches, on the other hand, treat language learning as closely related to a child's individual experiences and understandings. Acknowledging the work of Australian-based linguist Michael Halliday, they also recognise that languages function as semiotic systems for encoding collective experience (Halliday 1978) and that, through language, a child acquires a lens through which to understand the world. Empiricists still focus primarily on the linguistic *form* of utterances, but in this case as a window on the child's cognitive development in general and concept development in particular.

Recent research in the empiricist tradition has taken a turn back in the direction of behaviourism, recognising that, although much of any language is probably stored as a set of categories and rules, there is also a large element of rote learning or habit formation. This is captured in the neurological theory of connectionism, which predicts that 'learning occurs ... on the basis of associative processes'; it follows that 'rule-like behaviour' does not necessarily imply 'rule-governed behaviour' (Mitchell and Myles 1998: 79–80).

Much work in the empiricist tradition has concentrated on children's lexical development, with the emphasis on both quantification (key milestones in size of vocabulary) and classification (types of words produced). Thus, there are established inventories of young learners' comprehension and production of English words (e.g. Benedict 1979, reproduced in Bancroft 2007: 20). Aitchison

(1994: 170ff) has categorised the functions of these early words in helping the young child to understand that words are used to label entities in the world, that apparently diverse entities can be packaged under the same label and that words are related to each other in semantic networks. It has been widely observed that children tend to over-extend (or less commonly under-extend) the meanings of words, as they try to maximise their limited vocabulary and establish the concept boundaries that are available to them in English. Drawing on a range of diary studies of children's early word use, US psycholinguists Peter and Jill de Villiers (1979: 36) classify some typical over-extensions according to the apparent grounds for similarity: for example, movement ('bird' for any moving creature), shape ('moon' for round objects such as cakes, postmarks, the letter O), size ('fly' for crumbs, specks of dirt, toes), sound ('coco' = cockerel for music of all kinds) and texture ('bow-wow' for toy animals, slippers, fur coat). To this inventory Peccei (1994: 8) adds similarity in function, quoting an early example from Sully (1897/1971), where a child extends the notion of 'hat' to other objects linked to the head like a scarf and a hairbrush. Similarly, Aitchison (1994: 179) notes that young children's word associations, unlike those of adults, tend to focus on real-world collocation (as in dark–night), rather than decontextualised semantics (as in dark–light).

Beyond the level of lexis, researchers in the empiricist tradition have taken forward Brown's seminal early work on children's early meaning-making. According to de Villiers and de Villiers,

> English-speaking children . . . in their first sentences . . . talk [mainly] about actions . . . possession . . . location . . . recurrence . . . labelling . . . and non-existence . . . Children learning many different languages . . . seem to encode the same limited set of meanings in their first sentences. This lends credence to the notion that the meanings depend on, and are restricted by, the two-year-old's understanding of the world.
>
> (1979: 48–50)

SOME CRITIQUES OF EMPIRICISM

- Many critiques of the empiricist position are similar to those levelled against the nativist position, in that both often rely on the use of non-naturalistic experimental techniques, as well as the use of inference on the part of researchers.
- As with the nativist approach, there is still a tendency to focus on individual words, rather than formulaic sequences with social meaning.
- In developmental terms, it is well-established that comprehension precedes production (Bruner 1983; Wells and Nicholls 1985: 5) but how does one reliably test the comprehension of a pre-verbal child?
- It is clear that not all children's early utterances are simply a matter of *naming* objects or actions. Rather, words accompany actions in social context, and 'the child learns something about the meaning of words on the

basis of their occurrence in communicative acts' (Dore 1979: 343). And yet the context of children's utterances is rarely retrievable from the kinds of charts and inventories that are still common within the empiricist tradition.

• According to Sealey, both nativist and empiricist approaches tend to reify the language learning process, referring to 'child language acquisition', rather than 'children talking' (2000: 82).

THE SOCIAL PERSPECTIVE

Both nativist and empiricist perspectives are essentially cognitive in focus and view linguistic input merely as a trigger to processes internal to the child's mind. They also have a tendency to focus on the decontextualised forms of children's early utterances. The social perspective, on the other hand, is concerned with the role of language in social context and with the child's socialisation into a linguistic community with distinctive language practices. It is thus seen as the link between the individual and society. It emphasises the dialogic and pragmatic nature of language learning, focusing on how children learn to take part in conversations in dialogue with others, and how they use language to perform particular illocutionary acts such as requesting or refusing (Austin, 1962) and to express social identity. The focus is thus on the communicative function of language in 'meaning making' (Halliday 1975; Wells 1985b).

As Halliday first observed, children learn language in social situations where they, and other people, are trying to achieve certain goals: from an early age a child 'uses his voice to order people about, to get them to do things for him; he uses it to demand certain objects or services; he uses it to make contact with people, to feel close to them' (Halliday 1975: 11). According to this view, language is seen less as a system and more as a *resource* for its users: 'the production of grammatically well-formed sentences is not an end in itself, but a means for acting in the world' (Wells 1985c: 22).

An influential early volume of papers in the social tradition, edited by Elinor Ochs and Bambi Schieffelin (1979), argued that children begin by learning the pragmatics of speech acts and only gradually learn the language that corresponds to these. Ochs identifies a range of 'pragmatic alternatives that are available to young children even before single words emerge . . . touching, pointing, and eye gaze . . . reaching, holding up, waving . . . pushing away, head shaking, and the like' (1979: 13). She argues, moreover, that infants are fully effective communicators from an early age: there is no equivalent of the 'telegraphic' stage in pragmatic terms (1979: 17). Wells has likened this to a 'conversation without words' between infants and their caregivers; he argues that 'infants come to be able to have and express communicative intentions by being treated as if they could already have them' (Wells 1985c: 24).

Research in the social tradition usually takes an ethnographic or case study approach, where researchers 'situate their investigations in families and communities, taking account of the ways children learn . . . conventions of how things are interactionally achieved' (Sealey 2000: 84). Data are usually collected over an extended period from a small number of subjects and claim to be insightful, rather than representative. Because interaction is viewed as essentially context-dependent, great attention is paid in analysis to the *non*-linguistic context, exploring the interaction between different levels of language form and communicative function.

Whereas the focus of the nativist approach was on Chomsky's notion of *linguistic competence*, the focus of the social approach is on the child's *communicative competence*, a term generally attributed to US linguist Del Hymes:

> [A] normal child acquires knowledge of sentences, not only as grammatical, but also as appropriate. He or she acquires competence as to when to speak, when not, and as to what to talk about with whom, when, where, in what manner.
>
> (Hymes 1972: 277)

Because only a small proportion of the sentences permitted by the grammar of English is routinely used, children have to learn social appropriacy in the course of social interaction.

So what is it that children learn from interaction? It has been observed that, in some cultures, adults and older children in dialogue with young children adopt a highly inflected form of speech that has been called child-directed speech or CDS. This arguably helps to facilitate turn-taking in conversation by emphasising question-and-answer exchanges and other adjacency pairs (Sacks *et al.* 1974), and to direct the child's attention to key elements in the utterance. Cross-cultural studies (such as Heath 1983; Pye 1986) have demonstrated that CDS is by no means universal and certainly not essential to language acquisition, although the difference in input may well have an effect on the kind of language the child goes on to produce.

Whether or not particular features of CDS are involved, adults generally react to the *function* and truth-value of children's utterances and do not normally give explicit feedback on the *form*. Indeed, in interactional terms, adult feedback on the form of an utterance seems irregular, and appears to have little effect on the learner. Braine (1971: 160) quotes an exchange between a little girl and her father who, instead of responding to her request for another spoon, drills her repeatedly to produce the phrase *the other spoon*. As soon as the 'lesson' is over and the conversation resumes, she immediately reverts to her preferred expression *other one spoon*.

In the same way that the social perspective has shifted the focus of attention from the surface structures of children's language production towards their social practices, so a similar shift has taken place in the analysis of adult language input to children. Shoshana Blum-Kulka and Catherine Snow, comparing a collection of papers produced in 1977 with one produced in 1992, remark that the first 'operated from the presumption that characteristics such as phonological clarity, grammatical simplicity and redundancy were the crucial defining features of "baby talk"', whereas in the latter 'input was seen as conversational, interactive, transactional . . . with a primary emphasis always on the question of how these interactions simplify the problem of language acquisition for the learner' (2002: 2).

US psycholinguist Katherine Nelson (1981) was amongst the first to speculate that family patterns of interaction might influence the extent to which young children acquiring English learn how to name objects (the referential or ideational function) or engage in social interactions (the expressive or interpersonal function). This difference in emphasis has subsequently been related to different ways of understanding and producing chunks of language. Thus it is argued that one group of children – the so-called Analytic group – tend to process language analytically, with a focus on the form, and another – the so-called Gestalt group – tend to process it holistically with a focus on the function. Wray (2002: 116–17) has observed that parental level of education, presumably reflected in the more analytic kind of interactions they engage in with their children, appears to correlate with referentiality in the child. Conversely, it is argued that children who have experienced language primarily as a means of social control are more likely to be expressive in their own use of language. However, Wray points out that the language to which children are exposed also varies according to position in family:

> a first child is the most likely to receive predominantly referential input, as a great deal of carer attention is directed towards it in that vital early period. Children with older siblings are more likely to adopt an expressive style, because a sizeable proportion of the language that they witness is interaction between the mother and the other children, such as directives and requests.
>
> (Wray 2002: 116)

Recently, there has been increased interest in children's interaction with larger social groups, on the grounds that this exposes them to greater social role variation, audience design and participant rights (Blum-Kulka and Snow 2002: 4–9): 'Knowing what to say and knowing the rules of interaction that allow one to say it . . . who may talk to whom [and] what language performances are highly valued' (2002: 328, 3). Moreover, as Susan Ervin-Tripp (1979: 398) had earlier noted, turn-taking boundaries are more challenging for children to negotiate in larger groups and so require the development of more sophisticated skills.

Furthermore, there are particular kinds of social acts that children regularly get to perform *as children*, and this has led to increasing interest in children's language as an object of study in its own right (see Goodwin 1990 and 2006; Hoyle and Adger 1996; Sealey 2000). 'A crucial difference . . . between what adults and children can do with language in interactions is their respective locations in the domains of the social world' (Sealey 2000: 184). In order to choose the appropriate expression for the occasion, a child needs to be aware, not only of the range of linguistic forms available to perform acts like requesting, but also of how likely the addressee is to comply with the request. Children addressing adults usually resort to indirect means of getting what they want, such as asking questions or making hints (Shuy 1978: 272).

It is evident from the above that language learning, according to a social perspective, varies both sub-culturally and situationally. In our everyday lives we play a variety of social roles, and it is often through spoken language that we signal shifts in our social identity or relationship with others and perform 'acts of identity' (Le Page and Tabouret-Keller 1985). By deploying different varieties and styles of English, often alongside other languages, children learn to express different aspects of their identities and to become members of linguistic communities.

It was once thought (Labov 1964) that young children were not sensitive to social variation in language. However, there is now evidence that children start to learn the communicative norms of their community before they learn their first word. Even very young children are learning to use different varieties and mixtures of language to express their identities and achieve their goals, both as members of social groups and as individuals. From a very early age, they become aware of the social significance of different varieties of English, and learn how to vary their own language according to the perceived context and the desired outcomes, thus developing a *repertoire* of linguistic behaviour (Mayor 2007).

Valerie Youssef, for example, conducted a longitudinal case study of three children between the ages of two and four in Trinidad, where the characteristic differences between speakers are 'not outright distinctions in the use of particular forms, but rather differences in proportional usage of those forms' according to social class (1991: 89). She concluded that 'Overall [the children's] development reflected the extent and nature of expected usage of the respective markers for the social circumstances in which each lived' (1991: 93).

Different identities and social meanings are expressed in some communities via different dialects, in others via different languages, whereas in others codeswitching allows hybrid identities to be expressed and mixed messages to be conveyed. Classic research on code-switching conducted amongst the Hispanic populations of the USA (see, for example, Zentella 1997) and in Francophone Canadian communities (for an overview, see Genesee 2000: 335–7) has demonstrated the ways in which children effectively learn to reproduce the codeswitching norms of their communities. Codeswitching can be manipulated pragmatically in the micro-context of daily interaction within the family, where children may use different kinds of language with different people to convey subtle shifts in meaning (Harrison and Piette 1980; Li Wei 1994; Myers-Scotton and Bolonyai 2001; Al Khatib 2003).

Accent is obviously a key factor in the expression of social identity. Various researchers (for example, Payne 1980; Kerswill 1996) have investigated the extent to which young children acquire the accent of their peers rather than that of their parents. Payne's general conclusion was that children moving into an area before the age of eight stood a far better chance of sounding like a 'local' than those who arrived after eight, in other words their linguistic identity by this age had become relatively fixed.

The difference between pre- and post-adolescent children appears to relate to their individual psychological readiness to adopt new identities as much as to maturational factors *per se*. However, there is evidence that the phonological system, and to a lesser extent the grammar, becomes set at an earlier age than other levels of language such as vocabulary and pragmatics. Beyond adolescence, young people and adults will almost certainly have become more fixed in their linguistic identities, but will continue to extend their pragmatic repertoire as they enter new discourse communities and perform new roles.

SOME CRITIQUES OF A SOCIAL PERSPECTIVE

- Some early work in the social tradition placed inappropriate emphasis on the canonical form of illocutionary acts, such as the use of imperative verbs to issue commands, whereas in practice there are many linguistic ways to perform the act of commanding. In particular, we need to bear in mind that 'a child may use nouns to manipulate people as well as to refer to things' (Lieven *et al.* 1992: 292), posing a challenge to Nelson's (1981) expressive/ referential dichotomy.
- It is recognised that child-rearing practices are culturally specific, and yet there is still a bias towards the selection of academic researchers' own children and those of their colleagues and friends as the subjects of longitudinal research studies. Caution therefore needs to be exercised in generalising from the findings, since certain types of interaction are typical of certain types of home and, in particular, multilingual interactions are rarely treated as evidence in mainstream research. Furthermore, a bias towards first or only children has 'favoured the study of analytic children over Gestalt ones' (Wray 2002: 116).
- There is a tendency towards social stereotyping of families. It is not helpful to categorise children into definitive types since 'the strategy preferred at any given moment depends on the [linguistic] demands of the material and on the communicative situation' (Wray 2002: 14–15).
- Given the key roles of social context and individual motivation in a social perspective, this perspective relies particularly heavily on the provision of full contextual data and on social psychological insight as to a speaker's intended meaning. Indeed, it is arguable whether researcher intuition can ever be relied upon to fully interpret the complex intentions of speakers or the understandings of participants (Kramsch and Whiteside 2008). Even speakers themselves may not be fully aware of, or totally honest about, their own motivations.
- Work in this tradition has often been conducted by researchers whose disciplinary roots are not linguistic at all but lie rather in other areas of the social sciences, in particular in anthropology. It could be argued that they

effectively avoid some of the more problematic questions about the acquisition of language as a *system*.

CONCLUSION

Underlying the three perspectives described in this chapter runs a basic dichotomy in explanations of language acquisition, with the more cognitive perspectives (whether nativist or empiricist) giving greater prominence to analytic processes and rule formation, whilst other perspectives (from the early behaviourist to the social) give greater prominence to imitation and habit formation. Thus there exist parallel accounts which provide equally persuasive evidence for both telegraphic (essentially analytic) and formulaic (essentially imitative) speech in young children – reflecting a relative emphasis on linguistic structures or on communicative practices.

Writing from a social-psychological perspective, Nelson speculates that this relative emphasis may be attributable as much to individual differences in children as to different research traditions:

> how the child learns about the language initially is apparently determined to an important degree by what he or she supposes the language to be useful for . . . although the child cannot divide the language as we do . . . still the child can divide up the language in his or her own way and learn the pieces of each that fit together in appropriate contexts.

(1981: 187)

So, by this account, it is less a case of competing explanations as of individual cognitive style and self-expression on the part of the learner.

A more serious challenge, however, to the prevailing English-based models of language acquisition is raised by research into the acquisition of languages other than English. Although claims about the role of communicative practices in language acquisition are in principle transferable across cultural contexts, it is not possible to claim a similar universality with regard to the acquisition of linguistic structures. This process is inevitably more language-specific, since the structures of human languages differ fundamentally in terms of their basic building blocks (extending even to the concept of the 'word'), as well as their ways of mapping the world semantically. Indeed, a strong tradition of research on bilingual language acquisition (see Genesee 2000) has focused on whether children are in fact acquiring one system or two, and what principles govern their codeswitching between languages.

Despite these reservations, it would clearly be impossible to justify a focus on linguistic practices to the exclusion of linguistic structures or vice versa, and the three perspectives described in this chapter can be seen as essentially complementary. This complementarity is recognised even by researchers working primarily within one tradition rather than another. As New Zealand applied linguist Rod Ellis puts it, 'interaction . . . only facilitates acquisition; it does not *cause* acquisition to take place' (1999: 4). US psycholinguist John Dore, writing as early as 1979, likened the process to a two-sided axe: 'conversation is the immediate communicative context for language development, but the properties of conversation itself (together with all the child's experience) cannot explain the abstract structure of the language the child acquires', which 'exists independently of communication and is involved in non-communicative uses of language such as thinking' (1979: 339, 360).

Because of its very multi-disciplinarity, child language research has been able to benefit from such cross-fertilisation of ideas from different disciplines. It has contributed to, and occasionally challenged, the 'parent' disciplines by generating data on cognitive, linguistic and communicative systems in a process of emergence.

15

ACADEMIC LITERACIES

NEW DIRECTIONS IN THEORY AND PRACTICE

BRIAN STREET

INTRODUCTION

Until recently, the study of literacy was dominated by assumptions regarding the large consequences, for cognition and for society as a whole, of the acquisition of reading and writing. Psychologists in particular studied literacy in terms of the 'problems' of acquisition for individuals and the cognitive changes that occurred when 'successfully' mastered. While these studies continue, and in some cases still appear to dominate educational policy (cf. The National Literacy Strategy in the UK and No Child Left Behind in the US), a shift has taken place in recent years whereby emphasis in theory and research has been placed far more on understanding literacy practices in context, with greater caution regarding assumptions about the intrinsic nature or consequences of the medium. This more socially orientated approach, often referred to as the New Literacy Studies (Gee 1990), has been particularly influenced by those who have advocated an 'ethnographic' approach, in contrast with the experimental and often individual-istic character of previous studies, many of which now appear ethnocentric and culturally insensitive. Within the New Literacy Studies, literacy is treated as a social practice rather than a set of 'autonomous' cognitive skills and it is argued that, in order to understand and to teach literacy, we need to know the contexts in which it is being used and the meanings attached to it in those contexts. Recent applications of this approach have addressed the reading and writing requirements of Higher Education and treated these as examples of literacy in practice applying the same methodological and theoretical frame to their analysis as to the literacies outside the academy; in other words academics have been looking at their own literacy practices with the same kind of detached and curious eye as they do the literacies of 'other' people with which they are less familiar.

From this perspective, then, the term 'academic literacies' refers to the diverse and multiple literacies found in academic contexts such as disciplinary and subject matter courses (Street 2004). An academic literacies perspective treats reading and writing as social practices that vary with context, culture and genre (Barton and Hamilton 1998; Street 1984, 1995). The literacy practices of academic disciplines can be viewed as varied social practices associated with different communities. Those communities provide the broader social context within which the meanings of specific literacy practices are constrained and defined. An academic literacies perspective, then, takes account of literacies which are not simply associated with subjects and disciplines but with broader institutional discourses, for instance debates about 'plagiarism' and the use of scarce resources for feedback, student support and so on. It is within this context that student writing and learning are to be understood and it is argued that this involves issues of epistemology and identities rather than of skill acquisition or academic socialisation alone, although the perspectives are not mutually exclusive and individuals may move between them according to context and purpose.

For students, a dominant feature of academic literacy practices is the requirement to switch their writing styles and genres from one setting to another, to deploy a repertoire of literacy practices appropriate to each setting, and to handle the social meanings and identities that each evokes. Work in the field of academic literacies has been ethnographically oriented (e.g. Ivanic 1998; Lea and Street 1998, 2006; Lillis 1999, 2001; Ganobcsik-Williams 2006) and researchers working in this tradition have sought to explore actual practices and perceptions, rather than making value judgments about academic literacy. In particular, researchers such as Lea and Street, Ivanic, Lillis and others in the UK have explored mismatches between student and tutor expectations regarding written discourse and the variation in writing requirements across fields of study.

Recently, scholars have attempted to bring together work in the fields of academic literacies and of English as an Additional Language (EAL). Whilst work in the field of academic literacies has tended not to foreground EAL issues, research in school-based EAL has tended to focus on language use and diversity more than on literacy. Epistemologically, however, there is a fit between the two traditions and it is on this basis that the rest of this chapter proceeds. For many students it is this combination of language issues (both EAL and dialect variation amongst native speakers) and literacy issues that lies at the heart of their encounter with the academy and the judgments it makes about them. The academic literature in both EAL and 'academic literacies' studies demonstrates that the language and literacy learning issues involved in these activities are best understood as meaning-making in social practices (e.g. Boughey 2000; Gee 2004) rather than 'technical skills' or 'language deficit'.

These approaches to both literacy and language in the academy have a complex and uneven history and in this chapter there is space only to signal some of the major traditions and the movements currently taking place between and amongst them. The Writing Across the Curriculum movement in the USA, for instance, (Bazerman 1988; Russell 1991), arises from a different context than the UK academic literacy tradition outlined above and appears at first sight to offer a very different institutional and conceptual approach to writing support. However, there are also significant areas of overlap and current tendencies in both fields suggest that there may be increasing recognition of the need to review each other's research and practice. The US Writing Across the Curriculum movement, for instance, comes out of 'rhetoric and composition', a field that arose out of the professionalisation of teachers of first-year university general writing courses in the 1970s – with a strong humanities bent – and located in English departments primarily, with relatively little contact with linguistics.

At the same time, the adoption of the principles of Communicative Language Teaching (CLT) by English language teaching professionals broadened curriculum concerns to include notions of appropriateness and language norms in context (Canale and Swain 1980; McDonough and Shaw 2003). However, despite its conceptual foundations in ethnography of communication (with early references to Hymes), CLT practices have tended to rely on formal questionnaire and other self-report techniques for student needs identification, and native speaker insider knowledge for curriculum prescription (Dubin 1989; Leung 2005). A consequence of this is that, in English language teaching, pedagogy is culturally tuned to appropriateness in terms of formality of language discourse in general terms (as evidenced by most commercially published English Language Teaching textbooks), but it tends not to be able to offer specific guidance for particular domains of use, such as the variety of academic genres required in higher education (cf. Scarcella 2003; Crème and Lea 1997). This is a fundamental conceptual issue, with major pedagogic implications, that requires further research.

In this chapter, I will take account of these debates and alignments between the fields of academic literacies and EAL and, at the same time, I will also bring into the account another field that has deep significance for both of these traditions – that of multimodality. Scholars in this relatively new tradition focus on the role of other modes and genres, notably visual and gestural in both writing and in the classroom interaction that often precedes it (Kress and van Leeuven 2001). This approach to academic literacies enables a focus on the kinds of mode and genre switching (Scalone and Street 2006; see below) that occur in seminars and workshops and to which teachers seldom draw explicit attention, partly I would argue because they are so 'naturalized' (e.g. Fairclough 2003) as not to be immediately recognisable as factors in student learning. Likewise, the extent to which 'meanings' in written texts are conveyed by not only linguistic modes but also by such features of visual modality as layout, use of images, highlighting and so on may sometimes appear obvious or 'natural' but, in fact, are significant constitutive aspects of the communicative practice. In both cases, then, the 'problems' commonly associated with students acquiring academic discourse may lie not simply in their language proficiency or language varieties – such as EAL or regional varieties of English – or simply in their 'ability to write', but in their deployment of the range of registers, modes and genres conventionally associated with a particular subject, field or discipline (e.g. Lea and Street 2006; Bazerman and Prior 2004).

Any work in research or practice in the field of academic literacy will need to take account of the traditions signalled above, to recognise the multiple and complex nature of literacy and modality in the academy and to become comparative as people move across national boundaries and researchers learn more about other countries and traditions. This chapter offers two concrete examples of work going on in different contexts as an indication of what a comparative perspective can bring to the field.

ACADEMIC LITERACY AS DISCOURSE: AN EXAMPLE FROM SOUTH AFRICA

Boughey (2000) describes work in a first-year Systematic Philosophy class at a historically black South African university. She found that what was going on in terms of student writing challenged the assumptions on which she had based her practice as a teacher of English as a second language for many years. These assumptions focused on the perception of problems related to the production and reception of academic texts as solely, or even mainly, linguistic in origin, including the standard 'deficit', generic and cognitive approaches indicated above. She found from observations and interviews with students that in fact, although all were speakers of English as an additional language, the 'problems' in their writing stemmed mainly from their unfamiliarity with academic discourses rather than from linguistic deficits. Over a period of three years, she attempted, as a 'language specialist', to work alongside the mainstream lecturer teaching a Systemic Philosophy class in a way that resists an explanation of students' 'problems' as 'second language problems' and that fits more closely with the Writing Across the Curriculum, Academic Literacies and 'Embedded' approaches now being developed in the USA and UK. One source of her epistemological break was a reading of Jim Gee, from whom she cites a passage concerning a 'socio cultural' perspective on learning:

> Imagine that I park my motorcycle, enter my neighbourhood 'biker' bar, and say to my leather-jacketed and tattooed drinking buddy, as I sit down: 'May I have a match for my cigarette please?' What I have said is perfectly grammatical English, but it is 'wrong' nonetheless (unless I have used a heavily ironic tone of voice). It is not just what you say, but how you say it. In this bar, I haven't said it in the 'right' way. I should have said something like 'Gotta match?' or 'Give me a light, would 'ya?'.
> Now imagine that I say the 'right' thing ('Gotta match?' or 'Give me a light, would 'ya?'), but while saying it, I carefully wipe off the bar stool with a napkin to avoid getting my newly pressed designer jeans dirty. In this case, I've still got it wrong. In this bar, they just don't do that sort of thing: I have said the right thing, but my 'saying±doing' combination is nonetheless wrong. It's not just what you say or even just how you say it. It's also what you are and do while you say it. It is not enough just to say the right 'lines', one needs to get the whole 'role' right (like a role in a play or movie). In this bar, the biker bar, I need to play the role of a 'tough' guy, not a young urban professional (a 'yuppie') relaxing on the weekend. Other

bars cater to different roles, and if I want to, I can go to many bars so long as I play many different roles.

(Gee 1990 [second edition 1996]: xv)

Boughey notes how Gee in this passage uses the metaphor of a bar to explain the concept of a 'discourse',[1] and she attempts to apply the notion to university encounters. Just as those who are familiar with the bar discourse 'are welcomed there because other regular drinkers see that they share the same values, feelings and ways of acting and speaking as themselves', so those who are welcomed in the academy must 'demonstrate that they know how to act and speak like the people who are already there, and that they share the same feelings and values' (Boughey 2000: 280). In the case of the university, the transition is not always smooth, especially for those from 'non-traditional' backgrounds who 'might be able to pretend to speak and act in the same way but, sooner or later, their pretence will be exposed'. In the university 'bar', this process is enacted not only through speech but also through written materials. The university 'awards pieces of paper to show that newcomers have been accepted. These pieces of paper are called degrees, and the higher the degree, the greater the level of acceptance'. This, then, has implications for what counts as 'literacy' in the university:

> Literacy is not something that can be overtly taught in a convenient introductory series of lectures. People become literate by observing and interacting with other members of the discourse until the ways of speaking, acting, thinking, feeling and valuing common to that discourse become natural to them.
>
> (Boughey 2000: 281)

This understanding is especially important where universities are changing to include people from many different backgrounds. Perhaps in previous eras all the members of the university 'bar' shared a common discourse – but now, in South Africa as in the USA and UK, 'Widening Participation' means that it cannot be assumed everyone shares the 'discourse'. It is no longer sufficient, then, to treat students with 'problems' as needing technical assistance in their language skills – instead a rounder and fuller intervention is necessary to help them enter the discourse. This leads to a research and practice perspective that focuses on 'the differences between the ways of thinking, acting, valuing and speaking that students bring from home and school discourses and those that they must acquire in order to gain membership of academic discourses' (282).

Boughey proposes a set of headings under which we might explore these issues: Conceptions of learning; Negotiating voice; Rules for producing knowledge; and Forms of academic knowledge. But then she problematises these terms, denaturalises them so that they do not appear simply as 'givens' of the university discourse but as claims to knowledge that might be challenged. For instance, she discusses the need for students to shift from seeing their writing as the reproduction of old learning, to seeing it as a way of communicating new learning, and she points out the complex orchestration of different voices which students have to learn in order to produce written academic discourse. Ivanic and others in the UK academic literacies tradition would claim that such ethnographic style understanding needs to be used not simply to provide 'non traditional' students with 'access' to the dominant discourse but also to help change that discourse for all students (Ivanic 1998). Boughey cites Kramer-Dahl (1995: 22) as similarly recognising the tension between transformation and 'access'. She believes that:

> I should continue teaching the generic conventions, the ways of knowing and speaking, of academic discourse so that my students have a better chance of succeeding in the university. Yet, at the same time I should also make them aware that these conventions are not ideologically innocent, as they legitimate particular forms of knowledge which I, through my very activity of teaching, may help further entrench.

Likewise, the work described here from the UK and USA involves tutors in moving away from the 'study skills' and 'deficit' models of student writing in order to acknowledge issues of power and identity involved in producing academic discourse and the institutional nature of what counts as knowledge (Lea and Street 1998; Bazerman and Prior 2004). This chapter concludes with an example drawn from a project based on their work in the UK.

WIDENING PARTICIPATION: AN EXAMPLE FROM ENGLAND

This section describes one concrete example[2] of a writing support programme in the UK that builds upon the theoretical traditions outlined above and also combines with work in EAL to address issues of writing development for second language learners. The current UK government policy commitment to expanding British higher education – 50 per cent of the under-30 population to be in university by 2010 – has focused attention on widening participation of non-traditional students (Trainor 2003). This category of students includes (ethnically and linguistically diverse) individuals from low(er) socio-economic backgrounds. There is considerable official anxiety about the retention of non-traditional students. For instance, some 28,000 full-time and 87,000 part-time students who joined first-degree programmes in 2004/05 dropped out a year later (House of Commons Committee of Public Accounts, 2008). In addition, there are 100,000 non-European Union internationals enrolled as students on first-degree programmes in the UK at present. Again, this number is set to grow under the current government policy to expand recruitment.

From professional experience and research, linguistic minority students are likely to encounter considerable difficulties in meeting the different language and literacy requirements of a range of academic practices (e.g. Lea and Street 1998, 1999; Zamel and Spack 2004). These may include knowing how to participate in seminars, e.g. listening for meaning, interpreting information and recognising arguments. Similarly, knowing how to plan and organise the production of academic work (e.g. taking notes, summarising and presenting ideas, and constructing and supporting arguments). The traditional idea of teaching students 'standard' academic English has, as we have seen above, been found to be inappropriate – there is not one uniform thing that students can learn in a generic way. Instead, they need to be exposed to variation in the distinctive requirements of specific practices and genres in academic discourse. The socio-cognitive and linguistic demands of interacting in a tutorial group are quite different from listening to a lecture and taking effective notes. Similarly, writing an essay for a science-based subject is quite different from composing a personal statement for application to university. Language and literacy style require-ments vary between subjects (Lea and Street 1998; Lillis 1999).

It is in response both to these policy shifts and the findings of research in the academic literacies field that members of the Language and Literacy Group at King's College London have developed an 'Academic Language Development' programme for students from linguistic minority community backgrounds who are attending schools in the nearby area and who would like to move on to study at university (Leung and Safford 2005; Scalone and Street 2006; Mitchell 2006). It was hoped that participation in the programme would enhance both their performance in 'A' levels (national examinations taken by 18-year-old students in Britain) and their chances of entering higher education. The programme, consisting of three-hour sessions on most Saturday mornings from January to December, was not an English language programme per se, but rather focused on developing the use of academic English in Higher Educational contexts in the UK. Many of the students had spent limited time in the UK, and so might be unfamiliar with the academic language and literacy practices required for university courses.

As part of this programme, a team of tutors, including the author, conducted sessions based on some of the theoretical principles developed from the academic literacies model and from recent work on multi-modality and genre (cf. Kress 2003; Kress and Street 2006; Jewitt 2006). In these sessions students were required to interact with different categories of text that we defined as different genres and modes. We define genres as types of text, both spoken and written, such as student discussions, written notes, letters, academic essays. We wanted to help students be more aware of the different language and semiotic practices associated with the requirements of different genres in academic contexts.

In one of the early sessions, one of the tutors gave a presentation on genre switching (see Figure 15.1). He drew attention to the fact that prior to having a discussion, just having thoughts and ideas about a subject already involves certain kinds of representation, with different language entailments than those required in other forms or genres. Thoughts may, for instance, be free flowing, they may not always operate in sentences and they may include images and other non-linguistic semiosis such as colours. Then, when the students were asked to move into group talk and discussion, they were required to provide explicitness, to take account of their interlocutor and to employ specific language features and defined speech patterns. The shift from free flowing thoughts and ideas to some explicitness in discussion with others we identified as a shift to a different genre although, as Gunther Kress has pointed out (personal communication), it also involves a shift of 'mode' – from internal thought to external speech. Likewise, as the students shifted from talk and discussion to taking notes, new requirements came into play, such as the need for explicit attention to language structure, use of headings and use of visual as well as language 'modes' such as layout. The tutors encouraged students to make presentations to the whole class using overhead projector slides and again drew attention to the particular genre and mode features of an overhead slide, such as highlighting of key terms, use of single words and layout. Finally, students were asked to provide a page of written text based upon the discussions and overheads and these required joined-up sentences, attention to coherence and cohesion, use of formal conventions of academic writing and attention to editing and revision. Each genre and mode had different qualities. In their educational histories, students had not always been made explicitly aware of these qualities associated with different genres as they moved between genres in their school work. They had rarely been given time to dwell on and develop the distinctive features of each genre, or to address the question of the relationship of these different genres to each other, including the fluid overlap of their boundaries.

The use of the term 'genre' in this programme is related to ethnographic and multi-modal approaches to academic literacies, including the social practice perspective provided by 'New Literacy Studies'. This can be seen in the ways in which the teachers asked questions relating to the Mode and Genre Switching model illustrated in Figure 15.1. They asked, for instance, how do genres and modes vary across disciplines, subjects and fields? Students from science disciplines appeared less familiar with the 'genre' of extended prose but adept at structured layout and the use of visual signs incorporating more multi-modal strategies, whilst social science students had had more written work to do in their school practice but had not necessarily differentiated its features from those of talk and visual layout as explicitly as we were doing in these sessions. In some cases, the students reported that the teachers in their regular school would follow a discussion by asking them to 'write it up' without necessarily making explicit the different requirements as they switched genre and mode from speech to writing or from notes to essays. In the Academic Literacy Development Programme, explicit attention was focused on such switching, transformation and the changing of meanings and representations from one genre and mode to another and participants were encouraged to discuss how this often involves a different 'mix' of two or more genres and modes, such as the notion that writing always creates meaning through layout as well as through the use of words. Attention to these issues constituted a basic premise of the pedagogy in the course.

As we focused on the different genres that participants used within and across different activity frames, the issue of mode of representation also needed to be

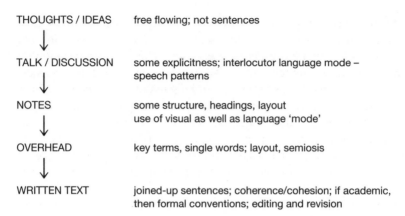

THOUGHTS / IDEAS   free flowing; not sentences

TALK / DISCUSSION   some explicitness; interlocutor language mode –
speech patterns

NOTES   some structure, headings, layout
use of visual as well as language 'mode'

OVERHEAD   key terms, single words; layout, semiosis

WRITTEN TEXT   joined-up sentences; coherence/cohesion; if academic,
then formal conventions; editing and revision

QUESTION: How do genres/modes vary across disciplines/subjects/fields?

GENRE: type of text, e.g. formal/informal, e.g. notes/letters/academic essay; genres vary with practice as well as with disciplines and have been described as 'typified rhetorical actions based in recurrent situations'

MODE: 'a regularised organised set of resources for meaning-making', e.g. image, gaze, gesture, movement, music, speech, writing

DISCIPLINE: field of study, academic subject, e.g. geography, chemistry; business studies; area studies

SWITCHING/TRANSFORMATION: changing meanings and representations from one mode (e.g. speech) into another mode (e.g. writing); often involves just a different 'mix' of both modes, e.g. writing/layout

Figure 15.1 Genre/mode switching.

addressed. Since the activities differed in terms of type of content represented, and genres used, a linguistic analysis of the texts produced was not sufficient to convey the range of semiotic resources used by participants. Multi-semiotic theories of communication emphasise the need to look at all forms of communication in terms of their representation across different modes: linguistic, actional and visual, that are differently organised and established meaning-making resources (cf. Kress and Van Leeuwen 2001, 2006). A multi-modal analysis enabled the teachers to depict and analyse the range of meanings expressed in the different activities and the genres associated with them. It also allowed them to theorise the multimodal nature of literacy, and thus of different genres, that students had to master in order to represent different types of curriculum content for different purposes, and therefore to participate in different activities. For instance, when students presented their own overhead projector slides of their discussions, we helped them to see the importance not simply of subject content – such as the themes necessary for filling in the statement about their personal background and interests required in the university application form – but also of layout, how they ordered the data using font, capitals, arrows and so on.

The team members who taught on the programme also engaged in ethnographic-style research. They were interested in the relationship between the programme objectives and actual experiences and perceptions of the sessions by the students and the tutors. As one of the tutors who both taught the course and engaged in research with it noted:

> The . . . programme tries to challenge some of the expectations students may have met at school . . . about language as narrowly defined . . . the course involves issues of discourse, genre, writing as social process . . . within a notion of building on what they already had and bring to the programme rather than treating them as a deficit and just fixing that.
>
> (Lea and Street 2006: 270)

By expressing personal styles and learning strategies during classroom activities and engaging with their related genres, students participated both in the community of the academy and in the community formed by the students during the course. Furthermore, by engaging with the types of literacy required in higher education in the UK, they collaboratively constructed an understanding of official requirements and participated in learning-oriented activities. Interaction with other students and with tutors was therefore fundamental in making explicit the different types of knowledge that students already used and that they needed to develop and customise to fit Higher Education standards.

CONCLUSION

The adoption of a social practices approach to literacy, then, leads to different understandings and practices in the academy itself regarding the nature of academic writing and how it might be taught. Whilst the traditional model focuses on skills and 'surface' language issues, the 'academic literacies' perspective that builds on New Literacy Studies focuses on broader features of the writing process, including student identities, epistemology and power. The relations between tutors and students become central to the learning of the new ways of writing required of those entering Higher Education and the issue of faculty feedback and student response requires explicit attention rather than remaining latent. The change of focus described in the examples above also involves some nuanced shifts in the underpinning traditions, for instance away from the College Composition focus on 'generic' courses of writing support previously favoured in the USA and away from the Australian 'genre' approach where that had been taken up in mechanistic and formulaic ways (as with the UK National Literacy Strategy in schools). At the same time, work in the field of multimodality has drawn attention to the wider range of modes through which communication is mediated, with visual, aural and kinaesthetic modes in particular playing a significant role in how members of the academy present their work and respond to that of others. In this chapter, I have briefly mapped some of these changes whilst recognising that the processes of adopting a social practice approach to literacy in the academy is ongoing and not simply a 'final' position rejecting all others. Indeed, even those who take on board this approach, recognise the importance of paying attention to skills and socialisation. Based on these perspectives, I have described two areas of work in which we can see these moves taking shape – one from South Africa involving a tutor who began by offering the usual language support to non-traditional students but then shifted to a more social practice and discursive approach as she recognised that the problems they were facing were to do with their entry into new discourse community norms and not simply matters of linguistic skill. Likewise, the example provided from the UK describes a widening participation programme that supports students in that country as they enter university, again calling upon social and multi-modal approaches. This chapter has presented working cases of applications of the new ideas developing in this field, which will contribute to a more refined theoretical and practical approach to the 'problems' of writing in the academy.

NOTES

1 That is, a socially established configuration of language use and other semiotic systems (e.g. imagery, personal appearance styling, ways of behaving), which represent reality from a particular perspective and sanction particular kinds of identities and relationships.
2 This account is adapted from Lea, M.R. and Street, B.V. (2006) 'The "Academic Literacies" Model: Theory and Applications' *Theory into Practice*, Fall, Vol. 45, no. 4: 368–77.

16

SPELLING AS A SOCIAL PRACTICE

MARK SEBBA

INTRODUCTION

In English-speaking countries, spelling is not just a set of rules for writing down words: it is a cultural preoccupation. This is clear not only from the range of apparatus which is provided to help, or force, writers to 'spell it correctly' – for example, dictionaries and spell-checking software – but also from the way that spelling is so explicitly part of the culture of literacy. Spelling tests are the norm at schools in Britain, the USA and elsewhere. In the USA, Spelling Bees – a type of competition where the contestants are required to spell words – are organised at all levels from individual schools up to nationally. In these and other countries, 'hard' spellings are material for quiz questions, while few of us reach adulthood without being asked by a friend or colleague: 'how do you spell . . . ?'

But surely, spelling *correctly* is not dependent on culture? It is just necessary and *natural*, it is 'the way things are'. Even if it is hard to do, is it not inevitable that we should try to spell according to a set of standards? History shows otherwise. As I shall describe in more detail in a later section, the notion of a 'correct' or 'incorrect' spelling in English is fairly recent, dating back around two centuries. Before that, there was no standard spelling and therefore no 'right' spelling; this concept developed after the publication of dictionaries which became accepted as authorities with the power to prescribe a unique correct spelling for any particular word. Thus, many of the classics of English literature were written in a period when the concept of 'correct spelling' simply did not exist.

In the history of the study of English, spelling has generally not been a major focus. Spellings from the period before standardisation, and more recently 'dialect spellings', have provided researchers with useful information (sometimes the *only* information) about local, dialectal and historical pronunciations. For linguists generally, the study of spelling is of interest for the light it sheds on how words and sounds are represented in the brain, and the relationship between these abstract representations and the writing system. Chomsky and Halle, two major linguists of the twentieth century, came to the conclusion on the basis of such a study that 'English orthography, despite its often cited inconsistencies, comes remarkably close to being an optimal orthographic system for English' (1968: 49): a conclusion which surprised and frustrated many of its users, who felt the opposite. Meanwhile, for those whose interests are in education and pedagogy, particularly in literacy, research has tended to focus on the strategies adopted by readers and writers for transforming sounds into written words and vice versa.

243

In this chapter I will take an entirely different approach, arguing that spelling is a social practice: in other words, it is not just something that is fixed and given, it is something that people *do*, an activity that they engage in, use for various purposes and about which they form attitudes and opinions. It is also something that may be manipulated in the construction of individual and group identities.

'SOCIAL PRACTICE' VS 'NEUTRAL TECHNOLOGY'

In his book *Literacy in Theory and Practice*, Brian Street describes the currently predominant model of literacy as based 'on the assumption that [literacy] is a neutral technology that can be detached from specific social contexts' (Street 1984: 1). According to this view, societies either have literacy or they don't; where they do, benefits result, while where they don't, there are problems, in particular a lack of economic development. In contrast to this model of literacy, which he calls 'autonomous', Street argues that a more explanatory and insightful approach to literacy would be an 'ideological' model which recognises the *culturally embedded* nature of social practices connected with reading and writing and 'stresses the significance of the socialisation process in the construction of the meaning of literacy for participants' (Street 1984: 2). This kind of approach requires a *practice account* of literacy (Barton 2007).

In the study of spelling, a similar distinction between approaches can be made. The dominant approach treats spelling as a technology, a *tool* which makes it possible to transfer language from spoken to written form. We can see this in the general approach taken by linguistics towards orthography (which for the purposes of this chapter can be defined as the design of spelling systems for specific languages). 'It is almost universally assumed that phonological study alone is what informs orthography' (Bird 2001: 52): in other words, it is seen to be something strictly to do with the relationship between sounds and the characters that represent them. The ideal, from this perspective, is to get a consistent one-to-one correspondence between sounds and letters since it is widely believed that 'a system based on this principle is necessarily easier than any other for natives to learn' (Jones and Plaatje 1916: xii). The lack of such a one-to-one correspondence is the basis of many criticisms of orthographies, and of the English spelling system in particular. For example, the Simplified Spelling Society, a group which presses for English spelling reform, says:

> over time, as pronunciation changes and new words enter the language, this match between letters and sounds can break down. Then learning to read and write becomes harder, and all education suffers.
>
> (Simplified Spelling Society n.d.)

In contrast to this view of spelling as a tool or set of skills, we can view spelling as 'culturally embedded', to use Street's expression, quoted above. We can look at the role which spelling plays in our culture, and look at the way that society and culture relate to spelling. For example, in mainstream Anglo-Saxon English-language culture great importance is placed on 'being able to spell correctly', an accomplishment which, in the USA, gives rise to the cultural institution already mentioned, the Spelling Bee. The existence of these competitions shows that spelling is governed by rules (it is either 'right' or 'wrong'), potentially difficult (or at least not easy for everyone), and is viewed as a legitimate basis for discrimination between those who 'can' and those who 'can't'. As Edward Carney puts it, 'Spelling errors have social penalties. If you cannot spell you are thought to be uneducated and, by a further savage twist, unintelligent' (1994: 79).)

The key to understanding spelling as a social practice (see Sebba 2007a, Chapter 2) is to see how it involves a set of *conventions*. A spelling convention can be thought of as a kind of 'social contract' to associate a particular word with a sequence of letters – or, if you prefer, a social practice whereby words are spelt in a particular way. Typically, the sound of the word is represented to some extent in the spelling in English, though the extent and nature of this relationship vary greatly from word to word.

In English, there are actually two sets of conventions. The first is the set of conventional rules whereby particular letters and combinations of letters are associated with particular sounds. Thus, it is conventional that the letter <i>[1] is used to represent a high front vowel, and the combination of letters <sh> is used to represent /ʃ/, a palatal fricative, in English. The first of these conventions is shared with many languages, the second with relatively few (Swahili, Zulu, Manx and Albanian among others). The other languages in the world which have the sound /ʃ/, or one similar to it, use a variety of different conventions to represent it (<x> and <ch> in Portuguese; <sch> in German; <sz> in Polish; <s> in Hungarian; <š> in Czech). Through its choice of these conventions, a written language can construct a unique identity for itself; no other language uses exactly the same conventions as English, though many languages have sets of conventions which overlap to a large extent.

A second set of conventions governs which of several ways of representing a given sound in English is used in a particular English word. In English, though <sh> is perhaps the most common or prototypical representation of /ʃ/, there are several others: <ti> (*nation*), <s> (*sugar*), <ss> (*issue*), <ch> (*charlatan*). Thus, in the following examples, the relationship between the letters and the sound they represent adheres to the convention, but the choice of the conventional representation is wrong for that particular word:

<shugar> , <nashon> , <ishue> = *sugar, nation, issue*

The result is a representation of a word which is recognisable, in the sense that if we know that <shugar> is representing a word of English, there is only one word it can be. However, writing <shugar> instead of <sugar> breaks the conventions and thereby produces an effect – the reader is aware that 'something is wrong'.

Learning the conventions of both types is part of learning to read and write a particular language – in this case, English. For example, my seven-year-old daughter wrote the following in a shopping list: *oyl, tothpast, Ritch tea* [biscuits], *oliv's, HP sors, Blue* [top] *milk*. This shows a typical stage of learning, where she has learnt some of the conventions, but not all. In the case of <oyl> , she has learnt that <oy> is a way of representing the dipthong /ɔɪ/ of English (for example, in *boy* and *toy*), but has not learnt the convention which requires that diphthong to be written in a different way in the word *oil*. Likewise, with <Ritch> , she has a conventionally correct correspondence between sound and letters: <tch> for /ʧ/, but, while this spelling is by convention the right one for *pitch*, it is not conventional in *rich*. There are therefore several possible ways in which variation in spelling can come about.

1. **The conventions themselves allow for a choice**. In British English, both <judgment> and <judgement> are acceptable, as are <swop> and <swap> , according to the Concise Oxford Dictionary – though the second one is preferred in each case. We can call this kind of variation *licensed*: it is in the dictionary. A slightly more complex case is that of words which have regional spelling variants, usually a 'British' and an 'American' variant, like <tyre> / <tire> , <defence> / <defense> . In such cases we may think of a particular variant as licensed for one region, but not for the other.

2. **The conventions themselves do not allow for a choice, but there exists the possibility of breaking the convention while still maintaining identification of the word.** This is possible when alternative conventional representations exist for the same sound, for example <ue> and <oo> . This makes <bloo> a recognisable spelling of *blue*, though by convention not the correct one. We can call this kind of variation *unlicensed*: the common interpretation of it would be that it is 'wrong', but this is not the only possible interpretation.

3. A third kind of variation is one which we could call **innovative**. This involves the use of written symbols which are not conventionally used as parts of words as substitutions for strings of characters, and/or using letters for the sound of their *names* rather than for the sounds they conventionally *represent*. English examples would be <gr8> for *great*, <good 4 U> for *good for you*, <some1> for *someone*, <ne1> for *anyone*. These practices were probably well entrenched in graffiti and other 'playful' uses of language before the arrival of e-mail and other computer-mediated forms of communication, but they have become particularly widespread through the the use of new media, especially text (SMS) messaging.

In the case of an adult who uses a non-conventional spelling, if we believe that the choice of representation was *un*intentional, we are likely to think that this was because the writer just did not know the conventional spelling. In our culture, where strict norms of spelling have been developing since the seventeenth century, this has come to be viewed as a form of ignorance and reflects badly on the writer: witness the regular 'moral panics' over spellings in text messaging and other computer-mediated practices (Thurlow 2006). Alternatively, if we think the choice to spell contrary to the convention was deliberate, we will have to conclude that the writer was trying to make some point or draw attention to the word for some purpose. Thus, the possibility of variation in spelling (as in other areas of language) allows us both to talk about spelling as a 'social practice' which involves choices, and to speak of 'social meaning' coming about through deliberate deviation from convention.

SPELLING AND SOCIAL MEANING

In a language like English, different word classes and textual genres provide different possibilities for introducing social meaning through spelling.

Personal names can be given an individual twist by using unconventional sound-letter correspondences: <Soozy> , <Konner> , <Khloe> for *Susy, Conor, Chloe*. Surnames are possibly even more susceptible to unusual spellings, though in this case they serve as family, rather than individual, emblems. As Carney puts it (1994: 449) 'the pressure of distinctive function puts a value on different and even bizarre spellings' of surnames, for example <Featherstonehaugh> (pronounced *Fanshaw*). Furthermore, spellings which retain recognisable archaisms or use French conventions like <Wylde> and <Beauchamp> may give added prestige by indicating a long pedigree (1994: 449). Here, the disjunction between the spelling and the pronunciation creates a kind of mystique for the name as only those 'in the know' will be able to read it correctly. The same applies to some names of institutions and places: <Caius> College, Cambridge (pronounced Keys), <Bicester> (Bister), <Quernmore> (Quormer, a place in Lancashire).

The potential for 'making strange' through deviating from convention is widely used in *product names*. Eirlys Davies (1987: 48) concludes that many non-standard spellings in trade names have the function of drawing attention to the product: 'innovative spelling may serve to attract the readers' attention, simply by virtue of its being different and unexpected'. However, at a more complex level, it may be to do with constructing identities – for the writer, the reader, for the object referred to or a combination of these. For example, the slogan *'It's Strickly Froots'* on the carton of apple juice (Figure 16.1) appears to be an attempt to construct the reader/customer in a certain way, and simultaneously to create a more exciting identity for what is otherwise an unremarkable product.

As a different kind of illustration of this more complex, identity-related, function of spelling, let us turn to Figures 16.2 to 16.5, which all are examples of an immediately recognisable genre – graffiti.

The texts in Figures 16.2–16.5 were almost certainly written by adolescents, and found in places typical of graffiti (walls, a park bench and a bus shelter). All

Figure 16.1 Strickly Froots.

Figure 16.2 Sarah. W. woz eya 2003!!!

Figure 16.3 AJ waz ere.

Figure 16.5 Emma Laura N Alice woz eya Munchin init 06.

Figure 16.4 KJ woz ere 9T7.

have a rather similar structure, with some obligatory and some optional elements, which we might represent like this (optional elements in brackets):

[name(s)] [was] [here] [(activity)] [(date)]

However, to dissect the texts in this way fails to reveal their most interesting aspects. From an ethnographic perspective they raise all sorts of questions about who the authors were, why they chose to perform this act of illegal (or at least disapproved-of) writing and what they were trying to communicate; while similar questions can be asked about the readers of the texts.

A striking fact about this type of graffiti is that the words *was here*, which are an obligatory part of the text, are never spelt in the conventional way. These are common words, and among the words taught in the earliest years of school. It is unlikely that the teenagers who wrote these texts, no matter how educationally challenged, did not know their conventional spelling. Notice also that in the examples given, both *was* and *here* have two variant spellings (neither of them the conventional spelling). Why should this be? First of all, it is fundamental that these particular texts are explicit acts of self-identification: they contain a name which is, or is claimed to be, the name of the writer or the group of people associated with the writer. So this text tells us something about the writer – his or her name, as well as the fact that he or she was at this particular place. But we also know, because this writing is graffiti, that the writer is prepared to break a law, or at least, to carry out an act which is frowned on by 'polite' society: namely, to write on a surface such as a park bench, where writing is not allowed. The use of the unconventional or *unlicensed* spellings therefore reinforces the use of an unlicensed surface for writing the message: it says 'I defy the rules'![2]

You could argue that the graffiti texts in Figures 16.2–16.5 are themselves conventional: they follow a formula. This is true, but the spellings are not actually conventionalised – they involve breaking the existing convention rather than following a new one: thus *was* is respelt as <woz> , <waz> or (less commonly) <wos> . Writers of graffiti are not required to spell these words in a particular way, they are just expected to go against the norm. They must, however, do what they do in such a way as to maintain intelligibility among their intended readers. In practice this usually means using a sound-to-letter convention which already exists in the language, but one which is regarded as wrong for the particular word in question. In the case of *was*, the sound /z/ is often spelt <z> in English, but <waz> is not the conventional spelling of the word; likewise the sound /ɒ/ is frequently represented by <o> , but not, by convention, in *was*.

This insistence on breaking the conventions is a common characteristic of graffiti and can be seen as one way in which its authors construct an identity for themselves which is resistant to the norms of the mainstream. In English-speaking countries, no particular group (other than perhaps 'adolescents' or 'youth' in general) is associated with anti-conventional spelling practices of this type. In other countries, this is not the case: in Spain, for example, there is a fairly strong association between certain spelling practices and subcultural groups. In Spanish, the sound /k/ is written as <k> only in words of foreign origin; in almost every word of Spanish origin, /k/ is represented by <c> (as in <color> 'colour') or <qu> (as in <queso> /keso/, 'cheese'). It has become a common practice for counter-cultural groups in Spain to use <k> in place of <c> and <qu> as a way of signalling opposition to the mainstream culture (see Sebba 2007a: 3–4). In the Basque country, a part of Spain which has regional autonomy under the Spanish constitution but where there is a separatist movement and public contention over language issues, the Basque language differentiates itself from Spanish (an unrelated language) by its choice of orthographic conventions for representing certain sounds which exist in both languages. The /k/ sound is one of these – represented by <k> in Basque but <c> and <qu> in

Spanish. This fact enables young Basques to engage in a practice of 'parodic spellings of Spanish words' and to communicate in written Spanish at the same time as undermining the authority of its spelling (Urla 2003: 219–20).

In Germany as well, the use of non-standard spellings is associated with subcultural identities. Androutsopoulos concluded from a study of German fanzines (music magazines produced by amateurs) that 'the more subculturally oriented a fanzine, the more non-standard spellings it can be expected to contain' (2000: 524).

'REGULATED SPACES' AND THE ZONE OF SOCIAL MEANING

In many types of text, spelling conventions are regarded as inviolable – e.g. academic texts such as the present chapter are patrolled by software, copy editors, publishers and readers. Kress comments on such constraints: 'Spelling is that bit of linguistic practice where issues of authority, of control, of conformity can be most sharply focused' (Kress 2000: x).

For other types of text, however, there is apparently great freedom to spell as you please, as long as your spelling keeps (just) on the right side of intelligibility. Table 16.1, adapted from Sebba (2007a: 47), gives an overview of how different types of contemporary writing can be located under different orthographic

Table 16.1 Orthographic regimes for different types of text

Regime	Writing types (examples)	Readership	Institution types
Most highly regulated	Texts for publication	General public	Publishing, journalism, etc.
	Texts for circulation (memos, business letters, work e-mail, etc.)	Colleagues/competitors	Business, employment
↓	'School' writing	Teachers	School
	Poetry, 'literary' writing	Identified (possibly elite) readership	Publishing
↓	Personal letters	Self/intimates	Not institutional
	Private diaries	Self/intimates	
↓	Personal memos (notes, lists)	Self/associates	
	Electronic media (personal e-mail, chat rooms)	Self/in-group	
	SMS text messaging		
	Fanzines, 'samizdat'	In-group	
Least regulated	Graffiti	In-group/general public	Oppositional

'regimes', ranging from the tightly regulated texts (typically produced for publication and/or distribution in an institutional setting such as recognised publishers, mainstream media, government, schools, etc.) to practically unregulated (graffiti, which is by its nature illegitimate and anti-institutional).

It should be emphasised that Table 16.1 represents the regulation of spelling in English at this particular stage in history. It is by no means fixed and unchanging. For example, some centuries ago practices were very different. During the Middle Ages, spelling was not standardised and scribes, especially lawyers' clerks, showed a tendency to favour more elaborate, French-based spellings, because they were paid for their work by the inch (Scragg 1974: 52). Somewhat later, after the advent of printing, printers might extend words (for example, by the addition of 'silent' letters) to justify margins or cut letters to compensate for shortages of movable type (Brengelman 1980: 333). These variations had nothing to do with identity construction, but demonstrate clearly that spelling was viewed as flexible. Still later, English spelling in printed texts underwent a rapid stanadardisation in the middle part of the seventeenth century, but spellings in *private* writing did not become standardised until a century later (Strang 1970: 107). The idea of a 'wrong' spelling thus dates back only to the end of the eighteenth century, and developed following the publication of authoritative dictionaries (those of Johnson in England and Webster in North America) (107), which clearly set out what was the 'right' spelling.

Until fairly recently, it would probably be true to say that the description of English spelling by Milroy and Milroy (1999: 56) as 'almost absolutely invariant'[3] was accurate, allowing for the possibility of deviation in only the most marginal and oppositional forms of writing, such as graffiti. However, since the arrival of computer-mediated communication (and, slightly later, text messaging), there has been a radical expansion of the range of genres in which variant spellings are tolerated or even valued.

If we compare the situation in the Middle Ages, where English spelling drew on several scribal traditions (the Anglo-Saxon, Latin and Norman French) but had no fixed standard, with the situation in the twentieth century, of 'almost absolute invariance', we can see that the possibility of spelling having social meaning derives from the fact that spelling is so standardised, and yet has potential for variant representations of the same sound. During the period when there was *no* standard spelling, it was not possible to use spelling to show resistance to the orthographic regime, since there was none. Similarly, if spelling were truly invariant, offering no options at all for variation (as in a few languages), it would not be possible to derive social meaning from variant spellings, since there would be none. The possibility of social meaning thus exists in a relatively narrow space between complete invariance and complete licence, which Sebba (2007a: 34) calls the 'zone of social meaning'.

In this chapter so far, the focus has been on the conventional spelling of Standard English – in other words, on standard spelling. However, it is worth mentioning that there are also texts written in English which intentionally use variant spellings to represent non-standard varieties of English, especially regional or local dialects. Historically, in the period before English itself was standardised, it was the norm for spellings to represent regional varieties, at least to some extent. Later, using non-standard spellings became a way of representing dialectal speech in opposition to the established standard, especially in literary works (several Scottish novelists have provided recent examples of this). Also in Scotland, the Scots language (sometimes known as Lallans, i.e. Lowland Scots) differentiates itself from English by a different, but less standardised, set of spelling conventions, some of which go back to the period when English and Scots were recognised as distinct written languages with different norms. Respellings to represent local pronunciations are also a feature of a kind of humorous publication, available in many places which have distinctive dialects: for example *A Rum Owd Dew* (a book by Charlie Haylock representing the Suffolk dialect) and *Essex – Sumfing Else!*, 'a cornucopia of Estuary English' by Steve Crancher.

CREATING GROUP IDENTITY THROUGH SPELLING: THE CASE OF AN ONLINE COMMUNITY

This section gives an example of an online community where non-standard spellings are used to create group identities. In the case of English (unlike Spanish, for example) this is where group identities constructed through spelling seem to be most likely to occur at the moment.

The online community is associated with the character 'Ali G' (a creation of the comedian Sasha Baron Cohen). Around the year 2000, Ali G became very popular in Britain, and subsequently elsewhere. The character is of ambiguous ethnicity but affects a hip-hop style of dress and language. Close examination of the language of Ali G reveals that his language is based on Southern British English (with a high proportion of stigmatised forms) with extensive influence from the British variety of Jamaican Creole.

In the wake of the success of Ali G, numerous websites were set up by (presumably mainly adolescent) fans. These websites include message boards, visitor books, spoof 'dictionaries' and other items, all of which involve written texts. A feature of postings to the bulletin boards, in particular, is the use of a special type of language, modelled on that of the Ali G character. Although this 'Ali G language' is not distinguished from English *solely* by its spelling – it has lexis and grammatical features from Creole and non-standard British English – it does depend heavily for its effect on respellings of common words.

This is illustrated by the following examples from the 'Ali G. Dreambook' (a guest book where visitors can insert their names, their 'Massive' (gang), and a message).

1   WE GOTZ MAD RESPECT 4 YO RANK FOR REAL, ME MAIN MAN
     DAVE SAYZ U IS REALLY WESTSIDE ESPECIALLY WHEN U IZ

MASHED ON DA TELLY INNIT SO KEEP DA PEACE AND KNOW
DAT YA HOMIEZ IN NZ GOT MAD RESPECT FOR YA RANK
AIIGHT, RESPECT
[March 20th 2001]
Homiez: friends
Aiight: all right (associated with Hip-hop culture)

2   I is bangin' on bout how all o' the court fields krew should be smokin'
da weed and havin a laff durin skool hours. I wanta get smashed in skool
as much as posible. Make it more fun. Well ... gotta be seeing yas.
Boyakasha!!
[March 27th 2001]
Krew: crew, gang
Boyakasha: used here as a greeting, origins probably in reggae culture

3   Tonight, thursday da 3rd hof may, iz gonna be a historic day fe da
Netherlands. dis iz gonna be da first time da Ali G show iz gonna be broad-
cast ova in ha house! geeza! can hardly wait to roll on da floor laughin!
everyone I nah iz told by me. all two hof dem! dis iz gonna be snoop!!
[May 3rd 2001]

(http://books.dreambook.com/rtevans/alig.html accessed 19 March 2008)

All three messages contain examples of modifications of the standard spelling
(there are some in the guestbook which do not), though not all the same ones:
thus *is* is spelt in the standard way in example 2 above, <iz> in 3 and both ways
in 1. Example 2 has several other non-conventional spellings, including <skool>,
<krew> and <laff> . In 1, *for* is represented as <4> while in 3 it is <fe> . In all
of these examples, the purpose of the spelling seems to be to flag 'otherness',
since the spelling does not reflect any difference in the sound (this is not true,
for example, of the spelling <da> for *the*, found in all three, which represents a
Creole/African-American pronunciation of *the* with an initial stop /d/ rather
than a fricative /ð/). Thus, it is clear that using non-standard spellings is an
important part of marking these messages as 'Ali G language' and therefore
appropriate contributions to this guestbook for Ali G fans, and it is through
using these spellings and other non-standard forms[4] that individuals can claim
membership of the online community of Ali G fans. Hence, spelling is an important aspect of identity construction for the people in this group. (For more
details on this work, see Sebba 2003b, 2007b.)

SPELLING REFORM IN ENGLISH

Few people will admit to liking English spelling. It is frequently denounced as
illogical, too difficult or a barrier to learning. In spite of this, there has never
been a mass movement to reform the spelling of English: rather, there have
been numerous proposals with the support of small minorities, which have made
little impact. This is not to say that the proponents of spelling reform are not

well organised: the Simplified Spelling Society was established in Britain in 1908 and remains the main campaigning organisation. Nor are they lacking in famous supporters: they can claim the distinguished phonetician Daniel Jones, the Members of Parliament Sir James Pitman and Dr Mont Follick, and perhaps most famous of all, the dramatist George Bernard Shaw, who provided in his will for a contest to establish a phonetic spelling system.

Given the level of support, why has spelling reform for English made so little progress? Once a standardised writing system has been established, it is extremely difficult to change it. Where few people use the system, where it is fairly new, where no one has a vested interest (such as being the publisher of a dictionary or author of a book) and where there are no identity issues involved, then change should be easy to achieve. In practice, spelling is hardly ever like this: even societies with relatively few readers and writers often have a strong attachment to their writing systems and there are always people with a vested interest in maintaining the existing system (see Johnson 2005; Sebba 2007a Chapter 6).

In the case of English, there is a very long tradition and vast numbers of readers, writers, authors and publishers, spread over a huge geographical area in a large number of countries, many of which have substantial publishing industries. The likelihood of getting agreement to changes – even small changes – from all these different stakeholders is very low. The case of German spelling reform in the late 1990s provides an instructive example. Even when an international agreement had been reached among the German-speaking countries, when the reforms had been put to the test in the constitutional courts by aggrieved members of the public, and the reform (which was estimated to affect only 0.05 per cent of all words in running text anyway[5]) had been put into practice, it was not long before some of the major players – the giant publishing houses Axel Springer and Spiegel – announced that they would revert to the old spelling and called on the rest to follow suit (Sebba 2007a: 159).

Whatever one's intellectual position on spelling reform, it is necessary to take account of the social, political and cultural conditions which make spelling reform so difficult to achieve. In this connection it is interesting to look at the position taken by the advocates of English spelling reform, such as the Simplified Spelling Society.[6] The Society, according to its website, 'does not currently advocate specific solutions' but does believe that 'the spelling of the written language should as far as possible conform to its pronunciation'.

The main motivation of the Simplified Spelling Society seems to be to do with the learning of reading and writing; according to their position statement,[7] the Society 'considers that the fundamental justification for any reform of Traditional Spelling is that it will improve literacy and cut learning costs in English among children and adults'. This motivation to improve 'literacy' (rather narrowly understood, it seems, as a tool or technology) comes across strongly in the statements of its supporters, who also have a tendency to link 'illiteracy' explicitly to social ills. For example, Sanford Silverman, author of a book on spelling reform was quoted as saying (on the occasion of a protest against the National Spelling Bee) 'If these people [illiterates] were able to read and write with a simplified spelling system, they would be able to fill out a job application, stay employed, and stay out of prison' (American Literacy Council 2004).

Interestingly, the Simplified Spelling Society does not argue against standardised spelling. According to their position statement,

> We wish to encourage a move to more regular spelling conventions rather than allow a free for all, which would probably lead to no overall improvement of literacy and might even impede written communication throughout the English Speaking World.

This is a little surprising, as easing up on the insistence on *right* spelling rather than *understandable* spelling might be one way of removing the stigma of 'illiteracy'. The supporters of simplified spelling protest against the way that the Spelling Bee creates a 'spelling elite' by exalting difficult spellings, but they do not, apparently, oppose the idea of *fixed* spelling as long as it is simple. The position of the Simplified Spelling Society is to reject the arguments that the reform of English spelling is too difficult, and to insist that a reform in the direction of more regular and phonemic spelling will benefit everyone. Yet, to adopt this attitude is to deny the culturally embedded nature of the English spelling system, and the extent to which users of English identify with their spelling system, which they see as troublesome and quirky, but satisfyingly difficult and somehow loveable.

CONCLUSION

Treating spelling as simply a way to get from the sound of a word to a representation of it on paper or on a screen is to overlook its social nature. Spellings create an identity for a written language as a whole, and for subgroups of its users as well. The potential for doing this is partly a consequence of the extent to which spelling has been standardised in English-speaking culture: so standardised that any deviation calls attention to itself, and is potentially imbued with social meaning. Some variation is allowed, but to different degrees in different genres and different contexts; writers exploit this potential in different ways, often for identity purposes. Spelling is not just a tool, but a social practice.

NOTES

1 Here, I follow the convention of using symbols within < > to represent spellings, and symbols within slashes / / to represent sounds (strictly, phonemes).
2 The spellings <ere> and <eya> are both likely to be intended to represent pronunciation. The first of these shows the dropping of the initial /h/, which is extremely widespread but is nevertheless stigmatised or seen as 'sloppy'. The spelling <eya> probably represents a regional two-syllable pronunciation of the word: both examples of this

were found in the north of England (though far apart from each other). This does not detract from the point that the spellings go counter to the convention for these words.

3 Milroy and Milroy actually apply this description to twentieth-century spelling.

4 Non-standard features of grammar in 'Ali G' language include *me* for *I*, and non-standard subject–verb agreement; lexical features include *homie, aiight, boyakasha, snoop*.

5 According to the *Institut für deutsche Sprache*, Mannheim.

6 www.spellingsociety.org/aboutsss/about.php, accessed 19 March 2008.

7 www.spellingsociety.org/aboutsss/position.php, accessed 19 March 2008.

17

MULTILINGUAL DISCOURSES ON WHEELS AND PUBLIC ENGLISH IN AFRICA

A CASE FOR 'VAGUE LINGUISTIQUE'

BUSI MAKONI AND SINFREE MAKONI

INTRODUCTION

This chapter briefly reviews some dominant research traditions in the use of English in Africa, questioning some of their assumptions about languages, and then focuses on a new emerging analytical framework based on the concept of *'vague linguistique'* (Thomas 2007). *'Vague linguistique'* differs from traditional structuralist approaches to language research in Africa, which tend to focus on the linguistic system, even if the researcher acknowledges the social context of their data. In contrast, *'vague linguistique'* is a plurilanguaging approach whose goal is to capture the dynamic and evolving relationships between English, other indigenous African languages and multiple open semiotic systems, from the point of view of the language users themselves; i.e. an insider or emic perspective. We apply this approach to a discussion of multimodal data from taxi culture in Ghana in the mid-twentieth century and South Africa in the early twenty-first century.

The chapter is divided into:

- a brief review of research traditions in the use of English in Africa;
- an outline of the *'vague linguistique'* approach;
- an analysis of taxi-lingua cultures in mid-twentieth-century Accra and early twenty-first-century Johannesburg.

RESEARCHING THE USE OF 'ENGLISH' IN AFRICA

In Africa, there are at least four main research traditions into the use of English and the role of African languages therein. The first tradition addresses the official status of English vis-à-vis that of African languages, as the media of instruction in post-colonial Africa. This approach focuses on the historical and contemporary status and functions of English and so-called indigenous African languages. English is the official language widely used for administrative and educational purposes whereas the use of African languages for educational purposes is often limited to the first four years of schooling. Thus African children initially experience mother-tongue education before switching to English.

During this period, exposure to English is very limited as it is only experienced by the children as one subject among many, before it is introduced as a language of instruction from the fifth grade onwards. The switch to English is often abrupt and this

> inadequate linguistic preparation of the pupils in the [English] language prior to its use as the medium of learning and the pupil's lack of exposure to the [English language] outside the classroom generally result in high failure rates and dropouts.
>
> (Kamwangamalu 2000)

An extended use of mother-tongue education has also been seen as contentious. Some educational linguists have argued that the use of indigenous African languages has advantages whereas others argue that research in support of mother-tongue education is inconclusive as there are no lifespan studies that show the longevity and sustainability of the gains. In fact, 'for every research report that indicates that mother tongue education is effective there is another one that indicates that it is not' (Fasold 1984: 312). A subtext to this argument is a body of research which is critical of the validity of the construct of mother tongue itself. Irrespective of the efficacy of mother-tongue education, there are suggestions that promoting it results in the separation of ethnic groups within the educational system, thus accentuating the ethnic divisions that are largely an artefact of colonialism.

This yin and yang argument, so to speak, has led to the suggestion that English should be the sole language used in education and that other languages should be limited in their functions. But the increasingly dominant use of English as an official language of business and education in some parts of Africa has led to an assumption that English poses a threat to the survival of indigenous African languages. Although English is an official language in some African countries, we would argue that it does not necessarily constitute a threat to the viability of African languages, whose position may be more seriously challenged by the Urban African Vernaculars which dominate popular culture and circulate widely.

The second research tradition involves identifying and mapping the number of languages in Africa and their geographical distribution. The underlying assumption is the countability (or numerability) of languages and speakers of each language. The countability of language as autonomous 'things' is a prerequisite for the management of states and 'countability' is an important philosophical trope for this research strand (Joseph 2006). However, radical social constructionists have begun to challenge the assumptions which form the basis for the countability of languages and the rationale in the differentiation of language from other semiotic systems (Reagan 2005; Yngve 2004). They argue that languages are historically contingent and political from the top down (Joseph 2006). Their view that languages are created on-line, in the context of multimodal social practice, challenges the notion that languages are 'natural'.

If languages cannot be readily separated from social context and other semiotic systems, they cannot be easily counted and counting them, although useful for 'governmentality' (Foucault 1991), is not otherwise very meaningful.

Radical social constructionism also questions the nineteenth- century notions in which languages are tied to specific geographical localities and speaker national identities (Mignolo 1996: 182) such as 'I live in France and speak French, therefore I am French'. The combined effects of migration in the nineteenth century from Europe to Africa and from Africa and Asia to Europe in the twentieth and twenty-first centuries have led to a 'disarticulation' in relations between language and territory (Shohamy 2006). This 'disarticulation' of language from geographical location has substantial epistemological consequences and researchers are beginning to develop conceptual frameworks which can accommodate subaltern knowledge practices and views about language (Mignolo 1996).

The third strand of research on English in Africa stresses how English is indigenized and localized in diverse African contexts, to produce 'New Englishes'. One of the main findings from research on New Englishes (or World Englishes, i.e. non-Anglo Englishes) is a cataloguing of linguistic features which are typical of each country (thus linking with the 'counting languages' approach above). Ghanaians speak Ghanaian English because they are Ghanaians and Zimbabweans speak Zimbabwean English because they are Zimbabweans. The nation state is one of the key units of analysis in spite of the fact that the validity of the construct *'state'* in contemporary African political philosophy is open to debate. Krishnaswamy and Burde (1998) state that this research tradition takes 'a nationalistic point of view' (1998: 30) to the extent that nations and their varieties of English are brought into being. Yet not only is there considerable diversity within states but also similarities between them, particularly along borders. Thus '[by] focusing centrally on the development of new national Englishes, the world Englishes approach reproduces the very linguistics it needs to escape from' (Pennycook 2007: 21).

The fourth and last research tradition is founded on notions of linguistic hybridity apparent from the characteristics of urban vernaculars in contemporary Africa. The examples used to support the so-called hybrid forms are words such as *smallinyana* (very tiny) which is a result of the English word 'small' inflected with the Nguni diminutive suffix-*nyana* (/small/tiny). *Smallinyana* is found in some varieties of language used in Southern Africa. Whilst this particular tradition is interesting as it touches on issues of creolization and languages in contact, it is also predicated on, and privileges, the notion of languages as discrete entities wherein one can determine where one language begins and the other ends.

In a bid to move away from the terminological trappings inherent in the use of the term 'hybridity', some researchers view this mélange of urban varieties (Githiora 2002) as 'vague linguistique', *courants/influences linguistiques* or *'linguistic current'*. It appears that '[t]erms such as *vagues* or flux waves [and] courants ... might be more appropriate and partially overcome the problems inherent in the notion of hybridity' (Thomas 2007: 3). In the *'courants'* research strand, varieties shown in the use of such lexical items as *smallinyana* or *huchest* (sweetest; drawn from *huchi* which means honey in Shona and -est which is the English superlative degree suffix) are viewed not from a formalist approach to hybridity which identifies segments from different languages, but as examples of linguistic fluidity that arise from exposure to multiple linguistic sources. The notion of *vague linguistique* focuses on the ongoing social process which involves a mobilization of diverse linguistic resources (plurilanguaging) in semantically open ways. It captures the unpredictability of the source of the *courants* situated in everyday life and the speaker's 'agency', both of which are overlooked in linguistic theories in which languages seem to operate independently of their speakers (Joseph 2006).

A *vague linguistique* approach accepts that speakers may have 'bits and pieces' of languages and partial semiotics, and uneven proficiencies in these languages. In the context of this approach it becomes difficult to sustain notions about the validity of English as a 'killer' language, because English, just like any other language, provides a linguistic resource amongst the other multiple resources (i.e. indigenous African languages) available to the speaker. *Vague linguistique* also challenges a dictionary perspective in which the relationships between form and meaning are fixed and predetermined in advance and not open-ended design systems. In an open-ended system, meanings are not wholly inherent in specific forms but their resonances vary depending on the speaker's agency. Recognition of open-ended meanings and of the disarticulation between the speaking self and geographical location (Mignolo 1996) challenge conceptual-izations founded on an assumption of the existence of an autonomous, agentive, truth-telling self (Robbins 2000).

TAXI CULTURE IN ACCRA AND JOHANNESBURG

In this section we extend *vague linguistique* research by focusing on the combina-tion of 'plurilanguaging' and multimodality within the lingua culture of taxis or what Wa Mungai in Kenya calls *'matatu culture'*. Wa Mungai (2007) defines *matatu culture* as

> a combined range of activities and symbolic acts, verbal or written, either deployed upon the vehicle or embodied by *matatu* workers and passengers, in interactions with each other upon and in reference to the site of the material culture object known as *matatu* taxi culture.
>
> (2007: 28)

Wa Mungai's study of matatu culture differs from our own study in that, whilst he focuses on popular media and the analysis of 'matatu discourse as a narrative of identity-making' (Ogude and Nyairo 2007), our focus is on language use and multimodality.

261

The empirical data presented in this chapter comes from the culture of *tro-tros* (lorry-taxis named after three-pence of Ghanaian currency) in 1950s and 1960s Accra and minibus taxis in Johannesburg in South Africa in the early twenty-first century. One of the defining features of public transport in African urban centres is taxi culture. Because taxis are the main modes of public transport in Ghana and South Africa, a relatively large number of Africans experience language used in the inscriptions on and inside taxis. They also encounter the interrelated semiotic systems of music and paintings on, in and through inscriptions and this complex semiotic environment shapes their language ideologies. The ways in which English is embedded in the taxi-lingua culture merits serious consideration because unmetered taxis are used extensively in African cities, and form an important part of people's everyday experience of English.

The Ghanaian data discussed below were gathered from inscriptions written on the wooden sides, front and back of the tro-tros or *'mammy lorries'* which first appeared in Ghana in 1948 (Kyei and Schreckenbach 1976). In the early 1950s and late 1960s Kyei and Schreckenbach[1] collected photographs of *mammy lorries* on Ghanaian roads and in the lorry dumping compounds referred to as *mammy grave yards*. They also carried out a series of interviews with the drivers on their motivations for using particular inscriptions, and for their choices of colour and font size. We have reanalyzed the photographs and interviews, focusing on the semantically open-ended nature of the *mammy lorry* inscriptions. The South African data were collected by ourselves and associates in Johannesburg in 2007, from a variety of African townships. Although the inscriptions on the Ghanian *mammy lorries* do not exhibit the vast array of popular visual images which we found on South African taxis in 2007, some of the paintings from both the 1950s Ghana *tro-tros* and the South African minibus taxis reflect the 'profusion of grotesque detached human and non-human bodies – wide eyed monstrosities with flaring nostrils and cavernous mouths drawn on these vehicles' which Wa Mungai (2007: 26) documents in contemporary Kenya. Some of these monstrosities appear to be human skeletons immersed in fire (see Figure 17.2).

INSCRIPTIONS AND DISCOURSES FROM GHANAIAN *TRO-TROS*

The inscriptions on the 1950s *tro-tros* were written mainly in standard English and forms of pidgin English used in and around Accra. They provide a social commentary on current affairs, reflecting engagement with prevailing political events, domestic issues and interpersonal relations with family members or neighbours. This social commentary, however, is often indeterminate: for example, in the inscription *'Blackman dei ibi trouble'* (A blackman is in trouble again) (Kyei and Schreckenbach 1976: 71) it is not clear whether the writer is admonishing the man, or praising his insurrection or commenting on a political state of affairs. In the category of inscriptions focusing on political issues, one *tro-tro* driver displayed the inscription *Congo* on his *tro-tro*, at a time when there was serious political upheaval in the newly independent Congo as a result of the assassination of the president Moise Tschombe in a military coup. The driver uses his inscription to point to a complex and intractable political reality, bringing it into the public domain. It is possible that the word *Congo* may have been used metaphorically, to capture the problematic nature of his taxi symbolically, drawing a mocking parallel with the disruption associated with the Congo. However, it is also possible that the use of the word *Congo* was unrelated to the political events taking place in the Congo and that the *tro-tro* driver used the word because he had heard it on radio or seen it through the print media.The meaning of the words is therefore indeterminate and open to a number of different possible interpretations.

In some cases the political commentary was, according to the drivers interviewed in the 1950s, unambiguously celebratory. For example, the industriousness of the Americans was reflected in the popular inscriptions of 'USA' or its variant 'the US' which the *tro-tro* drivers described as an acronym for *Uncle Sam*. The 1950s *mammy lorry* drivers also claimed that *Uncle Sam* was the name of rice that was imported from the USA. (In fact, the name of the rice that was imported from the USA was *Uncle Ben's*.)

Another category of inscriptions relates to domestic issues: happy moments, or tension and conflict within the family. For example, an inscription such as *'home hard Grow lanka lanka'* referred to hardships in the domestic space. When asked to provide a context and meaning for his use of this particular inscription, the *tro-tro* driver explained:

> *This struggle I struggle I go on empty stomach sometimes at times my wife and children and we **chop** (eat) only kenkey and shito and tatare for a week, like that then we grow **lanka lanka** (thin) like bamboo stick chief home hard.*
>
> (Kyei and Schreckenbach 1976: 6)

This inscription reflects the linguistic expertise of the *tro-tro* drivers who stretch the meaning of words to express individual opinions. For example, *'lanka lanka'* is drawn from the English word *'lanky'* and yet the grammatical from of *'lanka lanka'* is a duplicative verb form for emphasis and it comes from Twi; one of the African languages of Ghana. It appears that *'home hard'* could either be a basilect feature of linguistic resources which, from a strictly linguistic perspective, might be described as Ghanaian English in which there is no copula (see, however, our earlier critique of categories such as Ghanaian English and Nigerian English – our use of such categories reflects the problems of escaping the structuralist paradigm).

Part of the social commentary relates to interpersonal relations with other members of the community at large and the personal histories of individuals and their families are sometimes translated into taxi inscriptions. In fact, *mammy lorry* drivers not only transport people but also ideas and moral lessons. Hence, there are inscriptions that admonish others or talk back at society and share wisdom with the general populace, as in the following examples.

1   *Mind your own. In 99 out of 100 cases you find that you let sleeping dogs lie if you mind your own* (i.e. mind your own business);

2   *Stop poking your nyama nyama nose into other people's business* ('nyama nyama' means chunky, meaty);

3   *You pack your books and head for booze sessions instead of school sessions you pose a professor while actually a flop-ester* ('flop-ester' means a failure, a noun derived from the English verb to flop).

While inscriptions use fragments of English idiomatic expressions, most are written in a combination of English and African languages. For example, *'nyama nyama'* (nominal duplication for emphasis drawn from the local African languages) nose refers to a chunky nose. It seems that English is used as another local language, without any suggestion that it has a superior status. For example, in 1 above *'Mind your own'* would be incomplete as an idiomatic expression in standard English and yet, in this local version, it is an acceptable 'English expression' and used to humorous effect.

Inscriptions on the *tro-tros* also included the portrayal of foreign characters or situations, for example the inscriptions *'Big Boy'* and *'De Great'* seem to invoke the voice of the Black American boxer Muhammad Ali. The driver explained:

> I suppose you know me now de great it's not within accepted norms of modesty, but if you are the greatest, you are the greatest, you are the greatest, and you don't need actually need to wait for others to blow it for you.
>
> (Kyei and Schreckenbach 1976: 71)

The driver reproduces a version of what appear to be Muhammad Ali's phrases to acknowledge that he is bragging but justifies this by stating that if he does not indulge in self-praise, then it is highly unlikely that other people will blow his trumpet about his achievements. The inscription on his *tro-tro* could be either a parody or a straight reproduction of Muhammad Ali's familiar boasts.

In summary, the inscriptions by *mammy lorry* drivers are interesting examples of language use in the public space. They provide a social commentary on personal experience, political conflicts and national current issues and reflect a certain level of creativity in the use of linguistic resources drawn from a number of different languages, including English. The drivers make choices between languages and opt for a localized version of English or any one of the urban varieties that they are exposed to. In *'vague linguistique'* inscriptions are closely tied to the experiences which shape them and which they, in turn, shape. Inscriptions are situated in specific contexts and they drag with them the contexts of their creation as well. The various possible meanings of inscriptions like *'Congo'* or *'De Great'*, the indeterminate reference of 'I' and 'you' and the combination of features from different languages indicate the open-ended and flexible nature of the cultural resources, which are not necessarily constrained by the norms of any one particular language. There is thus an unusual degree of ambivalence in

the evaluative meanings and taxi drivers exercise considerable agency in manipulating the expressions in ways which suit them; depending on the 'voice' which
they seek to project (Blommaert 2006).

THE SOUTH AFRICAN TAXI INSCRIPTIONS: MULTILINGUALISM ON WHEELS

The inscriptions on South African taxis reflect modern-day South African poly-
glossia. They are written in what, from a western-educated linguist's perspective,
is a variety of different standard/official languages and non-standard 'languages'.
When we say that the inscriptions are in English or localized varieties of English,
we are therefore using an etic (outside) perspective, which is substantially
different from the emic experience which forms the focus of a *vague linguistique*
approach. The South African taxi inscriptions are embedded within a multitude
of semiotic systems and some of the social commentary challenges both socially
and linguistically prescribed norms.

The meaning or message in these inscriptions is also obfuscated and this is
one of the critical features of taxi-lingua culture which makes it amenable to
vague linguistique as a theoretical framework. It is not always clear who the
inscriptions are directed to and what the referent is. For example, in Figure 17.1
it is unclear who *'The outsider'* is or who is the 'me' in *'It's me against the world'*.
However, the driver does provoke social commentary with his inscription
'Legalise marijuana' found on the front of the taxi which enacts 'ideological

Figure 17.1 'The Outsider' inscription

insubordination' (Porter 1995: 101). This insubordination is also evident in the taxi drivers' well-known flagrant disregard of road regulations and in their use of unbridled obscenities in public. Their defiance is further expressed through a preference for Kwaito music, which emerged after the first democratic elections in 1994 and is usually construed as a South African version of American hip-hop. Kwaito is an aesthetic forum that taunts and defies social norms just like American hip-hop[2] and the language of the lyrics in Kwaito music is equally raw and colourful. In some instances the words are drawn from African-American Vernacular (AAV), suggesting that Kwaito musicians are avid devotees of American hip-hop. What is worth noting, is that both American hip-hop and Kwaito deal with ghetto life and brazenly challenge social norms. Thus, taxi-lingua culture is 'a space from which a subaltern category dabbling at subversion talks back at larger society' (Wa Mungai 2007: 30).

In fact, the expression '*It's me against the world*' is a song title of 2pac's[3] rap album whilst '*The outsider*' may be an album by American rap artist DJ Shadow, a film or a novel by the same name. Irrespective of what the source of the inscription is, it suggests an attempt at appropriating and glamorizing foreign material culture, possibly taking a celebratory stance like the USA inscription in the Ghanaian data. However, it is also possible that the use of music such as hip-hop has a linguistic impact on the inscriptions by the taxi drivers. Taxi drivers are able to 'pick' particular expressions from AAV which become part of their speech repertoire. One way in which language contact takes place between AAV and African languages is through hip-hop, which taps into the drivers' experiences of hardship in the townships and of growing up surrounded by violent conflict. The drivers thus, arguably, use music as an additional semiotic resource within taxi culture, alongside and related to their use of words and images.

The inscriptions written on the outside of the taxi in Figure 17.1 are in many colours and the words vary in terms of font size and type, reflecting the playful carnivalesque nature of taxi-lingua culture. The general trend, however, is to use very bright colors on the outside body of the vehicle as if to attract the attention of those who can read, while the more subversive inscriptions are written in places that will not immediately attract attention. For instance, in Figure 17.1, the inscription calling for legalizing marijuana is not emblazoned in bright red, orange or in as big a font as the inscription 'The Outsider', but more discretely placed below the front number plate of the vehicle.

The inscriptions on the outside of the taxi seem to be a commentary on the drivers themselves and an expression of their own views about their surroundings. For example, in the inscription from Figure 17.2 below the driver declares that he is '*Bad 2 Tha Bone*' and uses the saying '*IF YOU GOOD, YOU GOOD. BUT IF YOU BAD YOU BETTER*'. The meaning of '*bad*' in this inscription may be from AAV, in which case '*bad*' means 'good'. Because taxi drivers in South Africa are perceived as rude, uncouth and thuggish in their behaviour, it is therefore possible that when the taxi driver declares that he is '*Bad 2 Tha Bone*', he is, with tongue in cheek, reiterating this public perception or

Figure 17.2 'Bad 2 tha Bone'.

Figure 17.3 'If you good. . . .' inscription.

underscoring his insurrection by playing on the AAV meaning of '*bad*'. In emphasizing this message of how '*bad*' the driver is, there are also dark objects drawn on the body of the vehicle, for example a human skull or a dark demon vampire fleeing the fires of hell. Thus, the words on taxis are presented in combination with images which may reinforce or underscore the main message of the inscriptions.

In contrast to the inscriptions on the outside of the South African taxis, the discourses that emerge from the inscriptions inside the taxis (which are usually in a smaller font and handwritten) revolve around relationships between the drivers and the general public, or reflect drivers' attitudes to women. Some of these inscriptions read like instruction manuals, with instructions to the passengers expressed in a mixture of languages as if to suggest that they are engaged in a fictional dialogue with the driver:

1   *If you are late don't rush me, cos I'm on time.*
2   *Don't say dankie driver, say shot right or shot lef* (Don't say thank you driver, say turn right or turn left).
3   *Ungathi kealebokga driver, mina ngithi, kebatla tshelete yaka* (If you say thank you driver, me I will say I want my money).
4   *Don't say keatheokga driver, say shot lef, or shot right* (Don't say I am disembarking here driver, say turn left or turn right).

In these examples, the driver dialogically weaves together different South African languages. In example 3, he begins his instruction in Zulu then uses Tswana (*kealebokga* for thank you) to repeat what the imaginary passenger should not say, and then goes further to illustrate how he would respond to the passenger in Tswana. This 'template' for his instructional manual is also evident in examples 2 and 4 below. In example 2, the taxi driver uses English first and then Afrikaans in order to imitate the imaginary passenger. However, this time he goes further and instructs the 'passenger' in what has become popularly known as '*taxi lingua*' by saying '*shot lef*[4] *or shot right*' (i.e. take the road that turns to the left or the road that turns to the right).

The taxi industry in South Africa is predominantly male-dominated, rough and macho and this is evident in the sexually suggestive taunts directed at women in some inscriptions:

i   *Wamuhle G-string kodwa uyasidunusela* (Oh, what a nice g-string but you are showing me your bottom).
ii   *A beautiful woman is a multiplication of problems, an addition of enemies and subtraction of money.*
iii *How is your wife and my children.*
iv   *Nice g-string but angiyifuni iZ3.* (You have a nice g-string but I do not want to catch the HI virus).

These sexual fantasy discourses are reinforced by the loud Kwaito music played in the taxis, whose lyrics are replete with obscenities and the portrayal of women as sexual objects. Thus, music provides a framework within which the male taxi drivers' language, their harassment of women drivers and their 'eve teasing' (Khosa 1997), can be interpreted (Hansen 2006). Inscriptions are also read in the context of transgressive taxi-lingua culture: drivers mock the police, both on the road through their reckless driving and in the paintings on their windows which reinforce their defiance, for example in drawings of traffic police watching taxi drivers violate traffic regulations. The anti-establishment positions adopted by the taxi drivers are also apparent in their non-conventional spelling of English words, which challenges the standard language ideology (Milroy and Milroy 1999), in examples such as *Symp-athy* and *2nd 2 none*. Interestingly, while the written inscriptions draw on English, the use of spoken English by passengers in the taxis is strongly opposed and construed as putting on white mannerisms or claiming superior social class. Such passengers are described in a disparaging manner as 'biting [their] tongue' (Dlamini 2005: 127). The fact that written non-standard English is more acceptable than spoken English in this context suggests that discourse practices legitimated in one semiotic system are not necessarily admissible in another.

CONCLUDING REFLECTIONS

The inscriptions from Ghana were written in the middle of the last century and indicate the degree and extent to which English/pidgin had, by that time, permeated public life. They provide evidence of the drivers' engagement in social affairs, often with ambivalent evaluative meanings, and contribute to a taxi-lingua culture which is continued half a century later in South Africa. There are also differences, such as the more oppositional quality of the South African taxi inscriptions, and the more intensely interrelated use in the contemporary data of words, font and colour, images, music and driving behaviours.

The inscriptions on the *tro-tro*s and South African minibus taxis show creativity in the construction of multimodal discourses which can involve the appropriation and subversion of publicly available expressions as in '*driver is instructed to run away from the police*', or the culling of materials from different media sources, with expressions migrating from one medium to another. In contrast to research approaches referred to at the beginning of the chapter, a *vague linguistique* approach acknowledges the plurilanguaging, semantically open nature of the taxi inscriptions. We have extended this approach by focusing on the multi-semiotic nature of the inscriptions which have to be read against and at times in combination with other semiotic systems. These systems mutually reinforce one another, for instance in macho sexist discourses, and cannot be treated as discrete within the analysis. A multimodal analysis of the taxi-lingua culture enables us to move away from a structuralist orientation in the analysis of language practices in Africa, and is consistent with the more post-colonial and postmodern approach of *vague linguistique*.

NOTES

1 The data were collected as part of a photographic exhibition showing different constructions of self and social reality with the aim of establishing the role of culture and self in the construction of interdependence.
2 The similarity between Kwaito and American hip-hop is that both types of music are 'an expression and a validation of a modern, urban way of life, sung in street slang' (www.tsotsi.com/english/index.php?m1=pressandm2=Kwaito, accessed 19 April 2008). The South African street slang used in Kwaito is a mixture of South African languages.
3 2pac was a stage name for the American rap artist Tupac Amaru Shakur who gained recognition and endured a backlash for his controversial lyrics. He was killed in a drive-by shooting in 1996.
4 In township parlance, 'lef' is equivalent to the English word 'left'.

18

DOMESTICATING THE OTHER

ENGLISH AND TRANSLATION

SUSAN BASSNETT

TRANSLATION TODAY

It is an incontrovertible fact that English language readers are not very comfortable with translations. The percentage of published translations, at well under five per cent in Britain or the United States, is minute compared to the percentages of other European nations, where translated works can account for over 50 per cent of the book market. It is not uncommon for the name of an English translator to be printed in much smaller type than the name of the original author, or sometimes omitted altogether. In the theatre, it has long been acceptable for monolingual playwrights to be billed as having 'translated' a play by Chekhov or Brecht or Sophocles, and the justification for this practice is that they work from a so-called 'literal translation' which is then rewritten for performance. Perhaps most significant of all, however, is the absence of other contemporary literatures from British and American bookshops and review pages, an absence highlighted periodically when a writer who does not work in English wins the Nobel Prize for Literature and turns out to be all but unknown in the English-speaking world.

This chapter will examine how this state of affairs has come into being, and ask whether there are any signs of change. After all, the twenty-first century is one of global communication, through the internet and increased facility of travel. It is a time when millions of people are moving around the planet on a scale unprecedented in history, in search of employment, entertainment or sanctuary. The end of the Cold War saw millions of citizens living under former communist regimes suddenly able to travel, and the expansion of the European Community has further facilitated the large-scale movement of people in search of new job opportunities. In Asia, the opening up of China and the rise of a Chinese and Indian new middle class has also seen millions of people venture beyond their familiar boundaries.

As people move, so they acquire new languages and settle into new cultures. The age-old emigrant experience is one of moving to a new place, acquiring new knowledge and skills and, at the same, time retaining cultural ties with the place one is leaving. The advantages are enormous: the emigrant can occupy more than one cultural and linguistic space and be able to compare and contrast different societies, with their values and social practices. At a time when intercultural understanding is so crucial to the future of the world, in the post-9/11 age when there is genuine global anxiety about the planet's ecological survival and fears of a new nuclear arms race, it is perhaps more important than it has even been for there to be greater cross-cultural communication and for us all to learn more about each other's cultures. Yet, at such a time, the British government abolished foreign language learning in English secondary schools in 2004, with devastating results on university foreign language programmes and in the United States there are no signs of making Spanish a compulsory second language in the educational system, despite the millions of Spanish-speaking US citizens and strong commercial links with Central and Latin America.

GLOBAL ENGLISH(ES)

One simple explanation for cold-shouldering other languages is the dominance of global English. Why bother to learn another language, the argument goes, when the whole world is trying to acquire English? English is the language of international commerce and diplomacy, the dominant language of the internet and the language spoken by leading world powers in both the Northern and Southern hemispheres. This is true, of course, but it is only part of a much more complex story. For a start, we need to think, not in terms of English as a single language, but rather in terms of a range of linguistic variants, of Englishes in the plural, some of which are developing in quite specific ways. English may appear to be the common language of scientific congresses, for example, but the stylistic and semantic variations of English used in such contexts, that are a result of language interference and restricted language use in a particular field, can at times cause difficulties in understanding even for a native speaker. In short, though English may be widely used, no one variety of that language has precedence any longer. The whole world is learning not so much English, but the particular variant of English that will best suit their individual purpose. And the English language learner is adding English to whatever other language or languages he or she has already, with all the attendant cultural knowledge. This means that the native English speaker, who does not have access to any other language, is actively disadvantaged in a plurilingual and pluricultural world.

In such circumstances, we might therefore expect there to be a translation boom in the English-speaking world. If fewer people learn other languages, then their means of access to those languages has to be via translation. However, seeking an answer to the question of why there should be such resistance to other languages in this age of global English, it is important to remember the ruthless languages policy that prevailed for centuries in many parts of the British Isles as the pre-eminence of English was asserted at home, even as it began to be exported to colonies around the world. One aspect of the colonial project was a belief in the unifying power of a single language that would be able to hold barbarism at bay and be the bearer of civilisation. During the reign of Elizabeth

I, the Irish bards were savagely suppressed, and, within living memory, school-children have been punished for speaking Welsh or Scots Gaelic in class. Even the great Matthew Arnold, writing in 1867, in an essay on the study of Celtic literature, could declare that he quite shared the opinion of his brother Saxons 'as to the practical inconvenience of perpetuating the speaking of Welsh'. The Celtic languages were viewed not only as marginal but also as undesirable and not worthy of either study or retention. Brian Friel's play, *Translations*, which looks at the repression of Irish in the nineteenth century, is one of the best pieces of literature about the ideological implications of language policy that has been written in recent years. English was imposed on the Celtic world, and imposed also in the colonial world. Language is effectively the heart in the body of culture, so as someone learns another language or reads works translated from another language, so too do they begin to understand more about another culture. Rejecting a language implies the rejection of the culture that uses it and implies also a refusal to acknowledge the implicit relationship between language and identity. In oral cultures, songs, stories, riddles and linguistic games all ensure that the history of a people continues to be passed on to subsequent generations. In literate cultures, the written word becomes another form of transmission. Seamus Heaney has spoken about 'the spill of syllables' (Heaney 1984) that holds groups together and ensures their survival. Literature, including song and story-telling, is fundamental to cultural identity. But at the height of the imperial age, English was perceived as being more important than many other languages, a language to be exported around the world, and there was no comparable importation of other languages and their cultures into English.

LANGUAGES AND TRAVEL

This was certainly not the norm in the age of Romanticism and the early Victorians. Cultivated men and women in the eighteenth and early nineteenth centuries often had good spoken and written knowledge of several languages. George Eliot, for example, who did not have the benefit of a thorough educa-tion, nevertheless read French and Spanish and translated several philosophical works from German, including Ludwig Feuerbach's book on the essence of Christianity. Her male university-educated peers would have all had Greek and Latin, along with several European languages. Their level of linguistic compe-tence might vary, but the acquisition of languages and an ability to read other literatures was seen as important.

The age of the Grand Tour was followed by the growth of organised tourism, which began in Britain with the commercial venture of Thomas Cook in 1841. Cook was both a businessman and an idealist, and saw travel as a means of expanding people's knowledge and ultimately encouraging universal good will. In his *Physical, Moral, and Social Aspects of Excursions and Tours*, published in 1860, he declared that travel led to:

The expansion of the intellect, the grasping for information, the desire for books and the eagerness of their perusal, the benevolent sympathies excited by a more extended knowledge of the circumstances and sufferings of fellow-creatures.

(Pudney, 1953: 74)

How then to reconcile this idealism with a belief in the hegemony of English? To understand some of the forces at play, it is necessary to have an overview of the role played by translation in the growth of English literature and to look more closely at the ways in which a canon was formed as English became an object of study.

TRANSLATION IN THE PRE-MODERN PERIOD

From its very beginnings, English literature has involved translation. The growth of literature in the vernacular which took place in the Anglo-Saxon period was underpinned by translation. Arguably, the very emergence of vernacular literatures in Europe was a translation process, as scribes wrote interlingual glosses in the languages they used in their daily lives on manuscripts written in Latin,the high status language of scholarship and religious knowledge. During the reign of Alfred the Great (871–99), the vernacular language became firmly established as a medium for both prose and poetry, and the king himself produced five major works, including a translation of Boethius' *Consolation of Philosophy*, a translation of Pope Gregory the Great's *Pastoral Care*, and translations of works by St Augustine.

As English developed, acquiring Norse and Norman linguistic features which were amalgamated with the Anglo-Saxon base, so a growing variety of literary influences found their way into the literature. Across Europe, similarly, a massive shift was taking place, which Maria Tymoczko has termed one of the most significant transitions in Western culture, the shift from epic to romance (Tymoczko 1986). She points out that the new poetic parameters that led, not only to the poetry of the troubadours, but also to Dante, Petrarch, Chaucer and the great French Arthurian romances, came about through translation. Yet, so often, literary scholars have either overlooked the role of translation or have viewed it as of marginal significance. A typical example of this kind of thinking can be found in the introduction to the Penguin Classics *Medieval English Verse*. The author, Brian Stone, who also translated the poems into modern English, notes that:

The blend of the old Celtic stories – their visionary fury of passion, and myth set in cool green lands defies brief characterization – with the Provençal ideas of chivalry and courtly love, gave form to Romance and a basis to medieval secular literatures all over Europe.

(Stone 1964: 19)

He goes on to point out that the rise of the courtly love lyric may have been linked to a tradition of Arabic and Hebrew love-songs, but at no point in his essay does he mention the role that must have been played by translation. Translation, without which the transfer of the new forms and themes that revolutionised medieval poetry could never have happened, is entirely absent.

This attitude to translation is by no means uncommon. Despite the seminal significance of translation in the development of English literature, until relatively recently literary historians have tended to ignore it. A history of English literature written from the perspective of the role played by translation would look totally different from the established account which emphasises the individuality of English writers, decontextualising them from other influences.

Yet the history of English literature is also a history of translation. Without the Italian, French and Latin originals, Chaucer's great works would not have come into being. In an essay on Chaucer and translation, Barry Windeatt draws attention to the ambitious range of Chaucer's translations, which included Boethius, *Roman de la Rose*, saints' lives, penitential manuals and various other works, arguing that all this 'amounts to an ambitious career-long project of cultural importation' (Windeatt 2008: 139). When we approach the medieval world, we need to consider the ways in which ideas and literary genres appear to have been in a constant state of flux. The great cathedral builders travelled around Europe, exercising their art, so too did scholars and writers, borrowing from one another, rewriting and revising, reworking popular themes, experimenting and innovating.

The history of the Middle Ages is also the history of religious translation. Debates around the translation of the Bible and other religious texts into vernacular languages were intensely politicised, often leading to the burning of both books and translators. The French scholar, Edmond Cary has gone so far as to suggest that translation was at the very core of the Reformation:

> The Reformation, after all, was primarily a dispute between translators. Translation became an affair of State and a matter of Religion.
>
> (Cary 1963: 7)

The sonnet, developed into a high art form by Petrarch, came into English through the translations of Thomas Wyatt and Henry Howard, Earl of Surrey, and was then developed in interesting new ways later in the sixteenth century by Edward Spenser and William Shakespeare, to name but two of the best known. The way in which the sonnet came into English and was then transformed into something quite different from the Petrarchan sonnet is a classic example of how translation can act as a force for innovation and revitalisation.

The sonnet is a short poem of fourteen lines. In its early Italian manifestation, it was usually divided into two units of eight and six lines, with rhyme schemes of, for example, abab cdcd efeefe or some other variant of the eight/six division. What happened to the sonnet in English was that the organisation of the fourteen lines was altered so that there were three units of four lines each, variously rhymed, with a final couplet. The possibilities opened up by that final couplet have proved to be immense, and offer, in particular, a means of ending the sonnet very powerfully, often, as in so many of Shakespeare's sonnets, with an ironic twist.

TRANSLATION STUDIES

In the late 1970s, a new field of investigation emerged, that came to be known as Translation Studies. It appeared at a time when traditional English literary and language studies were being challenged in all kinds of ways, and its growth in the early years can be seen as parallel to the development of other radical approaches to English, such as feminist studies and gender criticism, in that scholars in all these fields posed major questions about the formation of the literary canon. The recovery of the lost history of women's writing, for example, is comparable to the way in which translation scholars around the world have sought to re-evaluate literary history by stressing the vital significance of translation in the shaping of national literatures. Translation studies has also striven to raise the status of translation, so as to see it recognised as a literary art in its own right. There was a common factor that underpinned feminist criticism, translation studies and, shortly after, postcolonial studies in its early manifestations, which was an exploration of that which had previously been invisible. Just as women and black writers had been written out of the pages of orthodox literary histories, so too had translators. Moreover, all too often, translations by well-known English writers have been ignored and studies of their work often fail to mention their translations. So, for example, Ted Hughes is remembered as a great English poet, while his translation opus, which is considerable, remains largely ignored. John Dryden (a leading translator of his day) or Alexander Pope are primarily remembered and taught as poets and their translation work barely noted, despite its prominence in the oeuvre of both writers. Indeed, Dryden can be said to be one of the earliest theorists of translation, and his remarks on translation reflect some of the most significant literary debates of his age. Generations of editors have tended to relegate translations to a category not unlike juvenilia, implying that translation does not deserve the same respect as other literary modes of writing.

In his book *The Translator's Invisibility*, subtitled 'A History of Translation', Lawrence Venuti looks at the way in which translation in the English-speaking world has been devalued to the extent that an ideal translation should not carry within it any signs of its foreign origin. A work written in another language should be translated so as to read as fluently as if it had been written in English in the first place. This translation strategy, which Venuti quite rightly notes has been the dominant one in English since the early modern period, is variously known as *domestication* or *acculturation*. He sees this Anglo-American attitude to translation as doubly disadvantageous to the translator:

> On the one hand, translation is defined as a second order representation: only the foreign text can be original, an authentic copy, true to the author's personality or

intention, whereas the translation is derivative, fake, potentially a false copy. On the other hand, translation is required to efface its second-order status with transparent discourse, producing the illusion of authorial presence whereby the translated text can be taken as the original.

(Venuti 1995: 6–7)

Venuti highlights a particular aspect of Anglo-American translation, the impulse to erase signs of the foreignness of a text which he terms a form of ethnocentric textual violence. He argues that this is a form of cultural imperialism, and proposes an alternative-*foreignisation*, a translation strategy that would retain signs of the Otherness of a work's origins elsewhere and would also remind readers that the text is being mediated through the work of a second writer, the actual translator. Here Venuti follows the ideas of André Lefevere, who called for an end to the distinction between a literary activity called 'translation' and another called 'original writing', pointing out that all translation is effectively rewriting, in a second language, a work that originated elsewhere. In his seminal book, *Translation, Rewriting and the Manipulation of Literary Fame*, Lefevere sees translation is the most obvious form of rewriting, since what the translator does is to recreate a work in a second language for a new set of readers, but he also makes the point that rewriting can take many forms:

Whether they produce translations, literary histories or their more compact spin-offs, reference works, anthologies, criticism or editions, rewriters adapt, manipulate the originals they work with to some extent, usually to make them fit in with the dominant, or one of the dominant ideological and poetological currents of their time.

(Lefevere 1992: 8)

What Lefevere is saying is that it is impossible to ensure the purity of a text, since editors, translators, anthologisers and literary historians all play a role in determining the fate of a work and of a writer. The case of Shakespeare's plays is a good example of how multiple forces have manipulated the work of one writer. There is no single 'authentic' collection of Shakespeare's plays, and editors have played a significant role in shaping the plays as we know them today. The importance of Shakespeare in the nationalist movements across Europe in the nineteenth century led to his being mythologised as a revolutionary playwright, very different from the high culture icon of the English. Lefevere reminds us that all kinds of forces are in play in the shaping of literary history.

Besides challenging the ideal of the pure text, Lefevere also invites us to consider the relationship between an original work and a translation. The crux of the problem lies here: can translation be considered to be a mode of writing equivalent in status to the original work? It is certainly true that, for a translation to succeed, the translator has to be both a highly skilled reader and a fine writer. Levefere goes one step further and argues that the translator *is* the writer, or rewriter in the second language. The one difference is that, while a writer engages with readers, a translator carries a double responsibility, to that original writer and to the second set of readers in the second language.

TRANSLATION AS A SHAPING FORCE

Another important founding figure in translation studies is Itamar Even-Zohar, a literary theorist of the Tel Aviv systems school. In an essay first published in 1978, and revised in 1990, Even-Zohar argues the case for the central importance of translation in literary history. He starts out with the notion of literature as a polysystem, made up of a range of distinct yet interconnected individual literary systems, and suggests that translated works should be considered, not on an individual basis, but as constituting a system in their own right:

> I conceive of translated literature not only as an integral system within any literary polysystem, but as the most active system within it.
>
> (Even-Zohar 2000: 193)

He goes on to argue that translation is often a driving force for innovation, when:

> No clear-cut distinction is maintained between 'original' and 'translated' writing, and ... often it is the leading writers (or members of the avant-garde who are about to become leading writers) who produce the most conspicuous or appreciated translations. Moreover, in such a state when new literary models are emerging, translation is likely to become one of the means of elaborating the new repertoire.
>
> (2000: 193)

Even-Zohar's essay is hugely important in the development of translation studies, because it represents the first serious attempt to set out a theory that foregrounds translation as a shaping force in literary history. The accepted view was, as has already been mentioned, that translation was somehow a second-class literary activity, less valuable than original writing and therefore less deserving of reward. Even-Zohar's proposal to view translation as crucially important for the transmission of literature across cultural boundaries involved a radical shift of perspective. Far from being a second-class, second-rate literary activity, translation could be re-evaluated as having been of major importance in the development of a literary system. Even-Zohar outlined three conditions that might prevail at times when translation activity was particularly high. The first is when a literature is in an early stage of development, 'not yet crystallized', as he puts it, which is precisely the case in early English literature when the first texts were being produced in the vernacular. The second is when a literature perceives itself to be 'weak' or peripheral to another group of correlated literatures, as was the case across Europe in the nineteenth century when writers in the Austro-

Hungarian empire, for example, began producing work in their own languages. Czech literature is a good case in point, and the role played by translating such writers as Byron or Shakespeare cannot be underestimated. Within a few years a language that had been banned as an educational or literary medium was producing extraordinarily fine writers and Czech had established itself as a major European literature.

Even-Zohar's third set of conditions is only vaguely formulated – 'when there are turning points, crises, or literary vacuums in a literature' (2000: 194). Nevertheless, this is a particularly interesting hypothesis, because he suggests that translation comes to the fore when there are specific cultural needs. The current translation boom taking place in China can be seen as one such turning point. We might also think of the conscious process of Westernisation undertaken by Kemal Ataturk in Turkey in the 1920s, when there was a huge government-funded initiative to translate those works which were deemed to be of potential use to citizens of the new republic. In England, in the fourteenth and fifteenth centuries, an era of civil conflict and economic instability when the Black Death ravaged Europe, translation was arguably the principal literary activity and laid the foundations for the English Renaissance of the sixteenth century.

Once we reconsider literary history in terms of translation, it becomes possible to see how patterns of influence crossed cultural and linguistic borders, and it also becomes possible to identify periods of greater and lesser translating activity. For example, the revival of theatre in the Restoration, when Charles II returned to the throne after the interregnum years of the Commonwealth, led to a proliferation of translations, often of very poor quality, that provided vehicles for leading actors of the time. In the nineteenth century, the emergence of the detective story, which was by no means due to Arthur Conan Doyle, though his Sherlock Holmes character remains the archetypal detective, was aided by the number of translations of popular novels from French sources. Both these cases are examples of translations filling a vacuum in response to a particular market need.

THE MIGHTY ORIGINAL

If we look broadly at the history of translation in English literature, it becomes apparent that a shift of consciousness took place at some point in the late seventeenth century, when works deemed to be 'originals' began to be considered more highly than works categorised as translations or versions. It is not accidental that the metaphor of the portrait or copy should have begun to be used to describe translation around this time. A copy would always be inferior to the real thing, a portrait less than the real-life subject, hence a translation would be less than the work from which it derived. Significantly, another metaphor of the period characterised translators as slaves or servants of the original. This has particular resonance if we consider that it came into use at a time when the colonial process was gathering momentum, when slaves were indeed labouring in many parts of the world to ensure prosperity for the European colonisers. The metaphor of the translator as slave reinforced the idea of translation as inferior. Copyright law, which privileged the original author, further added to a hierarchical distinction between writer and translator.

Perhaps the lowest point in the status of translation in English was the period following the First World War, when the expansion of English in schools and universities was characterised by a strong emphasis on the native tradition of English literature. This continued the trend begun in the nineteenth century of conceptualising literary history in terms of national traditions and origins, a trend that deliberately downplayed the extent to which a literature might have been influenced by the arrival of forms and ideas from elsewhere. F.R. Leavis devised the Great Tradition of the English novel, which sketched a map that downplayed the significance of French, Russian and German writers in the development of English fiction. The downplaying of translation at this time exemplifies Even-Zohar's hypothesis about cultures needing to translate at particular moments in their development and rejecting translation at times when they feel self-sufficient or when they are to some extent shutting out the foreign.

But although literary critics and historians may have downplayed translation, writers were still translating. D.H. Lawrence, held up as a quintessential English novelist, translated Giovanni Verga, for example, and remained influenced by the Sicilian writer's form of naturalism, *verismo*. In the 1960s, as the UK began to recover from the devastation of the Second World War, interest in translation began to revive. Ted Hughes and Daniel Weissbort founded *Modern Poetry in Translation*, the Aldwych World Theatre Season of 1967 brought new awareness of trends in theatre from around the world, and publishers, such as Cape and Penguin, embarked on ambitious translation projects.

In a very useful essay that summarises trends and tendencies in translation in the UK from the Victorians to the present day, Anthony Pym notes that, though many languages translate from English, English receives very few translations. He is unsure how to explain this, given that contemporary British culture appears 'more open in cuisine, music, painting and architecture' (Pym 2000: 80), but suggests that part of the problem may be an unwillingness to acknowledge closer cultural links with Europe. He is pessimistic, in that he sees global publishing in English as bolstering 'the sad illusion of a self-sufficient English literature' (2000: 81). Nor does he see the post-colonial developments in English writing as doing much to change this state of affairs.

Nevertheless, there are signs of change. More literary reviewers are now naming translators and crediting them as responsible for the success of a work. Newspapers such as *The Independent* regularly review translations, and *The Independent* sponsors a prize for the translation of foreign fiction, which is split equally between writer and translator, thereby signalling the parity of the roles of both. Translation is being talked about more frequently by literary theorists, often metaphorically as a tool for analysing the increasingly hybrid nature of much contemporary writing. Translation studies as a field of study is more closely linked today to research into comparative and world literature, and the importance of translation is beginning to be recognised in a whole variety of fields, including history, politics, business and globalisation studies. Bella Brodski opens her book *Can These Bones Live? Translation, Survival and Cultural Memory* with a strong statement about the importance of translation in the English-speaking world today:

> More than ever, translation is now understood to be a politics as well as a poetics, an ethics as well as an aesthetics. Translation is no longer seen to involve only narrowly circumscribed technical procedures of specialized or local interest, but rather to underwrite all cultural transactions, from the most benign to the most venal.
>
> (Brodski 2007: 2)

Brodski takes as her starting point Walter Benjamin's idea of translation as after-life, as the literary act that ensures the survival of a work and enables long-dead writers to reach new generations of readers. These subtle signs of change in attitudes to translation in the English-speaking world seem to suggest that, at some level, there is a growing awareness of the importance of inter-cultural communication for contemporary societies, and a willingness to reconsider the way in which English literary history has emphasised the local rather than acknowledging the importance of what has been imported into the native literature from outside.

BIBLIOGRAPHY

Adelsward, V. (1988) 'Styles of success: On impression management as a collaborative action in job interviews', *Linkoping Studies in Arts and Science*, 23, Linkoping: University of Linkoping.

Agar, M. (1985) 'Institutional Discourse', *Text*, 5(3): 147–68.

Aitchison, J. (1994) *Words in the Mind: An Introduction to the Mental Lexicon*, second edition, Oxford: Blackwell.

Al Khatib, H. (2003) 'Language alternation among Arabic and English youth bilinguals: reflecting or constructing social realities', *Bilingual Education and Bilingualism*, 6(6): 409–22.

Aldridge, M. (1991) 'How the language grows up: an outline of how children acquire English as a mother tongue', *English Today*, 25: 14–20.

Almanac, C.I. (2007) Worldwide Internet users, 2006, www.c-i-a.com/pr0207.htm accessed 1 April 2008.

American Literacy Council (2004) 'SPELLING BEE TO BE PICKETED'. American Literacy Council and Simplified Spelling Society Press release, 29 May 29, accessed online 5 December 2008 at http://www.spellingsociety.org/news/media/spellingbee.php.

Anderson, D. (2004) 'The script encoding initiative', *SIGNA*, 6: 1–12.

Andrews, R. (ed.) (1989) *Narrative and Argument*, Milton Keynes: Open University Press.

—— (2008) 'Ten years of strategies' (review article on *The Literacy Game* by Stannard and Huxford), *Changing English*, 15(1): 91–100.

Andrews, R., Torgerson, C., Beverton, S., Freeman, A., Locke, T., Low, G., Robinson, A. and Zhu, D. (2006) 'The effect of grammar teaching on writing development' in *British Educational Research Journal*, 32(1): 39–55.

Androutsopoulos, J. (2000) 'Non-standard spellings in media texts: the case of German fanzines', *Journal of Sociolinguistics*, 4(4): 514–33.

Appadurai, A. (1996) *Modernity at Large: Cultural Dimensions of Globalization*, Minneapolis: University of Minnesota Press.

Arends, J. (1993) 'Towards a gradualist model of creolization' in F. Byrne and J. Holm (eds) *Atlantic Meets Pacific*, Amsterdam: John Benjamins, 371–80.

Arnold, M. (1891) *Celtic Literature*, London: Smith and Elder and Co, access at http://www.gutenberg.org/dirs/etext04/celt10h.htm, accessed 10 February 2009.

Askehave, I. and Swales, J.M. (2001) 'Genre identification and communicative purpose: a problem and a possible solution', *Applied Linguistics*, 22: 195–212.

Atkinson, M. and Drew, P. (1979) *Order in Court: The Organization of Verbal Interaction in Judicial Settings*, Cambridge: Cambridge University Press.

Atkinson, P. (1995) *Medical Talk and Medical Work: The Liturgy of the Clinic*, London: Sage.

Attridge, D. (2004) *The Singularity of Literature*, London: Routledge.

Auer, P. and Kern, F. (2000) 'Three ways of analysing communication between East and West Germans as intercultural communication' in A. Di Luzio, S. Günthner and F. Orletti (eds) *Culture in Communication: Analysis of Intercultural Situations.* Amsterdam: John Benjamins.

Auerbach, E., Barahona, B., Midy, J., Vaquerano, F., Zambrano, A. and Arnaud, J. (1996) *Adult ESL Literacy from the Community to the Community: A Guidebook for Participatory Literacy Training*, Mahwah, NJ: Lawrence Erlbaum Associates.

Austin, J.L. (1962) *How to Do Things with Words*: The William James Lectures delivered at Harvard University in 1955, J.O. Urmson (ed.) Oxford: Clarendon.

Avgerinakou, A. (2003) 'Flaming in computer-mediated interaction', in C.B. Grant (ed.) *Rethinking Communicative Interaction*, Amsterdam: John Benjamins, 273–93.

Axelsson, A.-S., Abelin, Å. and Schroeder, R. (2003) 'Anyone speak Spanish?: Language encounters in multi-user virtual environments and the influence of technology', *New Media and Society*, 5(4): 475–98.

Baker, P. (1995) 'Motivation in Creole genesis', in P. Baker (ed.) *From Contact to Creole and Beyond*, London: University of Westminster Press.

Bakhtin, M. ([1953] 1986) *Speech Genres and Other Late Essays*, C. Emerson and M. Holquist (eds), trans. V.W. Mc Gee. Austin, TX: University of Texas Press.

—— ([1935] 1981) 'Discourse in the novel', in *The Dialogic Imagination: Four Essays by M.M.Bakhtin*, M. Holquist (ed.), trans. C. Emerson and M. Holquist. Austin, TX: University of Texas Press.

Bancroft, D. (2007) 'English as a first language' in N. Mercer, J. Swann and B. Mayor (eds) *Learning English*, Abingdon: Routledge, 5–37.

Barnes, D. and Barnes, D. with Clarke, S. (1984) *Versions of English*, New York: Harcourt Brace.

Barnes, D., Britton, J. and Rosen, H. (1969) *Language, the Learner and the School*, Harmondsworth: Pelican.

Baron, N.S. (1998) 'Letters by phone or speech by other means: the linguistics of email', *Language and Communication*, 18: 133–70.

—— (2000) *Alphabet to Email: How Written English Evolved and Where It's Heading*, New York: Routledge.

—— (2008) *Always On: Language in an Online and Mobile World*, New York: Oxford University Press.

Baron-Cohen, S. (2003) *The Essential Difference*, London: Allen Lane.

Barton, D. (2007) *Literacy: An Introduction to the Ecology of Written Language*, second edition, Oxford: Blackwell.

Barton, D. and Hamilton, M. (1998) *Local Literacies: Reading and Writing in One Community*, London: Routledge.

—— (2000) 'Literacy practices', in D. Barton, M. Hamilton and R. Ivanič, (eds) *Situated Literacies: Reading and Writing in Context*, London: Routledge.

Barton, D., Hamilton, M. and Ivanič, R. (eds) (2000) *Situated Literacies: Reading and Writing in Context*, London: Routledge.

Basso, K.H. (1970) '"To give up on words": Silence in Apache culture', *Southwest Journal of Anthropology*, 26(3): 213–30.

Bastow, T. (2003) *Friends and allies: binomials in a corpus of US defence speeches*, paper given at ASLA Symposium, Örebro University, 6 November.

Battenburg, J. (1997) 'English versus French: language rivalry in Tunisia', *World Englishes*, 16: 281–90.

Bauman, R. (1992) 'Performance', in R. Bauman (ed.) *Folklore, Cultural Performances, and Popular Entertainments*, New York: Oxford University Press, 41–49.

Baxter, J. (ed.) (2005) *Speaking Out: The Female Voice in Public Contexts*, Basingstoke: Palgrave Macmillan.

Bazerman, C. (1988) *Shaping Written Knowledge: The Genre and Activity of the Experimental Article in Science*, Madison, WI: University of Wisconsin Press.

Bazerman, C. and Prior, P. (2004) *What Writing Does and How it Does It: An Introduction to Analyzing Texts and Textual Practices*, Mahwah NJ: Lawrence Erlbaum.

Bechar-Israeli, H. (1995) 'From <Bonehead> to <Clonehead>: Nicknames, play and identity on Internet Relay Chat', *Journal of Computer-Mediated Communication*, 1(2), www.blackwell-synergy.com/toc/jcmc/1/2, accessed 27 April 2008.

Bednarek, M. (2008) 'Semantic preference and semantic prosody re-examined', *Corpus Linguistics and Linguistic Theory* 4(2): 119–139.

Bell, A. (1984) 'Language style as audience design', *Language in Society*, 13(2): 145–204.

—— (2001) 'Back in style: reworking audience design', in P. Eckert and J.R. Rickford (eds) *Style and Sociolinguistic Variation*, Cambridge: Cambridge University Press.

Benedict, H. (1979) 'Early lexical development: comprehension and production', *Journal of Child Language*, 6: 183–200.

Berger, P. and Luckmann, T. (1967) *The Social Construction of Reality: A Treatise in the Sociology of Knowledge*, New York: Anchor Books.

Bergson, H. (1911) *Creative Evolution*, New York: Henry Holt and Company.

Berk-Seligson, S. (2002) *The Bilingual Courtroom: Court Interpreters in the Judicial Process*, Chicago: University of Chicago Press.

Bernabé, J., Chamoiseau, P. and Confiant, R. (1993) *Éloge de la créolité*, Paris: Gallimard.

Besnier, N. (2003) 'Crossing genders, mixing languages: the linguistic construction of transgenderism in Tonga', in J. Holmes and M. Meyerhoff (eds) *The Handbook of Language and Gender*, Oxford: Blackwell Publishing, 289–301.

Biber, D., Conrad, S. and Reppen, R. (1998) *Corpus Linguistics: Investigating Language, Structure and Use*, Cambridge: Cambridge University Press.

Biber, D., Johansson, S., Leech, G., Conrad, S. and Finegan, E. (1999) *Longman Grammar of Spoken and Written English*, Harlow, Essex: Longman.

Biesenbach-Lucas, S. (2005) 'Communication topics and strategies in email consultation: Comparison between American and international university students', *Language Learning and Technology*, 9(2): 24–46.

Billig, M. (1999) 'Whose terms? Whose ordinariness? Rhetoric and ideology in conversation analysis', *Discourse and Society*, 10: 543–58.

Bird, S. (2001) 'Orthography and identity in Cameroon', *Written Language and Literacy*, 4(2): 131–62.

Birkner, K. (2004) 'Hegemonic struggles or transfer of knowledge? East and West Germans in job interviews', *Journal of Language and Politics*, 3(2): 293–322.

Bjørge, A.K. (2007) 'Power distance in English lingua franca email communication', *International Journal of Applied Linguistics*, 17(1): 60–80.

Blair, Tony (2002) 'Science matters' speech 23 May, full text: www.number-10.gov.uk/output/Page1715.asp, accessed 6 June 2003.

Bloch, J. (2004) 'Second language cyber rhetoric: A study of Chinese L2 writers in an online Usenet group', *Language Learning and Technology*, 8(3): 66–82.

Blommaert, J. (2006) *Discourse: A Critical Introduction*, Cambridge: Cambridge University Press.

Blommaert, J. and Bulcaen, C. (2000) 'Critical discourse analysis', *Annual Review of Anthropology*, 29: 447–66.

Bloome, D., Carter, S.P., Christian, B.M., Otto, S. and Shuart-Faris, N. (2005) *Discourse Analysis and the Study of Classroom Language and Literacy Events: A Microethnographic Perspective*, Mahwah, NJ: Lawrence Erlbaum.

Bloomfield, L. (1933 reprinted 1970) *Language*, London: Allen & Unwin.

Blum-Kulka, S. and Snow, C.E. (2002) *Talking to Adults: The Contribution of Multiparty Discourse to Language Acquisition*, Mahwah, NJ: Lawrence Erlbaum.

Boden, D. (1994) *The Business of Talk: Organisations in Action*, Cambridge: Polity Press.

Bohm, D. and Peat, D. (2000) *Science, Order and Creativity*, second edition, London: Routledge.

Bornstein, K. (1993) 'Interview with Shannon Bell', in A. Kroker and M. Kroker, *The Last Sex: Feminism and Outlaw Bodies*, New York: St Martins Press.

Boughey, C. (2000) 'Multiple metaphors in an understanding of academic literacy', *Teachers and Teaching Theory and Practice*, 6(3): 279–90.

Bourdieu, P. (1990) *The Logic of Practice*, trans. R. Nice. Cambridge: Polity Press.

——(1991) *Language and Symbolic Power*, in J.B. Thompson (ed.), trans. G. Raymond and M. Adamson. Cambridge: Harvard University Press/Polity Press.

Braine, G. (1999) *Non-native Educators in English Language Teaching*, Mahwah, NJ: Lawrence Erlbaum.

Braine, M.D.S. (1971) 'On two types of models of the internalisation of grammar' in D.I. Slobin (ed.) *The Ontogensis of Grammar: A Theoretical Symposium*, New York: Academic Press, 153–86.

Brazil, D. (1995) *A Grammar of Speech*, Oxford: Oxford University Press.

Brengelman, F.H. (1980) 'Orthoepists, printers, and the rationalization of English spelling', *Journal of English and Germanic Philology*, 79: 332–54.

Britton, J. (ed.) (1967) *Talking and Writing: A Handbook for English Teachers*, London: Methuen.

—— (1972) *Language and Learning*, Baltimore: Penguin Books Inc.

Britton, J., Burgess, T., Martin, N., McLeod, A. and Rosen, H. (1975) *The Development of Writing Abilities (11–18)*, London: Macmillan Education.

Brizendine, L. (2006) *The Female Brain*, New York: Morgan Road.

Brock-Utne, B. (ed.) (2005) *Language-in-Education Policies and Practices in Africa With a Special Focus on Tanzania and South Africa: Insight from Research in Progress*, Clevedon: Multilingual Matters.

Brodski, B. (2007) *Can These Bones Live? Translation, Survival and Cultural Memory*, Stanford: Stanford University Press.

Brown, J., Clark, S., Medway, P. and Stibbs, A., with Andrews, R. (1990), *Developing English for TVEI*, Leeds: University of Leeds, School of Education.

Brown, P. and Levinson, S. (1978) 'Universals in language usage: politeness phenomena', in E. Goody (ed.) *Questions and Politeness: Strategies in Social Interaction*, Cambridge: Cambridge University Press.

Brown, R. (1973) *A First Language: The Early Stages*, London: George Allen and Unwin Ltd.

Bruner, J. (1983) *Child's Talk: Learning to Use Language*, Oxford: Oxford University Press.

Bruthiaux, P. (2002a) 'Hold your courses: Language education, language choice, and economic development', *TESOL Quarterly*, 36(3): 275–96.

—— (2002b) 'Predicting challenges to English as a global language in the 21st century', *Language Problems and Language Planning*, 26(2): 129–57.

—— (2003) 'Squaring the circles: issues in modeling English worldwide', *International Journal of Applied Linguistics*, 13(2): 159–77.

Brutt-Griffler, J. (2002a) 'Class, ethnicity, and language rights: An analysis of British colonial policy in Lesotho and Sri Lanka and some implications for language policy', *Journal of Language, Identity, and Education*, 1: 207–34.

—— (2002b) *World English: A Study of Its Development*, Clevedon, UK: Multilingual Matters.

Bucholtz, M. (1999) '"Why be normal?" Language and identity practices in a community of nerd girls', *Language and Society*, 28(2): 203–23.

Bunyi, G. (ed.) (2005) *Language Classroom Practices in Kenya*, Clevedon, UK: Multilingual Matters.

Burton, D. (1981) 'Analysing spoken discourse', in M. Coulthard and M. Montgomery (eds) *Studies in Discourse Analysis*, London: Routledge and Kegan Paul.

Caldas-Coulthard, C. and Coulthard, M. (1996) *Texts and Practices: Readings in Critical Discourse Analysis*, London: Routledge.

Calkins, L. (1994) *The Art of Teaching Writing*, Exeter, NH: Heinemann.

Cameron, D. (2000) *Good to Talk? Living and Working in a Communication Culture*, London: Sage.

—— (2005) 'Language, gender and sexuality: current issues and new directions', *Applied Linguistics*, 26(4): 482–502.

Cameron, D. and Kulick, D. (2003) *Language and Sexuality*, Cambridge: Cambridge University Press.

Campbell, S. and Roberts, C. (2007) 'Migration, ethnicity and competing discourses in the job interview: synthesising the institutional and personal', *Discourse and Society*, 18(3): 243–71.

Canagarajah, A.S. (1999) *Resisting Linguistic Imperialism in English Teaching*, Oxford: Oxford University Press.

—— (2000) 'Constructing hybrid postcolonial subjects: codeswitching in Jaffna classrooms' in M. Heller and M. Martin-Jones (eds) *Voices of Authority: Education and Linguistic Difference*, London: Ablex.

—— (2006a) 'Changing communicative needs, revised assessment objectives: Testing English as an international language', *Language Assessment Quarterly*, 3: 229–42.

—— (2006b) 'Globalization of English and changing pedagogical priorities: The postmodern turn', in B. Beaven (ed.) *IATEFL 2005*, Canterbury, UK: Cardiff Conference Selections.

—— (2006c) Interview, in R. Rubdy and M. Saraceni (eds) (2006) *English in the World: Global Rules, Global Roles*, London: Continuum, 200–12.

—— (2007) 'Lingua Franca English, multilingual communities and language acquisition', *Modern Language Journal*, 91: 921–37.

Canale, M. and Swain, M. (1980) 'Theoretical basis of communicative approaches to second language teaching and testing', *Applied Linguistics*, 1: 1–47.

Carney, E. (1994) *A Survey of English Spelling*, London: Routledge.

Carr, J. and Pauwels, A. (2006) *Boys and Foreign Language Learning: Real Boys Don't Do Languages*, Basingstoke: Palgrave Macmillan.

Carter, R. (2004a) *Language and Creativity: The Art of Common Talk*, London: Routledge.

—— (2004b) 'Grammar and Spoken English', in C. Coffin, A. Hewings and K.A. O'Halloran (eds) *Applying English Grammar: functional and corpus approaches*, London: Hodder-Arnold.

Carter, R. and McCarthy, M. (1995) 'Grammar and the spoken language', *Applied Linguistics*, 16: 141–58.

—— (1997) *Exploring Spoken English*, Cambridge: Cambridge University Press.

Cary, E. (1963) *Les Grands Traducteurs Français*, Geneva: Librairie de l'Université.

Channell, J. (2000) 'Corpus-based analysis of evaluative lexis', in S. Hunston and G. Thompson (eds) *Evaluation in Text: Authorial Stance and the Construction of Discourse*, Oxford: Oxford University Press.

Chomsky, N. (1980) 'Rules and representations', *The Behavioural and Brain Sciences*, 3: 1–15.

—— (1986) *Knowledge of Language: Its Nature, Origin and Use*, New York: Praeger.

Chomsky, N. and Halle, M. (1968) *The Sound Pattern of English*, New York: Harper and Row.

Cicourel, A. (1968) *The Social Organisation of Juvenile Justice*, New York: Wiley.

—— (1981) 'Notes on the integration of micro- and macro-levels of analysis', in K. Knorr-Cetina and A. Cicourel (eds) *Advances in Social Theory and Methodology*, London: Routledge.

—— (1992) 'The interpenetration of communicative contexts: Examples from medical encounters', in A. Duranti and C. Goodwin (eds) *Rethinking Context: Language as an Interactional Phenomenon*, Cambridge: Cambridge University Press: 291–310.

CJC (Criminal Justice Commission) (1996) *Aboriginal Witnesses in Queensland's Criminal Courts*, Brisbane: Criminal Justice Commission.

Clemente, A. and Higgins, M.J. (2008) *Performing English with a Postcolonial Accent: Ethnographic Narratives from Mexico*, London: Tufnell.

Coates, J. (2003) *Women, Men, and Language*, third edition, London: Longman.

Coffin, C. and O'Halloran, K.A. (2005) 'Finding the Global Groove: Theorising and analysing dynamic reader positioning using APPRAISAL, Corpus and a concordancer', *Critical Discourse Studies*, 2(2): 143–63.

—— (2006) 'The role of appraisal and corpora in detecting covert evaluation', *Functions of Language*, 13(1): 77–110.

Coffin, C., Hewings, A. and O'Halloran, K.A. (eds) (2004) *Applying English Grammar: functional and corpus approaches*, London: Hodder-Arnold.

Cole, K. and Zuengler, J. (eds) (2003) *Engaging in an Authentic Science Project: Appropriating, Resisting, and Denying "Scientific" Identities*, Clevedon, UK: Multilingual Matters.

Collins, J. (1987) 'Conversation and knowledge in bureaucratic settings', *Discourses Processes*, 10: 303–19.

Collot, M. and Belmore, N. (1996) 'Electronic language: A new variety of English', in S. C. Herring (ed.) *Computer-mediated Communication*, 13–28, Amsterdam: John Benjamins.

Conley, J. and O'Barr, W.M. (1990) *Rules versus Relationships: The Ethnography of Legal Discourse*, Chicago: University of Chicago Press.

Cook, G. (1989) *Discourse*, Oxford: Oxford University Press.

—— (1992) *The Discourse of Advertising*, first edition, London: Routledge.

—— (2000) *Language Play, Language Learning*, Oxford: Oxford University Press.

—— (2001) *The Discourse of Advertising*, second edition, London: Routledge.

—— (2004) *Genetically Modified Language*, London: Routledge.

—— (ed.) (2007) *The Language of Advertising* (four volumes), London: Routledge.

Cook, G., Pieri, E. and Robbins, P.T. (2004) '"The scientists think and the public feels": expert perceptions of the discourse of GM food', *Discourse and Society*, 15(4): 433–49.

Cook, G., Reed, M. and Twiner, A. (2007) 'The Discourse of Organic Food Promotion: Language, Intentions and Effects', Research Report ESRC RES-000-22-1626, available: http://creet.open.ac.uk/projects/language-of-food-politics/projects.cfm

Cook, G., Robbins, P.T. and Pieri, E. (2006) '"Words of mass destruction": British newspaper coverage of the GM food debate, and expert and non-expert reactions', *Public Understanding of Science*, 15(1): 5–29.

Cook, G., Reed, M., Robbins, P.T. and Twiner, A. (2008) 'The Discourse of the School Dinners Debate', Research Report ESRC RES-000-22-1947, available: http://creet.open.ac.uk/projects/language-of-food-politics/projects.cfm

Cook, J. (2005) 'Creative writing as research method', in G. Griffin (ed.) *Research Methods for English Studies*, Edinburgh: Edinburgh University Press, 195–212.

Cook, V. (1999) 'Going beyond the native speaker in language teaching', *TESOL Quarterly*, 33: 185–209.

Cooper, R. (1982) *Language Spread*, Bloomington, IN: Indiana University Press.

Cotterill, J. (2003) *Language and Power in Court: A Linguistic Analysis of the O.J. Simpson Trial*, Houndmills, Basinstoke: Palgrave Macmillan.

Coupland, N. (1985) '"Hark, hark the lark": social motivations for phonological style-shifting', *Language and Communication*, 5(3): 153–71.

—— (2001a) 'Language, situation, and the relational self: theorizing dialect style in sociolinguistics,' in P. Eckert and J. Rickford, *Style and Sociolinguistic Variation*, New York: Cambridge University Press.

—— (2001b) 'Dialect stylization in radio talk', *Language in Society*, 30: 345–375.

Crancher, S. (2005) *Essex – Sumfing Else!*, Newbury, Berkshire: Countryside Books.

Crème, P. and Lea, M. (1997) *Writing at University: A Guide for Students*, Buckingham: Open University Press.

Crookes, G. (1986) 'Towards a validated analysis of scientific text structure', *Applied Linguistics*, 7: 57–70.

Crystal, D. (1997) *English as a Global Language*, Cambridge: Cambridge University Press.

—— (2003) *English as a Global Language*, second edition, Cambridge: Cambridge University Press.

—— (2004) *The Language Revolution*, Cambridge, UK: Polity.

—— (2006) *Language and the Internet*, second edition, Cambridge: Cambridge University Press.

Cunneen, C. (2001) *Conflict, Politics and Crime: Aboriginal Communities and the Police*, Sydney: Allen and Unwin.

Currie, M. (2002) 'Criticism and creativity: Poststructuralist theories' in Julian Wolfreys (ed.) *Introducing Criticism at the Twenty-first Century*, Edinburgh: Edinburgh University Press, 152–68.

Danet, B. (1997) 'Books, letters, documents: The changing aesthetics of texts in late print culture', *Journal of Material Culture*, 2(1): 5–38.

—— (1998) 'Text as mask: Gender, play and performance on the internet', in S.G. Jones (ed.) *Cybersociety 2.0: Revisiting Computer-mediated Communication and Community*, Thousand Oaks, CA and London: Sage, 129–58.

—— (2001) *Cyberpl@y: Communicating Online*, Oxford: Berg.

—— (forthcoming) 'Flaming and linguistic impoliteness in an English-based listserv for Israelis', in S.C. Herring, D. Stein and T. Virtanen (eds) *Handbook of Pragmatics in Computer-Mediated Communication*, Berlin: Mouton de Gruyter.

Danet, B. and Herring, S.C. (eds) (2003) 'The multilingual internet: Language, culture and communication in instant messaging, email and chat', *Journal of Computer-mediated Communication*, (9)1, available: www.blackwell-synergy.com/toc/jcmc/9/1, accessed 27 April 2008.

—— (2007a) 'Multilingualism on the internet', in M. Hellinger and A. Pauwels (eds) *Language and Communication: Diversity and Change*, Berlin: Mouton de Gruyter, 555–94.

—— (eds) (2007b) *The Multilingual Internet: Language, Culture, and Communication Online*, New York: Oxford University Press.

Danet, B., Wachenhauser, T., Bechar-Israeli, H., Cividalli, A. and Rosenbaum-Tamari, Y. (1995) 'Curtain time 20:00 GMT: Experiments in virtual theater on Internet Relay Chat', *Journal of Computer-Mediated Communication*, 1(2), available: www.blackwell-synergy.com/toc/jcmc/1/2, accessed 27 April 2008.

Daoud, M. (1997) 'English language development in Tunisia', *TESOL Quarterly*, 30: 598–605.

—— (2001) 'The language situation in Tunisia', *Current Issues in Language Planning*, 2, 1–52.

Davies, A. (2002) 'Whose language? Choosing a model for our language tests', *The International Conference on Language Testing and Language Teaching*, Shanghai.

Davies, E.E. (1987) 'Eyeplay: on some uses of nonstandard spelling', *Language and Communication*, 7(1): 47–58.

De Villiers, P.A. and de Villiers, J.G. (1979) *Early Language*, London: Open Books.

Defra UK (Department for Environment and Rural Affairs) (2003) 'GM crops: Effects on farmland wildlife', available: www.defra.gov.uk/environment/gm/fse/results/fse-summary.pdf, accessed 10 December 2003.

DeGraff, M. (2003) 'Against Creole exceptionalism', *Language*, 79(2): 391–410.

Deuchar, M. and Quay, S. (1998) 'One vs two systems in early bilingual syntax: two versions of the question', *Bilingualism: Language and Cognition*, 1(3): 231–43.

DfEE/DCMS (1999) *All Our Futures: creativity, culture and education*, Report of the National Advisory Committee on Creative and Cultural Education, London: Department for Education and Employment and Department for Culture, Media and Sport.

DfEE and QCA (1999) *The National Curriculum for England: English, key stages 1–4*, London: Department for Education and Employment and the Qualifications and Curriculum Authority.

Di Luzio, A., Günthner, S. and Orletti, F. (eds) (2000) *Culture in Communication: Analysis of Intercultural Situations*, Amsterdam: John Benjamins.

Dixon, J. (1967) *Growth through English: a report based on the Dartmouth seminar 1966*, Sheffield: National Association for the Teaching of English.

—— (1969) *Growth through English: Report based on the Dartmouth seminar, 1966*, Oxford: Oxford University Press.

Dixon, J. and Stratta, L. (1986) *Writing Narrative – and Beyond*, Ottawa: Canadian Council of Teachers of English.

Dlamini, S. (2005) *Youth and Identity Politics in South Africa*, Toronto: University of Toronto Press.

Dore, J. (1979) 'Conversational acts and the acquisition of language', in E. Ochs and B.B. Schieffelin (eds) *Developmental Pragmatics*, New York: Academic Press, 339–61.

Drew, P. and Heritage, J. (1992) *Talk at Work*, Cambridge: Cambridge University Press.

Dubin, F. (1989) 'Situating literacy within traditions of communicative competence', *Applied Linguistics*, 10(2): 171–81.

Duffy, C.A. (ed.) (2007) *Answering Back: Living Poets Reply to the Poetry of the Past*, London: Picador.

Dulay, H., Burt, M. and Krashen, S. (1982) *Language Two*, New York: Oxford University Press.

Durham, M. (2003) 'Language choice on a Swiss mailing list', *Journal of Computer-mediated Communication*, 9(1), available: www.blackwell-synergy.com/toc/jcmc/9/1, accessed 27 April 2008.

Dylan, Bob (2007 [1963]) 'A Hard Rain's A-Gonna Fall' in Mark Edwards *Hard Rain: Our Headlong Collision with Nature*, London: Still Pictures Moving Words.

Eades, D. (1991) 'Communicative strategies in Aboriginal English', in S. Romaine, (ed.) *Language in Australia*, Cambridge: Cambridge University Press, 84–93.

—— (1992) *Aboriginal English and the Law: Communicating with Aboriginal English Speaking Clients: A Handbook for Legal Practitioners*, Brisbane: Queensland Law Society.

—— (1996) 'Legal recognition of cultural differences in communication: The case of Robyn Kina', *Language and Communication*, 16(3): 215–27.

—— (2000) '"I don't think it's an answer to the question": Silencing Aboriginal witnesses in court', *Language in Society*, 29(2): 161–96.

—— (2006) 'Lexical struggle in court: Aboriginal Australians vs the state', *Journal of Sociolinguistics*, 10(2): 153–81.

—— (2007) 'Aboriginal English in the criminal justice system', in G. Leitner and I. Malcolm (eds) *The Habitat of Australia's Aboriginal Languages: Past, Present, and Future*, Berlin: Mouton de Gruyter, 299–326.

—— (2008) *Taken for a Ride: Courtroom Talk and Neocolonial Control*, Berlin: Mouton de Gruyter.

Eckert, P. (1996) 'Vowels and nailpolish: The emergence of linguistic style in the preadolescent heterosexual marketplace', in N. Warner, J. Ahlers, L. Bilmes, M. Oliver, S. Wertheim and M. Chen (eds) *Gender and Belief Systems*, Berkeley: Berkeley Women and Language Group.

—— (2000) *Linguistic Variation as Social Practice*, Oxford: Blackwell.

—— (2004) 'The meaning of style', in W.-F. Chiang, E. Chun, L. Mahalingappa, S. Mehus (eds) *Salsa 11*, Texas Linguistics Forum, 47.

Eckert, P. and McConnell-Ginet, S. (1992) 'Communities of practice: where language, gender, and power all live', in K. Hall, M. Bucholtz and B. Moonwomon (eds) *Locating Power: Proceedings of the Second Berkeley Women and Language Conference*, Berkeley, CA: Berkeley Women and Language Group.

—— (2003) *Language and Gender*, Cambridge: Cambridge University Press.

Edwards, R. and Usher, R. (2008) (second edition) *Globalisation and Pedagogy: Space, Place and Identity*, second edition, London: Routledge.

Eggins, S. and Slade, D. (1997) *Analysing Casual Conversation*, London: Cassell.

Ehrlich, S. (2001) *Representing Rape: Language and Sexual Consent*, London: Routledge.

Eklundh, K.S. and Macdonald, C. (1994) 'The use of quoting to preserve context in electronic mail dialogues', *IEEE Transactions on Professional Communication*, 37(4): 197–202.

Ellis, R. (1999) *Learning a Second Language Through Interaction*, Amsterdam: John Benjamins.

Erickson, F. and Shultz, J. (1982) *The Counsellor as Gatekeeper: Social Interaction in Interviews*, New York: Academic Press.

Erling, E.J. (2002) '"I learn English since ten years": The global English debate and the German university classroom', *English Today*, 70: 8–13.

Ervin-Tripp, S. (1979) 'Children's verbal turn-taking' in E. Ochs and B.B. Schieffelin (eds) *Developmental Pragmatics*, New York: Academic Press, 339–61.

Even-Zohar, I. (2000) 'The position of translated literature within the literary polysystem', in L. Venuti (ed.) *The Translation Studies Reader*, London: Routledge, 192–7.

Fahlman, S.E. (n.d.) 'Smiley lore :-)', available: www-2.cs.cmu.edu/~sef/sefSmiley.html, accessed 2 April 2008.

Fairclough, N. (1989) *Language and Power*, London: Longman.

—— (1992) *Discourse and Social Change*, Cambridge: Polity Press.

—— (1993) 'Critical discourse analysis and the marketisation of public discourse: The Universities', *Discourse & Society*, 4(2): 133–68.

—— (1995) *Media Discourse*, London: Edward Arnold.

—— (2000) *New Labour, New Language?*, London: Routledge.

—— (2003) *Analysing Discourse:Textual Analysis for Social Research*, London: Routledge.

Fairclough, N. and Wodak, R. (1997) 'Critical discourse analysis', in T.A. van Dijk (ed.) *Discourse as Social Interaction*, London: Sage.

Faraclas, N. (2004) 'Nigerian Pidgin English – morphology and syntax' in B. Kortmann, E.W. Schneider, K. Burridge, R. Mesthrie and C. Upton (eds) *A Handbook of Varieties of English*, vol. 2, Berlin: Mouton de Gruyter, 828–53.

Fasold, R. (1984) *The Sociolinguistics of Society*, Oxford: Basil Blackwell Ltd.

Ferguson, C.A. (1959) 'Diglossia', *Word*, 15: 325–40.

Ferguson, G. (2006) *Language Planning and Education*, Edinburgh: Edinburgh University Press.

Ferrara, K., Brunner, H. and Whittemore, G. (1991) 'Interactive written discourse as an emergent register', *Written Communication*, 8(1): 8–33.

Firbank, L.G. *et al.* (19 authors) (2003) 'The implications of spring-sown genetically modified herbicide-tolerant crops for farmland biodiversity: a commentary on the Farms Scale Evaluations of Spring Grown Crops', *Philosophical Transactions of the Royal Society (Biological Sciences)*, 358(149): 1773–913.

Firth, A. (1996) 'The discursive accomplishment of normality. On "lingua franca" English and conversation analysis', *Journal of Pragmatics*, 26: 237–59.

Firth, J.R. (1957) 'Ethnographic analysis and language with reference to Malinowski's views', in R. Firth (ed.) *Man and Culture: an evaluation of the work of Bronislaw Malinowski*, London: Routledge and Kegan Paul.

Fischer, J.A. (1958) 'Social influences on the choice of a linguistic variant', *Word*, 14: 47–56.

Fisher, S. and Todd, A. (eds) (1983) *The Social Organisation of Doctor–Patient Communication*, Washington DC: Centre for Applied Linguistics.

Fishman, J.A. (1964) 'Language maintenance and shift as fields of inquiry', *Linguistics*, 9: 32–70.

—— (1967) 'Bilingualism with and without diglossia, diglossia with and without bilingualism', *Journal of Social Issues*, 23(2): 29–38.

—— (1991) *Reversing Language Shift*, Clevedon, UK: Multilingual Matters.

Forceville, C. (1996) *Pictorial Metaphors in Advertising*, London: Routledge.

Foucault, M. ([1970] 1981) 'The order of discourse', trans I. McLeod, in R. Young (ed.) *Untying the Text: A Post-structuralist Reader*, London: Routledge and Kegan Paul.

—— ([1978] 1991) 'Governmentality', trans. R. Braidotti, in *The Foucault Effect: Studies in Governmentality*, G. Burchell, C. Gordon and P. Miller (eds) London: Harvester Wheatsheaf, 87–104.

Frankel, R. (1984) 'From sentence to sequence: Understanding the medical encounter through micro-interactional analysis', *Discourse Processes*, 7: 135–70.

Friel, B. (1981) *Translations*, London: Faber and Faber.

Fung, L. and Carter, R. (2007) 'New varieties, new creativities: ICQ and English-Cantonese e-discourse', *Language and Literature*, 16(4): 345–66.

Ganobcsik-Williams, L. (2006) (ed.) *Teaching Academic Writing in UK Higher Education: Theories, Practices and Models*, Basingstoke: Macmillan.

Gee, J.P. (1996) *Social Linguistics and Literacies: Ideology in Discourses*, second edition, London: Falmer Press.

—— (1999) *An Introduction to Discourse Analysis: Theory and Method*, London: Routledge.

—— (2000) 'The New Literacy Studies and the "social turn"', in D. Barton, M. Hamilton and R. Ivanič, (eds) *Situated Literacies: Reading and Writing in Context*, London: Routledge.

—— (2004) 'Learning language as a matter of learning social languages within discourses', in M.R. Hawkins (ed.) *Language Learning and Teacher Education: A Sociocultural Approach*, Clevedon, UK: Multilingual Matters, 13–31.

Gee, J.P., Hull, G. and Lankshear, C. (1996) *The New Work Order: Behind the Language of the New Capitalism*, St Leonards, UK: Allen & Unwin.

General Explanations to the New English Dictionary on Historical Principles (subsequently Oxford English Dictionary), 1933.

Genesee, F. (2000) 'Early bilingual language development: one language or two', in Li Wei (ed.) *The Bilingualism Reader*, London: Routledge, 327–43.

Gerrard, H. and Nakamura, S. (2004) 'Japanese speakers and the Internet', *International Journal on Multicultural Societies*, 6(1): 93–103.

Gibbons, J. (2003) *Forensic Linguistics*, Oxford: Blackwell.

Giddens, A. (1999) *Runaway World: How Globalisation is Reshaping our Lives*, London: Profile Books.

Giles, H. (1984) 'The dynamics of speech accommodation', *International Journal of the Sociology of Language*, 46.

Giles, H. and Powesland, R. (1975) *Speech Style and Social Evaluation*, London: Academic Press.

Giles, H., Bourhis, R.Y. and Taylor, D.M. (1977) 'Towards a theory of language in ethnic group relations', in H. Giles (ed.) *Language, Ethnicity and Intergroup Relations*, London: Academic Press.

Giles, H., Coupland, N. and Coupland, J. (1991) 'Accommodation theory: communica-tion, context and consequence', in H. Giles, H. Coupland and N. Coupland (eds) *Contexts of Accommodation: Developments in Applied Sociolinguistics*, Cambridge: Cambridge University Press.

Gill, V. and Maynard D. (2006) 'Explaining illness: patients' proposals and physicians' responses', in J. Heritage and D. Maynard (eds) *Communication in Medical Care: Interaction Between Primary Medical Care and Patients*, Cambridge, Cambridge University Press, 115–50.

Gimenez, J.C. (2000) 'Business e-mail communication: some emerging tendencies in register', *English for Specific Purposes*, 19(3): 237–51.

—— (2006) 'Embedded business emails: meeting new demands in international business communication', *English for Specific Purposes*, 25: 154–72.

Githiora, C. (2002) 'Sheng peer language Swahili dialect or emerging Creole', *Journal of African Cultural Studies*, 15(2): 159–81.

Gleason, J.B. and Weintraub, S. (1978) 'Input language and the acquisition of communi-cative competence' in K.E. Nelson (ed.) *Children's Language*, vol. 1, New York: Gardner Press Inc., 171–222.

Goatly, A. (2004) 'Nature and Grammar', in C. Coffin, A. Hewings and K. O'Halloran (eds) *Applying English Grammar: Functional and Corpus Approaches*, London: Hodder-Arnold.

Goddard, A. (1998) *The Language of Advertising*, London: Routledge.

Godin, S. (1993) *The Smiley Dictionary*, Berkeley, CA: Peachpit Press.

Goffman, E. (1959) *The Presentation of Self in Everyday Life*, New York: Doubleday.

—— (1961) *Asylums: Essays on the Social Situation of Mental Patients and Other Inmates*, New York: Doubleday Anchor.

—— (1974) *Frame Analysis*, Harmondsworth: Penguin.

—— (1981) *Forms of Talk*, Oxford: Blackwell.

Goodman, S. and O'Halloran, K. (eds) (2006) *The Art of English: Literary Creativity*, Basingstoke: Palgrave.

Goodson, I. and Medway, P. (eds) (1990) *Bringing English to Order: The History and Poli-tics of a School Subject*, London: Falmer Press.

Goodwin, M.H. (1990) *He-Said-She-Said: Talk as Social Organisation Among Black Chil-dren*, Bloomington, IN: Indiana University Press.

—— (2006) *The Hidden Life of Girls: Games of Stance, Status and Exclusion*, Malden, MA: Blackwell.

Goodwyn, A. and Findlay, K. (1999) 'The Cox Models revisited: English teachers' views of their subject and the National Curriculum' in *English in Education*, 33(2): 19–31.

Graddol, D. (1997/2000) *The Future of English*, London: The British Council, available: http://www.britishcouncil.org/learning-elt-future.pdf, accessed 4 February 2009.

—— (1999) 'The decline of the native speaker', *AILA Review*, 13, 57–68.

—— (2006) *English Next: Why Global English May Mean the End of 'English as a Foreign Language'*, British Council. Available: www.britishcouncil.org/files/documents/ learning-research-english-next.pdf, accessed 1 September 2008.

—— (2007) 'English manuscripts: the emergence of a visual identity' in S. Goodman, D. Graddol and T. Lillis (eds) *Redesigning English*, London: Routledge.

Graham, P., Luke, C. and Luke, A. (2007) 'Globalization, corporatism, and critical language education', *International Multilingual Research Journal*, 1(1).

Grant, D. and Iedema, R. (2005) 'Discourse Analysis and the study of organisations', *Text*, 25(1): 37–66.

Graves, D. (1983) *Writing: Teachers and Children at Work*, Exeter, NH: Heinemann Educational.

Gray, J. (1992) *Men are from Mars, Women are from Venus*, New York: Harper Collins.

Greatbatch, D. (1988) 'A turn-taking system for British news interviews', *Language in Society*, 17: 401–30.

Grice, H.P. (1975) 'Logic and conversation', in P. Cole and J. Morgan (eds) *Syntax and Semantics*, New York: Academic Press.

Grosjean, F. (1982) *Life with Two Languages: An Introduction to Bilingualism*, Cambridge, MA: Harvard University Press.

Gumperz, J. (1982a) *Discourse Strategies*, Cambridge: Cambridge University Press.

—— (1982b) *Language and Social Identity*, Cambridge: Cambridge University Press.

—— (1992) 'Interviewing in intercultural situations', in D. Drew and J. Heritage, *Talk at Work*, Cambridge: Cambridge University Press, 302–27.

—— (1999) 'On interactional sociolinguistic method', in S. Sarangi and C. Roberts (eds) *Talk, Work and Institutional Order*, Berlin: Mouton de Gruyter.

—— (2001) 'Contextualization and ideology in intercultural communication', in A. Di Luzio, S. Günther and F. Orletti (eds) *Culture in Communication: Analyses of Intercultural Situations*, Amsterdam: John Benjamins, 35–53.

Gurak, L., Antonijevic, S., Johnson, L., Ratliff, C. and Reyman, J. (eds) (2004) *Into the Blogosphere: Rhetoric, Community and the Culture of Weblog*, Minneapolis, MN: University of Minnesota Library, available: http://blog.lib.umn.edu/blogosphere, accessed 27 April 2008.

Gurrey, P. (1958) *Teaching the Mother Tongue in Secondary Schools*, London: Longmans, Green.

Habermas, J. (1979) *Communication and the Evolution of Society*, trans. Thomas McCarthy, Heinemann: London.

Hafner, K. and Lyon, M. (1996) *Where Wizards Stay Up Late: The Origins of the Internet*, New York: Simon and Schuster.

Hagège, C. (2006) *Combat pour le Français: Au nom de la diversité des langues et des cultures*, Paris: Odile Jacob.

Hall, C. (1997) *Social Work as Narrative*, Basingstoke: Avebury.

Hall, J. (ed.) (2002) *Dictionary of American Regional English*, vol. 4: P–Sk, Boston: Harvard University Press.

Hall, S. (ed.) (1997) *The Local and the Global: Globalization and Ethnicity*, Minneapolis, MN: University of Minnesota Press.

Halliday, M.A.K. (1975) *Learning How to Mean*, London: Edward Arnold.

—— (1978) *Language as Social Semiotic: The Social Interpretation of Language and Meaning*, London: Edward Arnold.

—— (1987) 'Spoken and written modes of meaning', in R. Horowitz and S.J. Samuels (eds) *Comprehending Oral and Written Language*, Orlando, FL: Academic Press.

—— (1989) *Spoken and Written Language*, Oxford: Oxford University Press.

—— (2002) 'Grammar and Daily Life: Concurrence and Complementarity', in J. Webster (ed.) *On Grammar*, London: Continuum.

Halliday, M.A.K. and Hasan, R. (1976) *Cohesion in English*, London: Longman.

Halliday, M.A.K. and Matthiessen, C. (2004) *Introduction to Functional Grammar*, third edition, London: Hodder Arnold.

Halliday, M.A.K., McIntosh, A. and Strevens, P. (1964) *The Linguistic Sciences and Language Teaching*, London: Longmans, Green and Co.

Hansen, T.B. (2006) 'Sounds of freedom: Music, taxis, and racial imagination', *Public Culture*, 18: 1185–208.

Hardt, M. and Negri, A. (2000) *Empire*, Cambridge, MA: Harvard University Press.

Harris, R., Leung, C. and Rampton, B. (eds) (2002) *Globalization, Diaspora and Language Education in England*, London: Routledge.

Harris, Z.S. (1952) 'Discourse analysis', *Language*, 28: 1–30.

Harrison, G.J. and Piette, A.B. (1980) 'Young bilingual children's language selection', *Journal of Multilingual and Multicultural Development*, 1(3): 217–30.

Harwayne, S. (2001) *Writing Through Childhood: Rethinking Process and Product*, Portsmouth, NH: Heinemann.

Haugen, E. (1966) 'Linguistics and language planning', in J.A. Fishman (ed.) *Readings in the Sociology of Language*, The Hague: Mouton.

Hayes, J. (1981) 'Gayspeak', in J.W. Chesebro (ed.) *Gayspeak: Gay Male and Lesbian Communication*, New York: The Pilgrim Press.

Haylock, C. (2006) *A Rum Owd Dew*, Newbury, Berkshire: Countryside Books.

Heaney, S. (1984) 'A Migration', in *Station Island*, London: Faber.

Heath, C. (1981) 'The opening sequence in doctor-patient interactions', in P. Atkinson and C. Heath (eds) *Medical Work: Realities and Routines*, Aldershot: Gower, 71–90.

Heath, S.B. (1982) 'What no bedtime story means: Narrative skills at home and school', *Language and Society*, 11: 49–76.

—— (1983) *Ways with Words: Language, Life and Work in Communities and Classrooms*, Cambridge: Cambridge University Press.

Hebdige, D. (1984) *Subculture: The Meaning of Style*, New York: Methuen.

Heller, M. (1992) 'The politics of codeswitching and language choice', *Journal of Multilingual and Multicultural Development*, 13(1/2): 123–42.

—— (2006) *Linguistic Advances and Modernity*, London: Continuum.

Heritage, J. and Maynard, D. (eds) (2006) *Communication in Medical Care: Interaction Between Primary Medical Care and Patients*, Cambridge: Cambridge University Press.

Heritage, J. and Sefi, S. (1992) 'Dilemmas of advice: aspects of the delivery and reception of advice in interactions between Health Visitors and first-time mothers', in P. Drew and J. Heritage (eds) *Talk at Work*, Cambridge: Cambridge University Press: 359–417.

Herring, S. (ed.) (1996) *Computer-mediated Communication: Linguistic, Social and Cross-cultural Perspectives*, Amsterdam: John Benjamins.

—— (2001) 'Computer-mediated discourse', in D. Tannen, D. Schiffrin and H. Hamilton (eds) *Handbook of Discourse Analysis*, Oxford: Blackwell.

—— (2004) 'Slouching toward the ordinary: Current trends in computer-mediated communication', *New Media and Society*, 6(1): 26–36.

Herring, S.C., Stein, D. and Virtunen, T. (eds) (forthcoming) *Handbook on the Pragmatics of Computer-mediated Communication*, Berlin: Mouton de Gruyter.

Heydon, G. (2005) *The Language of Police Interviewing*, Basingstoke: Palgrave.

Higgins, C. (2003) '"Ownership" of English in the outer circle: An alternative to the NS/NNS dichotomy', *TESOL Quarterly*, 34: 615–44.

Hinrichs, L. (2006) *Codeswitching on the Web: English and Jamaican Creole in E-Mail Communication*, Amsterdam: John Benjamins.

Hoey, M. (1983) *On the Surface of Discourse*, London: George Allen and Unwin.

—— (2001) *Textual Interaction: An Introduction to Written Discourse Analysis*, London: Routledge.

—— (2005) *Lexical Priming: A New Theory of Words and Language*, London: Routledge.

Holliday, A. (2003) *The Struggle to Teach English as an International Language*, Oxford: Oxford University Press.

Holmes, J. (1996) 'Women's role in language change: a place for quantification', in N. Warner, J. Ahlers, L. Bilmes, M. Oliver, S. Wertheim and M. Chen (eds) *Gender and Belief Systems: Proceedings of the Fourth Berkeley Women and Language Conference*, 19–21 April 1996, Berkeley, CA: Berkeley Women and Language Group.

—— (2006) *Gendered Talk at Work*, Malden, MA: Blackwell.

Horner, B. and Trimbur, J. (2002) 'English only and US college composition'. *College Composition and Communication*, 53: 594–630.

House of Commons Committee of Public Accounts (2008) Staying the Course: The Retention of Students on Higher Education Courses, London: The Stationery Office.

House, J. (2003) 'English as a lingua franca: A threat to multilingualism?', *Journal of Sociolinguistics*, 7: 556–78.

Hoyle, S.M. and Adger, C.T. (1996) (eds) *Kid's Talk: Strategic Language Use in Later Childhood*, New York: Oxford University Press.

Hu, G. (2002) 'Potential cultural resistance to pedagogical imports: The case of communicative language teaching in China', *Language, Culture and Curriculum*, 15: 93–105.

Hunston, S. (1995) 'A corpus study of some English verbs of attribution', *Functions of Language*, 2: 133–58.

—— (2002) *Corpora in Applied Linguistics*, Cambridge: Cambridge University Press.

Hunston, S. and Francis, G. (2000) *Pattern Grammar*, Amsterdam: John Benjamins.

Hutchby, I. and Barnett, S. (2005) 'Aspects of the sequential organization of mobile phone conversation', *Discourse Studies*, 7: 147–71.

Hyland, K. (2000) *Disciplinary Discourses: Social Interactions in Academic Writing*, Harlow, Essex: Pearson.

Hymes, D.H. (1962) 'The ethnography of speaking', in T. Gladwin and W.C. Sturtevant (eds) *Anthropology and Human Behavior*, Washington: The Anthropology Society of Washington.

—— (1972) 'On communicative competence' in J.B. Pride and J. Holmes (eds) *Sociolinguistics: Selected Readings*, Harmondsworth: Penguin Books.

—— (1974) *Foundations of Sociolinguistics: An Ethnographic Approach*, Philadelphia, PA: University of Pennsylvania Press.

Ibrahim, A.E.K.M. (1999) 'Becoming black: rap and hip-hop, race, gender, identity, and the politics of ESL learning', *TESOL Quarterly*, 33: 349–70.

Iedema, R. (2003) *Discourses of Post-Bureaucratic Organisation*, Amsterdam: John Benjamins.

Iedema, R. and Wodak, R. (1999) 'Organisational discourses and practices', *Discourse and Society*, 10(1): 5–20.

Ivanič, R. (1998) *Writing and Identity: The Discoursal Construction of Identity in Academic Writing*, Amsterdam: John Benjamins.

Jacquemet, M. (2005) 'Transidiomatic practices, language and power in the age of globalization', *Language & Communication*, 25: 257–77.

Jakobson, R. (1960) 'Closing statement: Linguistics and poetics', in T.A. Sebeok (ed.) *Style in Language*, Cambridge, MA: MIT Press.

Jefferson, G. (1989) 'Preliminary notes on a possible metric which provides for a "Standard Maximum" silence of approximately one second in a conversation', in D. Roger and P. Bull (eds) *Conversation: An Interdisciplinary Perspective*, Clevedon, UK: Multilingual Matters, 166–96.

Jenkins, J. (2000) *The Phonology of English as an International Language*, Oxford: Oxford University Press.

—— (2003) *World Englishes: A Resource Book for Students*, Oxon: Routledge.

—— (2006a) 'Current perspectives on teaching World Englishes and English as a lingua franca', *TESOL Quarterly*, 40(1): 157–81.

—— (2006b) 'Global intelligibility and local diversity: possibility or paradox?', in R. Rubdi and M. Saraceni (eds) *English in the World: Global Rules, Global Roles*, London: Continuum, 32–39.

Jewitt, C. (2006) *Technology, Literacy and Learning: A Multimodal Approach*, London: Routledge.

—— (ed.) (2009) *The Routledge Handbook for Multimodal Analysis*, London, Routledge.

Jewitt, C. and Kress, G. (2003) 'A multimodal approach to research in education', in S. Goodman, T. Lillis, J. Maybin and N. Mercer (eds) *Language, Literacy and Education: A Reader*, Stoke on Trent: Trentham Books in association with the Open University.

Johns, T. (1995) *Pedagogic Grammar*, teaching materials, University of Birmingham.

Johnson, S. (2005) *Spelling trouble? Language, Ideology and the Reform of German Orthography*, Clevedon, UK: Multilingual Matters.

Jones, D. and Plaatje, S.T. (1916) *Sechuana Reader in International Phonetic Orthography*, London: University of London Press; republished (1970) Farnborough, Hants: Gregg International Publishers.

Joseph, J.E. (2006) *Language and Politics*, Edinburgh: Edinburgh University Press.

Jourdan, A.C. (1991) 'Pidgins and creoles: the blurring of categories', *Annual Review of Anthropology*, 20: 187–209.

Kachru, B.B. (1986) *The Alchemy of English: The spread, Functions and Models of Non-native Englishes*, Oxford: Pergamon.

—— (ed.) (1992) *The Other Tongue. English Across Cultures*, second edition, Urbana: University of Illinois Press.

—— (1997) 'World Englishes and English-using communities', *Annual Review of Applied Linguistics*, 17: 66–87.

—— (2005) *Asian Englishes: Beyond the Canon*, Hong Kong: Hong Kong University Press.

Kachru, Y. and Nelson, C. (2006) *World Englishes in Asian Contexts*, Hong Kong: Hong Kong University Press.

Kalantzis, M. and Cope, B. (1993) *The Powers of Literacy: A Genre Approach to Teaching Writing*, London: Falmer Press.

Kamwangamalu, N.M. (2000) *Language Policy and Mother-tongue Education in South Africa: The Case for a Market-oriented Approach*, Georgetown University roundtable, available: http://digital.georgetown.edu/gurt/2000, accessed 12 April 2008.

Karmani, S. (2005) 'English, "Terror", and Islam', *Applied Linguistics*, 26(2): 262–7.

Kell, C. (2001) 'Ciphers and currencies: Literacy dilemmas and shifting knowledges', *Language and Education*, 15: 197–211.

Kerswill, P. (1996) 'Milton Keynes and dialect levelling in south-eastern British English' in D. Graddol, D. Leith and J. Swann (eds) *English: History, Diversity and Change*, London: Routledge in association with The Open University, 292–300.

—— (2006) 'Migration and Language' in K. Mattheier, U. Ammon and P. Trudgill (eds) *Sociolinguistics/Soziolinguistik – An International Handbook of the Science of Language and Society*, second edition, vol. 3, Berlin: Mouton de Gruyter.

Kerswill, P. and Williams, A. (2000) 'Creating a new town koinè: children and language change in Milton Keynes', *Language in Society*, 29: 65–115.

Khine, M.S., Yeap, L.L. and Lok, A.T.C. (2003) 'The quality of message ideas, thinking and interaction in an asynchronous cmc environment', *Educational Media International*, 40: 115–25.

Khosa, M.K. (1997) 'Sisters on slippery wheels: gender relations in the taxi industry in South Africa', *Transformation*, No. 33: 18–33.

Khubchandani, L.M. (1997) *Revisualizing Boundaries: A Plurilingual Ethos*, New Delhi, India: Sage.

Kiesling, S. (2002). 'Playing the straight man: maintaining and displaying male heterosexuality in discourse', in K. Campbell-Kibler, R. Podesva, S.J. Roberts and A. Wong, (eds) *Language and Sexuality*, Stanford: CSLI.

Kirkpatrick, A. (2006) 'Which model of English: Native-speaker, nativized or lingua franca?', in R. Rubdi and M. Saraceni (eds) *English in the World: Global Rules, Global Roles*, London: Continuum, 71–83.

Kitzinger, C. (2006) '"Speaking as a heterosexual": (how) does sexuality matter for talk in interaction?', in D. Cameron, and D. Kulick (eds) *The Language and Sexuality Reader*, London: Routledge.

Kloss, H. (1966) 'German-American language maintenance efforts', in J.A. Fishman (ed.) *Language Loyalty in the United States*, The Hague: Mouton, 206–52.

Knights, B. and Thurgar-Dawson, C. (2006) *Active Reading: Transformative Writing in Literary Studies*, London: Continuum.

Koch, H. (1985) 'Nonstandard English in an Aboriginal Land Claim', in Pride, J. (ed.) *Cross-cultural Encounters: Communication and Miscommunication*, Melbourne: River Seine Publications, 176–95.

Koller, V. (2004) *Metaphor and Gender in Business Media Discourse: A Critical Cognitive Study*, Basingstoke: Palgrave Macmillan.

Komter, M. (1991) *Conflict and Co-operation in Job Interviews*, Amsterdam: John Benjamins.

Kramer-Dahl, A. (1995) 'Reading and writing against the grain of academic discourse', *Discourse: Studies in the Cultural Politics of Education*, 16: 21–38.

Kramer-Dahl, L. (ed.) (2006) *Teaching Academic Writing in UK Higher Education: Theories, Practices and Models*, Basingstoke: Palgrave Macmillan.

Kramsch, C. and Whiteside, A. (2008) 'Language ecology in multilingual settings: towards a theory of symbolic competence', *Applied Linguistics*, 29(2): 1–27.

Kress, G. (2000) 'Multimodality', in B. Cope and M. Kalantzis (eds) *Multiliteracies: Literacy Learning and the Design of Social Futures*, London: Routledge.

—— (2003) *Literacy in the New Media Age*, London: Routledge.

Kress, G. and van Leeuwen, T. (2001) *Multimodal Discourse: The Modes and Media of Contemporary Communication*, London: Edward Arnold.

—— (2006) *Reading Images: The Grammar of Visual Design*, second edition, London: Routledge.

Kress, G. and Street, B. (2006) 'Multi-modality and literacy practices', in K. Pahl and J. Rowsell (eds) *Travel notes from the New Literacy Studies*, Bristol: Multilingual Matters.

Krishnaswamy, N. and Burde, A. (1998) *The Politics of Indians' English: Linguistic Colonialism and the Expanding English Empire*, Delhi: Oxford University Press.

Kristeva, J. (1986) 'Word, dialogue and novel' in T. Moi (ed.) *The Kristeva Reader*, Oxford: Blackwell Publishers.

Kulick, D. (2000) 'Gay and Lesbian Language', *Annual Review of Anthropology*, 29: 243–85.

Kumaravadivelu, B. (1994) 'The postmethod condition: (E)merging strategies for second/foreign language teaching', *TESOL Quarterly*, 28(1), 27–48.

—— (2008) *Cultural Globalization and Language Education*, New Haven: Yale University Press.

Kyei, G. and Schreckenbach, H. (1976) *No Time to Die*, Accra, Ghana: Catholic Press.

Labov, W. (1964) 'Stages in the acquisition of Standard English' in R.W. Shuy (ed.) *Social Dialects and Language Learning* (proceedings of the Bloomington, Indiana Conference), Champaign (IL), NCTE.

—— (1966) *The Social Stratification of English in New York City*, Washington, DC: Center for Applied Linguistics.

—— (1972) *Sociolinguistic Patterns*, Philadelphia: University of Pennsylvania Press.

—— (1991) 'The three dialects of English', in Eckert, P. (ed.) *New Ways of Analysing Social Change*, New York: Academic Press.

—— (2003) 'Pursuing the Cascade model' in D. Britain and J. Cheshire (eds) *Social Dialectology: In Honour of Peter Trudgill*, Amsterdam: John Benjamins.

Labov, W. and Fanshel, D. (1977) *Therapeutic Discourse: Psychotherapy as Conversation*, New York: Academic Press.

Labov, W., Ash, S. and Boberg, C. (2006) *The Atlas of North American English: Phonetics, Phonology and Sound Change*, Berlin: Mouton de Gruyter.

LaFarge, A. (1995) 'A World exhilarating and wrong: Theatrical improvisation on the Internet', *Leonardo*, 28(5), 415–22.

LaFarge, A. and Allen, R. (2005) 'Media commedia: The Roman forum project', *Leonardo*, 38(3), 213–18.

Lakoff, R.T. (1982) 'Some of my favorite writers are literate: The mingling of oral and literate strategies in written communication', in D. Tannen (ed.) *Spoken and Written Language*, Norwood, NJ: Ablex, 239–60.

Lam, W.S.E. (2000) 'L2 literacy and the design of the self: A case study of a teenager writing on the internet', *TESOL Quarterly*, 34: 457–82.

Langendoen, D.T. (1968) *The London School of Linguistics: A Study of the Linguistic Contributions of B. Malinowski and J. R. Firth*, Cambridge, MA: MIT Press.

Larkin, Philip (1974) 'This Be The Verse' in Philip Larkin *High Windows*, London: Faber.

Le Page, R. and Tabouret-Keller, A. (1985) *Acts of Identity: Creole-based Approaches to Language and Ethnicity*, Cambridge: Cambridge University Press.

Lea, M.R. and Street, B. (1998) 'Student writing in higher education: an academic literacies approach', *Studies in Higher Education*, 23: 157–72.

—— (1999) 'Writing as academic literacies: understanding textual practices in higher education', in C.N. Candlin and K. Hyland (eds) *Writing: Texts, Processes and Practices*, London: Longman, 62–81.

—— (2006) 'The "academic literacies" model: Theory and applications', *Theory into Practice*, 45(4): 368–77.

Leap, W.L. (1996) *Word's Out: Gay Men's English*, Minneapolis, MN: University of Minnesota Press.

Lee, C.K.M. (2007) 'Linguistic features of email and ICQ instant messaging in Hong Kong', in B. Danet and S.C. Herring (eds) *The Multilingual Internet: Language, Culture, and Communication Online*, New York: Oxford University Press, 184–208.

Leech, G.N. (1966) *English in Advertising*, London: Longman.

Lefevere, A. (1992) *Translation, Rewriting and the Manipulation of Literary Fame*, London and New York: Routledge.

Leith, D. (1997) *A Social History of English*, second edition, London: Routledge.

Lenhart, A., Madden, M., Macgill, A.R. and Smith, A. (2007) *Teens and social media*, Washington, DC: PEW Internet and American Life Project, available: www.pewinternet.org/pdfs/PIP_Teens_Social_Media_Final.pdf, accessed 28 April 2008.

Lenhart, A., Arafeh, S., Smith, A. and Macgill, A.R. (2008) *Writing, technology, and teens*, Washington, DC: PEW Internet and American Life Project and the National Commission on Writing, available: www.pewinternet.org/pdfs/PIP_Writing_Report_FINAL3.pdf, accessed 28 April 2008.

Leung, C. (2005) 'Convivial communication: recontextualising communicative competence', *International Journal of Applied Linguistics*, 15(2): 119–44.

Leung, C. and Safford, K. (2005) 'Nontraditional students in higher education in the United Kingdom: English as an additional language and literacies' in B.V. Street (ed.) *Literacies Across Educational Contexts: Mediating Learning and Teaching*, Philadelphia, PA: Caslon Publishing.

Levinson, S. (1992) 'Activity types and language', in P. Drew and J. Heritage (eds) *Talk at Work*, Cambridge: Cambridge University Press, 66–100.

Lévi-Strauss, C. ([1962] 1974) *The Savage Mind*, London: Weidenfeld and Nicolson.

Lewis, C. and Fabos, B. (2005) 'Instant messaging, literacies, and social identities', *Reading Research Quarterly*, 40(4): 470–501.

Li Wei (1994) *Three Generations, Two Languages, One Family*, Clevedon, UK: Multilingual Matters.

—— (1998) 'The "why" and "how" questions in the analysis of conversational code-switching' in P. Auer (ed.) *Code-Switching in Conversation: Language, Interaction and Identity*, London: Routledge, 156–179.

—— (ed.) (2000) *The Bilingualism Reader*, London: Routledge.

Lieven, E.V.M., Pine, J.M. and Barnes, H.D. (1992) 'Individual differences in early vocabulary development: redefining the referential-expressive distinction', *Journal of Child Language*, 19: 287–310.

Lillis, T.M. (1999) 'Whose common sense? Essayist literacy and the institutional practice of mystery' in C. Jones, J. Turner and B. Street (eds) *Student Writing in University: Cultural and Epistemological Issues*, Amsterdam: John Benjamins, 127–47.

—— (2001) *Student Writing: Access, Regulation, Desire*, London: Routledge.

Linell, P. and Thunquist, D. (2003) 'Moving in and out of framings: activity contexts in talks with young unemployed people within a training project', *Journal of Pragmatics*, 35: 409–34.

Ling, R. and Baron, N.S. (2007) 'Text messaging and IM: Linguistic comparison of American college data', *Journal of Language and Social Psychology*, 26(3): 291–8.

Livia, A. and Hall, K. (eds) (1997) *Queerly Phrased: Language, Gender and Sexuality*, New York: Oxford University Press.

Louw, W.E. (1993) 'Irony in the text or insincerity in the writer?', in M. Baker, G. Francis and E. Tognini-Bonelli (eds) *Text and Technology. In Honour of John M. Sinclair*, Philadelphia, PA: John Benjamins.

Lysandrou, P. and Lysandrou, Y. (2003) 'Global English and proregression: under-standing English language spread in the contemporary era', *Economy and Society*, 32(2): 207–33.

McArthur, T. (1987) 'The English languages?', *English Today*, 11: 9–13.

McCrum, R., Cran, W. and Macneil, R. (2002) *The Story of English*, third edition, London: Faber and Faber/BBC Books.

McDonough, J. and Shaw, C. (2003) *Materials and Methods in ELT: A Teacher's Guide*, second edition, Oxford: Blackwell.

McElhinny, B. (1995) 'Challenging hegemonic masculinities: Female and male police officers handling domestic violence', in K. Hall and M. Bucholtz (eds) *Gender Articu-lated*, London: Routledge.

McKay, S. (2005) 'Teaching the pragmatics of English as an International Language', *Guidelines*, 27: 3–9.

Macken-Horarik, M. (2003) 'Appraisal and the Special Instructiveness of Narrative', *TEXT* 23(2), special issue, M. Macken-Horarik and J.R. Martin (eds): 285–312.

Makitalo, A. and Saljo, R. (2002) 'Talk in institutional context and institutional context in talk: categories and situational practices', *Text*, 22: 57–82.

Makoni, S. and Pennycook, A. (eds) (2007) *Disinventing and Reconstituting Languages*, Clevedon, UK: Multilingual Matters.

Malinowski, B. (1923) 'The problem of meaning in primitive languages', in C.K. Ogden and I.A. Richards (eds) *The Meaning of Meaning*, New York: Harcourt Brace.

Mann, W.C. and Thompson, S.A. (1988) 'Rhetorical structure theory: toward a func-tional theory of text organization', *Text*, 8: 243–81.

Marshall, S. (1964) 'Memo to Plowden', *The Use of English*, XVI, 1: 3–7.

Martin, J.R. (1992) *English Text: Systems and Structure*, Amsterdam: John Benjamins.

—— (1993) 'Genre and literacy – modelling context in educational linguistics', *Annual Review of Applied Linguistics*, 13: 141–72.

—— (2004) 'Grammatical Structure: What do we mean?', in C. Coffin, A. Hewings and K. O'Halloran (eds) *Applying English Grammar: Functional and Corpus Approaches*, London: Hodder Arnold, 57–77.

Maryns, K. (2006) *The Asylum Speaker: Language in the Belgian Asylum Procedure*, Manchester: St Jerome.

Mason, I. and Stewart, M. (2001) 'Interactional pragmatics, face and the dialogue inter-preter', in I. Mason (ed.) *Triadic Exchanges: Studies in Dialogue Interpreting*, Manchester: St Jerome, 51–70.

Matthiessen, C. (2006) 'Frequency profiles of some basic grammatical systems: an interim report', in G. Thompson and S. Hunston (eds) *System and Corpus: Exploring Connections*, London: Equinox, 103–42.

Mautner, G. (2005) 'The entrepreneurial University: A discursive profile of a Higher Education buzzword', *Critical Discourse Studies*, 2(2): 1–26.

May, S. (2001) *Language and Minority Rights: Ethnicity, Nationalism and the Politics of Language*, London: Longman.

Maybin, J. (2002) '"What's the hottest part of the Sun? Page 3!" Children's exploration of adolescent gender identities through informal talk', in J. Sunderland, and L. Litos-seliti (eds) *Discourse Analysis and Gender Identities*, Amsterdam: John Benjamins.

—— (2006) *Children's Voices: Talk, Knowledge and Identity*, Basingstoke: Palgrave Macmillan.

Maybin, J. and Swann, J. (eds) (2006) *The Art of English: Everyday Creativity*, Basingstoke: Palgrave.

Maynard, D. (1992) 'On clinicians co-implicating recipients' perspectives in the delivery of diagnostic news', in P. Drew and J. Heritage (eds) *Talk at Work*, Cambridge: Cambridge University Press, 331–58.

Mayor, B. (2007) 'English in the repertoire' in N. Mercer, J. Swann, and B. Mayor (eds) *Learning English*, Abingdon: Routledge.

Meacher, M. (2003) *Are GM crops safe? Who can say? Not Blair, The Independent on Sunday*, 22 June 2003.

Medway, P. (1990) 'Into the Sixties: English and English society at a time of change', in I. Goodson and P. Medway (eds) *Bringing English to Order: The History and Politics of a School Subject*, London: Falmer Press, 1–46.

Mehan, H. (1979) *Learning Lessons: Social Organization in the Classroom*, Cambridge MA: Harvard University Press.

—— (1993) 'Beneath the skin and between the ears: A case study in the politics of representation', in S. Chaiklin and J. Lave (eds) *Understanding Practice*, Cambridge: Cambridge University Press, 241–68.

Meierkord, C. (2004) 'Syntactic variation in interactions across international Englishes', *English World-Wide*, 25: 109–32.

Mercer, N. (1995) *The Guided Construction of Knowledge: Talk Among Teachers and Learners*, Clevedon, UK: Multilingual Matters.

Mesthrie, R. and Bhatt, R. (2008) *World Englishes – the Study of New Linguistic Varieties*, Cambridge: Cambridge University Press.

Mignolo, D. (1996) 'Linguistic maps, literary geographies, and cultural landscapes: languages, languaging and (trans)nationalism', *Modern Language Quarterly*, 57(2): 181–97.

Mignolo, W. (2000) *Local Histories/Global Designs: Coloniality, Subaltern Knowledges, and Border Thinking*, Princeton, NJ: Princeton University Press.

Miller, C.R. (1984) 'Genre as social action', *Quarterly Journal of Speech*, 70: 151–67.

Milroy, L. (1987) *Language and Social Networks*, second edition, Oxford: Blackwell.

Milroy, J. and Milroy, L. (1999) *Authority in Language: Investigating Standard English*, third edition, London: Routledge.

Mishler, E. (1984) *The Discourse of Medicine: The Dialectics of Medical Interviews*, Norwood, NJ: Ablex.

Mitchell, B. and Robinson, F.C. (2001) *A Guide to Old English*, sixth edition, Oxford: Blackwell.

Mitchell, R. and Myles, F. (1998) *Second Language Learning Theories*, London: Arnold.

Mitchell, S. (2006) *Thinking Writing: News from the Writing in the Disciplines Initiative: Report on Consortium for Writing in the Disciplines*, Newsletter Autumn 2006, Language and Learning Unit, Queen Mary, University of London.

Mitchell, T. (2001) *Global Noise: Rap and Hip-hop Outside the USA*, Middletown, CT: Wesleyan University Press.

Moffett, J. (1969) *Teaching the Universe of Discourse*, Boston: Houghton Mifflin.

Moloney, K. (2006) *Rethinking Public Relations: The Spin and the Substance*, second edition, London: Routledge.

Mufwene, S. (2001) *The Ecology of Language Evolution*, Cambridge: Cambridge University Press.

Myers, G. (1990) *Writing Biology: Texts in the Social Construction of Scientific Knowledge*, Wisconsin: The University of Wisconsin Press.

—— (1994) *Words in Ads*, London: Arnold.

—— (1999) *Ad Worlds: Brands, Media, Audience*, London: Arnold.

Myers-Scotton, C. (1993) *Social Motivations for Codeswitching: Evidence from Africa*, Oxford: Clarendon.

Myers-Scotton, C. and Bolonyai, A. (2001) 'Calculating speakers: codeswitching in a rational choice model', *Language in Society*, 30(1): 1–28.

Nardi, B.A., Whittaker, S. and Bradner, E. (2000) 'Interaction and outeraction: Instant messaging in action', in *Proceedings of the ACM Conference on Computer-Supported Cooperative Work*, New York: ACM Press, 79–88.

Nash, C.M. (2005) 'Cohesion and reference in English chatroom discourse', in *Proceedings of the 38th Annual Hawaii International Conference on System Sciences (HICSS'05) – Track 4*, The Institute of Electrical and Electronics Engineers, available: http://doi.ieeecomputersociety.org/10.1109/HICSS.2005.143

Nelson, K. (1981) 'Individual differences in language development: implications for development and language', *Developmental Psychology*, 17(2): 170–87.

Nettle, D. and Romaine, S. (2000) *Vanishing Voices: The Extinction of the World's Languages*, Oxford: Oxford University Press.

Nicholls, J. and Wells, G. (1985) 'Editors' introduction' in G. Wells and J. Nicholls (eds) *Language and Learning: an interactional perspective*, London: Falmer Press, 1–19.

Norrick, N.R. (1997) 'Twice-told tales: collaborative narration of familiar stories', *Language in Society*, 26: 199–220.

Nunan, D. (2003) 'The impact of English as a global language on educational policies and practices in the Asia-Pacific region', *TESOL Quarterly*, 37: 589–613.

O'Halloran, K.A. (2007) 'Critical discourse analysis and the corpus-based interpretation of metaphor at the register level', *Applied Linguistics*, 28(1): 1–24.

O'Halloran, K. and Coffin, C. (2004) 'Checking overinterpretation and underinterpretation: help from corpora in critical linguistics', in C. Coffin, A. Hewings and K. O'Halloran (eds) *Applying English Grammar*, London: Arnold.

Oates, J. and Grayson, A. (2004) 'Introduction: perspectives on cognitive and language development' in J. Oates and A. Grayson (eds) *Cognitive and Language Development in Children*, Oxford: Blackwell in association with The Open University, 8–20.

Ochs, E. (1979) 'Introduction: What child language can contribute to pragmatics' in E. Ochs and B.B. Schieffelin (eds) *Developmental Pragmatics*, New York: Academic Press, 1–17.

—— (1992) 'Indexing gender' in A. Duranti and C. Goodwin (eds) *Rethinking Context: Language as an Interactive Phenomenon*, Cambridge: Cambridge University Press.

Ochs, E. and Schieffelin, B.B. (eds) (1979) *Developmental Pragmatics*, New York: Academic Press.

Ogude, J. and Nyairo, J. (eds) (2007) *Urban Legends, Colonial Myths Popular Culture and Literature*, Trenton: Africa World Press.

Omoniyi, T. (2006) 'Hip-hop through the WE lens', in Y. Kachru and J. Lee (eds) *World Englishes and Global Popular Cultures*, Oxford: Oxford University Press.

Orton, H. and Wright, N. (1974) *A Word Geography of England*, London: Seminar Press.

O'Sullivan, P.B. and Flanagin, A.J. (2003) 'Reconceptualizing "flaming" and other problematic messages', *New Media and Society*, 5(1): 69–94.

Painter, C. (1984) *Into the Mother Tongue: A Case Study in Early Language Development*, London: Frances Pinter.

Pakir, A. (2005) 'The measurement of World Englishes: Kachruvian concerns', *14th World Congress of Applied Linguistics*, Madison, WI.

Palfreyman, D. and Al Khalil, M. (2003) '"A funky language for teenzz to use": Representing Gulf Arabic in instant messaging', *Journal of Computer-Mediated Communication*, (9)1, available: www.blackwell-synergy.com/toc/jcmc/9/1, accessed 28 April 2008.

Paolillo, J. (2007) 'How much multilingualism? Linguistic diversity on the Internet', in B. Danet and S.C. Herring (eds) *The Multilingual Internet: Language, Culture and Communication Online*, New York: Oxford University Press, 408–30.

Paradis, M. (1998) 'Neurolinguistic aspects of the native speaker' in R. Singh (ed.) *The Native Speaker: Multilingual Perspectives*, New Delhi: Sage, 205–19.

Parakrama, A. (1995) *De-hegemonizing Language Standards: Learning from (Post)Colonial Englishes about 'English'*, Basingstoke: Macmillan.

Pavel, T.G. (1986) *Fictional Worlds*, Cambridge, MA: Harvard University Press.

Payne, A. (1980) 'Factors controlling the acquisition of the Philadelphia dialect by out-of-state children' in W. Labov (ed.) *Locating Language in Time and Space*, New York: Academic Press.

Peccei, J.S. (1994) *Child Language*, London: Routledge.

Pennycook, A. (1994) *The Cultural Politics of English as International Language*, London: Longman.

—— (2003a) 'Beyond homogeny and heterogeny: English as a global and worldly language', in C. Mair (ed.) *The Cultural Politics of English*, Amsterdam: Rodopi, 3–17.

—— (2003b) 'Global Englishes, rip slyme and performativity', *Journal of Sociolinguistics*, 7(4): 513–33.

—— (2007) *Global Englishes and Transcultural Flows*, London: Routledge.

Pennycook, A. and Coutand-Marin, S. (2003) 'Teaching English as a missionary language', *Discourse: Studies in the Cultural Politics of Education*, 17/3: 337–53.

Petyt, K.M. (1980) *The Study of Dialect*, London: Andre Deutsch.

Philips, S.U. (1993) *The Invisible Culture: Communication in Classroom and Community on the Warm Springs Indian Reservation*, second edition, New York: Longman.

Phillipson, R. (1992) *Linguistic Imperialism*, Oxford: Oxford University Press.

—— (1999) 'Voice in global English: Unheard chords in Crystal loud and clear', review of D. Crystal, *English as a Global Language*, Cambridge: Cambridge University Press, *Applied Linguistics*, 20(2): 265–76.

—— (2003) *English Only Europe? Challenging Language Policy*, London: Routledge.

Phillipson, R. and Skutnabb-Kangas, T. (1996) 'English only worldwide or language ecology?', *TESOL Quarterly*, 30(3): 429–52.

Piller, I. and Takahashi, K. (2006) 'A passion for English: Desire and the language market', in A. Pavlenko (ed.) *Bilingual Minds: Emotional Experience, Expression and Respresentation*, Clevedon, UK: Multilingual Matters, 59–83.

Pinker, S. (1994) *The Language Instinct: A New Science of Language and Mind*, London: Penguin.

—— (1995) 'Why the child holded the baby rabbits: a case study in language acquisition', in L.R. Gleitman and M. Liberman (eds) *An Invitation to Cognitive Science*, vol. 1, second edition, Cambridge, MA: MIT Press, 107–34.

Platt, J.T., Weber, H. and Ho, M.L. (1984) *The New Englishes*, London: Routledge.

Plunkett, K. and Wood, C. (2006) 'The development of children's understanding of grammar', in J. Oates and A. Grayson (eds) *Cognitive and Language Development in Children*, Oxford: Blackwell in association with The Open University, 163–200.

Pope, R. (1995) *Textual Intervention: Critical and Creative Strategies for Literary Studies*, London: Routledge.

—— (2005a) *Creativity: Theory, History, Practice*, London: Routledge.

—— (2005b) 'The Return of Creativity: common, singular and otherwise', *Language and Literature*, 14(4): 276–96, including responses by R. Carter and D. Attridge.

Popper, K.R. (1972) *Objective Knowledge: An Evolutionary Approach*, Oxford: The Clarendon Press.

Porter, R.A. (1995) *Spectacular Vernaculars: Hip Hop and the Politics of Post-modernism*, Albany: State University of New York.

Prabhu, N.S. (1990) 'There is no best method – Why?', *TESOL Quarterly*, 24: 161–76.

Prior, P. (2004) 'Tracing process: How texts come into being', in C. Bazerman and P. Prior (eds) *What Writing Does and How it Does It*, Mahwah, NJ: Lawrence Erlbaum.

Pudney, J. (1953) *The Thomas Cook Story*, London: Michael Joseph.

Pye, C. (1986) 'Quiché Mayan speech to children', *Journal of Child Language*, 13: 85–100.

Pym, A. (2000) 'Late Victorian to the present', in P. France (ed.) *The Oxford Guide to Literature in English Translation*, Oxford: Oxford University Press, 73–81.

QCA (2005) *Taking English Forward*, London: Qualifications and Curriculum Authority.

—— (2008) *English 21*, available: www.qca.org.uk/qca_5640.aspx, accessed 13 February 2008.

Quirk, R. (1985) 'The English language in a global context', in R. Quirk and N.S. Widdowson (eds) *English in the World: Teaching and Learning the Language and Literatures*, Cambridge: Cambridge University Press for The British Council.

Quirk, R., Greenbaum, S., Leech, G. and Svartvik, J. (1985) *A Comprehensive Grammar of the English Language*, London: Longman.

R v. *Kina* (1993) Unreported, Queensland Court of Appeal, 29 November.

Radford, A. (1990) *Syntactic Theory and the Acquisition of English Syntax: The Nature of Early Child Grammars of English*, Oxford: Blackwell.

Radhakrishnan, R. (2003) *Theory in an Uneven World*, Oxford: Blackwell.

—— (2007) 'Globality is not worldliness', in R. Radhakrishnan, K. Nayak, R. Shashidhar, R.R. Parinitha and D.R. Shashidhara (eds) *Theory as Variation*, New Delhi: Pencraft International, 313–28.

Ramanathan, V. (2005) *The English-Vernacular Divide: Postcolonial Language Politics and Practice*, Clevedon, UK: Multilingual Matters.

Rampton, B. (1990) 'Displacing the "native speaker": Expertise, affiliation, and inheritance', *ELT Journal*, 44: 97–101.

—— (1998) 'Language crossing and the redefinition of reality', in P. Auer (ed.) *Code-Switching in Conversation: language, interaction and identity*, London: Routledge.

—— (2005a second edition) *Crossing: Language and Ethnicity Among Adolescents*, Manchester: St Jerome Press.

—— (2005b) *Language in Late Modernity: Interaction in an Urban School*, Cambridge: Cambridge University Press.

Rampton, B., Tusting, K., Maybin, J., Barwell, R., Creese, A. and Lytra, V. (2004) 'UK Linguistic Ethnography: a discussion paper', available: www.lancs.ac.uk/fss/organisations/lingethn

Ravem, R. (1974) 'The development of *wh*-questions in first and second language learners', in J. Richards (ed.) *Error Analysis: Perspectives on Second Language Acquisition*, London: Longman.

Raymond, E.S. (1996) *The New Hacker's Dictionary*, third edition, Cambridge, MA: M.I.T. Press.

Redish, J.C. (1985) *The Plain Language Movement*, New York: Pergamon.

Reagan, T. (2005) *Critical Questions, Critical Perspectives: Language and the Second Language Educator*, Greenwich, CT: Information Age Publishing Inc.

Robbins, J. (2000) 'God is nothing but talk modernity, language, and prayer in a Papua New Guinea society', *American Anthropologist*, 103(4): 901–12.

Roberts, C., Davies, E. and Jupp, T. (1992) *Language and Discrimination: A Study of Communication in Multi-Ethnic Workplaces*, London: Longman.

Roberts, C. and Campbell, S. (2005) 'Fitting stories into boxes: Rhetorical and textual constraints on candidates' performances in British job interviews', *Journal of Applied Linguistics*, 2(1): 45–73.

Roberts, C. and Sarangi, S. (2005) 'Theme-orientated discourse analysis of medical encounters', *Medical Education*, 39: 632–40.

Robertson, R. (2003) *Three Waves of Globalization: A History of a Developing Global Consciousness*, London: Zed Books.

Rock, F. (2007) *Communicating Rights: The Language of Arrest and Detention*, Basingstoke: Palgrave Macmillan.

Romaine, S. (1995) *Bilingualism*, second edition, Oxford: Blackwell.

Rosen, H. (1987) *Stories and Meanings*, Sheffield: National Association for the Teaching of English.

Rothery, J. (1996) 'Making changes: developing an educational linguistics', in R. Hasan and G. Williams (eds) *Literacy in Society*, Harlow: Addison Wesley Longman.

Rubdy, R. and Saraceni, M. (2006) 'Introduction', in R. Rubdi and M. Saraceni (eds) *English in the World: Global Rules, Global Roles*, London: Continuum, 5–16.

Rumens, Carol (2007) 'This Be The Verse' in Carol Ann Duffy (ed.) *Answering Back: Living poets reply to the poetry of the past*, London: Picador.

Russell, D. (1991) *Writing in the Academic Disciplines 1870–1990: A Curricular History*, Carbondale: South Illinois University Press.

Sacks, H., Schegloff, E. and Jefferson, G. (1974) 'A simplest systematics for the organisation of turn-taking in conversation', *Language*, 50(4): 696–735.

Samraj, B. (2004) 'Discourse features of the student-produced academic research paper: variations across disciplinary courses', *Journal of English for Academic Purposes*, 3: 5–22.

Sanders, E.K. (1961) 'When are speech sounds learned?' *Journal of Speech and Hearing Disorders*, (37): 55–63.

Sarangi, S. and Roberts, C. (1999) 'The dynamics of interactional and institutional orders', in S. Sarangi and C. Roberts (eds) *Talk, Work and Institutional Order: Discourse in Medical, Mediation and Management Settings*, Berlin: Mouton de Gruyter, 1–57.

—— (1999) (eds) *Talk, Work and Institutional Order: Discourse in Medical, Mediation and Management Settings*, Berlin: Mouton de Gruyter.

Sarangi, S. and Slembrouck, S. (1996) *Language, Bureaucracy and Social Control*, London: Longman.

Saville-Troike, M. (2003) *The Ethnography of Communication: An Introduction*, third edition, Oxford: Blackwell.

Scalone, P. and Street, B. (2006) 'An academic language development programme (widening participation)', in C. Leung and J. Jenkins (eds) *Reconfiguring Europe: The Contribution of Applied Linguistics*, London: Equinox, 123–37.

Scarcella, R. (2003) *Academic English: A Conceptual Framework*, Irvine: Linguistic Minority Research Institute, University of California.

Schegloff, E.A. (1997) 'Whose text? Whose context?', *Discourse and Society*, 8: 165–87.

Schegloff, E.A. and Sacks, H. (1973) 'Opening up closings', *Semiotica*, 7: 289–327.

Scheuer, J. (2001) 'Recontextualisation and communicative styles in job interviews', *Discourse Studies*, 3: 223–48.

Schmitt, N. and Carter, R. (2004) 'Formulaic sequences in action: an introduction', in Schmitt, N. (ed.) *Formulaic Sequences: Acquisition, Processing and Use*, Amsterdam: John Benjamins, 1–22.

Schmitt, N., Grandage, S. and Adolphs, S. (2004) 'Are corpus-derived recurrent clusters psycholinguistically valid?', in Schmitt, N. (ed.) *Formulaic Sequences: Acquisition, Processing and Use*, Amsterdam: John Benjamins, 127–51.

Schneider, E. (2007) *Postcolonial English: Varieties around the World*, Cambridge: Cambridge University Press.

Scollon, R. and Wong Scollon, S. (1983) 'Face in interethnic communication', in J.C. Richards and R.W. Schmidt (eds) *Language and Communication*, Harlow, Essex: Longman.

—— (2003) *Discourse in Place: Language in the Material World*, London: Routledge.

Scragg, D.G. (1974) *A History of English Spelling*, Manchester: Manchester University Press.

Sealey, A. (2000) *Childly Language: Children, Language and the Social World*, Harlow: Pearson Education Ltd.

Searle, J.R. (1969) *Speech Acts: An Essay in the Philosophy of Language*, Cambridge: Cambridge University Press.

—— (1979) *Expression and Meaning*, Cambridge: Cambridge University Press.

Sebba, M. (2003a) 'Spelling rebellion', in J.K. Androutsopoulos and A. Georgakopoulou (eds) *Discourse Constructions of Youth Identities*, Amsterdam: John Benjamins, 151–72.

—— (2003b) 'Will the real impersonator please stand up? Language and identity in the Ali G websites', *Arbeiten aus Anglistik and Amerikanistik*, 28(2): 279–304.

—— (2007a) *Spelling and Society: The Culture and Politics of Orthography Around the World*, Cambridge: Cambridge University Press.

—— (2007b) 'Identity and language construction in an online community: the case of "Ali G"', in P. Auer (ed.) *Style and Social Identities: Alternative Approaches to Linguistic Heterogeneity*, Berlin: Mouton de Gruyter, 361–92.

Seedhouse, P. (2004) *The Interactional Architecture of the Language Classroom: A conversation analysis perspective*, Oxford: Blackwell.

Seidlhofer, B. (2001) 'Closing a conceptual gap: The case for a description of English as a lingua franca', *International Review of Applied Linguistics*, 11(2): 133–58.

—— (2004) 'Research perspectives on teaching English as a lingua franca', *Annual Review of Applied Linguistics*, 24: 209–39.

Selinker, L. (1972) 'Interlanguage', *International Review of Applied Linguistics*, 10: 209–31.

Serote, Mongane Wally (1974) 'The Actual Dialogue' in Robert Royston (ed.) *Black Poets in South Africa*, London: Heinemann.

Shaw, S. (2006) 'Governed by the rules? The female voice in Parliamentary debates', in J. Baxter (ed.) *Speaking Out*, Basingstoke: Palgrave Macmillan.

Sherwood, J.C. (1960) 'Dr Kinsey and Professor Fries', *College English*, 21: 275–80.

Shiu, E. and Lenhart, A. (2004) *How Americans Use Instant Messaging*, Washington, DC: PEW Internet and American Life Project, available: www.pewinternet.org/pdfs/PIP_Instantmessage_Report.pdf, accessed 28 April 2008.

Shohamy, E. (2006) 'Reinterpreting Globalization in Multilingual Contexts', *International Multilingual Research Journal*, 1(2): 127–33.

Shuy, R. (1978) 'What children's functional language can tell us about reading or how Joanna got herself invited to dinner', in R. Beach (ed.) *Perspectives on Literacy: Proceedings of the 1977 Perspectives on Literacy Conference*, Minneapolis, MN: University of Minnesota.

Silberstein, S. (2002) *War of Words: Language, Politics and 9/11*, London: Routledge.

Silverman, D. (1999) 'Warriors or collaborators: reworking methodological controversies in the study of institutional interaction', in S. Sarangi and C. Roberts (eds) *Talk, Work and Institutional Order: Discourse in Medical, Mediation and Management Settings*, Berlin: Mouton de Gruyter, 401–26.

Silverstein, M. and Urban, G. (eds) (1996) *Natural Histories of Discourse*, Chicago: University of Chicago Press.

Simões Lucas Freitas, E. (2008) *Taboo in Advertising*, Amsterdam: John Benjamins.

Simplified Spelling Society (n.d.) *Modernizing English Spelling: Principles and Practicalities*, leaflet, downloaded on 21 February 2008 from: www.spellingsociety.org/aboutsss/leaflets/leaflets.php

Sinclair, J. (1991) *Corpus, Concordance, Collocation*, Oxford: Oxford University Press.

—— (2003) *Reading Concordances*, Harlow: Longman.

—— (2004) *Trust the Text: Language, Corpus and Discourse*, London: Routledge.

Sinclair, J.M. and Coulthard, M. (1975) *Towards an Analysis of Discourse: The English used by Teachers and Pupils*, Oxford: Oxford University Press.

Singh, P. and Doherty, C. (2004) 'Global cultural flows and pedagogic dilemmas: Teaching in the global university contact zone', *TESOL Quarterly*, 38(1): 9–42.

Singh, R. (ed.) (1998) *The Native Speaker – Multilingual Perspectives*, New Delhi: Sage.

Singler, J.V. (1996) 'Theories of Creole genesis, sociohistorical considerations, and the evaluation of evidence: the case of Haitian Creole and the Relexification hypothesis', *Journal of Pidgin and Creole Languages*, 11: 185–230.

Skutnabb-Kangas, T. (2000) *Linguistic Genocide in Education – Or Worldwide Diversity and Human Rights?* Mahwah, NJ: Lawrence Erlbaum.

Smith, D. (1987) *The Everyday World as Problematic: A Feminist Sociology*, Boston: Northeastern University Press.

Smith, J.M. (2003) *Seeds of Deception*, Fairfield, Iowa: Yes Books.

Snyder, I. (2008) *The Literacy Wars*, Crows Nest, NSW: Allen and Unwin.

Sonntag, S. (2003) *The Local Politics of Global English: Case Studies in Linguistic Globalization*, Lanham, MD: Lexington Books.

Spatafora, J.N. (2008) *IM learning 2 write? A study on how instant messaging shapes student writing.* Unpublished MA thesis, Queen's University, Kingston, Ontario, available: http://qspace.library.queensu.ca/dspace/bitstream/1974/1001/1/Spatafora_Julia_N_200801_MEd.pdf, accessed 28 April 2008.

Sperber, D. and Wilson, D. (1995) *Relevance: Communication and Cognition*, second edition, Oxford: Blackwell.

Stannard, J. and Huxford, L. (2007) *The Literacy Game: The Story of the National Literacy Strategy*, London: Routledge.

Steger, M. (2003) *Globalization: A Very Short Introduction*, Oxford: Oxford University Press.

Sternberg, R. (ed.) (1999) *Handbook of Creativity*, Cambridge: Cambridge University Press.

Stevens, J.A. (1990) *From Masculine to Feminine and All Points In Between: A Practical Guide*, Cambridge, MA: Different Path.

Stillar, G. (1998) *Analysing Everyday Texts: Discourse, Rhetoric and Social Perspectives*, Thousand Oaks, CA: Sage.

Stone, B. (1964) 'Introduction' in *Medieval English Verse*, Harmondsworth: Penguin.

Strang, B.M.H. (1970) *A History of English*, London: Methuen.

Street, B. (1984) *Literacy in Theory and Practice*, Cambridge: Cambridge University Press.

—— (1995) *Social Literacies*, London: Longman.

—— (2004) 'Academic literacies and the "New Orders": Implications for research and practice in student writing', *HE Learning and Teaching in the Social Sciences*, 1(1): 9–32.

Stubbs, M. (1996) *Text and Corpus Analysis: Computer-assisted Studies of Language and Culture*, Oxford: Blackwell.

—— (2001) *Words and Phrases: Corpus Studies of Lexical Semantics*, Oxford: Blackwell.

—— (2007) 'Quantitative data on multi-word sequences in English: the case of the word *world*', in M. Hoey, M. Mahlberg, M. Stubbs and W. Teubert (eds) *Text, Discourse and Corpora: Theory and Analysis*, London: Continuum, 163–89.

Su, H.-Y. (2003) 'The multilingual and multi-orthographic Taiwan-based Internet: Creative uses of writing systems on college-affiliated BBSs', *Journal of Computer-Mediated Communication*, 9(1), available: www.blackwell-synergy.com/toc/jcmc/9/1, accessed 28 April 2008.

Sully, J. (1897/1971) 'Children's ways', reproduced in A. Bar-Adon and W.F. Leopold (eds) *Child Language: A Book of Readings*, Englewood Cliffs, NJ: Prentice Hall.

Summerfield, G. (1965) *Topics in English for the Secondary School*, London: Batsford.

—— (ed.) (1968) *Voices*, Harmondsworth: Penguin Education.

—— (ed.) (1970) *Junior Voices*, Harmondsworth: Penguin Education.

—— (ed.) (1979) *Worlds*, Harmondsworth: Penguin Education.

Swain, M. (1972) *Bilingualism as a First Language*, PhD dissertation, Irvine, University of California.

Swales, J. (1981) *Aspects of Article Introductions*, Aston ESP Reports No. 1, The Language Studies Unit, Birmingham: Aston University.

—— (1990) *Genre Analysis: English in Academic and Research Settings*, Cambridge: Cambridge University Press.

—— (1998) *Other Floors, Other Voices: A Textography of a Small University Building*, Mahwah, NJ: Lawrence Erlbaum.

—— (2004) *Research Genres*, Cambridge: Cambridge University Press.

Swales, J.N and Rogers, P. (1995) 'Discourse and the projection of corporate culture: the mission statement', *Discourse and Society*, 6(2): 233–42.

Swann, J. (2002) 'Yes, but is it gender?', in L. Litosseliti and J. Sunderland (eds) *Gender Identity and Discourse Analysis*, Amsterdam: John Benjamins, 43–67.

Swann, J., Deumert, A., Lillis, T. and Mesthrie, R. (2004) *A Dictionary of Sociolinguistics*, Edinburgh: Edinburgh University Press.

Taboada, M. (2007) *Rhetorical Structure Theory*, available: www.sfu.ca/rst, accessed 30 November 2007.

Tannen, D. (1989) *Talking Voices: Repetition, Dialogue and Imagery in Conversational Discourse*, Cambridge: Cambridge University Press.

Tannen, D. and Wallat, C. (1993) 'Interactive frames and knowledge schemas in interaction: examples from a medical examination/interview', in D. Tannen (ed.) *Framing in Discourse*, Oxford: Oxford University Press.

Tanskanen, S.-K. (2001) 'Avoiding conflict in computer-mediated discussions, or, fear of flaming', in R.R. Hiltunen, K. Battarbee, M. Peikola and S.-K. Tanskanen (eds) *English in Zigs and Zags (Anglicana Turkuensia 23)*, Turku: University of Turku, 227–42.

The Sun online Thursday 23 November 2006, available: www.thesun.co.uk/sol/homepage, accessed 24 November 2007.

—— Friday 24 November 2006, available: www.thesun.co.uk/sol/homepage/news/article72563.ece, accessed 8 November 2007.

Thomas, D. (2007) *Black France: Colonialism, Immigration and Transnationalism*, Indiana University Press.

Thomason, S.G. and Kaufman, T. (1988) *Language Contact, Creolization and Genetic Linguistics*, Berkeley, CA: University of California Press.

Thompson, G. and Hunston, S. (eds) (2006) *System and Corpus: Exploring Connections*, London: Equinox.

Thornborrow, J. (2002) *Power Talk: Language and Interaction in Institutional Discourse*, Longman: London.

Thurlow, C. (2006) 'From statistical panic to moral panic: The metadiscursive construction and popular exaggeration of new media language in the print media', *Journal of Computer-Mediated Communication*, 11: 667–701.

Thurlow, C. and Brown, A. (2003) 'Generation txt? The discourses of young people's text-messaging', *Discourse Analysis Online*, 1(1), available: www.shu.ac.uk/daol/articles/v1/n1/a3/thurlow2002003-t.html, accessed 28 April 2008.

Tognini-Bonelli, E. (2001) *Corpus Linguistics at Work*, Amsterdam: John Benjamins.

Tollefson, J. (2000) 'Policy and ideology in the spread of English', in J.K. Hall and W. Eggington (eds) *The Sociopolitics of English Language Teaching*, Clevedon, UK: Multilingual Matters, 7–21.

Toolan, M.J. (2001) *Narrative: A Critical Linguistic Introduction*, second edition, London: Routledge.

Tormey, S. (2007) 'Consumption, resistance and everyday life: Ruptures and continuities', *Journal of Consumer Policy*, 30(3): 63–280.

Trainor, R.H. (2003) 'The social impact of British universities since 1850', in F. Bosbach, K. Robbins and K. Urbach (eds) *Birth or talent? The formation of elites in a British–German comparison*, München: K.G. Saur, 217–28.

Trinch, S. (2003) *Latinas' Narratives of Domestic Abuse: Discrepant Versions of Violence*, Amsterdam: John Benjamins.

Trudgill, P. (1974) 'Linguistic change and diffusion: description and explanation in sociolinguistic dialect geography', *Language in Society*, 3: 215–46.

—— (1978) 'Sex, covert prestige, and linguistic change in the urban British English of Norwich', *Language in Society*, 1: 179–96.

—— (2004) *New Dialect Formation: The Inevitability of Colonial Englishes*, Oxford: Oxford University Press.

Tseliga, T. (2007) '"It's all *Greeklish* to Me!" Linguistic and sociocultural perspectives on Greeklish (Roman-alphabeted Greek) in asynchronous CMC', in B. Danet and S.C. Herring (eds) *The Multilingual Internet: Language, Culture, and Communication Online*, New York: Oxford University Press, 116–43.

Tsui, A.B.M. (2003) *Understanding Expertise in Teaching*, Cambridge: Cambridge University Press.

Tupas, R. (2006) 'Standard Englishes, pedagogical paradigms and conditions of (im)possibility', in R. Rubdy and M. Saraceni (eds) *English in the World: Global Rules, Global Roles*, London: Continuum, 169–85.

Turkle, S. (1995) *Life on the Screen: Identity in the Age of the Internet*, New York: Simon and Schuster.

Tymoczko, M. (1986) 'Translation as a force for literary revolution in the twelfth-century shift from epic to romance', *New Comparison*, 1, Summer: 7–27.

Underwood, G., Schmitt, N. and Galpin, A. (2004) 'The eyes have it: an eye-movement study into the processing of formulaic sequences', in N. Schmitt (ed.) *Formulaic Sequences: Acquisition, Processing and Use*, Amsterdam: John Benjamins, 153–72.

Upton, C. and Widdowson, J.D.A. (2006) *An Atlas of English Dialects*, second edition, London: Routledge.

Urla, J. (2003 [1995]) 'Outlaw Language: Creating Alternative Public Spheres in Basque Free Radio', in R. Harris and B. Rampton (eds) *The Language, Ethnicity, and Race Reader*, London: Routledge, 211–24. Originally published (1995) in *Pragmatics*, 5(2): 245–61.

van Kruijsdijk, J. with Reitsma, R. (2005) *Instant messaging in the UK: An MSN Affair*, Cambridge: Forrester Research, available: www.forrester.com/Research/Document/Excerpt/0,7211,37784,00.html, accessed 28 April 2008.

Varghese, M. and Johnston, B. (2007) 'Evangelical Christians and English language teaching', *TESOL Quarterly*, 41(1): 5–31.

Venuti, L. (1995) *The Translator's Invisibility. A History of Translation*, London: Routledge.

Vera, V. (1997) *Miss Vera's Finishing School for Boys who Want to be Girls*, New York: Doubleday.

Vestergaard, T. and Schrøder, K. (1985) *The Language of Advertising*, Oxford: Blackwell.

Vickers, B. (1988) *In Defence of Rhetoric*, Oxford: Clarendon.

Wa Mungai, M (2007) 'Kaa Masaa, Grapple with spiders: the myriad threads of Nairobi matatu discourse', in J. Ogude and J. Nyairo (eds) *Urban Legends, Colonial Myths Popular Culture and Literature*, Trenton: Africa World Press, 25–58.

Walsh, C. (2001) *Gender and Discourse: Language and Power in Politics, the Church and Organizations*, London: Longman.

Wandor, M. (2008) *The Author is Not Dead, Merely Somewhere Else: Creative Writing Reconceived*, Basingstoke: Palgrave.

Warschauer, M. (2000) 'The changing global economy and the future of English teaching', *TESOL Quarterly*, 34, 511–36.

Warschauer, M., El Said, G.R. and Zohry, A. (2002) 'Language choice online: Globalization and identity in Egypt', *Journal of Computer-Mediated Communication*, 7(4), available: www.blackwell-synergy.com/toc/jcmc/7/4, accessed 28 April 2008.

Waters, M. (1995) *Globalisation*, London: Routledge.

Weber, M. (1947) *The Theory of Social and Economic Organisation*, trans. M. Henderson and T. Parsons, Glencoe, IL: The Free Press.

Wei, C.Y. and Kolko, B.E. (2005) 'Resistance to globalization: Language and internet diffusion', *New Review of Hypermedia and Multimedia*, 11(2): 205–20.

Weinreich, U. ([1953] 1968) *Languages in Contact*, The Hague: Mouton de Gruyter.

Wells, C.G. (1981) *Learning Through Interaction: The Study of Language Development (Language at Home and at School Volume 1)*, Cambridge: Cambridge University Press.

—— (1985a) *Language Development in the Pre-school Years (Language at Home and at School Volume 2)*, Cambridge: Cambridge University Press.

—— (1985b) *The Meaning Makers: Children Learning Language and Using Language to Learn*, Oxford: Heinemann.

—— (1985c) 'Language and learning: an interactional perspective' in G. Wells and J. Nicholls (eds) *Language and Learning: An Interactional Perspective*, London: Falmer Press, 21–40.

Wells, G. (1993) 'Reevaluating the IRF sequence: A proposal for the articulation of theories of activity and discourse for the analysis of teaching and learning in the classroom', *Linguistics in Education*, 5: 1–37.

Wells, G. and Nicholls, J. (1985) (eds) *Language and Learning: An Interactional Perspective*, London: Falmer Press.

West, C. (1984) *Routine Complications: Troubles in Talk between Doctors and Patients*, Bloomington, IN: Indiana University Press.

Wetherell, M. (1998) 'Positioning and interpretative repertoires: Conversation analysis and post-structuralism in dialogue', *Discourse and Society*, 9: 387–412.

Whitehead, A. N. (1926) *Religion in the Making*, New York: Fordham University Press.

Widdowson, H. (1995) 'Review of Fairclough's *Discourse and Social Change*', *Applied Linguistics*, 16: 510–16.

—— (2000) 'On the limitations of linguistics applied', *Applied Linguistics*, 21: 3–25.

—— (2004a) *Text, Context, Pretext: Critical Issues in Discourse Analysis*, Oxford: Blackwell.

Widdowson, H.G. (2004b) 'A perspective on recent trends', in A.P.R. Howatt with H.G. Widdowson *A History of English Language Teaching*, second edition, Oxford: Oxford University Press.

Wierzbicka, A. (1991) *Cross-Cultural Pragmatics: The Semantics of Human Interaction*, Berlin: Mouton de Gruyter.

Windeatt, B. (2008) 'Geoffrey Chaucer', in R. Ellis (ed.) *The Oxford History of Literary Translation in English, Vol.1 to 1550*, Oxford: Oxford University Press, 137–48.

Winter, E. (1994) 'Clause relations as information structure: two basic text structures in English', in M. Coulthard (ed.) *Advances in Written Text Analysis*, London: Routledge.

Wodak, R. (1996) *Disorders of Discourse*, London: Longman.

Wodak, R. and Wright, S. (2007) 'The European Union in Cyberspace: Democratic Participation via Online Multilingual Discussion Boards?', in B. Danet and S.C. Herring (eds) *The Multilingual Internet: Language, Culture and Communication Online*, New York: Oxford University Press, 385–407.

Woodbury, H. (1984) 'The strategic use of questions in court', *Semiotica*, 48(3/4): 197–228.

Wray, A. (2002) *Formulaic Language and the Lexicon*, Cambridge: Cambridge University Press.

Wright, S. (ed.) (2004) 'Multilingualism on the internet', special issue, *International Journal on Multicultural Societies*, 6(1).

Yajun, J. (2003) 'English as a Chinese language', *English Today*, 19: 3–8.

Yates, J. (1989) *Control Through Communication*, Baltimore: Johns Hopkins University Press.

Yngve, V.H. (2004) 'Issues in Hard Science Linguistics', in V.H. Yngve and Z. Wasik (eds) *Hard-Science Linguistics*, New York: Continuum. 14–27.

Youssef, V. (1991) 'The acquisition of varilingual competence', *English World-Wide*, 12(1): 87–102.

Zamel, V. and Spack, R. (eds) (2004) *Crossing the Curriculum: Multilingual Learners in College Classrooms*, Mahwah, NJ: Lawrence Erlbaum Associates Publishers.

Zentella, A.C. (1997) *Growing up Bilingual: Puerto Rican Children in New York*, Oxford: Blackwell.

Zimmerman, D. (1992) 'The interactional organisation of calls for emergency assistance', in P. Drew and J. Heritage (eds) *Talk at Work*, Cambridge: Cambridge University Press, 418–69.

INDEX

314